eleven DAYS

eleven DAYS

From 35 million to food stamps... what a family gains when losing the American dream

JC Cochrane

R HOUSE PUBLISHING LLC – DALLAS, TEXAS

R HOUSE PUBLISHING LLC FIRST EDITION, AUGUST 2016

PUBLISHED IN THE UNITED STATES BY R HOUSE PUBLISHING LLC, ROWLETT, TEXAS
R House publishing titles may be purchased in bulk for educational, business, fundraising, or sales promotional use. For information contact RHOUSEPUBLISHING.CO.

ISBN : 0997692308
ISBN-13: 9780997692303
Library of Congress Control Number: 2016957817
r house publishing
Rowlett, TX

WWW.RHOUSEPUBLISHING.CO
R HOUSE PUBLISHING LLC
DALLAS, TEXAS

cover design : Dennis Rhodes
author photo : Laura Bravo Mertz

10 9 8 7 6 5 4 3 2 1

ALSO BY JC COCHRANE
(coming soon)

Includes excerpts in the back:

CARRY ON – the secret language, lessons and heart wrenching love a family experiences when a child endures addiction. (copyright 2014)

YOU CRACK ME UP – from broken bones to broken homes and monsters, bullies & stuff – is one of 11 books in a children's series called OAKIE DOAKIE (copyright 2016)

JCCOCHRANE.COM

THIS BOOK IS MY SONG
& THIS SONG IS FOR YOU

to Bill, Marcus, Clint & Nicole

82188

CONTENTS

AUTHOR'S NOTE

This story is about our family of five enduring a financial fall from $35 million to food stamps.

Three years after the fall, I spent 11 days house-sitting in Santa Barbara, California, by myself.

During those 11 days, my husband Bill and I rarely spoke. He stayed home in Tucson, Arizona, with the kids (Marcus, 11; Clint, 9; and Nicole, 7) His personal experience during this time was also transformative and then indirectly explained to me via phone calls with the kids, as well as reports from friends, co-workers and our attorney at the time.

To write about this, I relied on emotional memory, past notes, and journals I'd accumulated over those 11 days. At times, to bring clarity and relevance, time was collapsed and events compressed. Strategic omission's, embellishments and some combining of characters were meant to disguise people, places, and things. When necessary, names of some individuals were changed, and identifying details were modified to preserve privacy.

After I had returned home, Bill's story, the kids' stories, and my story became clear. Following with 11 years of processing, I finally put pen to paper.

It's been 11 years since the 11-day trip. This is the 11th house we have lived in. Bill is on his 11th job. And Marcus turned 11, a week before the 11 day house-sitting trip in Santa Barbara.

This is based on a true story.

In 9 months, high-tech firm zips through growth cycles

i360 inc. goes full circle

By Alan D. Fischer
ARIZONA DAILY STAR

A Tucson high-tech company recently sold for $90 million — less than nine months after it launched.

And i360 inc.'s Feb. 23 acquisition by InfoCast Corp. should help push the company's fast-track growth, said Bill Cochrane, president and CEO of the local firm.

The company was conceived July 7, in guest rooms at a local resort.

"It started at the Westward Look Resort," Cochrane said. "We worked 24 hours a day, around the clock, and had beds and desks in the same room.

"We had six or seven PCs, and we just sat working on the computers with phone lines coming in through the windows," he said. "It was a great incubator — we worked together and lived together for six weeks."

The company rose from the ashes of a failed business attempt — a proposed cellular voice-over Internet company that didn't pan out, he said. But the core talent remained together and launched another Internet-related operation: i360.

Cochrane said the initial months were enlightening, but trying. "I had never been involved in a start-up. I heard a lot of people tell me a lot of things about start-ups," he said. "It's the best thing I've ever done, and the hardest thing I've ever done.

"I had no idea — it ranged from making payroll out of my own pocket to the merger. There have been tremendous upswings and downswings."

The first few weeks' intense workload planted the seeds for success. "It showed we had a good idea of how we wanted to do it, what we were going to do, and what the principles of what we wanted to do were," he said.

"Then we started to do some acquisitions, finding the pieces to help accelerate our growth — and then there was a steep acceleration," he said. "Then it was a lot of grunt work again."

Cochrane said the project's mix of people aided in the success.

"What we do is very complex, and there is a ton of different pieces to it," he said. "We went out and found the very best people," he said.

"We had a tremendously diverse pool of people, with radically different views on things," he said. "By being committed to the same basic end result ... we accelerated, we built a better product, and we did things we did not even plan on to begin with."

He said what the company does is a bit difficult to describe.

"What we do is create a content-rich, information-rich private network — a private environment for people in an affinity group who need specific information from that group," he said. "It is an online community."

i360 creates *content- and information-rich private networks for groups*

"It's the best thing I've ever done": *Bill Cochrane, CEO of i360, credits the best people, commitment for firm's success*
Chris Richards/Staff

The company also offers dial-up Internet service over a network that can reach 93 percent of the U.S. population using local phone numbers.

For example, a church organization could use i360's services to offer Internet service to members, and give them a virtual community where they could get information, activity schedules, links to other related Web sites, and communicate with other members.

The church group would also share in the project's revenues, he said.

John D. Grabo, vice president at the Greater Tucson Economic Council, said he was impressed with i360's rapid development and sale.

"In my opinion, that's a pretty phenomenal dollar value in such a short time," Grabo said. "But this is not out of the ordinary in the high-tech, knowledge-based economy, where the purchase of technology is second only to the formation of technology.

"Speed is of the essence in the knowledge-based economy, so companies acquire rather than develop their own technology," Grabo said. "Enabling technologies are probably more ripe for acquisition than the e-businesses themselves."

"We anticipate this merger will accelerate InfoCast's business model by six months, and be a catalyst for more rapid growth," said Jim Leech, InfoCast's president and CEO, when the deal was announced in February.

"InfoCast is well positioned to provide infrastructure-on-demand for i360's rapidly-growing customer base," Leech said.

i360 is housed on the ground level of a five-floor building at 407 W. Congress St., next to the new federal courthouse downtown. Cochrane said it will soon expand to use the top two levels of the leased, 60,000-square-foot building.

"We do need some more space. We're moving our Jacksonville (Fla.) office here, and we anticipate moving in some of the folks from InfoCast," he said.

Even considering all the hard work that has gone into the business, Cochrane is still amazed at the rapid development.

"All this stuff wouldn't have happened if there wasn't really a higher power," Cochrane said. "The moon and stars were aligned and it worked out perfectly."

i360 at a glance

- Address: 407 W. Congress St.
- Number of employees: 35
- Launch date: July 7, 1999
- Sale date: Feb. 23, 2000
- Purchaser: InfoCast Corp.
- Purchase price: $90 million

eleven DAYS

PART ONE

THE LAY OF THE LAND

WHAT MONEY CAN BUY

The only light I could see at the end of the tunnel was a train heading our direction. I tried to convince myself everything was going to be all right... it's just money.

In a trance like state, I slowly moved my hands around the soft leather steering wheel of my Porsche parked outside the garage on our cobblestone driveway. As I studied our soon-to-be-sold home located in Tucson, Arizona, a sense of panicked intuition warned me of what might be coming next. *How the hell did we sell a company for 90 million and end up here?*

After some time, I shut the car door with a deep thud leaving me to feel I entered a vessel of some kind. The scent of leather permeated the interior, and I couldn't help but acknowledge, out of all the vehicles my husband, Bill, had collected and sold over the last 18 years, this Porsche 911 twin turbo was the first car I admitted liking. Which is funny because, initially, I was embarrassed that its cost was close to that of our first home. For years, I teased Bill about his detailed knowledge and adoration of automobiles. He had, by this point, owned so many clunkers and brand new cars, I couldn't even count them, much less name them. Up until now, I had never felt the same about a car, but understood a love like that. Art, music, crystals and even finding a heart-shaped rock would excite me and draw me in just the same. But money *could* buy you some things; the price tag on the Porsche was around $125,000.

For me, this vehicle symbolized an arrival of sorts. We had always stood strong that we weren't our money, house, or cars. So, I wasn't concerned with others being impressed with it. It just reminded me of how hard we had to work to have something like this.

The Porsche was flat-out fun, and it carried an energy that belonged in the fast lane. A Tiptronic built into the wheel made it easy to glide into manual driving so you could hear the individual six gears of the engine. After reaching 75 mph, the tail lifted. I once followed behind it in Bill's lapis-blue metallic Porsche in order to see it lift on the open road. It also came with a feature allowing you to set the tail up even when not reaching those speeds. I kept it up all the time.

It was a powerful machine that demanded you take it seriously. I can't say I always drove the speed limit in it because it went 0 to 60 in 4.2 seconds, but I can say I was always present when I sunk into the race car's black leather seats trimmed with yellow stitching, matching the custom Ferrari yellow exterior paint. The combination of yellow and black had never been appealing to me in the past, but somehow it screamed "happy face." I wouldn't go all out and say it made me happy, but it did bring me some joy. Plus, it was the most well-received and approachable of any of the cars I had driven. At stoplights, people would wave, smile or give me a thumbs-up. In the past, it wasn't uncommon to be driving one of Bill's red Corvettes and get flipped off for no reason, or aggressively challenged to race.

Bill and I didn't grow up in wealth; we grew up near it. We did not attend private schools or Ivy League colleges. There were no trust funds to lean on, and we weren't in line for an inheritance in this lifetime. But this *climb* up a hill of hope, to a destination where we thought we'd finally arrived, was proof that with money, there does come a bit of freedom and stability. It was a feeling we were relieved to experience. In college, our only assets were Bill's '85 Honda motorcycle, and my $250 '72 Olds. Our net worth after the sale of the company, i360: $35 million.

As a little girl growing up, I had hoped for a future filled with abundance. There was a part of me that felt I was living the definition of the American Dream: you learn as much as you can; you do what's right; you work your ass off, harder than what's required; and, with a little luck, you arrive somewhere better from where you came. But, on the flip side, I was surprised to find that I had some difficulty owning it at times, which threw off an air of guilt. I imagined it was because I just wasn't used to this way of life.

After college, our wealth grew like crumbs that make the cake, and the sale of i360 threw everything into hyper-abundance gear. This financial standing was the opposite of how I grew up, and I noticed I'd occasionally overcompensate by purchasing toys I would have liked to have had as a child, only to find my kids playing in the big cardboard boxes they came in. I was so grateful for easily managed Christmas shopping lists, being able to pay the bills, and to spontaneously write checks for any club, sport, tutor or any other kids' needs. The most fun was no longer having to wait for anything to go on sale. It's what I always imagined security to feel like.

Gratitude for this life we created on our own enriched us, but we held on to one important thing: often, we felt blessed by whatever power and current might be guiding the Universe, which in our case, we called God. Our belief was reinforced throughout the years while watching divine moments where things came together and also fell apart in perfect order, an order we couldn't take credit for. This was especially true at i360. The luck we needed, and the unique players showed up, with divine timing, making us feel humbly aware of a higher power than ourselves.

Unfortunately, this venture wasn't always filled with ease and grace due to its fast track. Minute by minute, the office would shift from peace to fiercely furious exchanges caused by internal power struggles. On some days, greed ran like the plague while Bill and his corporate team spoke with potential buyers. At times, the energy in the office turned urgent because some felt entitled to be paid more as if we had already arrived. All along, he had been generously giving stock to these employees, so much, in fact, he was highly criticized by investors for having given too much. He stood in front of them, time and time again, defending his over-sharing of stock and explaining his purpose: "I want them to run their divisions like they own it."

Those individuals who stayed focused on doing what was best for the company inspired us, at the same time, former employees that left pissed off, distracted us. But then, local Tucson investment companies romanced i360 in hopes of being a part of it all, while in the same week aggressive competitors in the national market threatened to steal the company's top programmers. It was a rollercoaster. I observed only brief segments of treachery while Bill acted as chief, putting out the fires during his 15 to 20 hour days; seven days a week. As much as I worried about the stress on him, I knew that in order to build a company of this magnitude, he needed to stay fully engaged to watch its proverbial back. Somehow, the $90 million dollar sale divinely took place, despite the interruptions, and we celebrated, as we focused on the good of it all.

It was shocking that it was only one year ago.

Pricey champagne bottles were popping to the right and left of me. Hugs, high-fives, and kisses on the cheek with overwhelming joy and relief poured through after selling the company. Bill had invited only the top executives to our home and had a limo outside waiting to take a small group of executives and wives to the larger celebration, where the rest of the employees of the two merged companies waited. I was thrilled to be among them all that night, unlike the past, where I complained to Bill about the phony element present during the fancy dinners, trips, parties, and fundraisers I attended with him. I'd much rather be with my hair in a ponytail, at home, with the kids. Which always made me feel like I wasn't the best partner for Bill while he built his career. Somehow, over the years, I learned to politely and appropriately play in the sandbox even though I didn't love the chase of it all. But this party was different and tonight it was easy for me to raise my glass. I knew how hard they all worked, and it felt more like winning a championship football game with teammates you worked your asses off with. The wives and I connected on a deeper level as we were able to see the triumph on paper and we had at least one thing in common: we were proud of our husband's. I, silently, was screaming with joy for Bill. I knew how hard he had worked behind the scenes. This merger made headlines and so had my husband, for good reason. As for this town I adored, Tucson finally had its cutting edge, high-tech company that had sold to a publicly traded company, listed on the NASDAQ.

He did it. We did it. We finally did it.

While the champagne bubbled and the appetizers passed around the room, I exited the party area and moved down the wide hallway, which connected the kitchen leading me to their rooms. Even though we had someone to watch them, I wanted to check on the kids. I wore a full-length, deep V-neck, red silk dress that I picked up while I walked so it wouldn't get tangled. I knew the kids would most likely be asleep so I tried to keep my high heels quiet as they clicked across the travertine floor. It was one of those glorious nights where I let go of criticism about being able to pull this outfit off and so I wore it like I belonged in it. While making my way, I felt Bill on my heels and turned to him. He pulled me into his arms and kissed me as he gently pushed me back up against the wall, holding my slightly raised hands and arms out to the sides. I felt the cold texture through the back of my silk dress, but his lips warmed me through. This kiss felt different, and I opened my eyes. His remained closed. With his lips lightly on top of mine, he whispered, "I love you."

I let this moment sink in. As my hands released from his, I let my fingertips move to the corners of his mouth, my favorite part of him, and I felt our breath move in and out of each other. I didn't have to say it back because we learned long ago that getting into a habit of saying it only to hear it said back was not healthy. He knew I loved him. He was my best friend, and we had been married for 12 years, together for 15, and had gone through enough up until now that we were comfortable with the depth of our love. Somehow, after the kiss, in a silent gaze, nothing was said, and everything was said.

I took his hand and whispered, "Follow me."

We quietly opened Nicole's door to her bedroom and slowly tiptoed in. Her room decorated with her typical toddler art on the walls and various dolls and doll clothes were scattered on the berber carpet.

"We've lived here a year. Is this room ever getting decorated?" Bill teased.

I pointed to her colorful abstract paintings and smiled and whispered, "Probably not. Every time I come in here with the designer's paint swatches, she gets inspired and whips out her paints and creates these. For now, this works. Look at her dresser. She colored these little wood shapes with colored pencils and glued them onto the dresser to make flowers."

"That's actually cool," he whispered. Then he pointed and said, "Her window is open, and the air conditioning is on."

Quietly giggling, I replied, "Shhh, don't shut it, she likes the smell of that tree we had planted, the Texas Mountain Laurel, ' 'cause its' 'big purple flowers smell like grape candy.' "

I tucked her in and gently kissed her forehead. Bill gave her a kiss and gave me a nod that humbly and gratefully said, "So grateful for our baby girl."

I nodded in agreement. "I can't believe she's already 4."

We quietly shut the door and moved into the boys' room. Marcus, age 8, was on the bottom bunk, and we took turns kissing him good night. Bill found a light blue and orange, metal model GT 40 racecar, meant for display on a shelf, lying next to him like a teddy bear. We quietly laughed as he put it onto the nightstand. Bill then helped guide my high heels onto the wooden ladder that went up to Clint, age 6. Marcus hadn't moved, so I was pleased with my stealth mode. Clint's back was to me while he lay on his side, and as I leaned in to kiss him, he abruptly flipped over and screamed, "Boo!"

I would have slipped off the ladder if it hadn't been for Bill. We all broke out into laughter and had to quickly explain to a startled Marcus what had happened. He laughed and rolled back into slumber. I lay on the top bunk cuddling with Clint for a few minutes while Bill tickled him. *Life is good.* Reluctantly, we felt the pull to return to our guests but wished we could stay.

Bill and I walked hand in hand through the kids' corridor. High above was a stunning handcrafted, bull-nose vaulted ceiling. It gave the appearance of a small white cathedral ceiling 15-feet above. *A place fit for Angels.* We passed the media room, and were about to enter the kitchen that led to the living room, but stopped. I was thinking of how amazing and huge this sale and merger was and how proud I was of Bill. I recognized that I was the only one in his life today that knew him better than anyone, and I knew he was capable of this and even more. *This is just the beginning.*

Bill turned to me and raised my hands to his chest, while his two fingers twirled my wedding ring around my finger and he said, "Thank you. Thank you for being there... for me, and for the kids. I couldn't have done it without you."

————

While sitting in the Porsche in the driveway, I felt myself sigh, knowing I needed to temporarily release these memories as the raw truth of what was happening today desperately needed my attention. *Our hard work looked to be ending in despair.* I scanned the garage, *what should stay and what should go?* I thought while taking note of the silver Volvo station wagon and the custom Suburban for our drives to California, equipped with drop-down movie projectors connected to theater sound systems, wired for hours of on-board kid entertainment. I wondered which one made sense to keep *if* we could afford it.

The engine rumbled as I pulled out onto the cobblestone drive. Like clock-work, Marcus and Clint dropped what they were doing and raced out to see my departure. Nicole stayed inside with our nanny. In the front turnaround, I saw the boys in my rearview mirror, one standing with their bike and the other with a skateboard. While I slipped into neutral and revved the engine, they didn't cheer. They smiled in silence, glancing at one another and back at the car. I knew they, like their dad, had an activated gene for loving vehicles, and now I had a mutated gene, too. Even though I was only going to be gone a few hours, my heart melted while watching them stand there. There's something about the way a child re-minds you of how much you're loved and needed in the stance they take, as they watch you drive away. It's as if you see their whole truth, nothing but the truth, through their tears or their smile. *God, I love them.*

The boys gave me a quick wave and a smile as I honked, and pulled out onto the cobblestone roads that led to the gate of our development, The Canyons. It was a small, exclusive development most people in Tucson weren't aware of. Instead of leaving right away, I felt pulled to drive through the developments twisted and turning roads, while I embraced the feel of the wide racing tires grip-ping the bulky stones below.

A recent fight with Bill gripped my mind. It went down as a memory I may hold forever. I officially named it a "Come to Jesus" meeting. Truth was told, and it unleashed our financial status, which was painful. We agreed the house and a couple of cars needed to be sold, immediately. Not sure of when the move would take place, I wanted to soak in all of the surrounding beauty back here in the high foothills of Tucson. So I drove to the back of the development. A simultaneous urge to scream at the top of my lungs arose, but I stifled it with the distraction of the bright sunny 80-degree day.

Living large may become a memory or a launching pad for something bigger in the future. Who knew? I was born with a positive nature and held onto it as much as possible. Although today, it felt like a fine thread amidst ropes of omitted truth, greed, behind-door positioning, and mounting lawsuits. We thought we'd already been through the gauntlet with i360 before the sale, but things had stepped up a notch in the world of the crashing Telecom industry, and I was guessing we might not be experienced or equipped enough to be playing on this level.

As far as business, we would need to endure some big changes. Trying to stay positive, I thought back to our past years where we showed signs of being somewhat durable, so I had a shred of confidence we might persevere. As for our marriage, we were tired and distracted by our busy, over-scheduled household. We had, yet again, in the last year, coasted into something I named *parallel and pretty mode* and I had a sinking feeling that only a deep marriage would be able to take a hit like this one.

TRUTH BE TOLD

I listened to Bill while I sat on a small patch of grass in our backyard under the stars. We discussed a year's worth of details in this "Come to Jesus" meeting. Some of which he had kept to himself, hoping he'd find a way through some gritty obstacles that came up immediately after the sale. Two companies had become one, but this was not a merger filled with ease. The severity of our situation sunk in whole-heartedly; I now knew the lay of the land. I fixated on the negative-edge pool and watched the water gently tip over the pool's edge, mirroring our own financial stability slipping away.

Pieces of our life's puzzle started to fall into place as I remembered the soon-after-the-sale calls from former employees and investors, blowing Bill's phone up. I recalled seeing him sitting in our elaborate home office with the phone against his ear and his hands cradling his head, bent over his enormous mahogany desk. I wanted to give him a nudge to make him aware of his beaten and broken posture. We had read enough self-help and motivational books by now; he knew better. Our floor to ceiling, thick wood shelves held thousands of well-worn books and tape series, collected and studied since college. Topics ranged from business, religion, and philosophy to self-help, meditation, and the healing arts. A water bottle filled with chewing tobacco spit sat next to the papers sprawled in front of him. I hadn't seen that since his college football days. Documents had been flooding the fax machine all morning, and I wondered what was going on. In hindsight, I recognized my denial as I was hoping for another promising venture.

At the time he didn't share the details, and I didn't ask.

Turns out, Bill and some investors decided that he fly to Canada to discuss things with the merger; things that were happening due to the recent stock market crash. Employees in Tucson were being let go; they released the original president, and they were declaring a full relocation to Canada. None of which was part of the plan, pre-merger. But because of the upset in this industry, they were trying to keep things afloat. Bill arranged to stay several days with the i360 Inc. corporate attorney but returned after one day.

He explained it this way: "Their lawyers picked me up at the airport, which was not expected. They drove me straight to the office boardroom where the board members and I sat. Since part of the sale included I stay involved and working for them for three years, I felt comfortable to discuss these new concerns. I was well prepared by our investors on the outside, and we had a strategy to get things back on track. I wasn't fearful of delivering the information. I knew it would be a battle, but saw it as simple and fair; it made perfect business sense."

Then he said this, "I was ready for a boxing match, except, when the board room door closed, it was a bloody street fight. No gloves, no ring, no rules, and no refs. The game had changed: I hadn't realized the significance of this telecom crash that hit. It was ten times bigger than the dotcom crash. They're saying it's the biggest and fastest in all history at 2.9 trillion… that's a potential recession. Bottom line was that numbers weren't hit, and there was no way for me to make it happen quickly in this industry. I gave up some shares to help stabilize, but that didn't seem to help. We just simply all got our asses handed to us in this crash and were trying to build it back."

"Judy, don't look at me like that."

I said, "We shouldn't have built this house. It was a gamble, I get it, but…"

"But, we can sell it and probably walk away with 750K. We can use that for living expenses and buy something else."

"I just don't see how the hell we ended up here. Where's the cash we had before this company? It's sickening," I said. I felt the cool grassy earth under my fingers as I grasped for something, anything to hold onto. This meeting was far from over. Bill kept speaking as my stomach kept tightening.

"Look, it's simple. We dumped a million into the house we built. We were the first investors with a million into the company. I also bridged the financial gap for a while, so there's 800K there. We have about 350K in legal fees and settlements that I'll explain in a minute. Also, I've been deferring taking income from the company for two years, that's 500K, times two, of our own money we've blown through. And you know I did that in order to get equity in $2.5 million shares. It's restricted, but it won't be forever. Listen, this is important and may make you feel better, the stock was at $17 and dropped, but hear me out, in the last few months, the new CEO they just put in place, actually asked me to step back in to help resurrect the company and funding. So the stock could go back up. This guy has brought a new boardroom of people with business pedigrees you wouldn't believe. I've always wanted to work with a group like this. The stock is at $14 a share right now, but that would still leave us with 35 million-ish."

Looking back at the last year, I could now see his initial disappointment scream so loud through the silence he had hung onto. His trust in the lay of this land was void. He had shut down and kept me out of the loop, and it made me feel for him. But at the same time, I was angry. I didn't know how I hadn't tapped into this. He hid it so well, but I knew him so well, or so I thought. In contrast, I could see that this new group had stirred some hope in him. So I listened on.

He continued to fill me in on the details regarding lawsuits that had surfaced. Bill's name listed as a top executive, made him a legal target for anyone who wanted to get paid for something. On top of that, he inadvertently had signed a personal guarantee, locking him in to being a sure target. Within a short period, lawsuits flooded in.

"I did my best to protect us over the last year. I've been battling to get the personal guarantee cleared, but with no avail. So I attempted to settle the first lawsuits. Legal advisors suggested coming up with settlement checks for $30,000 to $100,000 at a time. Unfortunately, that didn't end our battles; it emboldened them. You follow me? I've been trying to get us liquid again and get the business back on track."

I nodded without relief, feeling my anxiety rising.

"For a guy who hates to gamble, I can't believe you're participating like this. I get you want to save the world, Atlas, but who's gonna save you? You were going to retire. Coach middle school football. Spend more time with the kids."

He didn't respond.

I won't say I saw desperation in him because it wasn't that. He was in pure action mode, seeking every angle to make things right again. It was more a warrior overdrive kicking in. My warrior, the guy that never gives up. Whether it's on a football field, in a board room, at a bar fight, or in our marriage therapist's office, his keen dissection of all moving parts in most circumstances served him well in all arenas. The typical Libra, with balanced scales, sought ways to make it a win-win for all. Back in the day, when he recognized his sales team at Motorola was lackadaisical, he personally paid for his 25 employees to walk on hot coals at a Tony Robbins event. When the members of the next sales crew that came up the ranks were overly aggressive, and at times, anxiously fired up, he sent all of them and himself to a Deepak Chopra primordial sound meditation seminar for five days. Each group became No.1 in the country afterward.

In the past, his balance had come from devouring any marketing, management, sales or self-help book I shared with him. He enjoyed absorbing stories of historians and the biographies of past Presidents in order to uncover the hero in them. Now tonight—he was ferociously seeking balanced scales in his own life and was on the hunt for the hero in himself.

I was horrified to learn of the lawsuits. But it became clear, as the company looked more vulnerable, the dent in finances was potentially going to deepen, and more lawsuits would attach to the ship going down. *I need to get ready. Get stronger. He was right. We need to sell this house and some cars and hope that new financing is secured. Soon.*

The only thing I could hold onto after our talk was, I knew the truth, but I can't say it was setting me free.

We moved inside to the kitchen, where the tall granite counter island served as a barrier between us. After learning all the details of our situation, I dove into a fight to be right—foreign territory for a woman who hates confrontation.

He sensed my anger and asked me to "not freak out." He needed me to "stay calm and strong."

"Seriously? You're asking me to not freak out? First of all, with all of our experience in marriage counseling, didn't you realize that you pushed me to the end of your line? I thought we were in this together. I could have helped. And now you finally let me in, in the 11th hour, to let me know how bad things are? All I can do now is pack!"

"Listen," raising his voice, "You haven't asked. And you don't work there everyday. It's impossible to get you up to speed. And, no offense, but I can't hear about your intuitive hits on it all. I need to trust my own gut."

"Well, I was right about a lot of them," I blurted.

"Maybe, but I don't think you get it. I've worked my whole life to be here, and you expect me to just give up? It's what I know."

"But it's not all you are," I said.

He shrugged and nodded with a reluctant air of agreement.

I continued, "Sounds like throwing good money at bad. You're so driven to make this work, to save all the people their jobs, I'm afraid you may drive right into a dead end. Are you going to be able to see that?"

"I will," he answered bluntly, "Just keep the faith. We need to resurrect this company. There's no other way."

"And so you're staying in this game, then? Can't you just get another job? 'Cause with all the lawsuits, stress, and no income; we won't last long. We definitely need to sell it all to stay afloat, right?"

"Right. We have about a 120-day window to secure new financing. We're just about there. Meanwhile, I'm gonna keep an eye out for another job."

I had never felt doubt about his direction, but this one shook me to the core.

Shifting into a kind of crazy gear as panic took over I yelled, "You tell the kids they have to move again. We've already moved twice in less than two years, just waiting for this house. You let them know they will, most likely, have to switch schools. Holy shit, Bill! You're the only one dumping money in. You're literally the nice guy that will potentially finish last!"

"You don't get it. We don't have a choice, and IT TAKES MONEY TO MAKE MONEY!" he said as he threw his arms up to the house, "You want ALL of this? Well, it takes hard work! And you can't just quit 'cause it gets hard, Judy."

Exhaling with a deep breath, he continued, "And, no, Judy, don't even say it… I didn't manifest all of this. People have free will and on top of that… shit actually happens! And when it does, sometimes you have to fight. 'Cause it's the right fucking thing to do! You can't just meditate the lawsuits and challenges away," he said, taking a jab at my last 25 years of studying healing arts, meditation, yoga, and visualization.

He locked eyes with mine, "If I'm going down, I'm goin' down swinging."

I flashbacked on all my years of praying, believing and counting on God—it all looked and felt different now. I panicked with the realization of how fragile my faith must be.

Speechless and now furious, I stared him down. His neck turned a disturbing shade of red as he took a deep breath. He squatted down, elbows on bent knees. His 6'2" 240-pound frame reminded me of his linebacker stance back in college. He shot up with full force and slammed his hands widely apart on the counter, his eyes darting from right to left, never looking into mine, which were locked in on him. Dramatically, he kicked the heavy bar stool out of his way, landing on the Italian travertine floor with a huge bang echoing through the high ceilings. *He is so screwed. We are so screwed.*

I had never seen him like this.

"F u c k!" he screamed.

Without thinking, he grabbed a coffee mug and whipped it across the room, just missing our glass-topped kitchen table. The mug smashed against the wall, breaking into tiny pieces, spraying all over the floor.

Trying to uncover the source of the bang from the stool, and also our yelling, Marcus, Clint and Nicole dashed into the kitchen. We were well-trained as healthy communicators, so this heated vocal exchange shocked them. Cautiously, they stood there, wide-eyed, waiting for our next move.

Scared by Bill's unnatural violence, I overreacted and uncontrollably screamed, "Fucking loser!"

I had never said nor ever thought that of him before.

This confirms my immediate disintegration of faith in God, myself and him.

I grew up with siblings who never verbally fought with me, so I didn't even know how to engage in battle. I just said the first thing that came to mind. He, on the other hand, was an expert debater and arguer because of his vocal family. He had a way to deliver his point, but not destroy someone. For me, not speaking up when I should have had always been a known weakness of mine. Yet here, while my innocent children watched, I said something when I shouldn't have. And I felt exponentially worse. I had just ended this fight by letting it escalate to the point of no return. There was nothing more to say. I did damage. And I did it in front of the kids, who stood there stunned.

In unison, all three kids started backing up and then scattered off to the top of the boys' bunk bed where they quietly sat, waiting for one of us to come to them.

I had no plans to make dinner but busied myself by turning my back to Bill while slamming open a cabinet below, grabbing a soup pan and dropping it with inappropriate distance onto the gas stove. I took a deep breath and yanked the pot filler from the wall to fill the pan with water. Out of the corner of my eye, I watched him awkwardly open and close cabinets in a separate area of the kitchen designed for vegetable prepping. He searched for paper towels or anything to help clean up his mess. Annoyed, knowing that's not where cleaning supplies would have been, I refused to help. Eventually, he gave up the search and sat down with his head hung over the round glass kitchen table. His shoes were pressed up against the hand carved Cantera stone base. The pillars in the foyer were made of the same material, and I immediately thought how strange and parallel we were to the stone. One of our contractors, born and raised in Mexico, had shared how the pyramids there were made of Cantera, which was surprisingly fragile. He actually snapped a 12x12 tile in half to show me. He explained that when the stone was kept in large volume, it was unbreakable and extremely heavy. In the past, I had always recognized the strength Bill and I had together, but as I studied him sitting at the kitchen table, I saw our fragility. And it scared me.

I knew he would not be sharing much more information with me based on his startled and severe disappointment in my crazed response. Eventually, the details of our "meeting" all started to make sense. Like my old voice coach from Chicago had told me, "You're too nice for the music industry. Go sing in a church." I was hoping the same advice would not be true for Bill in this type of business world, but I wondered if his defeat might be telling us something. *Maybe we don't belong here.*

In general, since college, I noticed that the business world was sometimes filled with unfair advantages; there were some that aggressively dominated by lying while not seeming to lose any sleep at night, some justified their actions with the mantra, "It's business, not personal," when at times it really was personal. Some gave fair warning, "I'm going to be brutally honest," and excitedly pounced to slice you to the core. Some started off by saying, "With all due respect," but didn't really have any respect for you. Some hid behind thoughts convincing themselves that morals and character could take a back seat if it were legal. "Legal" made anything acceptable.

Recognizing my cynicism had grown throughout the years, I sensed a loose grip on my old genuine belief in the goodness of others. A wall was going up, and I was afraid it would block the good from entering. Fear won out, and I began barricading myself into protection mode, as I tried to hold on to a deep down belief, there may be a silver lining.

I attempted counseling myself, that maybe we wouldn't have to fall too far. From what I'd read, a real hard time for someone in this position might last six months to a year. To stay calm, I rationalized that selling the house and extra cars may give us breathing room. However, it was clear, as quickly as the stars aligned to bring everything together, it felt like the stars were aligning just as fast, to dismantle it all.

Truth be told, our belief that our financial blessings were on loan from God was easier to believe when the money kept flowing. I just wondered how that would hold up now. I hoped for the best but strategically started preparing for the worst. And I started considering Karma. *Where did we go wrong? And was this now going to serve us right?*

THE CANYONS

The Porsche tightly hugged a curve leading up a steep hill, which took me up to the back of the development. The exhaust system was not overdone, but just right to alert someone, a magnificent machine was arriving. I shifted with each hill, twist and turn to hear the sound bounce off the nearby Santa Catalina Mountains. *I'm gonna miss this neighborhood.*

The award-winning architectural homes filling the development were master-pieces. The copper and steel contemporary angles with full walls of glass over-looking these Mountains and vast Tucson city views were stunning. Every house had its own personality; a 6,000-square-foot contemporary would sit comfortably next door to an exquisite 14,000-square-foot Mediterranean-style mansion nes-tled into the mountainside behind us. The homes were purposely designed and situated where all had privacy. Even today, I was still noticing aspects I hadn't seen before in these beautiful pieces of art. Occasionally, you may see someone over-50 walking a little dog, but, besides that, we felt like we were nestled all alone. Being one of only two families with children living here, I loved the cocoon-like feel.

I downshifted from third gear and stopped for a moment around a bend in the road to take in the full view of the Tucson skyline, the same I saw from the entire front of our home. Of all the houses we had lived in, this one had it all; both city and mountain views. We appreciated the mountains all day long from the enormous glass, floor-to-ceiling windows on the back of the house. The sun and occasional rare clouds shifted the colors and displayed different textures from one minute to the next, leaving me with a new piece of Mother Earth's art everyday. It was like the Mountain was alive, and I could see her breathe. Monsoons in July created one of my favorite displays of nature. Massive rains, with violent thunder and lightning strikes, would take my breath away. I'd literally stay clear of the win-dows while peeking around brick walls and demand the kids take cover while the fascinating and captivating show seemed to rumble and roll through and around the house.

Sunsets in Arizona are real life post cards. Hot pink and bright orange streaked the turquoise blue skies like a priceless watercolor. I felt my mouth drop open when I first saw one. In the evening, bright stars popped out of the black night, making you feel as if you could reach out and touch a few. From the front of the house, we were graced with the vast twinkling city lights, spanning the entire valley. Doors off the dining area led out to a balcony that overlooked the city. It was ethereal-like to stand high up there and see the hustle and bustle of cars zipping around but hear none of it. The silence was deafening, and I liked it. It felt easy to think clearer here.

As our realtor was taking photos of our place to put in the portfolio she was preparing for the sale of the house, I threw open the French doors and stepped outside onto the patio, "This may be a strong selling point for a buyer."

"Good God, Judy! Put some shoes on. You know better than to stand out there in bare feet with centipedes, scorpions and rattlesnakes!" she exclaimed.

"Oh, I've never been bitten. I belong here. They know that" I winked.

I wasn't at peace with selling this place, but trying to keep it light, I recited a verse from "The Red River Valley," calmly, I spoke, "…from this valley they say you're going… we will miss your bright eyes and sweet smile…"

She turned to me with an empathetic hint of apology and a compassionate smile and said, "If we price it right Judy, we'll unload this fast. It's a stunning home… it's a mix of Spanish cathedral with all the modern goodies. It has an exquisite courtyard with a gorgeous Cantera water fountain leading to a separate guest house. And this majestic foyer, with the many traverse windows, set high above, lets in the most extraordinary light. The location and views are what everyone wants—numerous outdoor living areas, four fireplaces and how 'bout that negative edge pool? You only have $1.2 million in it, and I think I can list for $2.2. The market has dipped, but not in this price bracket, so I think it'll move quickly."

I nodded in agreement as I studied the twinkling lights below. *Everything was moving quickly.*

Realizing I was late for a luncheon; I headed out towards the gatehouse which was a literal boulder that the developer cut and fashioned into a heavily secured entrance. It was apparently the most expensive, per square foot, structure made in Tucson. Security was top notch, and even my own mother, who visited regularly, was often declined entry.

The Canyons privately hid at the top of Alvernon Way. Often, I would startle a hiker making their way to the Finger Rock Trailhead because they didn't even know the development was there. The kids got a kick out of Finger Rock because it was a rock structure that sat above The Canyons that looked like a hand with the index finger standing straight up, like a number one. While in town, playing sports on a field or at someone's house, it wasn't uncommon for one of the kids to point to finger rock and say, "That's home." One night after football practice, Clint plopped himself into the backseat of another mom's car and when she asked, "Where do you live honey?" He responded by pointing up to Finger Rock.

The gates began to open, and I revved the engine and tore through them before it was appropriate. Eddie, our main security guard, peeked his head out from the gatehouse as he waved for me to go faster. I appreciated Eddie. On a daily basis, he remained genuinely interested in all that passed through the gates, always embracing someone's smile, their hello, and their good and even rude mood. I waved as I passed him, and he waved back with a big smile, "Go get 'em, Tiger!"

ENOUGH IS ENOUGH

The drive down into town was glorious, and I let myself briefly disconnect from worry on this perfect sunny day. After lowering the windows, I opened the sunroof and allowed my left arm to flap like an eagle on the way down the steep hill. The stereo's volume was up to only three, but the thump of the bass made my heart feel like it skipped a beat as Lenny Kravitz's "American Woman" blasted through the Bose speakers and outside the Porsche. And, like always, at the first red light I came to, with this song still blasting, I received a thumbs-up from someone in the next lane.

I pulled into the entrance of La Paloma Resort and up to the valet area. As usual, the rumble of my engine downshifting caught the attention of the young male valet attendants. This resort was close to home, but we never purchased a membership because Bill and I liked having the kids to ourselves. I was trying hard to not have typical "country club kids," but they ended up spending plenty of time there, attending numerous birthdays, bar mitzvahs, play dates, Halloween's, and Fourth of Julys.

Jimmy, the head valet, excitedly waved and smiled when I pulled up. He was always cheerful and even though I wasn't mirroring that back today, I pushed myself to wave and smile in return, deciding to fake it until I made it, just like the books told me.

I got out of the car before he could open the door for me.

"Uh-uh. Nope, get back in there lady. We're gonna do this right."

All the other valets turned towards me as they watched and laughed because they had seen this show before.

"Oh, geez, I'm late, Jimmy," as I turned and got back in the seat, waiting for him to re-open my door. After he did, I stepped out and handed him the keys.

"Uh-uh. Nope," handing me back the keys.

I continued to play along. After all, I thought, this may be the last we see of this *happy* Porsche. With a playful catwalk, I threw the Porsche keys high up in the air behind me. I didn't look back to make sure Jimmy caught them—he always did. The valet guys were laughing, hooting and hollering.

When I had first driven this Porsche, I did exactly what I had today: just pulled up, let myself out and handed Jimmy the keys. But, because of the occasional slight air of guilt I had for material things, he noted, "Geez, lady, you should have some attitude getting outta a car like that.

Ever since then, I played the girl with the make-believe attitude, and we all got a kick out of it.

The plan for today was to meet with a charitable group of women with whom I had regularly met with over the last few years. Two of them were wives of the husbands working for Bill at i360. I was running about 20 minutes late as I hurried over to our regular luncheon table. I quickly but carefully walked with high heels across the polished, cream-marble floors through the lobby of this premiere resort. I passed by a massive marble pillar near our table when I heard my name. Stopping dead in my tracks, and curious to hear what they were saying about me, I tucked myself behind one of the pillars.

Abby, a woman married to one of Bill's employees, was in full rant mode. I immediately felt exposed as I realized she was laying out the lay of *our* land. Her husband, Frank, had been sharing detailed information with her about how he felt certain Bill could have sold the company for more and clearly he was incompetent for not doing so. She continued on and on about all the accused incompetents.

"Apparently they are being sued, big time. They could lose it all," she excitedly explained.

"Serves them right," said one of the other women at the table who was known for having a spiritual side. I could feel my face contort. *Ouch.* Her words struck home because I had just been contemplating the same karmic idea.

Still, behind the pillar, I felt small beads of sweat pop up along my hairline. I could feel droplets begin to drip down into my cleavage. I slightly lifted my arms and pinched a piece of my blouse into my fingers, tenting it as I moved it like a flag in order to get air onto my damp skin. I was worried my blouse would tell all. I placed my warm, flushed face against the cold marble pillar. *Dear God, this is humiliating. Please land us a quick sale of our home and help us find the next job, which hopefully will be in a place far from here.*

On a roll and unable to stop herself, Abby seemed to revel in sinking the ship Bill was trying to bail out and keep afloat. She even went so far as to make fun of Bill's enormous window in his office where he wrote, *KEEP THE FAITH* with a dry erase marker.

"Hope their faith sees them through!" she mocked, as it had become not just a talking point, but a laughing point as well. *Who does that?*

"I'm not even sure Judy is going to be effective in this group. Maybe it's time for her to go."

Trying to both sooth and empower myself before I faced them, I thought, *Get a grip, Jude.* But something deep inside me was being dragged up to the surface—a strong belief system—that scared me. *Why do I always feel like I'm not enough?*

Embracing a pause due to awkward silence at the table, I came around the pillar as if I had heard nothing. This wasn't a game I liked to play, but it was a game I knew I had to play. Their words about me quickly changed to "How are YOU? The kids? We heard the bad news." The small talk settled, and I silenced their fake concern for this trying time for Bill and me, by saying, "This too shall pass." *I only wished I believed it.*

I encouraged them to talk about the next order of business: which charity to fund, and how much we needed to raise.

Abby said, "If you have too much on your plate, and this isn't a good time for you, you don't have to come to these meetings anymore."

I knew her real agenda. She had been pitching a charity that we already had assisted. If she chaired the event, she would most likely be recognized publicly, and all of Tucson would know of this. In addition, the establishment where we would have the event would be right here at her country club. Her natural desire to control situations was obvious, so I wasn't surprised by her excitability over this idea. I let her pitch the whole thing without interruption, and listened to all the agreeable ladies chime in.

Spreadsheets highlighting all the charities discussed today, plus monetary needs, present position and also dates on when we last funded them were in individual packets for each one of us to look over. I had been sifting through the information while the ladies were only talking about this one charity. I'm no business guru, but it looked pretty ridiculous and obvious to me that her charity was not the right choice. Their conversations continuously got hooked on when they would schedule their dress shopping trip to Scottsdale. Each time I'd try to push them back on topic, they'd trail off about the appropriate hairstyle for certain types of necklines and which jewelry they could pull from their safes. Trying to get used to more frugal living again, I casually suggested we should borrow each other's dresses this year as a statement of savings.

Silence filled the table. Finally, one of the ladies responded with an insulted tone, "Um, excuse me. That won't work. We aren't all the same size."

I silently disagreed.

When first meeting these women, I couldn't get over how much they all resembled each other. They were similar in height and weight, and all went to the same personal trainers. They each had the same boob job, the same hairdress-er, practically the same hair cut and same shade of highlights. Even the same manicurist performed the same perfect acrylic french manicures on each of them. They were all white, and they all had blue eyes. I was born and raised outside of Chicago. *Where are all the different shapes, sizes, and colors?*

To me, these ladies looked related. And then it hit me: *Shit. I look like them.* I didn't resemble them in every way, but I found myself sitting at a table with women, who at this moment, reflected me.

After all the paths I have taken in religion and self-help... directing me to be trans-parent, genuine and grounded, it made me question... *How the hell did I get here?*

I certainly had clinked champagne glasses with a few of them when times were good, but the truth was I wouldn't call one of these women in crisis. They were a tribe, but not one I'd step on a battlefield with. I always hoped the friend-ships would have gone deeper, but it seemed we were far from that.

I couldn't stand to hear one more word. I noticed my tolerance had shifted to another gear while standing behind the pillar, but my voice surfacing at the table surprised me.

Calmly at first, I said, "Two years ago we raised funds for this group. They look sufficiently well-funded for now. How about we look at them again for next year and focus on this one here that could use our support: The Tucson Food Bank. The function could be held on the premises, which would be a bit more casual, but perhaps people would give more money because of having a more affordable ticket price. They need help in building an enormous organic garden for a green-house someone donated. We could have butterflies released, serve simple foods, organic vegetables, organic fruit tarts and have a cash bar. And for music, we could have a local mariachi band or maybe just a DJ. Tickets could be $75. More people could afford to come. Our profits could be substantial, and we would most certainly meet their needs and also bring awareness to the food bank, which may increase donor support for years to come."

Feeling they did not like this direction, I explained further, "The ticket price you're looking at for the event here at La Paloma will be $150 and may mean sales of $45,000. But the resort will charge us for their full course dinner, ballroom fee, and alcohol. In addition, you want a casino, silent auctioneer, a live band *and a* DJ, a photo booth, and thank-you gifts at each seat. I get it. But... cha ching! It's glamorous, but is it really meeting a need? We'd barely break even."

Dead silence filled the table again.

I could see the illusion of respect they had for me disappear from their eyes as I scanned the table. It wasn't surprising. It was disappointing. This platform... This once-solid ground Bill and I had stood upon was crumbling.

I don't belong here.

And then Abby spoke, "Umm, okay. Let's see, how do I explain this to you? You see, people want to have fun, or they aren't going to come. If you think I'm attending the Tucson Food Bank to eat pork and beans in my jeans and get my hands dirty in manure, you're crazy. I have a gardener that does that for me." She laughed and looked around the table for her tribe to join in.

The stress had officially gotten to me. The information downloaded in the fight I had with Bill, and now Abby's condescending response pushed me over an edge I was unaware of standing on. Until now. I sunk my teeth into the first thing that came to mind. I tried to pull in grace as I delivered the information, but it didn't come out the way I wanted.

I went into full preach mode, and I couldn't stop. "Your past fundraisers have failed miserably. You overspend simply to attend a party that is fun. And afterward, you deliver a check that doesn't meet needs. Frankly, it's embarrassing. Your attention to fucking dresses, hairstyles and which diamond to take from the safe is ridiculous!"

I drew an imaginary circle around the table, "You're a group of women that are not about giving or empowering other women. You even hide your beauty secrets from each other for fear another will be more radiant than yourself."

I pointed to a woman across the table, "Your husband went through a tough financial hit before and instead of sharing something supportive about this time to help ease my and Bill's suffering, you seem more pleased watching us squirm. The most disturbing of all is you would still be kissing my ass if I had money. Do you see how fucked up that is?"

Their arms crossed in front of them, showing great offense was taken. But I didn't care. *Enough was finally enough.*

BEING HONEST MAY NOT GET YOU A LOT OF FRIENDS BUT IT'LL ALWAYS GET YOU THE RIGHT ONES. JOHN LENNON

NO PLACE TO CALL HOME

I left that day and never attended another meeting. Immediately after, I had one fire after another to put out. I recognized the work I'd have to do on myself. However, my unstable life made it easy to stay distracted with the chaos in our lives.

Just as our realtor had guessed, our house sold immediately for a full cash offer of $2.2 with a 30-day closing. But the number of lawsuits quadrupled and the profit from the sale of the home disappeared in payment to the lawyers. Debt collectors would call relentlessly day and night. They were well-trained people, masterful at fighting for money. I lacked experience with this combat and was torn up after almost every call. The last-ditch efforts to keep the company alive rapidly drained our checking and savings accounts. Our high-limit credit cards, with minimal debt incurred, were shut down due to a couple of missed minimum payments. I had made numerous phone calls arranging future payments, but they closed the accounts anyway. After we sold the house and paid the mortgage off in full, our bank called to thank us for doing business with them, and they would now be dismissing the personal banker they had originally assigned to us and that we should feel free to ask for assistance at the teller window in any of their local branches.

As if on a staircase, we took a step down every year in terms of living conditions. At first, we rented our Canyons house back from the new owners for $10,000 a month, just to give ourselves a few months to find a place to live. Then we moved mid-year to Ventana Country Club & Resort and rented a fully-furnished home on the golf course. The development was directly across the street from the kids' elementary school. Because of not being able to show income, the landlord asked us to pay up front. We used our last chunk of money to pay the entire year in full. We hoped that by doing this, it would take the pressure of rent payments off our radar so that we could focus on Bill or me attaining employment. On the outside, it appeared we were still somewhat living, in the same way, we were accustomed. But every time I would find 9 to 5 kind of work for myself, I would consider the costs of hiring people, or finding places, to take care of our three kids, and it never made financial sense.

Because I was a hypnotherapist by trade, I continued to try and grow my own small business, working within school hours. It was strictly word of mouth, and I was getting good results, so it kept me busy, but not financially stable. I saw adults for smoking and weight loss to depression and anorexia. I met with many children who were suffering from bedwetting, night terrors, or addiction. When kids were concerned, I would often help desperate families at no charge. Bill was not pleased with the many hours I would spend at work. Energetically, I was too weak to handle their suffering and started to feel ill after each session. But I kept going, as I was never able to say no.

Over the next two years, Bill secured four different jobs selling life insurance and mortgages exactly when the banking industry was in a down turn. Each job was worse than the previous one. At one company, after arriving early in the morning to work, security guards quickly escorted him out of the building and told him he had been let go. Turns out, this company declined a Hispanic grandfather for a small life insurance policy. He was seeking this policy because his children and grandchildren had to move in with him and he wanted to make sure things would be covered if he passed away. Bill apologetically declined him on behalf of the insurance company, but then made a call to a small insurance company in town that was known for helping provide local Hispanics with small policies like this. Bill thought it was a perfect fit. Apparently, though, his current employer mistakenly assumed he was going to be making a commission off the policy that he had simply helped arrange. Luckily, within days of hearing Bill was fired, the smaller insurance company he referred the Hispanic grandfather to, hired Bill and he started working there immediately.

Bill worked from home, more often than not. At this point, he was barely making enough money to make our ends meet, so a large part of his time was spent trying to secure a more permanent executive position. He was also still seeking a resurrection of funding for the merger, hoping to salvage the still-sinking ship. Having him here, working at our kitchen table, and over-hearing his disappointing phone calls was taking its toll. The kids loved having him around at first, but quickly realized this was not playtime with daddy. He kept his nose to the grindstone and didn't spend much time away from the table or phone, trying to find a way out of this hellhole we were in.

Bill continued to stay off our family's grid while submerged in private warrior mode. A man certain that he was the only one to fix it, was determined to be on his own. He had stopped reaching out to me, and the only sex he wanted now was emotionless. I rejected that kind of lovemaking, and the wedge grew deeper between us.

Even though he was at home all the time, I never wavered from my role as primary caregiver for the kids. I flew all over town, picking up and dropping off kids at baseball parks, football fields, skate parks, playgrounds, play dates, karate class, dance lessons, chess club, sleepovers, and occasionally school to drop off forgotten lunches and homework. Like a lot of mothers, I made it easy for him to enjoy the kids for an hour or so at night before bed.

As much as I had complained over the years about Bill working 15-20 hours a day, seven days a week, I wanted my space again. I looked forward to him leaving to coach Pop Warner football and baseball games so that I could have the house to myself. He was overwhelmed by and annoyed to see the dis-organization of our stuff crammed into our temporary houses with boxes stacked in random places that never seemed to have what we needed to find. I was annoyed because I just want-ed him to shut up, rip open a box, and put the shit somewhere that made sense.

We stepped down another stair on the staircase and moved to an even smaller rental. Our credit score had plummeted, and the landlord required a $3,000 secu-rity deposit because of it. I borrowed money from my mom, but we also had to ask our friend, again, to co-sign the lease. I remember watching her sign the papers, and after we silently walked out of the building, the disappointment ran deep be-cause we both thought this was all going to be over by now. The rough six months or so I had originally expected extended to three years, with no hope in sight.

Upon arrival at the new rental, I prepped Bill and the kids for the poor condition it was in.

"It's kind of rundown, but it's good cause it's close to your school, the bus stops in front of our house, and there are lots of kids in the neighborhood to play with." Turning to Bill, I added, "And it's cheap, for the foothills."

I opened the front door, and a smelly gust of musty mold hit us all as we crowded into the tiny foyer. The popcorn ceilings hung low, and the windows didn't allow enough light in. The grout around the cheap broken white-tile floor was caked with dirt that would most likely never get clean. As I fought with the broken track to pull back the yellowed plastic vertical blinds from the living room window, I said to the kids, "Go... go take a look around..."

But all three kids stayed close following Bill and I from room to room. I didn't push exploration. I let them follow as I knew by the cautious looks on their faces that they were now feeling the same as me—tired, dirty and small—just like this place. The outdated bathrooms left me wondering if I would even be able to brush my teeth in the old cracked and permanently brown stained ceramic sinks. And I made a mental plan to pour bleach on the black mold in the tiled corners of the shower. The filthy carpets in the bedrooms were matted down where padding was exposed from years of traffic patterns from other renters, and I imagined I would never allow myself or the kids to walk barefoot on them. No one said a word as we looked around. Their discouragement was obvious, but I was drawn to their politeness by not saying exactly what was on their mind. And then Nicole, without knowledge of our code of silence screamed, "This is Horrrrible!"

The boys' wide eyes turned toward us to see how we would react. Because of her speech impediment and lisp, it sounded like she said, 'Horehole.'

"Ohhhhhhhh, that's a bad word Nicole," Marcus warned.

"Yeah Nicole," said Clint.

Bill and I turned to each other and stifled our reaction. We excused ourselves to the back yard and both burst out laughing. Whore hole. The more we repeated her version of horrible, the funnier it became. In the past, we had named cars and houses and so without further discussion, the name stuck. We, of course, restricted it to our adult conversations. As sleazy as it may have been, it gave us a laugh… which we needed more of. *Horehole.*

We emptied our friends' storage area that held our furniture from the 6000 square-foot home and stuffed it into this 1000 square-foot home, which left the walls lined with boxes stacked floor to ceiling. My intention was to sell as much as possible in a garage sale since we were out of cash. Because of my role, CEO of household, I had become the expert and the one in charge of all aspects having to do with a move. I had moved us from Chicago to North Carolina, basically on my own. And then, North Carolina to Tucson; I packed an entire house and then drove a minivan pulling a U-Haul with my sister and three kids in tow. Hours were spent planning, organizing and delegating and also physically moving by myself because Bill was always out of town for work. I wasn't as bothered by the task when he was making good money. *But now that we were moving into Horehole, it was a different story.* Getting close to the end of my rope was an understatement. I was tired of doing this without resources like trucks and movers. Many marathon-like days of multiple car trips filled to the rim with stuffed garbage bags and used grocery boxes became the only way to transport our belongings.

Disgusted with this rental, I felt like a vacationer that kept arriving in the most disappointing seedy hotel imaginable. Besides that, my natural nesting desire was strong and made me yearn for a place to call home. Even if we had the money, fixing up a rental would be a waste. I would have partially felt satisfied if we could purchase anything at this point, a n y t h i n g to call our own.

Regretting this move from Day One, I wanted to run and hide... Mexico, California, somewhere, anywhere. The exhaustion, coupled with endless disappointments was getting to me, and I was feeling restless on a dangerous level. I thought it was interesting that I spent more time considering running away in the past three years than I ever had as a child.

THE ROLEX

Luck and breaks seemed to evade us daily. While working at mortgage and insurance companies, Bill also juggled one interview after another over the three-year period, but nothing panned out. Then, *finally*, Bill made it through to his sixth interview for a VP sales position with a Phoenix company. We were hopeful. The salary was decent enough, and the potential for commissions and bonuses based on sales generated made it promising. Unfortunately, despite all the reasons to hire him, there was resistance at the board level given the decline of i360 and Infocast. This dead end happened so often, we lost count.

I had garage sales in each neighborhood we moved to. I stood in each space and wrestled with what we could live with and without, as I rifled through the last of our storage location as well. Grudgingly, we sold every piece of jewelry worth something, and, one by one, we were letting go of Bill's small Rolex collection—except one.

Bill stood in our bedroom doorway staring down at the submariner Rolex, moving through his fingers. I'll never forget his strong hands in contrast to his breaking heart that wouldn't allow him to look me in the eye. He couldn't bear to personally go into the jewelry store to do it, as he had with the others. It was the Rolex he had bought and given to his father, who had since passed. I could tell he probably thought of him daily as his dad was his biggest fan and he longed for someone on his side these days. Bill had given his dad this gift when we lived in Chicago; it was long before he could afford to do so. I remember feeling financially pinched at the time. Bill had once asked his father while still alive, "Is there anything you wanted to do, or anything you feel you missed in your life?"

"Wish I could drive my old 1965 Shelby GT350 again, and I guess I'll never own a Rolex."

But today, I was so grateful that his dad wore it religiously for a few years, while I imagined it filled him with love and pride for his adored, Billy. Besides his dad's ashes, the Rolex was the last material thing connecting them and watching him battle through the release of this, just to pay rent, left me numb. There was nothing to say and nothing to do, to ease his pain.

Bill Sr. stood 6'4 at 300 lbs, with full sleeves of tattoos which ranged from a naked lady to the Marine Corps motto, Semper Fi. At times, he wore his gray hair in a short ponytail or swept the full head of hair back over the top of his head. With attractive German features and blue piercing eyes that squinted when he talked to you, he looked like an old man Thor, with a gait of a monstrous warrior. Objects on shelves rattled as he walked by. Literally, things broke when he moved through a room.

My dad called him a *man's man*. He never took no for an answer, and he would fight anyone to the death as long as they started it. His unique character, full of life, demanded full attention. Bill's dad launched numerous paramedic and fire programs in Illinois and Iowa. It's impossible to count the number of lives he saved. His nickname, which headlined in newspapers, was the *Tattooed Angel of Mercy,* but most called him Chief. He recruited Billy in as the youngest paramedic cadet at 15 and they created a bond from sharing bloody, tragic memories to witnessing miracles together.

Bill Sr. was rough around the edges and he intimidated most. But his edges softened for only one, his Billy.

As my Bill stood in our doorway, my heart softened for him. I saw a glimpse of the warrior in him, so similar to his father. A warrior who would do whatever it took to take care of his family. His strength of character showed me he could rise from wreckage. Coming from a heavily staffed office with a huge desk, to plugging away in a tiny cubicle among clients with a language he could not speak, humbled him. Bill's generous nature of giving us unexpected gifts and providing financial security was a known trait by anyone that knew him well. Not being able to be generous in nature and provide for our needs whether it was a new tire or a movie night, added to Bill's new humility. *Things can always get worse,* so we never dared to say the opposite out loud.

After selling the Rolex, I returned to the house and found Bill sitting at the kitchen table. I knew he was waiting for me.

"Done?" he asked.

I nodded cautiously and apologetically said, "It's done. I'm sorry Bill."

He nodded with a resigned shrug.

I proceeded to get the kids to bed early that night and carried a six-pack of Coors Light out to the backyard. Gently dropping into the faded yellow plastic lounge chair left behind by the last renter, I let myself finally relax. Half- snapped plastic straps dangled below. I sunk into them wondering if they would hold me just one more night. I drank enough that I knew I'd have to do some creative recycling to hide the cans.

From the backyard, I was able to watch Bill through the window sitting at the kitchen table. It crushed me when I imagined Bill Sr. looking down on *his Billy* now. Shadows cast on his face from the 1970's brass kitchen table light above, making him unrecognizable.

I spent a couple of hours reflecting back on the day. Kindness dripped from the jewelry owner, as he was sincerely sorry to be a part of these sales, "I'll hold onto it as long as I can Judy, and you can buy it back."

For a brief moment, and now emboldened by five beers of liquid courage, I thought, "I *will* buy that watch back!"

But with everything going on, I put myself back in place and thought, *Be real.* Knowing this was the final item of real value clarified we had no more cushion. Friends and family had helped enough and were no longer offering. We hit the wall. I opened up another can of beer, now warmed by the concrete patio where it had been sitting. I took a sip, laid my head back and studied the bright Arizona sparkling stars and wished they were sending some kind of Morse code against the pitch-black sky. I continued to drink hoping to forget about it all.

Bill emerged from the sliding-glass doorway and asked, "Hey, did you pay the rent? And did they wave the late fee 'cause we were only three days late?"

"SHIT," I said as I rolled off the lawn chair and headed inside.

Originally, the wife of the landlord had waived the $150 late fee, but the husband called this morning with what seemed to be enjoyment, which I took offense to, and said, "Absolutely not. My wife shared your unfortunate story, however, need I remind you that you have signed a legal document agreeing to late fees and by law you owe me?"

No. You don't need to fing remind me.

"Fine," I agreed, too tired to fight with what felt like an opportunist with a misuse of power.

I plopped myself down in front of the pile of bills. Out of anger, I pressed my pen into the check, ripping it a little as I scribbled, in place of my signature, "Go fuck yourself," legible enough for him to read. I planned on a call from the bank asking, "Mrs. Cochrane, have you made a name change we should be aware of?"

Not my best work.

ALL IN A DAY

The next day, the phone rang at the same time the alarm went off. Springing from bed while holding my pounding head, I grabbed the call. The alcohol-rich blood pumped through my veins as I listened and followed directions.

"Judy, it's Nick Mahoney. I need both you and Bill on speaker. Is he available?"

I made my way back to the bedroom. "Hey, get up," I said nudging him while covering the receiver.

Out of habit, Bill obediently followed me out to the family room. Slipping the switch to speaker, I waited to hear what Nick seemed urgent to share. Like always, we braced ourselves when one of our attorneys called.

"Seems your enemies have somehow found out you're considering bankruptcy. You know how I feel about a BK-a bankruptcy. It's a bad move for two reasons. Number one, you're in line to win these battles, and I advise you to keep fighting. Number two, the city of Phoenix runs all BK's through the state of Arizona. Someone has anonymously informed them, in writing, that your potential BK is fraudulent. They have written details about 'Judy's hidden jewelry and fur coats' and that you, Bill, have a collection of watches, along with hidden cash."

We glanced at each other, and Bill said with a laugh, "Whoever it is, they don't know Judy. A fur coat would be out of the question. As for jewelry and watches, they're gone."

"Bill, I don't think you're getting the gist of this. If the city of Phoenix arrives at your door, searches the house and declares you fraudulent, you could do jail time."

"What the fuck, Nick. Can't you intervene somehow and just tell them these idiots are lying? We aren't hiding anything!"

"I can't control them. They will do what they want to do and what if they find something you forgot about?"

Exasperated with Nick's logic, Bill said, "I don't know what to tell ya. We're gonna continue to consider a BK, Nick. I'll get back to you after I put some more thought into it. And it's a joke that there is even a lawsuit. After three years, we're tapped. I'm working in a mortgage industry when the banks are getting bailouts and not pushing any loans through. And don't they know our stock is still restricted and dangling from a fine thread? All they have to do is watch the NASDAQ. I think the stock is at five cents now."

Nick said, "All they know is you still have a hand in trying to resurrect this company, and if you do, you still own 30% of the shares—if there's a comeback, that stock is something worth waiting for."

After the call, silence took over, and we went off in separate ways. It was time for the kids to wake up for school, so I headed for their rooms.

Failed attempts of trying to shine the light on Bill and our situation so he could see his unique strength and to encourage him to keep pushing on was a role I no longer played well, so I didn't even try this morning. He wasn't having it anyway. Even though cars, houses, and jobs had not defined us in the past, I found now that poverty had; it highlighted a family consumed with failures, bad luck and lack of comeback.

Bankruptcy had begun to feel as if it were the only solution to the unending lawsuits that spilled out of our fax machine every Friday. Until that stock hit zero, those lawsuits were not going away. We tried hard to strategize, to prepare and to combat the legal and financial issues, but it was as if we had lost our magic, and every decision we made seemed wrong.

Faxes with updates on more bad news always left us in the worst mood at the start of the weekend with the kids. We tried to shake it off, but I noticed all three kids would go off and play together instead of urging us to play with them. *Bankruptcy could equal 7-to-10 years of unknown consequences, but what would a clean slate feel like?* I imagined a life without lawsuits and felt a smile spread across my face.

After getting the kids off to school, I found myself listening in on one of Bill's calls. I was so desperate for him to secure another job, I was willing to have him talk with a previous business associate who had an inappropriate attraction to him. I overheard her suggestion to have him live in California during the week and commute to Tucson every weekend, which sent a red flag up. Our marriage was fragile at best.

I nursed my hangover and nausea with a Power Ranger ice pack on my forehead while taking small sips of water to be gentle on my upset stomach. For the rest of the morning, I was a prisoner to managing harassing phone calls from collectors, stacking the bills in order of which to pay next, juggling legal and tax paperwork, and trying to make it to the cafeteria before Marc's lunch period because he had left his little brown bag on the counter.

Still hung-over, I found myself standing by the heavy metal doors at the elementary school, scanning the horrifically loud and stinky cafeteria for Marc's sweet face. He had his back to me, and because of being a bit of a target for bullies, he was sitting alone at the end of a long table. With my broken heart, I slipped onto the bench and sat face to face, "Hey!"

Excitedly, "Hi Mom!"

Handing him the brown paper bag, I said, "I put something inside your bag. A surprise from a hidden stash."

As if it were Christmas morning, he ripped open the bag and found a ziplock of cheddar cheese goldfish crackers—a rare treat in our house.

Smiling ear to ear, "YES! Thanks, Momma. You're the best," he said as he savored them, eating one at a time. From his backpack, he pulled out and handed me a small bag of generic brand saltines. "We'll save these for tomorrow," he suggested.

Clint's teacher had come up from behind me and placed her hand on my shoulder. "Good to see you finally arrived. Want to head out with me to the bus?"

"What bus?" I asked.

She laughed, and then stopped after seeing the look of confusion on my face. I had totally forgotten my commitment to volunteer for a field trip to Bisbee, Arizona. A bus filled with the entire third-grade class and Clint was leaving in 15 minutes. This trip would take at least an hour and 45 minutes, and as that sunk in, I felt sweat drip down my back realizing a hangover, an empty stomach and a bus filled with excited kids wasn't going to be a smooth ride. I made a plan to eat the saltines and after giving Marcus a big hug and squeeze, I stood in the chocolate-milk line searching for a dime at the bottom of my purse. My wallet was empty. Just as I was about to give up the search, a little girl tapped me from behind, "Here Mrs. Cochrane, I have a whole bunch." She held a dime out to me. I gave her a hug and said, "Oh, my goodness. You sweetheart. Thank you. I'll have Marcus buy you milk someday."

"Oh, no worries Mrs. Cochrane."

Struck by her adult-like comment, I thought, *I want my kids to be able to feel like they can say 'no worries.'*

Being poor kept me busy and buried in worry. There was always something to manage, prove, deflect, pay, or explain. It was the little things that left me scrambling. Teachers would often request supplies for the classrooms and money for field trips. Throughout the year, I spent endless hours going from one classroom to the next, offering to volunteer, pleading for scholarship money or negotiating to pay half of the amount asked. I made some progress there, but I would always be driving up in this spotless, shiny dark green Denali SUV and carrying my Coach purse, which gave the illusion of well-to-do. Upside down financially, this vehicle and the gas expenses were killing us, but if we unloaded it, it wouldn't be enough to pay off the loan, and with our horrible credit, and now with a re-possessed Volvo under our name, we wouldn't be able to purchase anything to replace it.

On top of that, spontaneous financial needs like birthday presents, increases in fees for sport uniforms, and equipment costs popped up often like a scary jack-in-the-box. Volunteering Bill to coach both boys' baseball and football teams helped waive fees, but it still stung to pay for the rest.

To cut costs further, I even went as far as combining a birthday party for Nicole with a wealthy friend's daughter so that she wouldn't notice the difference between a birthday at The Canyons compared to one at Horehole. Unfortunately, the party bombed because when the guests arrived, only her daughter received gifts. Nicole didn't seem to be bothered, as she spent the whole day swimming in and out from under a waterfall in their pool. *Thank God.*

Entering the bus filled to the rim with little bodies and big voices, I saw Clint sitting near the back. He liked this spot because he could 'bounce a lot.' Anything he could feel movement with—that was the place he wanted to be. He was the only quiet one on the bus, but the excitement in his eyes screamed of joy as he saw me come up the bus stairs and it melted my heart. His leg was sprawled over the entire area so as to save a seat for me. He moved toward the window and patted the empty space next to him.

Oh my God. What would his face have looked like if they had shut and locked those bus doors with no sight of me?

Barely able to stop myself from bursting into tears, I slid in next to him.

"Hi there, buddy." I pulled him into me with a big bear hug.

Looking around me with concern, "Did you bring our sack lunches? There were two Lunchables. One for me and one for you. You got them special for this trip. Member? Did you forget them?"

Oh, Dear God.

I pulled the saltines out of my purse. "Oh honey, I'm so sorry, I did forget."

Panicked, I realized I had nothing in our checking account and recapped not even one dollar in my wallet. I could not be more unprepared. He started rifling through his backpack, showing me an applesauce and a small bag of gummy bears that looked like they may have been there since second grade. He announced proudly, "I got you. We can share these."

Clint's teacher found her way back to us. She crouched down in the aisle facing us, but not allowing Clint to hear, "Hey Judy. I've heard through the grapevine that things for your family are still rough. So, no worries about forgetting about the trip. You have a lot to manage, I'm sure. I was glad you were going on this trip though cause something funny was said recently, and I thought you'd get a kick out of it. Even though I don't have kids of my own yet, I can really appreciate your three. We've all been watching your family come through our school system the last few years. I just wanted to say; I don't know how you're staying so positive and keeping it all together, but just know a lot of teachers here support your family so you'll think this is funny. In a recent staff meeting, after one of the teachers was told who would be assigned to her next year's class, she exclaimed, "Well, if I have to take the unruly kid, then give me a Cochrane kid."

We both laughed out loud, and I squeezed her hand and mouthed, "Thank you," afraid that if I used my voice it would turn into a full-fledged cry. And I didn't want to blow my strong cover.

She slipped me a $10 dollar bill, saying, "Take it. Please. I know you don't have lunches. Those of us that don't have a bagged lunch will be eating at the café in Bisbee." She took off down the aisle before I could reject it.

Scarcity on this day kept meeting up with abundance, and I grabbed Clint's little hand in mine and felt deeply grateful as we bounced along the highway.

The field trip centered around the financial rise and fall of Bisbee. In the early 1900s, it was one of the largest cities between St. Louis and San Francisco. The entire town flourished because of the mining of copper, azurite, and malachite, mostly. A fire ravaged the entire city in 1908, and they completely rebuilt. But what it was last remembered for is the notorious 1970 large-scale mining crash. The courthouse had pieces of stock certificates behind glass-framed boxes showing the promise of riches and the fall to poverty. It was interesting that this town was living large back in its day, financially dominant over Tucson and Phoenix.

We put on raincoats and helmets with headlamps and rolled off on carts deep into the mines. I was shocked that they allowed the kids to do this. We parents had signed waivers the week previous, but I did not imagine it would be this scary. The sunny 80-degree day disappeared behind us, as we rolled in silence, deep into pitch-black darkness.

"Turn your headlamps on," the conductor shouted. We all scrambled to find the switches and, one by one, the cave walls started lighting up from 35 little kids' helmets. There were yelps and comments laced with fear, and I wondered again, whether this was actually a good idea. The conductor, who sat behind me, decided to give me a private history lesson on the background of these caves and as he would shout some general information over the top of me, and then he would tap my helmet and direct my attention to other boarded-off entry ways, privately sharing how many people were known to have been buried alive.

That information hit me hard. That desire, that passion, and that drive of individuals finding their fortune has never changed. These men had risked their lives to provide for their families. I imagined their family relationships suffered from the stress. Bill's desire to provide was similar and because of his toughness, if we had been alive in those days, he would have been one of the fearless ones to risk his life to do the same.

At the end of the field trip, I felt lifted. So much good happened today. And this was a special trip with Clint. Because of his quiet middle-child nature, he never asked for attention, but as I poured it out on him today, he lit up. The hopelessness I felt was slightly replaced with the potential to persevere. It was good for me to take a break from Tucson, our bad news, and bad luck. *Bisbee took a financial beating and had a decent comeback. Why not us?*

FOOD STAMPS

During this period, one of our constant concerns became the overwhelming fear that one of the kids would have an accident, and we'd not be able to cover expenses, or, worse, we'd be turned away from emergency services because of our lack of finances. Clint had just chipped his front tooth and it wiped us out financially. I ended up begging the dentist to set up a payment plan for the remainder due. It was three years ago when I wondered *what if we fall and we can't get back up?* A severe accident or illness would crush us today. So, I broke down, let go and admitted we needed help. The only thing that made sense now was to start the time-consuming process of getting food stamps and state health insurance.

These processes demanded massive amounts of paperwork, including copies of full past and present tax returns, current utility bills, and some papers were required to be notarized. This seemed more involved than purchasing a home. In addition, there were always long lines, with a three-to-four-hour wait for the numerous follow-up appointments to keep proving low income. I had heard of people cheating the system, but after going through this process, I couldn't figure out how they would manage it. I never filled out more detailed or more intimate paperwork in my life. The people who knew the system well found ways to cut in line. Yet even this stopped bothering me when I recognized the same fine thread of greed having the potential to weave through it all... boardrooms, food stamp office (D.E.S. Department of Economic Security) and even at Disneyland.

I recalled a past trip where cheerful Disney music blasting all around us while I watched parents aggressively push their kids up to the front of the line while following on their heels with an air of this behavior being acceptable and deserved.

THE WORLD HAS ENOUGH FOR EVERYONE'S NEED, BUT NOT ENOUGH FOR EVERYONE'S GREED. MAHATMA GANDHI

On the first day of getting food stamps, I got up early in the morning, dressed in sweats, threw my hair in a ponytail and left my face makeup-free. I had called earlier to ask how to qualify and find out what documents I'd need, and for the average wait time. Overly prepared, I arrived and sat in my car for a half-hour, watching people pull up and walk in. The wait was going to be long, but I just couldn't bring myself to get out of the car. I had the urge to buy a pack of cigarettes. Why? I don't know. I restrained from adding to my list of expenses and potential addictions. Besides, according to the website, food stamps won't pay for those. I was disappointed to learn that they also would not cover alcohol. My love for Coors Light had grown. Bill had recently made a comment about my new habit and seemed annoyed with my level of consumption. I was surprised I hadn't caught myself before he did. Alcoholism and some drug addiction ran rampant on my side of the family, and I had a concern, but thought I would relax after Bill got a job. I often reasoned with myself; I need it! I need to relax after I get the kids to bed.

An hour passed while sitting in the car. *Get off your ass and get in there. Your kids need health insurance and food for God's sake.*

I cautiously entered the business strip mall where the food-stamp office was located and got in line. Like a sheep, I followed the people in front of me and feverishly read all the signs explaining details about this process. I noticed I caught the attention of many others in the room. I wish I could say they were welcoming looks, but they were not. I drew back on my Chicago city-girl instinct and confidence; like a lioness, there to protect her cubs, I stared down every person that stared at me first. I didn't like this side of me, but I got comfortable with it while standing in line.

I was there so long, that out of boredom, I studied the signs in Spanish while testing myself to see what I could understand. Finally, my number was called, and I entered a small cubical with a woman in her 30's. Administrative paperwork tacked to her cubicle walls covered every square inch. All of it was in Spanish. It was times like these when I wished I knew this language. I felt an instant barrier between us as I sensed she didn't like me right away. Agitated, she pointed to a chair for me to sit in. Impolitely, she demanded my paperwork while looking me up and down. I had all my identification, documents and required paperwork completely filled out, in a manila folder. I purposely did not bring my Coach purse. *Thank God.* I already felt out of place and uncomfortable with her edgy anger, which she seemed to display with immediacy. After overhearing other conversations while standing in line, I noticed she asked me ten times more questions than the others. *Did she think I was a fraud? I know the system has loopholes, and people may abuse them, but why single me out?*

Without warning, she whipped out a camera lens in my direction, and the flash blinded me for a couple of seconds. The lady next to me got fair warning for her photo. She then whipped out a tray with black ink and grabbed each finger and took my prints. She pressed harder than I thought she needed to and I wanted to slap her across the face and say, *Are you kidding me right now? According to the taxes we have paid in abundance since 1985, I think we should be helped here without judgment. This is a short-term thing to feed children and have peace of mind to have some kind of health insurance, for God's sake! Once Bill gets a job, we will be off of these! What the fuck kind of system is this?*

I was then told to wait in the lobby for my card to be made. I could smell the laminating machines hard at work today and waited for my name to be called. Out of boredom, I started counting the dirty white linoleum squares on the floor. An hour passed, and I realized that people who originally were behind me this morning now were going up to a window marked "C" to pick up their new food-stamp card. I cautiously approached the window and asked if my card was back there. The lady behind the glass seemed cheerful and said, "Oh, yes, you've been approved." She smiled. "And, I'm sorry, girl. I was wondering what you were waiting there for. I thought you needed to see the original attendant again."

She handed me the debit-like card.

"Thank you," I said with sincere relief.

I went directly to the grocery store near our rental in the foothills. Filled with gratitude for this plastic card, I let myself feel relief that the way-too-familiar Ramen noodles we had been eating were not going in the cart today! I caught myself humming while I shopped and couldn't remember the last time I had done that in the grocery store. *What a life saver food stamps are.* I was only familiar with the weekly sales at a certain grocery store in the foothills, so the risk of running into someone I knew, was likely.

Standing in line after buying $150 worth of groceries, I slid the card through the machine and looked up to see the giant screen in front of the cashier flash FOOD STAMP DEBIT. She swiveled the screen towards me where I and the rest of the line could see.

Annoyed, she asked, "What is this?"

Embarrassed, I responded as quickly as possible as to not draw even more attention. "This is a food stamp debit-card. I received it today. It supposed to work like a debit card. Is it not valid? I can put these items back and come back another time."

She picked up her microphone and spoke loud and clear, "Mr. Reynolds, can you please come to register three? We have a FOOD STAMP DEBIT CARD here that I don't know how to process!"

Holy shit. I could be wrong, but she seemed to display a hint of enjoyment.

The woman in my line toward the back was a mom from one of the boys' classes, and I was so ashamed. I appreciated that she pretended not to know what was going on, but that made it even more awkward. Mr. Reynolds asked for my card, manually inputted the information off the card, and said, "Sorry, ma'am, we've never had one of these up here in the foothills."

About a month after getting our food stamp card, I received a registered letter and a call from the Department of Economic Security. They informed me that they believed I was fraudulent, and I was instructed to be in their court in three weeks to stand before a Judge, in order to prove my innocence. I planned on defending myself, as we had no money and had tapped all free attorney resources.

I was given an address in a part of town I'd never been. It was an obscure location, and I got lost. Because I was now three minutes late for my hearing, I told Nicole to stay in the car, keep it running with the air on, and lock the door.

"I'll be right back to get you after I check if I can still be seen."

Being so mature at the age of seven, I felt comfortable leaving her temporarily.

I heard the bolted doors to the courtroom being locked from the inside just as I ran into the building. "I'm sorry I'm late. Name is Judy Cochrane." A woman behind the glass window sternly informed me that my card would now be shut down, and I was found to be fraudulent for not showing up.

"But I'm here. Wait, fraudulent?" I explained about the obscure address being hard to find and begged for the Judge to re-open my case.

There was a second woman behind the glass window as well, with a nicer attitude. The first one came off seeming to have fun announcing my fate due to the rules in place. The kinder lady seemed embarrassed and confused as how to help me and she even agreed about the obscure location and mentioned that a lot of people get lost. She rustled papers and gave the other girl the eye like, "Are you sure? It's *only three* minutes."

They rescheduled my hearing for the following month.

I ran back to the car to find Nicole lethargic. I had to bang on the window to wake her. I had picked her up at a sleepover earlier and now wondered if she'd eaten something she was allergic to. She was sweating profusely, and her hair was soaked and clinging to her head and face. I started the car immediately and realized she must have turned the key back, so only the fans were blowing the hot air in, from outside. With the windows closed, the 90 degrees outside quickly created an oven inside the car. She was literally sweating to death. I peeled out of the parking lot with my finger on 911 and pulled in right next door to a 7-11.

I opened all the doors and blasted the air and asked an older man in the car next to me, "Please sir, can you watch her?!" as I bolted in the store and grabbed a Gatorade and water from the cooler and ran out.

The young male cashier noticed me immediately, "HEY LADY! GET BACK HERE! I'm calling the POLICE!"

"DO IT!" I screamed.

When I returned, the older man had gotten Nicole to talk to him, and she was alert, but I forced her to drink the Gatorade and water. The clerk from the counter followed me out with his phone in hand and after looking at Nicole's drenched head, had figured out what was going on. "OH shit, sorry lady. Don't worry. I didn't call. Gatorade and water are on the house."

The older man stood with a concerned look. I could tell he wanted to scold me for leaving a kid in the car to overheat like this. But he restrained himself long enough to see me drop my head in Nicole's lap and sob. "I'm so sorry, baby. You could've died. I practically made an unlivable mistake. I will never leave you again."

And in her sweet lisp, she replied, "It's all right Momma," as she patted me on my head that laid in her lap.

I immediately knew I needed to let this incident *serve me right*. I needed to wake up. I could clearly see now that everyday I'd been running on empty and in full anxiety mode; my adrenals were on overload and in massive overdrive. One crisis after another found me, but this one would have devoured me. By now, I was manifesting dangerous shit more often than not. I took full responsibility and recalled the many inspirational books that support what this small wise master shared; it is *all right*. This near disaster can and will serve me right. No more hiding behind how painful and distracting my life had become. I felt myself surrender to the crazed part of me while deeply thanking God that I wouldn't have to endure that particular unnecessary lesson.

I returned to the courtroom much earlier the second time and went before the Judge. He barely looked up and was rude. I took it personally and suppressed my anger the best I could. The last month's episode with Nicole was still raw, making me overly sensitive. I had all the paperwork necessary to prove my innocence. He showed no interest in looking at it and explained that someone in the office had found my needs suspicious based on all the addresses I lived in.

"Anybody that lives in *The Canyons* certainly does not need food stamps. In addition, your hypnotherapy business must be doing well in order to have the office address listed here, also in a very upscale area."

I took a deep breath and told the Cliff Note's version: that we *had* lived in The Canyons and were in a rental now. The office address was a friend's law office that let me periodically work out of there when he didn't have it occupied. I explained that we did indeed need this assistance, and I sincerely questioned, "Isn't it there for people like us?"

My voice cracked, revealing my stress and exhaustion. I was having trouble catching my breath. I fought back the tears, but the tremble in my hands and body made it clear. "I'm beat, sir. I beg you to reinstate the card and our health care and let me leave here and try to get back on our feet. I have three little kids with no health insurance. This is dreadfully time-consuming and being here frankly keeps me from getting ahead. I need help sir, and I need it today."

My anger was slipping into vulnerability, humility and now reaching hopelessness.

The people in the pews behind me got quiet, and I knew I had the attention of everyone in the room, but I didn't care. I was too tired to care.

He slammed down his gavel and unemotionally handed me a pile of papers while a friendly-faced, heavy-set lady wrapped her arm around my shoulders and led me to the glass window where I started the whole process of getting a new card again.

"There, there," she said as she stood behind me, literally holding me together with her two hands on each shoulder. I wanted to crawl into her lap. Her genuine comfort warmed my heart. Compassion emanated from her as she recognized my pain. She was the nice woman behind the glass when I had left Nicole outside in the car.

You see it, don't you? You see me, and you see my pain. Thank you.

I felt safe with her. I loved her beautiful black, flawless skin and her twinkling, dark golden brown eyes. As I kept maintaining eye contact with her, she kept pointing me back to where I had to sign the paperwork. She knew this paperwork well. Her body heat warmed me in the freezing air-conditioned courthouse, and the heat allowed her hair product to give off a light perfumed scent. She reminded me of a friend back home. Where I used to feel safe. Oh, how I missed my sweet home Chicago, where our kids were born, and we trusted what was coming next.

Upon returning to Horehole, I studied the boxes lining the walls of the dumpy family room, briefly considering emptying a couple of them, but every time I tried to dig down into my empty energy reserves to open a box, I'd get distracted with another urgent phone call or a kid needing something. Besides, the last month's memory of what I had just put myself and Nicole through, made me care less about this mess. It felt good to finally have a handle on something so clear—by almost losing Nicole; it narrowed the path to my heart and to what really, really mattered in my life. And most importantly, I saw a pattern of how and what I had been manifesting as of late.

Just being in the presence of the boxes smothered me, so I moved outside to sit on the front steps. My heart warmed as I watched Marcus and Nicole play with the neighbor kids. Other parents were spending time catching up with each other, and for the first time in my life, I didn't want to engage. I liked these hard working people, they seemed nice, but I didn't want to talk to them as I always had back in the day. *I'm too raw, too real, too much. Too far from successful small-talk. I'm guessing I won't be well-received in this state.*

Clint rounded the corner on his BMX bike and jumped a ramp he'd made from a board and some dirt at the end of the driveway. In mid-air, I realized he had a helmet on, but it wasn't his regular bike helmet. It was Bill's football helmet from college. The entire surface was covered with little-circled Panther stickers— awarded for tackles made. Clint landed upright, but looked like a bobble head, and I panicked he may snap his neck.

"Clint! Bring that helmet to me and put yours on please."

He slid his bike sideways, effortlessly coming to a screeching halt, stopping at my feet while handing me the helmet. Everyone in our house knew the importance of this helmet; the hard work, the hits it absorbed, the scholarship it earned, the blood and the sweat that soaked into the padded lining. I held it in my hands, moving it around to see it close up. The stickers earned were doubled up in some areas and had started to curl back from under and around the violent scrapes that left the opponents color of helmet behind. Some stickers had become part of the deep dents, evidence of the many concussions Bill endured over those years. I hadn't looked at it since college. Ironically, it looked delicate today, and I felt like we would need to take better care and handle it less, in order to preserve it.

Reflecting on our college days, I barely recognized us, compared to the us back then. The world was at our feet, time was on our side, and our love would see us through. Sure there's been wisdom gained, but it felt like it replaced hope. Dropping my chin down to my folded arms, which rested on the helmet in my lap, I recalled the first time I met Bill in 1985 at Eastern Illinois University in a southern city called Charleston. I couldn't help but think, *where'd that girl go?*

IT MUST BE LOVE

When Marie, my best friend in college, suggested 50-cent beers and shooting pool, I was the first one to close my math homework and push it aside. At 19, I stood in front of the small dorm mirror as I pulled my Eastern Illinois football sweatshirt over my head and patted down my electrostatic hair, reaching for the ceiling. It was February, and the heater vent blasted hot air through our tiny dorm rooms creating electrical shocks in and on everything we touched. I gave up on the static and pulled my hair into a long ponytail. Examining the makeup I had applied in the morning, I turned my head left to right in the mirror. Half approving it, I threw another zipper hoodie over my sweatshirt to protect against the cool Charleston, Illinois evening. I could smell rain coming and hoped we wouldn't have to walk home in it later tonight. Spring was in the air as scents of mud and grass were finally thawing. But being born and raised in Illinois, I knew better than to get my hopes up for warmer temperatures and sunshine, which we may not see until the end of May. As I walked over to my desk, where all my un-done homework would wait, I applied some neutral lip-gloss. Feeling rich, I grabbed a five-dollar bill on my desk and stuck it in my front pocket, knowing I could splurge for us all because of the 50-cent beer night.

In record time, I was first out the door and stood in front of Marie and Shannon's room ready to go. I loved going out with them. We weren't flashy like a dolled-up group of sorority girls, but pretty enough with a wholesome feel. We didn't turn every head but usually turned a few.

They weren't ready to go yet, so I told Shannon I was going to grab my mail downstairs, and I'd meet them in the lobby. I made my way down the staircase, but not without greeting every person along the way. Somehow, in only one year of college, it felt as if I had met everyone on campus.

I checked the mail and had nothing there. Looking up, I noticed the announcement on the wall: "VOTE FRIDAY FOR OUR SPRING QUEEN". Underneath the sign, there were 8x10 photos of me and four other girls. I was sure I was nominated more for my personality and not just by looks. The photo wasn't complementary either. My hair looked dark brown. All you could see were my *wannabe* Farrah Fawcett bangs because my long hair was tossed to the back. The others photographed better than I. Their blue eyes portrayed a doll-like look. A look I thought to be the epitome of the title. I secretly did not want to win. Plus, the pressure was on. I just learned I had an admirer on the football team, and I wondered if it was because I was up for this prestigious Queen title.

Earlier that same evening, at the basement floor cafeteria, I went with my roommates and floor mates of our dorm to eat together, as usual. Lined up single file, pushing our trays along the metal grates, while in my regular playful mood, I began teasing Shannon about a boy she liked. Never really paying attention to who was in the cafeteria, and not caring we were in complete view of a large audience, I kept teasing her all the way through the line where the ladies with hairnets were getting annoyed. They tried to push me along faster. One of the hair-netted ladies pointed over my head to show me we had a full house tonight in the cafeteria and a long line behind us.

Glancing over my shoulder I said, "What the heck?" I had never seen the place packed.

The netted lady said, "The football players' private cafeteria had a fire in the kitchen and so they're all eatin' here t'night?"

Sarcastically, I said, "Aw, well what a shame for them. So they don't get their regular steaks, twice-baked potatoes, fresh tossed salads and steamed veggies? How horrible they have to eat the prison food with us?"

The netted lady didn't find me amusing, but Shannon did. From day one, living here, we had been complaining of having to smell their delicious food and fresh baked desserts, right next to our cafeteria. One day, with success, we had begged the cooks to give us some of their melt-in-your-mouth, chocolate cake. Shannon was super skinny, so I had explained, "Come on now, look at her! She needs some cake!"

I nudged Shannon in front of me, "Tonight's the night girl. Let's be sure to 'share' some of our veggies with the football players."

A wink from me was enough for Shannon to realize we would transform the veggies from food to projectiles. This wasn't our first rodeo when it came to food fights.

I loaded my tray, her's and Marie's, with a big bowl of steaming Brussels sprouts. Marie hadn't been listening to our conversation, but being a good veggie eater, she politely accepted the Brussels sprouts on her tray. Shannon giggled with her hand over her mouth, trying to stifle her laughter and stay quiet. I laughed out loud as I normally do and unfortunately captured the attention of an entire table of football players. Embarrassed, I quickly turned back towards the netted ladies and kept pushing my tray along.

We found our way to a table in the back corner opposite the football players. I couldn't get over the fact they looked like cartoon characters of overgrown people. All huddled and hunched over their food piled high, eating in unison, as if from a trough. Only muffled grunts could be heard coming from their table. *Did they actually talk to each other? Did they talk at all?* Their bodies screamed so loud; I could not hear a word they'd say anyway. The muscles on their backs were rippled and could be seen under their tight heather gray t-shirts. The short sleeves left nothing to the imagination. There were veins popping and muscles bulging in areas I'd never seen before. One of them reached over his head to stretch, and I saw equally as many veins and muscles on the inside of his arm as there were on top. Their shoulders created a wall of muscle where they nearly touched each other and then each one's waist, with the exception of a lineman, dropped into a "V". I couldn't imagine the hours of work it took to sculpt such physique, but for the first time, I found myself intrigued. It started to remind me of watching animals in the wild. Occasionally one would lift their head, scan the room, check for predators and then go back to their food. They were aware we watched them, but they weren't bothered by it.

One of our dear friends at our table, Lacey, was a sorority girl, and she was "in" with all the football players. I guess they liked to attend her particular sorority's parties. They did seem to have the prettiest girls on campus. So Lacey, being her bubbly and polite, outgoing self, headed over to the table to say hi. She knew all of them by their first names. I studied each one and observed how they addressed her. They were a lot more polite than I thought they'd be. And I noticed a quiet confidence about them, which I wasn't expecting. I guess I assumed arrogance, big egos, and inappropriate comments, but I was wrong. They seemed pretty cool.

She stayed a long time, and I almost went over to join her, but remembered our stock pile of Brussels sprouts and started gathering them up in front of me. Marie had eaten hers, but I still had Shannon's and mine. I grabbed one sprout, winked at Shannon, and whipped it right at the table of football players Lacey was speaking to. A guy we knew sitting at a table next to us said, "WHAT THE FUCK JUDY? YOU TRYIN' TO GET US ALL KILLED? That dark haired guy and the guy with the Fu Manchu, flipped a car completely over last weekend when they were leaving a bar. I saw it. I was there. And I ran. Those dudes eat frickin' bar glasses for fun. There's something wrong with a person that does that. Stop throwing that shit!"

I don't know why it struck me as funny, but it did. Maybe the fear of getting caught ignited the laughter. I pushed Shannon's bowl in front of her and gave her the nod. Our aim was perfect, and the sprouts exploded into little green pieces, as they hit the players' shoulders, the table, and then bounced off to the floor. The football players briefly scanned the cafeteria, looking for the culprits, but then quickly turned back to their food and continued eating and talking to Lacey. Shannon found it funny too, and we were so proud of our poker faces when they turned to see if they could catch the "veggie snipers."

Our neighbor at the table next to us was getting more and more anxious, and it just simply made it all funnier. Lacey was ducking from our sprouts and handling the whole thing with a light heart. She turned a couple times and said to the entire cafeteria, "HEY, whoever is doin' that is really askin' for it. May wanna stop now."

Shannon and I thought it was so funny we hadn't been caught, that our hysterics made us slip off our chair and under the table. When we popped our heads back up, we saw Lacey heading our direction. She had a smile on her face while staring right at me.

"What?" I asked, thinking I was busted for the sprout attack.

"That guy, Bill Cochrane, with the brown hair... he likes you," pointing towards him.

I thought silently, *Oh great, the guy that flips cars?*

I replied, "What? How? I've never met him."

"He said he saw you at the beginning of the year in the lobby and then never saw you again and just recently was happy to see your picture for Spring Queen because he didn't know your name. He has been hot on the trail, wantin' to meet you. Apparently, all of the guys at the table have been on strict orders that if they see you at a bar or party to call him, and he'll come over. But it has been months, and nobody's bumped into you."

The girls at the table started giving me the entire scoop on what they knew, heard and what they thought about Bill Cochrane: He was the Captain of the football team, an All-American linebacker, he was frequently in the newspaper because he was making the highlights with bone crushing plays every Saturday. He recently left a full-time job and transferred to Eastern because he wanted to give it one last shot to play ball. One of the guys at the table next to us chimed in and added that he looked to be not just a football player, but a "player." They said he has a rowdy group of friends and a brother that comes to watch games from his hometown, and they have all been seen piling out of a hand-painted pink Cadillac on occasion. In addition, these guys said he bounced at Krackers Bar, and apparently the owners embroidered the name, Clark Kent, instead of his real name, on his uniform polo. Lacey also shared that he was a phenomenal dancer, and was a gentleman at the sorority parties and kind of treated the girls more like his sisters and friends than anything else. He looked familiar to me, but I couldn't place where I might have seen him.

The preconceptions I had about potentially dumb football players being sexually loose were flooding my mind, and I told her, "No way."

Besides, he was attracted first to me, 'a girl he *saw*, not a girl he *knew*.' He probably thinks of me *all wrong*. He probably wants and desires the Spring Queen. She goes perfectly with the Captain of a football team. But I need a boyfriend that doesn't put pressure on me to be *that*.

Lacey grabbed my wrist and said excitedly, "C'mon, just meet him. I got a feeling about you two."

I tapped the back of her hand and said, "Sorry, no, don't set that up for me."

Lacey reluctantly went back to the table and quietly explained to Bill, "She's already taken, maybe some other time."

The netted ladies were in the back cleaning dishes, so we decided to act on the silverware heist we planned on earlier. Our plans were to return them at the end of the year. Immediately, we carefully stashed forks, knives and spoons for our late night cereal and pudding, into our socks, under our pant legs. Slowly we walked through the cafeteria, as if it were a serious heist, making it to the large open staircase, where you could see down through each step to the cafeteria floor below. I had a clear view of the football players table. I had made it halfway up to the landing, stepping onto the next stair, when I felt the cold metal begin to shift and fall out of my sock. One piece of silverware after another started to dislodge and fall to the ground. I panicked and laughed at the same time and ran up as quickly as I could, hunched over, using my fingers for balance against the slippery linoleum stairs in front of me, so as to not fall or slip. The silverware continued to fall out of my sock and hit the stairs and floor with loud 'pinging' noises. After sliding through the open stairs, they landed right next to the table where the football players sat. I saw Bill Cochrane get up from his seat. Eyes calmly locked on me. And with a great big smile, while holding a handful of knives, forks and spoons up for all to see, he said, "Did you lose something here?"

His entire table broke out in laughter, and I took off back to my dorm room. But not without seeing all of the green Brussels sprouts sprawled over their table and around their chairs, as well. *Oh, the netted ladies were going to be pissed at the football players tonight.*

SUPERMAN

Panther Lounge, a typical Midwest college bar, is where Bill and I first talked face-to-face. The scent of stale beer from the previous night hung in the air over the four dimly lit pool tables. The thick dark-wood counters, covered in layers of polyurethane, were nicked and scraped from many years of drunken college students stumbling on and off their barstools.

This was the best bar for shooting pool and the "favorite guy hangout" for students at Eastern, with an occasional visitor from Southern Illinois and the University of Illinois. Because guys generally came to shoot pool, it lacked the "meat market vibe" so I felt comfortable here. It also reminded me of the bars frequented by my dad and brother, Johnny, where I spent endless hours in my early teens perfecting my pool game with random old men that wouldn't just "let me win." I had to earn it, fair and square.

I looked forward to accepting a game of pool tonight and watching their faces when I started to sink the balls, one after another. As a kid, my brother, Johnny, bought a table with his first paychecks from a pizza place and assembled it in our basement. We certainly weren't the richest on our block, but we were the only ones with a slate pool table in our basement that kids were allowed to play on. Johnny taught me how to plan my future shots and strategize accordingly. It wasn't uncommon for him to run the table, and even though I never accomplished that, I was good for a 19-year-old girl who wouldn't normally be mistaken for a pool shark.

We headed straight up to the bar and ordered beers. Out of the corner of my eye, I saw one of the football players from the cafeteria run for the payphone. He had a short conversation, hung up and returned to his pool game. All the guys shooting pool were the same we had just seen earlier in the cafeteria. About fifteen minutes later, Bill Cochrane walked into Panther Lounge. His dark blue eyes darted right towards me as if they specifically told him what barstool I'd be sitting on. As he got closer to me, I instantly recalled seeing him in the papers. I wasn't a football fan, but I sold advertising in the local paper and would sometimes read about him by skimming over the football stats. Not just hoping to see a championship game in our future, but more because I like to see the underdog win. Bits and pieces of his story came back to me.

He was almost 23 years old and already had been a full-time paramedic. I wondered, *why quit that, to come back to football and college life?* He had excelled in wrestling and football in high school in his hometown, Lake Zurich, Illinois. Apparently, he had plans to attend med school. I wondered if that was still on his radar.

He made his way across the room, and his eyes never left mine. I could tell he wasn't intimidated by any woman. It's as if you could feel his experience just by watching him walk. It wasn't the cocky strut of an egomaniac; it was simply forceful, direct and true.

Shannon and Marie were already deep in conversation at a booth nearby, but as he walked past them, he caught their attention, and they watched his approach. He nodded a "hello" to the bartender and within seconds Bill had a beer and a Jack and Coke sitting in front of him. He tried to pay, but the bartender said, "On the house, buddy."

"Can I buy you a drink?" he asked.

"I have one, thanks," I raised my beer as if I had to show him.

He smiled, "Can I buy you a beer *after* you finish that one?"

"Maybe," I replied.

I wasn't as impressed by his height as I was with his width. He was 6'2" and weighed 272 pounds; never in my life had I seen shoulders like his. The men in my family were known for big Scandinavian shoulders, but his were crazy wide with mounds of muscle covering them. I asked him to sit down on the stool because his size was overwhelming. I wondered if he even knew how intimidating he was. *Is he one of those guys that doesn't know his effect on the world? Or worse, is he someone who would misuse his power to purposely intimidate others in order to feel more powerful?* I needed to know this about him before this conversation continued.

He reached towards me, and I watched my hand disappear into his.

"Sorry, I didn't formally introduce myself. I'm Bill."

His handshake was gentle, but not too gentle. The calluses on the inside of his hand gently scratched the palm of mine. That and the actual superhuman size and warmth of his hand screamed; *warrior. strong. protector.* His fingernails were torn down the middle of his nail bed from ripping into other player's jerseys. Sportswriters had documented his fierce ability to be the lead in tackles, and I could see the wear and tear close up. The top of his nose displayed a still-healing laceration caused by, according to the paper, a broken helmet, and facemask during the final game of the season. His bruised eyes were seeing their last days, apparently the result of a broken nose from a previous scrimmage. I studied his full head of short brown hair, perfectly groomed in a contemporary high-and-tight, with the top tussled in a non-shiny pomade and wondered if it ever got messed up. His complexion was perfect, and the whites of his eyes were so bright they made his dark blue eyes pop. His matching navy-blue Eastern Illinois football jacket and sweats were embroidered with his last name and his number 59. He smelled good, freshly showered, but with a hint of Polo cologne. Somehow this guy was feeling *right* to me, but my head was screaming, *NO f'ing way!*

I replied to his proper introduction, "Judy Wilson."

My head won out. I don't know how I found the courage to say what I said next. But I wonder, in hindsight, whether I was testing him as if I sensed I would marry this man and have children with him. I needed to get things clear fast.

"Listen, Lacey mentioned you had interest in meeting me, but I should tell you that this whole huge muscle, college-football-player-thing," swirling my finger while outlining his upper torso, "is not for me. I'm more interested in artists and musicians." More playfully, I said with a smile, "And I have no interest in being a groupie either. Besides, I don't have the collection of high heels and mini skirts to parade around in, while following you to all the bars."

Undeterred, he laughed and answered calmly, "Judy," he said my name like he had known me for years, "I get it. It's just I saw you a long time ago and just knew I had to meet you. I can't exactly explain it, but I heard your laugh first, and then saw your smile. I get where you're comin' from, and you're right, I have a lot of people judge me before meeting me, both good and bad. Sometime when you'd be open to it, I'd like to talk more and see where that goes."

"Hmm," I said, while studying his eyes to see if I could pick up on anything, anything at all, that would clarify whether this was the right or wrong guy for me. I could hear the voices in my head. Not just my own, but my mother's and sister's, strongly cautioning me to stay away from potentially unintelligent, emotionally immature and dangerous athletes.

Marie and Shannon studied us from across the room. Their heads were bent towards each other not taking their eyes off of us. Their dialogue seemed intense. I needed to hear what they were most likely going to confirm: that they did not approve of Bill Cochrane #59, starting middle linebacker, Captain of the E.I.U. Football team.

From the corner of my eye, I saw this Thor look-alike, sporting a stylish Fu Manchu, stampeding in our direction with a pool stick in hand. I instinctively wanted to get off the stool and take a step back but then remembered how physically safe I felt with Bill. Plus, quickly it became clear they were happy to see each other and besides the different last name and number embroidered on the other guy's jacket, their matching shiny sweat outfits made them look like brothers.

"Billlly my brotha! Well, well, well, FINALLY!" he said while he half hugged and wrapped his hand into Bill's and pulled him into his chest.

Turning to me, "Finally! The two of you meet! Ya know how long I've had you on my radar, lil' lady?"

Now with his hand on Bill's chest, "THIS GUY has been looking for you for a loooong time!" He motioned to the bartender by raising his glass, to get him another.

A few moments later the bartender handed him a drink.

"Jack & Coke, Tommy," the bartender announced.

"Thank you, sir!" he replied as he raised his glass to him.

Tommy had a warmth that made me instantly like him. I couldn't put my finger on it, but he was just extremely light-hearted and big-hearted at the same time. He didn't carry the ego you'd think he would have. Strangers in the bar were coming up to him to talk about his past games, and he was friendly and grateful for their attention. He was strikingly handsome, with flawless physique like Bill's, so I imagined he'd had his way with quite a few women. He kept playing songs on the jukebox and obviously had a love for rock'n'roll and Elvis. Being a music lover myself, I was impressed he knew the lyrics of practically every song played. Earlier, he moved his hips around the pool table and now, while standing with us, he thrust his hips to the beat in a way I thought, surely this is a man comfortable with his body.

Then Tommy asked, "What are you doing this weekend? My girl Sandy, from home, comes every weekend. Maybe the four of us can go out?"

His girl from home? Sandy was his high school sweetheart, and they had promised to marry shortly after college, but before Tommy attained his dream of becoming a professional football player. My affection for him increased when he danced in place to the music, pretending to hold Sandy in his arms. He was only a few short days away from seeing her.

Watching Bill as he interacted with Tommy and the other players demonstrated a true brotherhood, a tribe; you could tell they had each other's backs. They shared a deep respect for one another and the unique bond created from competing together in a sport. Because of Bill's age and being one of the Captains of the team, he had an authority that, I had to admit, I was drawn to. His vocabulary was advanced, maybe because of his exposure to the medical world. I liked it.

My dad and brother both have extremely high IQ's, and I was raised listening to them argue about the definitions of words I couldn't pronounce, have confusing discussions about the meaning of life, and go over details on religion and politics I didn't understand. In addition, they would recite and share quotes, name every capital of every single place in the world, quiz each other without calculators on complicated mathematical calculations and decipher exact percentages of things. They regularly alternated the first and second positions on the national trivia games available in bars and restaurants, so bringing home a male friend of below-average intelligence simply was not going to fly.

I watched Bill raise the frosted grooved beer glass to his lips as if it were a teacup. I raised mine with two hands; I was always extra careful not to chip or damage my one gift, straight teeth. I hadn't noticed them before, but his lips may have been the most perfect lips I'd seen. They were the lips you see on models in a GQ magazine. Masculine but inviting, they were full, unlike mine, and I found myself wondering what it would be like to kiss him.

I abandoned this dreamy path and sternly reminded myself to re-evaluate what exactly was going on here. Was it that I just wanted to kiss any random pair of full, inviting lips, or was it *him* I wanted to kiss? My head was starting to change its mind. How and why? *This most certainly has to be a bad idea.*

A fellow student had been watching the players around me and made his way over to us. He was a bit shy, but a huge football fan. He went right up to Bill and cautiously put his hand out. Bill grabbed it immediately, and before the guy said anything, he said, "Hey brotha. How you doin'?"

The guy stuttered and mentioned an interception from last season, where Bill ran it in for a 85-yard touchdown. Bill graciously thanked him for coming to the games and told him he hoped the "football Angels" would provide again.

I stopped dead in my tracks, on full alert now, and wondered if he really believed in Angels. After several remarkable experiences I'd already had at my age, I was a believer. *Does he call on them before games, or was this just a passing, random comment?*

He couldn't possibly know my connection to Angels, but I needed him to if we were ever to move forward. He needs to know that when I found out at the age of 7 that I had not been baptized, I urgently demanded it. The Pastor tried to convince me to take a Bible study class with kids my age as a prerequisite. I declined and insisted on an immediate baptism which was then scheduled the following Sunday. During my entire childhood, I stood on top of a fan making my voice vibrate while I preached from the Bible. The neighbor kids sat cross-legged around me and listened until the end when I sang, "Jesus Loves Me," while I strummed the strings of my mom's guitar. Unfortunately for my friends, this was before I started guitar lessons.

It was also important for Bill to know of my encounter with and connection to Angels after enduring the loss of my 5th-grade friend, Monty Klemmer, who unexpectedly died. He had visited me in my dreams for years, and I always felt he became an Angel of mine.

I would need this guy to know about all the other times in my life when I reached to the Heavens for support: when my dog was put to sleep without my knowledge; the night my parents announced their plans for divorce; the two weeks my sister disappeared as a runaway; her overdose, which she barely survived; the fire I accidentally started as a kid, which destroyed our house; the day my dad moved out; the day my stepfather moved in; the switch to a new high school at 15; adapting to a new home and new town; and coping with a wealthier social class, in which I was the odd one. All of these childhood challenges became a current that pulled me toward God, Spirit, Saints, the Universe, my Ancestors and my Angels, which I believed I heard and saw in my dreams as well as in my waking life. And although I had no hard proof, I felt I met with them daily. From the age of 7, each occurrence built on the next and I kept feeling a deeper urge to look at things in a bigger way and to seek spiritual solutions.

Bill didn't look much like a nature lover, and that was also a concern for me. In addition to the Angels, he would need to understand my love and connection to nature. Nature was always a refuge in which I could seek peace and solitude. It's where I found comfort in God's hands and in the arms of my Angels. Picking raspberries on the side of our house (where just beyond the bushes was a busy highway) became a private sanctuary. Forts built out of old doors burnt from the fire became my favorite place to escape. I would stay out there until I couldn't stand another mosquito bite or in the wintertime until the tips of my toes, nose and fingers went numb.

If Bill and I were to move forward, he would need to know about my experiences while working at "Here's Health" health food store during high school, where I saw very ill people turn to prayer through the intervention of God, Angels, the Universe, Saints, Source, Buddha, Jesus, their Rabbi's, their Priest's, and Shamanic healers. I was convinced that Bill needed to know how meditation, yoga, hypno-therapy, hands-on-healing, juicing and seaweed diets in unique combinations appeared to heal the customers I had met. I wasn't insanely certain about all of this, but I will always be deeply intrigued.

He should know I had worked a second job cleaning a synagogue. It was there, after hours, that I ravenously learned about the Jewish religion, while I had the Rabbi to myself. In addition, the Priest of my next-door neighbor's church explained the power of prayer, Angels & Saints and he'd also taught me about the purpose of incense and how it cleanses space in the holy areas. And, back to present, I felt Bill should simply know the only food I brought to college this fall was a few jars of peanut butter and a case of rice cakes. I felt he needed this information so he wouldn't waste his time, or mine, chasing the wrong girl.

I didn't expect this guy to believe in the natural and alternative healing modalities I was exposed to, and he is certainly not going to feel full on my rice cakes, but if he is mocking the Angels, this for sure will not be a fit for me.

It was clear that I felt physically safe with Bill. I worried, though, that he might have the potential to wreck me emotionally. I was safe with past boyfriends, physically and emotionally, but with Bill, he would be comparing me to the many women he'd already been with and to the hundreds of women he could potentially have. This was a ladies' man; a real player in a game with which I wasn't experienced.

Bill noticed me studying his friends and, mostly, Tommy's dancing, who was now sliding across the floor like Michael Jackson, to "Billy Jean." Tommy saw my amusement and continued to show off his moves. I loved this guy's free spirit and love for life. He was comfortable in his body and wasn't embarrassed about who he was. He seemed to be the kind of guy who could enjoy his own company.

Bill was quietly confident, and like Tommy didn't seem to try to be anything other than who he was. These guys were comfortable being warriors, and, although I didn't expect it, they were artists in their own ways. Their artistry challenged the preconception I had in my head. The box I would have put them in was now blowing wide open. But as silly as it may sound, I still needed to find a way to address Bill's concept of Angels.

The bartender approached with baskets of chicken fingers, wings, nachos and onion rings. "On the house," he announced.

I'm not sure how they did it, but the food was devoured in less than five minutes, though I was offered "first dibs."

I turned to Tommy and said, "A guy in the cafeteria tonight mentioned you and Bill flipped a car over last weekend and you both were seen in a bar eating the bar glasses. Is that true?"

Tommy's light blue eyes crinkled around the edges. He smiled and said, "I will neither confirm nor deny."

The bartender sighed as he turned and made his way to the back room to prepare for what was coming next. He returned shortly after with a fresh box of the thick beer glasses.

Tommy locked his eyes on mine while he bit a piece of his glass off and chewed. It made me want to pee my pants. *Holy shit, I loved these silly college games. Why? What the hell is wrong with me? These guys are not my type!*

Before I had a chance to address them, one of the guys standing there grabbed a phone book and gave it to Bill. "Billy, do your thing."

Embarrassed, he said, "No, no, that's stupid. She doesn't need to see that."

I could tell he didn't want to use these tactics to get my attention. In fact, I think he knew they could potentially do the opposite. But with continued peer pressure and me finally saying, "What are you gonna do with that?" he succumbed and held the very thick phone book in two hands, ripped it in half and set the two pieces on the counter. They all roared with laughter. One by one, Bill's teammates tried to do the same. They weren't successful. I liked Bill's modesty and chalked it up as being healthy.

Bill put his hand on my thigh, "Hey, it's just stupid things we do."

I could sense he didn't want me to know he spent time eating glasses and tearing phone books in half, and I also had a feeling he may never do such things in front of me again. I couldn't put my finger on it, but there was something different about Bill Cochrane. I saw depth and wanted to know more about where that may have come from.

He didn't mean it to be because it was more of a pat of friendly concern, but his huge hand on my thigh was beyond sensual. The combination of his warm hand and size reminded me of a heating pad. Seemingly arriving out of thin air, he tilted another frosty glass of foamy beer against his full lips. The jury was still out on whether or not I would ever kiss him, but I was starting to lean towards a yes. The bartender was well-trained and kept my beers coming, so I became quite buzzed. I was used to having a few dollars and only drinking a total of three beers. I think I may have drunk four or five by this point. *Was this part of the game; was this how they got girls into bed?*

I'm not sure what exactly came over me, but the glass eating and phone book ripping inspired me to share a bar trick my dad and brother helped me to perfect. After my parents had divorced, I'd spent many Saturday and Sunday afternoons visiting my dad in his favorite local downtown Chicago hangouts: Tiny Tap and Egan's. I also spent a lot of time in Wisconsin with my brother and cousins after the age of fifteen, hanging out in bars perfecting bar tricks, shooting pool and becoming skilled at darts.

I placed three bar stools all in a line. As I arranged the stools, the clang of the heavy metal hit the cement floors, and I captured attention from most of the people in the bar. I put my butt on the middle one, I leaned back with my head and neck on one of them and placed the heels of my feet on the last one. I balanced myself there, like a board, facing upward.

Tommy ceased his dancing around the pool table and turned toward me to see me in action.

I reached underneath and pulled the middle barstool away, keeping myself balanced in the plank position across the other two. I swung it over the top of my body, staying balanced on just two stools, and then replaced it under my rear end. I jumped off the stool and took a bow. The bar erupted in laughter and claps. Tommy was delighted with this trick and immediately started setting up his own stools to do the same.

He successfully accomplished the feat, and many followed afterward.

"I need to take a piss," Tommy said as he nodded his head towards the bathroom to Bill. Bill got up right away and headed in that direction. It was like they had a silent language; I could tell Tommy wanted to tell him something in private. The other guys politely scattered. When I was alone at the bar, I tapped the thick grooved beer glass on my teeth and clamped down just to get a feel of what they felt.

Marie and Shannon bee-lined over and wanted the scoop.

I asked, "Did you see that guy eat the glass?" They had, and we all laughed.

Marie asked, "Soooo, what do you think of him?"

I replied, "Not sure yet."

Shannon and Marie looked at each other and giggled.

"What?" I asked.

"Well," Marie paused, "I think this'll be the last boyfriend you have."

"WHAT!? Are you kiddin' me? Oh no, no way."

Or was I? What is this gut feeling? Am I just young and blind, or is there something right here?

The Foreigner song "I Want To Know What Love Is" came on as Bill and Tommy came out of the bathroom. Tommy, with arms opened wide, belted the song out as we all cracked up.

After we had been left alone at the bar, Bill asked cautiously, "What'd ya think of Tommy?"

"I liked him."

"He totally liked you," Bill replied.

Bill was a bit embarrassed but wanted to say what was on his mind: "Tommy told me in the bathroom, 'That's her Billy. That's your girl. Your future wife. I'm not kiddin' you, brotha'. I'm fuckin' serious right now. I'll be standin' up in this wedding.'

CAN'T FIGHT IT

A week after that night at the Panther Lounge, Bill and I sat in the crowded dorm lobby on one of the ten couches. We had one couch to ourselves, turned slightly toward each other. He smelled good again. He was wearing a snug turquoise short-sleeve Polo shirt and some tight jeans, both of which required tailoring to fit his trim waist and broad shoulders.

Away from the barroom atmosphere, I was able to ask questions about his past relationships. He freely shared what he liked and didn't like, and I found we had a lot in common, but I wasn't about to admit that yet.

I was distracted by his tight-fitting jeans and the physique they hugged. His hand, that monstrous hand that could tear a phone book in half, rested on his massive thigh. For the first time, I noticed his fingers, which were close to the size of Italian sausages. I teased him about this and sensed that most girls he dated were less playful than me.

The more he talked, the more I liked him. He showed sensitivity, but I had to ignore his exterior to see it. The chemistry between us was obvious, and I simply found him interesting. He seemed worldly in that he hadn't lived the easiest life, but he also seemed to have learned a lot from everything he'd been exposed to. He was street-smart, for sure. His position of authority on the field and his standing in class were evidence of a great work ethic. He seemed a little more serious than playful, but that wasn't a total deal-breaker for me.

Bill and I proceeded to talk until the sun came up. My cheeks hurt from smiling, and my throat was sore from talking. I could smell scrambled eggs and sausage wafting up the stairs from the cafeteria. There was no more fighting the truth after this marathon-get-together. The lobby speakers had been turned down low all evening and tuned into a radio station that continuously played the new hit song "Can't Fight This Feeling" by REO Speedwagon. As it played for maybe the 20th time, we continued to lock eyes. I stood up as to say, "Let's call it a night, or should I say morning."

I wanted him to kiss me. *It was time! I was ready. But I'm not the one dripping with experience. He is.* I had only two serious loves up until now. He should initiate. Right? He reached his arms out to mine and pulled me close. I could feel the whole front side of his solid body against me, a massive wall of warmth. Just as before, when my hand disappeared into his, my body disappeared in the same way. He smelled so good, and it wasn't the cologne. That had worn off. It was him, his scent. I let my head rest against his massive chest. I could feel the pocket of muscles on his pecs. I wanted to reach under his shirt to feel them. We stood there a long time. *Why wasn't he kissing me?*

After our night at Panther Lounge and the last 13 hours of conversations about his past, which included many women, I had a feeling he was going to be extra careful about making moves with me. I was going to probably have to make the first move. Maybe the second, too.

And then, like a gentleman, he said, "Lemme' walk you to your dorm."

Our lobby connected his dorm, Stevenson, co-ed and mostly athletes, to my dorm, Lincoln, which was all girls, as well as to the all-male dorm, Douglas. He pulled the heavy entrance door to Lincoln open, and it made a deep suction noise as the wind from the corridor whipped up against my back and into his face. My long hair blew all over and across my face, and I finally saw his hair messed up. We were laughing and awkwardly trying to figure out whether to shut the door so we could have that first kiss, or simply to go our separate ways.

He said, "Hey, may the wind be at your back," an old Irish sentiment I coincidentally loved. I loosely held his hand. "See you later, Bill Cochrane."

I made my way back to the dorm, smiling at the fact that I had just met someone who would change the course of my life. I reviewed the 13 hours that had flown by. We'd covered what we knew of politics, racism, psychology, world suffering, God and religion, Angels, war, the death penalty, marriage, vows, family, love of animals and children, our college majors, our dream jobs and incomes, dream houses, health, parts of the country we wanted to live in, cars, vacations, friends, weddings, funerals, deaths, our highs and lows, honesty, lies and white lies, what we knew of some of our weaknesses and strengths, our functional and dysfunctional families, and we even spent ten minutes discussing the best way to eat Oreo cookies.

NO DOUBT

After Bill and I both graduated from Eastern Illinois University in 1987, I was offered a job selling Cover Girl makeup to stores. They offered a decent salary and a small commission structure, along with a company car, but Bill and I had discussed bigger goals. We spent no time being fearful of commission jobs, where the income relied on what you could sell—the return seemed worth the risk. What we did have, was 100 percent faith in ourselves and in each other. We had no doubt that time was on our side, and love would see us through. We each had a sense of our capabilities, and they exceeded stocking shelves day after day. We wanted to sell a competitive product that demanded we be the best at what we did. We hunted for high-end, high-tech, high-quality, and the highest-cost product we could find; cell phones and copiers held the greatest return. I quickly landed a risky, commission-only sales job, selling the highest-end cellular phones for Motorola, Inc., with offices out of Schaumburg, Illinois, and downtown, Chicago.

Bill accepted a similar 100-percent-commission sales job, but with Harris 3M, selling copiers. Together, we rented the most luxurious apartment we could find, with private garage parking for the new cars we had just financed. We were off and running. We secured two memberships at a fitness club and spent numerous hours exercising when we weren't working ridiculous hours, far surpassing our peers. Between the two of us, Bill was the better shopper, so he took the lead when it came to our new grown-up wardrobes, in contrast to the casual wear of college life. He was decisive and generously free with money. I was thrilled to wear high-end suits, with traditional cotton, button-down blouses. The navy blue and black pumps were higher than most women would wear while walking around downtown, but I'd grown to like this businesswoman look.

While standing in the store, I hadn't paid attention at first when Bill asked the seamstress measuring the navy suit and blouse, "What other fabrics do you have?"

She gave him a ring of fabrics to choose from, and he pulled some out and handed them to her, "We'll take these, too."

He whipped out his credit card and off we went. When I went back to pick up my tailored suits in seven different colors with seven different blouses, as well as four different pairs of high heels, I was shocked to see we'd spent a small fortune on my new wardrobe.

I called him from the car, "What the hell were you thinkin'? That totaled seven grand!"

He laughed and calmly said, "It's simple, we got this. We need to sell about 13 phones and copiers. To paraphrase, 'We just need to believe it and then we will see it,' just like we heard Wayne Dyer say at that conference."

We had created a blueprint for bliss from our studies of psychology, and spiritual audiotapes and inspirational books with complimentary workbooks. We included business, sales and management series such as Norman Vincent Peale's *The Power of Positive Thinking*, Dale Carnegie's 10 *Keys To Success*, Napoleon Hill's *Law of Success*, *Think and Grow Rich* and of course, Tony Robbins was included in our main focus during this time. Our first purchase for the apartment was a huge bookshelf that covered one entire wall. Our place captured the look of an inspirational and motivational bookstore.

In short order, we graduated, moved in together, got engaged and now had five months to plan our wedding, which would take place on August 21, 1988. We knew it wasn't going to be financed by my parents, nor his, and so with no hesitation, we planned a formal 250-person church ceremony with a Radisson Hotel reception in Glenview, Illinois, just north of Chicago. We naively opted for upgrades in everything they offered as far as food and alcohol and happily flipped the bill for about 15 extra guests who were not even invited. *The more, the merrier.*

Bill attended my Motorola Christmas party. He met my boss and the boss's boss, and by the end of the evening, they hired Bill, and he joined our sales team. Within months, we combined our efforts to create a stronger sales force and became the top producers in the country. We began showing others how to pair up in the office, and our entire Schaumburg and Libertyville offices grew rapidly and far surpassed sales across the entire country.

Always thinking of new business opportunities, Bill was inspired by his past experience and love for firehouses, and he found some creative engineers to electronically attach a cell phone to an EKG unit. They worked after hours and on weekends in our garage for months. This unit was the first of its kind. It transmitted the EKG of a patient in the field to an ER doctor's computer so he could advise the paramedic on the next steps. Bill ended up selling that product to Motorola within a few months. This sale helped to pay for our wedding.

Bill also strategically financed our first home purchase, rolling his sleeves up and making that happen shortly after we married. He sold his two motorcycles and also bought, fixed up and then sold a limited-edition Corvette. He had a knack for knowing what to clean up, detail, add or take away from anything with a motor.

While he continued to flip vehicles and motorcycles, he turned a profit rather than breaking even, and it continued to be a creative outlet and moneymaker for us.

With a wad of cash in my hand, I once asked him how he knew what to do, to make these cars more sellable.

He simply said, "I just make them the way I'd want them. Pulling labels off to change the factory look makes them a little different."

Cars and motorcycles were like works of art to him. He would spend hours on his knees and back with toothbrushes, toothpicks and cleaning polishes, leaving not one speck of dirt behind. He invested in a professional power washer, only using the most expensive polishes and waxes. He was such a perfectionist, in fact, that eating and drinking in the cars was off limits.

Our first house was the highest-end of the track homes in a northern suburb outside of Chicago. We did exactly what we were *not* supposed to do. We bought the most expensive house in the neighborhood, loaded with every extra, but that's how we did things.

We were on the roll we thought we'd be on. More and more, I believed in the climb we were making. It was supposed to be this way. You make a plan, you do the right thing, you work your ass off, and you get a pay-off. Trajectory always followed and off we went. The money started to roll in, just as we expected, planned on, worked for and strategized for. Bill was soon promoted to Sales Manager. The office environment was filled with high-pressured quotas, but that made it fun.

Two of our great producers were ex-Chicago Bears football players, and they were a blast to hang out with. This group of both young and old salespeople worked hard and played hard. It was a great foundation to learn the world of balance in life and work, but Bill leaned more towards work than play. Which kept his team ranked perpetually among the top producers in the country.

His nickname became "The Magician" because of his magical way of transforming an employee, who might not have appeared to be polished, into a dominating force in nationwide sales. He said it wasn't magic. He just encouraged sales reps to be genuine, to solely give the customer only what they wanted and to never oversell. He would say, "If you genuinely earn their trust, you will eventually earn their referral."

Bill became the youngest National Sales Director in the company, and as a result started to travel extensively. He was described by upper management as one that, "runs it like he owns it." He continued to exceed sales quotas each quarter, while referrals to work with Bill and his sales team flooded the office. The clientele at Motorola grew rapidly and became even more exciting and fun. Walter

Payton became a customer first and then a friend of Bill's soon after. Another client owned the largest private collection of Ferraris, as well as a famous Italian restaurant in downtown Chicago. He asked Bill and me to drive a red '72 Ferrari to the Milwaukee Mile track one weekend, and when Bill officially drove on the track, a lot faster than a practice lap should be driven. We were not surprised and the owner and I broke out in laughter. The top defense attorney in Chicago became a close friend, as well. The most mysterious were the clients asking to meet us after hours. These appointments felt like something you'd see in the movies, related to secret government missions of some kind. We learned much from contacts with the many types of businesses and executives that comprised the Motorola clientele. Working, and playing, in those circles, suited us. And as quotas and salaries increased, so did our dreams and goals.

Until we moved to Tucson, where we were stopped in our tracks.

YES, SIR!

In Tucson, periodically, I would often work through anxiety by kicking off my flip-flops and walking on the hard dirt outside in the backyard in order to get grounded. Once in a while, I'd feel the great sensation of being planted into the earth. At times, if alone, I'd get so into it that it wasn't uncommon for me to stomp as if somehow the thump brought it all home. But, it wasn't helping this time, and I retired back inside, feeling my baked, dry skin had scorched from the summer sun. I lay down on my back, onto Horehole's cold, white tile and I let it cool me like the air-conditioner couldn't.

Most of our close friends were thriving financially. I kept thinking that should be more of an inspiration for me to see others thrive, but it kept back-firing. The mother of one of my girlfriends won a $13-million lottery. Another friend seemed to win every raffle she played; she actually won a car and a 10-day Hawaiian vacation in the same year. Our next-door neighbor took a small company public and was selling his product so successfully to major outfits he could barely keep up with supply and demand. He used my kids as models on the front of the boxes, so I saw their sweet faces everywhere I went. I was excited about his company's growth and the marketing expertise behind it, as it was always a dream of mine. But all the hard work and years of experience that got him there was looking impossible for me. I barely had the energy to wash dishes, cook, do laundry, help with homework and get kids to bed.

My friend, Cami, actually kept finding money everywhere we went.

She exclaimed, "Oh my God, This *only* happens when I'm with you! *You* are my lucky charm!"

She'd shout, "Yay for me! I wonder why *you* aren't manifesting any of this?"

I wondered the same, especially having read and studied both very old and current books on the magic and power of believing and visualization. Until now, I actually believed my metaphysical studies had played a big role in the success Bill and I had experienced over the years. *What the hell is wrong with me that I can't create what everyone else around me seems to be doing? I'm literally someone else's lucky charm, and I hold none of the luck for myself?* I instantly became an-noyed that this newbie to self-development was having such an easy time with it all. Which I found ridiculous: Did I think I was going to be somehow left behind by the universe? I felt jealous and lost. *I'm losin' it.*

I began examining our relations with friends more carefully. *What are the real reasons for these friendships? What kind of a friend do I deserve and what kind of a friend am I?* After these rough months, it became clear to me that some of our so-called friends were more interested in the novelty of our rise and fall. Some of them fell off when they got bored with it all. Some dumped us because we couldn't afford the extracurricular activities that our friendships centered around. Some seemed strangely uplifted by it because it gave them a false sense of stability for themselves. I could imagine their inner dialogues: "Whew, glad that's not me and my family," or worse, "We're smarter. That would never happen to us."

The beat on our hearts, minds, and emotions continued as our connections disintegrated, along with respect that we once felt from our community. At the same time, we felt dis-membered from some of our immediate families, who started suggesting that we wanted too much to begin with, that we were too risky, too ambitious, with way too lofty of goals. There was an unspoken implication from some family members that they believed the current situation served us right. There was even one family member that made fun of us for being on food stamps, and behind our backs, called us "*white trash.*"

We started being compared to others in the family that were having success; ones with less eventful career paths that turned out successfully, and somehow, we were scorned for not taking those paths. Family get-together's, and out of town visitors with good intentions would unintentionally rifle Bill for the download on his job situation; details on what he's doing now, what interviews are lined up, or they would seek an update on probable moves to another rental. Quite a few would re-hash "the fall of it all" and make ridiculous, but usually well-intentioned, suggestions of what Bill should have done to make it work. When we finally did discuss some of the cutthroat actions of others, a few members of the family looked at us like *we* did something wrong. As much as they sometimes wanted to support and back us up, our family had a long history of never being in a business like this or any of the businesses we'd been in. As a result, their advice and suggestions were not always helpful. They actually hurt. Family, who had happily accepted thousands of dollars of gifts from us in the past were now counseling us on our ethics and ambitions. I pulled further and further away from them, hoping I'd have minimal to no contact with most, especially the one using the words "white trash."

I literally began to take "news fasts" in order to not let my mind and heart absorb more bad news. At first, I thought it was a healthy distraction to stop obsessing with my own problems, but on updates 9-11, continued terrorist threats, bank bailouts, dot-com, telecom and stock market crash became unbearable to watch. Bill was feeling as hopeless and beat as I was. His silence told me so. Unless he was on a football or a baseball field, Bill seemed to carry a heavy body language, and we all knew to step back. His occasional temper came on quickly and made you feel like it was too late to run. He often expressed his annoyance wordlessly, but we felt it loud and clear. Bill had a strong history of shared brotherhood from football fields and firehouses. I suspected that his current restlessness was connected to the fact that he was living the opposite today. He was no longer a part of a team where men had each other's backs. In his world, nobody had his back, and if they did, it would be more likely that they'd stab him there. He often talked about enlisting in the military, and would have if his age hadn't been a factor.

The kids' sporting events became our new vehicles for experiencing victory because it wasn't manifesting anywhere else. At games, I started noticing my loud voice and Bill's intense silence on the sidelines. Both of which showed our pressing desire to excel and win again, even if it was Little League softball, baseball or a Pop Warner football game. Coaching these young boys was turning out to be Bill's salvation. Win or lose; he always walked around on those fields with a spring in his step. I'm not sure what would have become of Bill without these players and parents. He didn't talk in detail about what this did for him, but I knew his words of wisdom for his players tied so deeply into his personal processing of the current situation. Privately, I wished he could be satisfied with becoming a teacher and a football coach. He seemed to love it that much. *But I had to honestly ask myself, would I truly be satisfied?*

Off the field, his potential depression was turning into anger. This became a growing concern for me. Occasionally, we would be in the car and watch him easily become agitated with the wide corners and slow, erratic driving of the predominantly retired drivers in the foothills. They didn't drive like Chicago motorists. His family history of suicide, both attempted and successful, haunted me. There were other dotcom and telecom companies going down the tubes, just like ours had, and I'd been reading stories about men taking their own lives because of it.

It happened nearby to another foothills family with two young children. The father parked his running car in the garage and shut the door. I was well aware that could be us. *Why not us?*

Because we were no stranger to marriage therapy, I suggested that maybe I could get us in somewhere through our state health insurance. He adamantly declined, and I dropped it.

When Bill first started coaching football during their first season years ago, parents started asking permission to be a part of the after-practice and after-game chats with the kids because they, too, left inspired by Bill's words. Soon after, parents and players from other teams would meander over to hear his closing remarks. I agreed they were awesome, and often asked him to repeat what he said when we'd return home, or at least write it down so we would have record of these. But he could never remember them.

Thinking back to the time when we parents shared a tough time watching our little kids develop, I thought of the second to the last game of a past season, when the heads hung low as the little pee-wee football team exited the field after a very close game. They had now endured nine losses, with their final game of the season remaining which was going to be the following week, against the first-ranked team in the city. As parents, we were heartbroken for them. Somehow, Bill had kept the kids' attitudes miraculously positive despite the mounting losses. We thought for sure the team would squeak a win out on this day, and so did the kids. We silently exited the stands and met up with the team sitting in a horseshoe shape around Bill. He was kneeling to maintain eye contact with the players. He waited for the parents to gather before he started his speech. The kids' wide eyes waited for what Coach Bill would say. They had shame written all over them. Marcus and Nicole stood on each side of me, and we all wanted to reach out to Clint, who had tears in his eyes as he waited for his dad to speak.

"Guys. Look, we were so close, but you couldn't have done anything more than you did. You played your butts off, with all your heart and you played hard for each other. So, this loss is mine. I'll take it. You did everything I could have asked you to do. So, we tip our hats to their victory, and we move forward. Sometimes you give all you have, and you lose. Just like life. Sure, we could give excuses like—most of you have never played tackle football and that it's a tough sport. But that's not what we do. We work harder, and we work together. You played a heck of a game. You were courageous and selfless. We moved the ball on one of the best defenses in the city. And a team that thought they'd run right over us had to fight for their win."

He continued: "I want you to feel great about your effort, bring that same effort to our last practice this week and we'll finish this season like champions. Now I want ya to go to your parents standing behind you and thank 'em. Thank 'em for driving you to practice every day. And thank your siblings, while you're at it. They come to watch all your games. Tonight, I want you to get ready for a great week. Do your homework, wash your own uniforms, and do your chores. You're growin' up. You guys have learned a lot this season, nothing more important than doing your part. You'll get through this season with a victory cause you worked hard, you never gave up, you believed in yourselves, and you believed in each other. I am very proud of you guys."

He scanned the boys around him, "Look to your right and now to your left. Look your brothers in the eyes. You want to see them succeed?"

And they nodded and yelled, "YES, SIR!"

"If they win, who wins?"

"WE DO, SIR!"

Bill continued, "We're not playing for a championship trophy next week. But let me ask you this: If you play as hard as you can, and you play to honor each other, and to honor the game, doesn't that make you a champion? Well, let me be the one to tell you…" and he started pointing to each and every kid… "You are… in my eyes… in my heart… CHAMPIONS. Here's the deal: Being a champion is a choice. And it all starts here with the heart of a champion, your heart. I expect you to take that heart of a champion and to be great. Now, one last question: Will you play like champions next week?

"YES SIR!" they screamed in unison.

Bill's pee-wee football team experienced the most dreadful season that year, but it turned glorious, a week later, after miraculously winning the last game against one of the toughest teams in the city.

…And they dominated in the seasons after that, with trophies and division championships in the many years to follow.

ASK AND YE SHALL RECEIVE

My best friend in Tucson kept trying to pull me out for drinks and eventually became tired of my declines and withdrawal.

"Okay, forget the drinks, fun and laughter. What about you get out of the house and just come over here to cry? You need to express yourself. You can't just keep up this strong-girl front."

Without admitting out loud that she was right, I could see how my constant worry about Bill's potential depression masked my own. It was becoming clear that the emotional trauma I was privately suffering also highlighted the loss of my super powers: superwife, supermom, superdaughter, supersister, superfriend… all the superwomen I spent a lifetime trying to be. I had always been willing to accept the praise I'd received for seeming to have it all together. I'd spent years expecting and counting on that feedback. But today, I was supertired. That truth silenced me. It created a barrier where I tried to hide from judgment—theirs and my own.

I found myself spending every free minute studying any books that helped me get a deeper spiritual, mental and emotional handle on the world, myself, the kids, the marriage and our financial status. It was like I was a junkie. I would find golden nuggets of peace in all of the books I read, but it wasn't nearly enough. Like an addict, the more exposed I became to what I didn't know, the more ravenous I became to know more.

I also started to recognize that I might have potentially overcompensated for our lack of money by diving into my spirituality to disguise our poverty. *If I'm at zero financial value, I better seek my spiritual worth.* I questioned whether or not I should keep diving; it was turning others off, and since Bill wasn't participating with me, it actually became more of a barrier between us. But I kept at it.

One day I surprised myself as I started getting more real about how I felt after picking up a book about *staying positive*. The author wrote about how important it was to find one thing for which to be grateful. I had read this so many other times, but this time, it infuriated me. Going to my regular places of gratitude, I tried calming myself down while listing off the kid's names but stopped. It's not that I wasn't grateful for them, I was. It just wasn't moving me out of the state I was in; it seemed to drive me deeper. Wrapped up and attached to how hard these times were for them had stifled my ability to feel gratitude. In direct relation to them, heavy guilt surfaced that I hadn't noticed before. Sure, they seemed okay, but the belief I bought into today was that *they didn't know any better*. Little did they know that we could easily be homeless in 30 days or less at any given time. I studied the cars we owned and mentally planned what we would be able to take with us if we had to leave fast. Bill and I were supposed to protect and provide, but we were dangerously close to another fall, worse than the last one. Just one health crisis could do us in. The guilt immediately turned to anger, and I sarcastically mocked the idea of choosing "one thing to be grateful for." And I whipped the book across the room, making a hole in the rental wall and said, "I'm grateful for walls I can break through!"

On a positive note, though, a few days later, I had to admit that I was thankful that my understanding of others suffering had deepened, and as my clients would trickle in, they saw positive, sometimes miraculous results. Unfortunately, my stomach problems became worse. I just didn't have the healthy boundaries to protect me from the empathetic nature of this practice. I slowly shut the door on my work, becoming an emergency last-resort resource for a few doctors in town, who knew I would only accept children in crisis. However, I wrestled with the fact that I was a certified hypnotherapist, who understands the power of words and thoughts, but could not personally keep it together in the face of our continual bad news.

My health screamed for attention, and I was diagnosed with ulcers and acid reflux. I was rushed to the emergency room for various things—vomiting, diarrhea, blood in my urine and the feeling like something was stuck in my throat. Eventually, I found myself in the hands of an ER gastrointestinal doctor.

He studied his clipboard, looking at me while I sat on a cold, hard chair while doing a double-take. He said, "Hmm. You spent the whole night in the ER? You don't look sick... it's hard to believe this chart. You look healthy as a horse."

Yeah, yeah, I know.

I don't know if it was that old Coach purse, the Arizona tan from sitting in the stands at outdoor sports for the kids or the general put together look I was carrying, but I was feeling invisible—completely undercover. What I appeared to be was not at all what was going on. I was like a 100-year-old saguaro that stood tall with big thick, healthy green arms, covered with needled armor, but one that had a shallow root system and could fall in a mild thunderstorm. There was a part of me that wanted to stand at the top of the bleachers and scream out loud, telling everyone every detail of my life. And there was another part of me that was ashamed and hoped that if I kept faking it before I made it, I would arrive back to where I was, and no one would even need to know my truth. Not even me.

The ER doctor scribbled some acid prevention medicines on a pad, handed it to me and said "This is just stress. Your husband should take you to Hawaii and feed you margaritas on the beach."

Literally, he said that.

Little did he know, that coming up with the $15 dollar copay on state health insurance for this visit was challenging enough. And a trip to Maui was not at all likely.

The medicine didn't help, and I grew more concerned, as my condition got worse. I reached out to people in my network of alternative health to address the obvious scientific connections which proved ulcers can be caused by stress. So, I called Katie Campano, an intuitive, from Santa Barbara. She had been referred to me by a friend. She mentioned my throat issues might be because I was either not speaking my truth, or perhaps I had been speaking it too much. She was shocked I had not been practicing self-hypnosis.

My present belief, which I tried banking on, was that a new job and more money would aid in the healing of my health issues, so I first wanted to hear what she saw for us in the near future, as far as work and money were concerned. I specifically asked about an upcoming interview for Bill, and, to my delight, she mentioned there was a light at the end of the tunnel.

Thrilled, I said, "Oh, thank God, I wasn't sure how much more waiting we could do."

She quickly added, "Oh, wait. Honey, hold on. I saw it wrong. The light is a symbol that it's good, but it's going to be rough. And, Judy, this looks to be somewhere around a decade of growth, learning and repair. You need to put your seat-belt on, dear. Wait, no. Put a racing harness on. It isn't that your marriage can't endure things, it can. I can see snippets of the past solid work you've both done. And, sometimes, if it is time for something to end, it must. You have spent time appreciating and owning who you are, but for the last few years, you have not. You, like many busy mothers and wives, have gotten away from your true Goddess nature."

If this has something to do with chanting in a white gown while standing under a waterfall in Maui, I'm going to scream.

She went on: "Buddha said, 'If your compassion only includes others and not yourself, it is incomplete.' "

Shit! I thought, as my stomach and esophagus burned while reacting to this information. I was fascinated to see disease show itself like this, but also terrified because I couldn't stop it. Not only was my financial world a disaster, physically, mentally, emotionally and spiritually, but I was severely disconnect-ed and unhealthily connected in the wrong way as well. I was making myself sicker!

I didn't know what to say or ask of her. I had just agreed to pay money I didn't have, to a woman I never met, who may have just given me the worst news I could have imagined about our financial future. On top of that, I didn't appear to be able to do anything with this information.

Tucson was going to thoroughly kick our ass. The Native American's named her Death Valley and often spoke about her healing nature. If disrespected, she would fight you harder. Strangely, I had watched people come and go from here. If they left with a middle finger in the air, they seemed to live with suffering of some kind. I was not new to respecting the energy of the land I lived in and on. There may be no rest in sight for a while. *Arizona wasn't done with us yet. She's going to rip us apart. Then what?*

About an hour after the call with the intuitive, Katie, I called her back. Not sure what made me do it, but I asked her to keep a look out for anyone who may need a house-sitter this summer, preferably someone with a dog, cat or both. I was so done with people, and I deeply missed having an animal. *I need to be alone, get grounded and align with Source.* I knew Bill would be really pissed off, but I couldn't care. It was something I had to ask for. Katie was agreeable, but also let me know most people do not leave Santa Barbara in the summer. Unlike Tucson, where it's a ghost town. I had spent the last three months watch-ing practically every friend and neighbor escape, seeking water and cooler temperatures.

That evening, I was surprised to hear back from Katie. She said she announced my desire to a small group of her regular clients and was thrilled to tell me that a Santa Barbara couple, Tracy and Ed Martin, needed someone to watch their two dogs and one cat, for 11 days. They were going to Greensboro, North Carolina, to visit family.

"What do you say?" she asked.

"I say YES! And GREENSBORO? That's where we lived before Tucson. How bizarre!"

"Or, should we admit, how Divine? I'm thinking the Universe is showing you this may be the right path," Katie reassured.

"YES. YES. This feels so right."

"When you get here, be sure to call Skye Hawkins for an appointment. She's an intuitive healer here. Lives in a celebrity neighborhood. She resides in a guest-house of another person I can't give you the name of. Just trust me, you'll love her. She's perfect for you right now. She has a complete private referral base only. You will never find this woman in a newspaper ad. I'm personally referring you so that she will take your call. If you see anyone famous entering or leaving when you get there, be sure to stay cool and ignore him or her."

Nervously intrigued, I said, "Okay, will do, sounds interesting for sure."

I hung up and immediately dropped into panic mode. My upcoming to-do list hit me hard, and Marc's 11th birthday was the next week. I'd be leaving shortly after that, and school registration for all three kids was the day after I returned. I headed to the front door to check on the kids. Having never done anything like this before, I wondered how they'd do. Starting to feel a hint of regret, as I opened the door, the 100-plus-degree heat wave hit me in the face. Gulping in the hot air, my throat went dry, leaving me barely able to swallow. In the past, I had appreciated the dry heat and less sweat in this part of the country, but today I couldn't go there. I hated Tucson, this proverbial bitch in heat, and she hated me back.

I reminded myself of how effortless this 11-day trip had just come together. I aligned my thoughts and started strategizing on what I could do beforehand to make this as simple as possible for Bill and the kids.

I called my friend Cami, the one I was a good luck charm for, and told her what had evolved. I expected her to reassure me that I needed this and that it was a sound idea. I shared the date of my departure and return. I also asked if she wouldn't mind carpooling with Bill for the floor hockey camp we both had our kids scheduled for, and maybe even setting up a sleep over or two to give Bill a break at times. Our kids liked to play together. She was the most perfect to help out.

Dead silence on her end.

"Hello, did I lose ya?" I asked.

"Nope, I'm here."

She was pissed. I could now only imagine Bill would be at least the same, and based on his temper these days, probably worse.

"What's up?" I cautiously asked.

"Oh, I don't know, Judy. I've been here for you all along, but, seriously, I think you just crossed a line. I'm shocked you think this is an appropriate time to be taking off and not caring for your kids and Bill. Of all people, I would have never imagined you to become selfish during this trying time. Like, where's all your

Wayne Dyer, Deepak Chopra and spiritual philosophy shit now? You really believe going away for 11-days right before the kids go back to school and making Bill take care of kids' stuff is okay? Honestly, I have always admired your ways of diving into spirituality—you got me interested in it, but do you really think this is going to help? You seem desperate and unsure. I will never be convinced that this will be a good move for you or your family."

FOR A SEED TO ACHIEVE ITS GREATEST EXPRESSION, IT MUST COME COMPLETELY UNDONE. THE SHELL CRACKS, ITS INSIDES COME OUT AND EVERYTHING CHANGES. TO SOMEONE WHO DOESN'T UNDERSTAND GROWTH, IT WOULD LOOK LIKE COMPLETE DESTRUCTION. CYNTHIA OCCELLI

THE ART OF LEAVING

The following day was a Saturday. Bill came in from the garage as the phone started to ring. I grabbed it and was happy to hear George Shiftman's voice. There were a few lone survivors from i360 that went on to thrive in other businesses, and I was relieved to see George was one of them. He and his wife were in their early 70s. They were a couple we deeply admired and cherished. They had a solid marriage and in the 1980s, together, they built the National MLS listing system for realtors. He was a strong force, bringing investors into i360, and a huge fan of Bill. They lived on the East Coast. His friends were powerful New York executives and heavily-medaled military and political leaders. Because he was a busy man, we had never heard from George on a Saturday before. But he went out of his way, on speakerphone, to tell us something he felt he needed to say. Apparently, he'd been closely following Bill's attempts to keep the ship afloat.

"Kids, I've been thinking a lot about your situation. The sale was well done, and it is unfortunate it didn't evolve into retirement for the two of you. But the way the company is trying to resurrect and add to their platform to find new financing is making things sloppy. I want you both to *listen* to me very carefully. This is important. In life, there is sometimes *an art to leaving*. I trust you to do what you think you need, and Billy, you know how much I appreciate your ability to be an unstoppable missile locked into a target, but it's been a brutal three years for you, and I want you to consider what I'm saying. Take it to heart and know I have been where you have been before. If you feel this is destroying the good in your life in any way, then you should consider my advice and prepare for *the art of leaving*. I suggest you tap into making this decision with both the heart and mind in equal measure. I'm an old man. As you know, I have had and lost fortunes a few times. The only thing with importance is what you have right here between the two of you and those three kids."

I was so moved by George's call. I longed for Bill to grab me around the waist and pull me close to him and dance with me the way he used to in college. I yearned for him to say, "Hey, we're all right, everything is gonna be all right, I got this." But instead, he told the truth by saying nothing at all. He wasn't moved by George's words, and he wasn't okay. He was not sure things would work out, and he didn't feel like dancing; he was drowning after all.

Maybe it was time to let George's words speak to me directly. Maybe the whole Santa Barbara trip was the first step to *the art of leaving Bill*. I continued bracing for every scenario; including being a divorced single mother. There was a part of me that thought I might just need to be alone now. This stage of my life may require solitude. A recent talk show discussed how many women in history had left or been left by a man and shortly following, they thrived emotionally, financially, mentally and spiritually. Maybe this was our time to separate and start again on our own, on different paths. Bill always held a belief that I was 'going to be somebody.' Maybe I needed to be that 'somebody' without him.

The stand I was taking today was that I didn't want to stand by his side. It seemed the only thing keeping us together was that we couldn't afford a divorce. We'd already had numerous arguments about the woman from his old company that was so obviously ready and willing to pounce. So be it. At this point, I was tired. Tired of being married to someone who showed no signs of wanting to be married to me. I wanted to tell her, "Take him, he's yours."

Contemplating my departure, I calculated how much money I needed for gas, food, and for the healer. The major thing I needed was silence, and it felt good that something I wanted, for once, was finally free.

It's time. I have to tell him. Oh my, God, this could put him over the edge.

I don't even know how to start this conversation. 'Um, hey honey, ya know how you love to take care of the kids and all the details surrounding the kids?',

NOT!

'And you know how lighthearted and free you feel right now and that having the time to play with the kids would be really fun for you all?'

NOT!

'And since we aren't really enjoying each other's company, maybe a break would be good for us.'

NOT!

He hated when we were apart under any circumstance. This is the guy who would rather have me by his side. It wasn't just the fact that he didn't like the guy he was alone with—he was a true Libra, super-social and liked to stay connected to those whom he is closest, especially when things were turbulent.

I, on the other hand, was told I was a monk in a past life. Which might explain my *love* to be alone and have had to balance that part of myself. I can't be certain of a past life, but it is true, I do like having time alone. Luckily, in the past, my interest in people of all different backgrounds kept me engaged in the outside world.

Bill was in the garage organizing boxes from our most recent move. These were the boxes for the future garage sale; the one I decided would have to be this coming Saturday.

"Hey, I think the garage sale should be Saturday. Will be good to get this stuff out of the house, have the cash to pay bills, what do you think?"

"I think you're smokin' crack. Look at this shit, and have you looked inside the house? This is gonna take fricken' forever to organize what to keep and what to sell," he growled as he senselessly whipped a box of small bike parts and bolts into a larger box.

I watched the beads of sweat build over his brow and drip into his eyes. His shirt was soaking wet and clinging to him as he bent over and slid boxes from one wall to the next. He didn't seem to be putting things in order; he was just shuffling stuff around. It annoyed me. I followed the rules: one box at a time and the goal was to touch it once; put the stuff away, break down the box and throw it in recycling. Most definitely, I would have to retouch every box he was slamming and stacking up against the wall now. As much as I agreed with him on bad timing, I played the expert mover card and reminded him, "I had to do this in Chicago, North Carolina and here in Tucson a few times, I really think it's manageable. We'll be fine. We can do this."

"Well, fine. But I have a lot of meetings this week, I have another mortgage test to pass, and I'm gonna need to spend a lot of time working on combatting these lawsuits with Nick. These guys are fricken jacking us again and some Utah lawyer is sending us shit now."

"Wait, what? Another lawsuit?"

"Yes, fricken' landlord for the i360 building is personally coming after us cause Infocast bailed on the lease payments. It's legal. But shit. I'm getting hit so hard, I'll never fuckin' get back up."

Just as the textbooks had written, Bill's character was interestingly revealing itself during this trying time. All traits, good and bad, became amplified. His core still contained valiant desires that were noble and moral where he still fit the mold to be a lover of all heroes. His favorite movies now were always bloody

and involved warriors with a good dramatic cause. He despised the lack of mo-
rality and honesty he'd seen over the years in business but learned to play in the
sand box alongside it, the best he could. Until now—where he was kicked out
of the sandbox. The pretentious and smug had always been intolerable to him,
especially if they had money and privileges. These days, whether he saw that in
real life or on TV, his emotions easily ignited and went up a whole other level.
He had always been the guy who would most definitely draw a sword on any
that drew it first, but the difference today was he didn't appear to have a sword.

As he aggressively shuffled boxes around, with a hint of guilt, I trailed off, visualizing myself on my long beach walks, ocean breezes cooling my skin, moisture
in the air, sand under my toes and cool ocean waves crashing up and over my feet
and ankles.

"So you really want to do this garage sale next week?" he asked, pulling me
out of my dreamland.

"Yeah. Um, the main reason is, I want to get the house in order here. I have
an opportunity to housesit for someone for 11 days in Santa Barbara, and I don't
want to leave you with this mess."

He stopped dead in his tracks and locked eyes with me. "Are you fucking
kidding me right now?"

Oh geez, here we go. Am I asking him for the unthinkable?

He's not the primary caregiver; there are a lot of details that go into the kid's
days and mine. He knows this fact, but I haven't seen any signs of respect for it
these days. He's in so much pain, he just wants me to keep trucking along and not
interfere with his own duties and painful path.

"How the hell am I gonna get stuff done at the lawyer's office and this sloppy
business-shit George just mentioned and keep job interviews coming *and* work?
Do you expect me to bring the kids to all of that?"

I suggested, "Well, I think my mom can help out…"

He paused as he wiped his entire face, starting with his forehead down to his
chin, with one aggressive, forceful swoop from the palm of his whole hand. "So
let me get this straight; I'll finish unpacking, cause there's no way you'll have this
house in order by then, get kids up and dressed in the morning, make three meals
a day, drive Nicole, Clint and Marcus to their camps, pick them up, do car pools,
attend three different sports, coach football practice, grocery shop, do laundry,
read nighttime stories, and set up and deliver them to play dates?"

I guess I could be somewhat pleased he'd actually been paying some attention. He had the regular to-do list down at least, except he didn't know about the

birthday party for one of Nicole's friends, who'd requested homemade presents *only*, or a cash donation to the animal shelter.

He blankly stared at me. Then turned to move things from one box to another with what continued to seemingly have no rhyme or reason.

And then the amazing happened.

He was quiet for a while, and then turned to face me and said, "Fine. Go."

For a second, I thought about how hurt he was by all this, and then I somehow popped out the other side and started feeling more comfortable with leaving. Not for him, not for the kids, not for money or lack of, not for love, not for punishment, but *for me*. For the first time in a long time, this felt more right than anything I had done. I knew it would be hard to leave them, but I also knew if I didn't, a part of me, a *big* part of me would stay broken and wrecked and for the rest of my life, I would live in an emotional house out of order, until I couldn't stand it any longer. Which is when I would finally leave him.

He walked to the opposite part of the garage. He was done talking. I wasn't sure if it was because he was thinking about the backup girl in the wings, or if he simply was beat and letting go. Honestly, I couldn't blame him. I was no good in the kitchen, never had been. I had no interest in the bedroom as of late. I was overly sensitive and overreacted to most everything now. When I finally talked, I talked too much about myself, and for a girl that used to be known for laughter, I was devoid of that emotion most days. *I've changed.*

I knew this small town would hear I left, and the rumors might fly. That wouldn't be his first rodeo with rumors. Bill had already brushed off a lot of hearsay after the sale of the company. And as a teen, some of his own family and friends supported an unfavorable rumor about him, which was eventually unfounded, so he learned to develop an armor I wished I had for myself. *If the rumors fly, he could take it.*

I attended to the never-ending dishes piled so quickly in our house. But for the first time in quite some time, I felt a tiny lift in mood. I contemplated the art of leaving and how it applied to all things: love, marriage, career, school, town, friendships… Doing these dishes didn't bother me as much today. When I let off the gas pedal of guilt, I could actually feel a little spring in my step with anticipation of this trip. I turned the radio on in the kitchen and one of my favorites, an oldie but goodie from my childhood came on, "I Can See Clearly Now." The lyrics reminded me of a time of hope and happiness. A time when rains come and then they go, clearing all obstacles in our way. That the darkness we temporarily visit, will eventually lift to a bright sunshiny day.

While rinsing a plate, I watched the soapy suds slide off and slip down the drain, and without realizing it, I said out loud, "Lord, is this the rainbow I've been praying for?"

LETTING GO

Horehole was the perfect neighborhood for a garage sale. Unlike The Canyons, where they were not allowed.

These days, we were living in more of the familiarity of how we grew up, but that didn't bring me comfort. I studied the lines on my mom's face in the sun. She was here to help with the garage sale. Recalling how annoyed she was when I was a little girl and how I interrupted her going through our piled up bills, made me realize I was the same these days with my family. Over the last few years, everyone learned to give me space during those bill-paying hours.

My mom, a natural athlete, chose to embrace life more often than not. She regularly ran short marathons, played tennis twice in a day, attended 5 A.M. daily cross-fit workouts, and even learned to race a Porsche. Basically, she was game to try most anything. In fact, she walked over the hot coals at the Tony Robbins event with us and the Motorola sales team. She stood 5'11", with a lean muscular build, wore little-to-no makeup and let her medium-length blonde hair dry naturally after a shower. She was strong inside and out. She rarely hesitated to offer her bold opinions, but if she was aware it was too sharp, her heart boldly took over, where she would course-correct, so feelings were mended.

While placing stickers on items for sale, she shared concern with my house-sitting job and was focused on what Bill must be feeling. She took his side after almost every single fight, and as much as that annoyed me at times, I appreciated her not doing what was easy and just telling me what I wanted to hear. Her marriage to my dad and now my step-dad were not the exact marriages I wanted to mirror, but there were parts I liked about each of them. The bottom line was, I always felt like she was on my side, even by taking Bill's.

She came from the field of social work, and I knew she would understand when I assured her that I never felt more right and wrong at the same time.

I said, "I *am* doing this, no matter what, Mom. In addition, I'm not gonna' be calling and touching base during these 11 days. I don't want to lean on you. I want to force myself to just be alone. Reconnect to Source. No offense to anyone, Mom. I just need to temporarily shed these roles. I just wanna BE."

She answered, "Ok. Fine. I guess I'll just look forward to hearing about it when you get back."

She always loved to tell or hear a good story. For a minute, though, my stomach flipped, and I quickly reassured myself of my purpose for going. This was for me, not for her or anyone else that would like the story. I could tell just by my reaction that I needed to go where no one knew me, and no one was watching, and most importantly, nobody cared about what I was doing or not doing. I liked the feeling that whatever transpired there for me was my very own and whether it was good or bad, it was *mine*. If I so chose, I could keep it a secret, unlike the Tucson foothills neighborhoods, where I felt I was among many who thought they had me all figured out. I was free to be *Me*, whoever that was... .

Even though I sensed a misunderstanding coming from my mom about me not wanting to have contact with her, that too, felt good. It felt healthy and right.

Today was a good day. It was time to *let go* at this garage sale. I'd been so consumed on how to hold onto material things that kept leaving our life, I forgot how therapeutic it was to take charge of the things that you want to let go. Seeing the joy on people's faces when they found something they liked in our pile of belongings was fun. I played board games on the driveway with children who were waiting for their parents to shop, and afterward, I gladly snuck whatever toy or game they had their eye on into their parents' bag of purchases. At one point, my mom and I laughed hysterically when my kids marched out, inspired to let it *all* go, with items from inside the house that were not for sale; my guitar, a hand-carved wood flute a Native American Indian had given me and a teapot that I used daily. After a blistering hot day of walking in and out of the house and packing people's cars, left me feeling that my clothes were glued to parts of me, but the garage sale ended up a successful $650 dollar day.

Bill was right about the unpacking of all the boxes. It was overwhelming. We squeezed Marc's birthday sleepover into the week as well. I was running on my adrenaline rush produced by planning the trip to Santa Barbara, and I had stayed up until 2 and 3 A.M. in the morning frantically unpacking boxes and trying to find ways to organize quickly, but it was a task too big to complete in just over a week. While caught up in appointments with business associates, lawyers, the food stamp check-in appointments and now a tax attorney (who needed various paperwork that would take considerable time and focus to gather), I simply ran out of time. I didn't get the house the way I wanted, before my departure. I never uncovered the box with my crafts, and so I didn't get to the homemade birthday present Nicole would need at the upcoming birthday party. I painfully laid a $20 dollar bill, from the garage sale, on the counter with a note explaining this will be the birthday donation. I hoped that brought Bill at least a little relief.

Laundry and packing were done when he wasn't around. I never mentioned my daily tracking of the weather in Santa Barbara: partly cloudy and 78 degrees, which could not have been better. Our rental's old air conditioner was losing the fight against the 100-plus-degree temperatures in Tucson. It was blazing hot, and now Bill was starting to vocally demand an answer to the question, "Why are we even living here? There are no jobs. This is for the rich and retired, trust-fund families or University of Arizona college students."

He knew why we were here. He wanted to start that fight. I had told him in college, "If you really think you want a future with me, then start seeing it in Tucson."

In the past, I loved Tucson. She was a valley of healing, and the Indians worshiped her as I did from a young age of 7. My grandparents had retired here, and I would come visit them every spring to warm up from the freezing cold, depressing gray skies of Illinois.

Each and every single middle-school and high-school spring break, I would kick off my shoes and hardly put them back on for 10 days. My grandparents would parade me from house to house, during cocktail hour, in their retired village of condos, showing me off to all their friends. I would go from one place to the next, catching up or meeting new, interesting and vibrant, elderly people who could not get enough of my below-par guitar playing and the singing of new lyrics and music I had created over the previous year. I was a star here, and each spring they would look forward to and encourage my shining visits.

After many trips, at the age of 15, I started showing up with lists of questions like, "What's the meaning of life?" I found this generation a wealth of information and pushed and probed for their answers. A.P. was my favorite. He's the one I asked, "What is love?" My feelings were so hurt because he seemed to purposely avoid me afterward and he wouldn't respond to the question. Each day, I would see him at the pool, he would wave and smile, but he wasn't engaging the way he always had. He was 98 at the time, and my Grandma explained he wasn't feeling his best and had been sleeping a lot so he may just be too weak to answer the enormous inquiry. I had played this game with him for quite a few years now, and I was so sad he might be out of the game. I watched him while I lay there on my stomach in my bikini, on the plastic lounge chairs. I could feel the straps leaving their mark on my stomach and thighs. I had laid there too long, and I knew when I played Spite and Malice with Grandma tonight, my sunburn was going to be screaming like a bitch when I sat on her burlap-textured davenport. My head rested on my folded arms as I continued to study A.P. and his solid silver hair as it shimmered in the scorching sun.

"Hey A.P., did you golf this morning?" I asked.

Each condo backed up to the golf course and he usually played golf every morning.

"No, Doll, I didn't," he replied.

"You feeling all right?" I asked.

"Never better," he answered, with his head still down, immersed in his note-pad, which wasn't uncommon because he loved to write poetry.

His close friend was Norman Vincent Peale, and I happen to know he wrote him a lot too. He looked like he wanted to be left alone, so I gave him his space. I had a feeling that this might be the last spring break I would see him, and it broke my heart.

As always, the 10-day break went too fast. My Grandpa Milt stood in the doorway and watched me pack my belongings. Because of his engineering back-ground, he couldn't resist suggesting how to pack my things in a more orderly way. I let him insist because I could do no wrong in his eyes, and neither could he in mine.

The doorbell rang, and in walked A.P. He now stood in the doorway with a large stack of about 10 notepads in his hands. It looked like a manuscript in the works. A huge smile covered his whole face while his blue eyes sparkled with pride. He raised the pads up and said, "What is Love? Here is my version, Doll. Read it on the plane and call me with your comments upon your return to Chicago."

Year after year, my grandparents unknowingly created a space for me here in Tucson to fall in love here—with the desert—and also with the people attracted to this valley. I felt rich here. My grandparents had a way of not coddling me, but at the same time, I knew they deeply loved me. I knew their personal experiences during the Depression of the 1930s made them passionately push going to col-lege, to think deeper about things, to have discernment, but also to create a way to make a solid living. My grandmother was a school principal back in the day, and my intelligent grandfather built grain elevators for Cargill. They both always inspired me to learn about the history of Tucson and her beginnings, but they got me hooked first with showing me all the desert animals. The combination of all of these elements left me with a knowing, even at that age, I belonged there someday. I always requested a window seat so upon arrival, with glee, I could see her from up high. And, on departures, I could turn towards the window and quietly cry as I left her behind.

For Bill, Tucson was never close enough to water. It was hot and dusty, and it was a hard place to make money. And now I was leaving him here to care for the children, to fight the fights and to battle the fires and the heat. Alone.

I made sure to gather and pack my favorite books and CDs from those I had spent the most time silently arguing and agreeing with: Deepak, Wayne, Harold, Byron, Eckhart, Napoleon, Louise, Khalil, Joseph, The Tao, Mother Theresa, the Dalai Lama, Mary, Joseph, and Jesus. I tossed in my collections of meditation and my own recorded hypnotherapy CDs, my yoga mat, and some hand-me-down brainless fashion magazines a girlfriend gave me. I also packed an expensive soy candle in a glass jar, I had received as a gift, and was saving for a special occasion. I threw my tarot cards in the pile hoping those would look better in California. Last, while looking forward to feeling a chill in the early morning and evening air, I threw my favorite beach sweater in. *Done.*

My expensive highlights were long gone, and I hoped the sun would lighten my roots the way it used to do. I packed makeup and hair products left from the days of wealth. I grabbed one of the kids' partially used spiral notebooks from the last school year, and I left the used scribbled pages, knowing I would like to see that when I was missing them. *Maybe I'll journal or write lyrics.*

The pile on the bed was growing, and an urgency to get all this into a bag and into the car before Bill could see, took over. It looked like *too much... too much* to look forward to. I was exposing all things I took comfort and joy in. I didn't want him to have a reason to confront me with annoyance. His silence was easier for me to deal with.

One last time, I scanned the closet to make sure I had everything I'd need. My guitar, ALVAREZ, stood in the corner. I hadn't touched that in a long time.

"You're comin' with me, Alvarez."

I quickly started loading the truck. I wanted to be all packed, so all I needed to do was say goodbye in the morning and go. I didn't want to give the kids a chance to be sad about this. Right now, they liked the whole idea of it being 'an adventure for mommy,' and they started making lists of what I could bring back for them. Clint, my nature boy, wanted a surfboard, or any rocks and sticks he could make a sling shot out of. Marc wanted a bag of ocean sand. Nicole requested a mermaid.

Just the thought of them tonight brought on guilt. *Should I call Katie back and tell her this is off?*

While taking extra-long on bedtime stories this past week, I noticed it felt good to be present with them. And I felt that getting each of their bedrooms in order, so they easily knew where everything was, took away the ammunition for Bill to ever say, "See? This was a bad idea."

Bill stayed stuck to his cell phone in the backyard while he watched me make several trips to the truck.

At one point, he pressed his phone into his chest and said, "What's with all the luggage, you movin' there for good?"

It wasn't a playful comment. He had finally become outwardly annoyed about my departure, which was tomorrow morning.

That evening, while the kids were tucked away in their rooms sound asleep, we lay awake on our backs, in bed. I assumed Bill would try to reach out. So I planned on picking my excuse: headache, stress, ulcer kicking up, and the usual—tired. I was disgusted that I wasn't a better lover to him, but I was also comfortable that I was a woman who wouldn't prostitute herself.

As always, my first thoughts went to finances. It felt good to have made $650 on the last of our big garage items: a power washer, tools, tires, two of Bill's trumpets and a lawn mower. I paid some bills, and earmarked a chunk for gas and food, and maybe even a total splurge for something decadent like a manicure in Santa Barbara. I left the rest for Bill and the kids to get what they needed, and maybe even an ice cream or something fun. I made sure to grocery shop at the food bank the day before, but I would leave him the food stamp card for emergency groceries I may have forgotten.

Like a board, I laid there for quite some time before I heard him drift away into a deep slumber. He never reached out, didn't lean in for a kiss and his hand never moved toward mine. We were so far from that now. He just rolled to his left side, and his back created a wall that I welcomed. I watched his shoulders move with his breath, and I felt relief.

What was not so surprising, though, is that we had slipped off into parallel and pretty mode again. It was as if we gave each other silent permission to go there during this time. However, I could feel the tracks made here today were deep. We had stayed here too long. Just like in Greensboro, North Carolina.

PART TWO

THE LAND OF REFLECTION

HER

With those North Carolina days on my mind, I let Bill's breath and the gentle rise and fall of his back lull me back to the time when we couldn't look prettier on paper. We were both in our 30s, and the kids were the adorable ages of 2,4 and 6. Everyone was healthy, money was flowing, and we owned a magnificent home in a beautiful neighborhood. It had only been about five years ago since we lived in North Carolina, but I remembered it like it was yesterday. It was a time frame that rocked my world. I especially recalled one day in particular...

The cold paper crunched under my back while my feet made their way into the metal stirrups. I hated gynecological visits, but luckily this doctor was a dear friend. I met her right after we moved to Greensboro. Dr. Kate Stewart was an MD, but also studied alternative medicines, meditation, medicinal herbs and had an understanding of energetic dis-ease and healing. After having some unusual symptoms, I first ran out and did a pregnancy test that turned out negative. I then realized I'd better get checked out.

I rested my hands on top of the paper blanket across my abdomen. As I lay there, I prepared for our always-amazing conversations, during which we shared many discoveries about our kids and husbands. Her husband, Alex, was an accomplished author and spoke nationally about the art of doing business with a conscious heart. He was as dynamic as she. Alex was the only guy whose company Bill enjoyed. That was a rare thing because of Bill's extensive travel. He was hardly interested in meeting new people or dining out because he entertained enough as a VP of sales for a Fortune 100 company.

When she entered, we quickly updated each other on the kids. She tapped my leg to silently say, 'Spread your legs.' She slid her white gloves on with a snap. I felt her small fingers effortlessly slide in, and she gently swabbed the inside of my cervix.

"Hmmm," she said.

Suddenly, I felt warm tears drop down the sides of my face. Surprised, I quickly patted them dry with my fingers. Her light blue eyes and naturally curly light brown hair rose from between my legs. She didn't say a word. She didn't have to; we had this remarkable ability to read each other. I sensed she was tapping into her medical intuition and would share what may be going on in my body and how that may be attached to my emotions.

It reminded me of one of the books on my nightstand, Louise L. Hay's "Heal Your Body." Louise defined the phrase, *metaphysical causations* as how the power of words and thoughts can create experiences. In her book, she lists possible mental or emotional causes for various health conditions, and if it feels true for you, you can sit quietly with the issue and consider any thoughts in you that might have helped create the problem. Once you are done, you can repeat to yourself, "I am willing to release the pattern in my consciousness that has created this condition." She then listed a "new thought pattern" which you would begin to repeat several times and then take yourself to a place where you assume the healing is already in process.

This book always resonated with me because Hay clearly states that her book does not "heal" anyone, but it is intended to awaken the ability to contribute to one's own healing process. Louise healed vaginal cancer in herself. Her doctors grudgingly gave her three months to work on herself while at the same time warning her that she was endangering her life with the delay. It was a journey of self-discovery, where she healed the emotional damage of years of sexual abuse, while at the same time assertively changing her diet and detoxifying her body. When she returned to the doctor, six months later, with no signs of cancer, she was not surprised.

Something was bubbling up to the surface, and I didn't know why, but I was certain of one thing: I wanted it to stop. I knew I was in a safe place with Kate, but I also knew I didn't want to hear what she might say next. She became even more serious as she removed the metal clamp and warned me her whole hand would be entering. Her other hand rested on my abdomen. The warmth felt good, but the tears increased. I was looking at the ceiling but felt her eyes on me as I turned to look at her. We still said nothing.

I immediately recognized a familiar symptom—the cramp I'd been feeling for a month. Since I tended to be a hypochondriac, I hoped the cramp was only due to too much caffeine.

Her eyes softened, "Do you feel anything?"

I confirmed with a nod and laid my head back down. She placed the paper over my lap, sat back down on her stool and sighed.

"How are you and Bill doing?"

Looking up at her, I shrugged.

"Has he been out of town a lot?"

I nodded.

"Are you guys connecting sexually?" she asked.

"Once every few weeks or so, maybe. I don't know. Why?"

"Your cervix is abnormally bleeding and looks to be slightly cramping when touched."

She paused and then said, "Okay. So I'm just gonna come out and ask this: Do you think Bill has been faithful? 'Cause sometimes a cervix will react this way if fighting an STD."

"An STD!?" I shot upright, "Are you fuckin' kiddin' me!? A sexually transmitted disease?!"

The room went dark, started to spin and heaviness settled in. Having always being told my healthy pap smears in the past may have been partly due to having minimal intercourse partners, I was shocked when thoughts of betrayal took over. "What kind of STDs are we talking about? Syphilis, AIDS? Oh my God."

Calmly, she said, "Maybe the womb wants to tell us something. It wouldn't be uncommon to have an *infidelity interruption* like this right now. I'm guessing based on Bill's extensive travel, and perhaps his dislike for his job, the 'parallel and pretty' mode you told me you guys have been experiencing, may be calling your attention… or not. Let's just start by getting some tests done."

Then she said, "Don't worry Judy, whatever 'this' is, you'll find your way through it."

Kate stepped out to consult with a male colleague. Louise's book sat on the bookshelf over her desk, so I wrapped the paper around my waist and made my way over to it. I opened to V—*Venereal Disease*: **The mental state:** Sexual guilt. Need for punishment. Belief that the genitals are sinful or dirty. Abusing another.

The new thought pattern: *I lovingly and joyously accept my sexuality and its expression. I accept only thoughts that support me and make me feel good.*

All I could think at that moment was, *if this is an STD, someone's gonna pay.*

In a panic to try to stay positive, I quickly turned to my symptom,

Bleeding—**The mental state**: Joy running out. Anger. But where?

The new thought pattern: *I am the joy of Life expressing and receiving in perfect rhythm.*

I felt like I could live with that one easier than the first and after slightly settling down, I made my way back onto the table.

Kate's partner entered the room. He practiced more of the Western medicine way of thinking. He asked the regular questions, "Have you had any new partners, Mrs. Cochrane?"

"What? New partners? No. None."

If not totally in love with these three tiny beings, I was far too busy to consider the luxury of another lover between the glamorous rounds of life with small children: driving to and from preschool, play dates, pink eye, chicken pox, potty training, lice, ear infections, stomach flus, head colds, strep throat and ring worm…

On his pad, he checked off what seemed to be a hundred boxes for every STD imaginable, most I had never heard of, and I scribbled my signature for approval to run them all. I couldn't wait to get out of there. When I got in the car, recalling my suspicion about the woman working for him at Motorola, back in Illinois, I thought, *I may have been right!*

When I got home, my best friend, Claire, who was also the next-door neighbor's nanny, was standing in my front yard burning white sage. She held it up high in the air, swinging it from right to left, but switched to in front and behind her like she was directing a plane to land on a runway.

She let out a theatrical scream of joy with my arrival, "HEY Sweetie! All clear here!"

Claire had been in charge of my kids, and the neighbor's kids and they were all hanging out in our 'A' frame playroom above the garage. In a neighborhood full of mostly doctors and lawyers, it became a welcomed sight to see her hippy gypsy self, just doin' her thing, without a care of how she looked to others.

Claire was 40, about 5' tall and voluptuous, a born-and-raised Southern gal who gave bear hugs infused with unconditional love. Her hugs always left behind the scent of her custom-created essence of essential oils. Claire's hair hung long, with brown and natural gray streaks. She regularly wore an oversized, tie-dyed crew-neck T-shirt, with black leggings and Birkenstocks. Her fingernails held various colors of paint, glitter, and glue because she was a craft queen, and she entertained the kids with projects even Martha Stewart would have been in awe of. Her hearty laugh came easily and was real. It had a magic that made her jokes even funnier. A walking encyclopedia of alternative health information, Claire was able to talk and recite all the natural and healing modalities from the East to the West.

If I mentioned having a sore throat, she would run over to the house with a shot of pure ginger and/or oil of oregano to hold under my tongue. She seemed to have an answer for everything, and because of my similar interests, we enjoyed sharing each other's findings regarding alternative wellness. It wasn't uncommon for us to spend up to three hours discussing one modality or herb.

Thanks to Claire, about a month after arriving in Greensboro, I had met Dr. Kate Stewart, my current OB/GYN, David Cree, an energy healer; and Enmei, a Buddhist psychotherapist, whose name meant "bright circle." Claire even introduced me to the owners of a health food store and somehow managed to get me a discount on all the essential oils, supplements, and vitamins I needed. I was now wondering if she intuitively knew to set me up, to be ready for crises of any kind.

The kids heard my car arrive and came running down the back staircase, through the garage. Entering the house, I noticed the smell of sage indoors, as well. Claire explained, "I lightly saged to make it feel lighter upon your arrival, but I didn't touch the wine cellar. I know how you like the smell of the cedar shelving down there."

"Hey, thanks for the clearing and for watching the kids. I have to take care of something, can I touch base with ya later?"

She could tell something was up but knew not to ask for details.

"Of course," with a wink.

The kids sat quietly at the kitchen island while I placed celery sticks with scoops of peanut butter in front of them while pouring three small glasses of organic cranberry juice. After they had finished, I suggested they run back up to the playroom. It was the farthest point to put them, and I hoped my call with Bill would run smoothly. But just in case it didn't, they would be safe up there, where they couldn't hear anything. Claire would have been happy to take them, but this was a time where I wanted all chicks in the nest.

The playroom was enormous and connected to a breezeway with floor-to-ceiling windows featuring two 'A' frame skylights. It gave you a cocoon-like view of the tall long-leaf-needled pine trees outside. We had a TV, small fridge and workout equipment there. A hallway led to an open office with built-in floor-to-ceiling shelves and drawers. Three huge bedrooms for the kids were down the hall, and a big open library followed, opening up to the top of the stairs. The kids loved the deep, cushy leather chairs that hugged us while I read books to them.

I made my way downstairs and into our parlor/sitting room, grabbing the nearest home phone ensuring a good connection on my part and hoping his cellphone would be clear. I knew he was hanging out at the Ferrari dealership, with his friend, the general manager. I carefully planned where I wanted to sit for this call and even scolded myself for being so pathetic about contemplating that.

Just make the fucking call, Judy! Where you sit means nothing compared to what his answer is.

I dialed his number and waited for him to pick up.

He answered, "Hello."

"Hi,"

"What's up?" he asked.

"Um, nothin'… Well, not nothing, just wondering what you're doin' and when you might be comin' home."

"Well, I was plannin' on hanging here a while and havin' some dinner with Neil. Why? What's up? You sound weird."

"Yeah. Well, I feel kinda weird. I'm havin' a slight health issue. I saw Kate today. I don't feel right, and my body's doing some strange stuff. Don't know if I have an actual 'thing' goin' on, or if this is a Louise Hay thing or what."

Dead silence on his end.

I knew what he was probably thinking: '*Here she goes again with this psychic, psycho, hypochondriac, mumbo-jumbo, crazy energy bullshit… attaching every emotion to an ache and pain connected to disease.*' He had admitted to being somewhat interested in the same stuff when we were back in Illinois, but my studies had now become annoying to him.

He pushed, "What's really up Judy? What's goin' on here?"

"Ok. I need to know one thing. As crazy as this may sound, like I said, my body is reacting to 'something.' I need to know if you've had any recent sexual partners."

And then he said something I never expected to hear. "I'll be home in 15."

I dropped the phone to the floor without even hanging up, and I stood and slowly walked to the top of stairs. I could hear the kids playing and giggling as I headed down the hallway towards them. In the playroom, an entire wall had been made into an enormous chalkboard. Before I realized what I was doing, I picked up a piece of yellow chalk and wrote: "Where troubles melt like lemon drops."

That described this 'A' framed ceiling-playroom for me. It was full of their laughter, toys, books, puzzles, a craft table with multicolored construction paper and crayons, chalk and glue sticks. I loved this creative place. I loved these kids and, oh my God, I loved being their mom.

What the fuck just happened? Was this someone he's in love with or was it a one-night stand?! Fuck fuck fuck!

Thoughts dumped into my mind. *We failed. We finally did it. The biggest fuckup. One of us caved. He was weak and deep down, there was a part of me that kinda knew he would do this. Yep. Up until now, I'd been a bit asleep and also a doormat for him, and when he gets home, he will deal with the fiercest of fierce.*

I could feel an eruption of anger rise in me that I had not felt before. He was going to meet a new woman today, a lioness. He will be sorry to see who I've become, just in the last 15 minutes.

As I stood in the middle of the room, an immediate change of plan came to mind. I may scream on this battleground I was about to step on. *I need to get the kids out of here!* I walked into our exercise area, which was basically a massive hallway connecting to the main part of the house. Peering out the square awning windows lining the walls, I looked outside. The windows opened out toward the ground, and I saw Claire in her backyard.

I knelt down and yelled out the window, "Hey, Claire, can you grab the kids and take them for a while?"

She replied, "Sure, Sweetie, send 'em on over."

READY OR NOT

I calmly shuffled the kids off, down the back staircase so they could exit quickly. After making my way back through the house, I somehow was still able to recognize the artful craftsmanship in the massive white crown molding running along the floors and ceiling. It was no wonder this was featured in The Metropolitan Home magazine a few years back, having won awards from a husband-wife team who built it together. When I got downstairs and entered the foyer, I stood frozen between our back door and front door, which were directly across from each other.

The tall, heavy front door was one of a kind. The hand-cut stained glass reminded me of a contemporary church window. Bill had arrived, and I could see his distorted figure through the stained glass, nervously fumbling for his keys while cautiously walking up the few steps and onto our freshly painted white wood porch. I watched his every move and then he must have noticed me on the other side of the glass, as well. We both stood there for quite some time, like statues in a museum. I wanted to scream out, *'Ready or not'* anticipating that the truth of our marriage was going to unveil itself today.

Bill finally entered. I didn't want to look at him, at first, but then, on the other hand, I wanted to tie him up in a chair and stare him down, nose to nose. No words came to mind. My heart was breaking. Physically, it ached like heartburn. *Or was it a heart attack?* It ached for what I thought we had and apparently did not have. Humiliation crept in and made me question, *was I not enough? Or is he not man enough? What's it gonna be? 'Cause somebody's going down for this!*

He cautiously nodded toward the parlor. He knew I loved this room, a typical Southern sitting room… *a peaceful parlor.* A room with a view where you could read or nap. The L-shaped windows followed the wrap-around porch just outside of it. "I may never leave this room," I told the realtor when viewing the house. Now, this room had become something else. I started to hate it in here, and I felt like bolting. Having trouble making eye contact, I found myself focusing on my bare feet pressed against the cool wood floors, and I was surprised to think how strange it was to focus on that right now.

Off and on, I could feel everything moving either in slow motion or moving lightning fast. My growing anxiety kept me far from having the ability to formulate words. I fixated on the outside porch swing swaying alongside the two rocking chairs, gently rocking in unison. I'd read enough and attended enough counseling to know I needed to stick with *how I was feeling.* But I was afraid to let myself fully feel.

So, I started preparing: maybe this is the end. He and his new wife would enjoy those rocking chairs. As far as I could tell, if there was going to be a divorce, I wanted no part of another man. *They can have the fucking chairs.*

He sat next to me. Way too close to me. I could feel the heat of his thigh next to mine, and I motioned for him to move further away. He then noticed the phone I had dropped to the floor earlier, so he hung it up and cautiously placed it on the coffee table. He noticed me adjusting myself on the couch, trying to get comfortable, and handed me a pillow, which I pushed away. I felt like running out the door, but couldn't think of a place to go. *This is all I have. All my friends are busy with little kids. I can't hysterically barge in their door right now and scare their kids. I don't have work friends, a project to dive into or an office to hide behind.*

At this moment, I wanted to be as far from Bill as possible, but at the same time, I needed him close so I could get answers.

Any questions about me not being enough started to shift to, *I was more than enough!* I noticed it right away and thought it was interesting. It made me wonder whether it was a natural defense mechanism. I think Bill sensed the shift because he awkwardly started to explain.

He cautiously described feelings of being disconnected from me for quite some time. He mentioned a weak moment during a business trip to Atlanta, Georgia, when he found himself attracted to someone who was giving him attention. *Blah, blah blah* was going off in my head. I may not have been showing him attention, but he sure hadn't been showering me with it either. Mighty anger began to boil with each word he spoke. I didn't want to hear any of this, and yet I wanted to hear *all* of it. I demanded details I couldn't believe I was asking for. I wanted to know what she looked like, clothed and unclothed. I wanted to know the color and even the texture of her hair and the style of clothes she was wearing. What did her skin feel like? How did she look at him? Did she have full lips or thin? He obediently explained every detail, with caution, searching for a way to make some kind of sense.

It's strange how I can remember almost every word that came out of his mouth that day.

I paid great attention to his tone, continuing to demand and then dissect each and every word. I hunted for his lies, discrepancies, and his truth. *He promised me. How could this have happened?*

Bill was willing to take all the blame. And as much as I thought I'd like that, I found it pathetic. My emotions flipped back and forth like a crazed woman. He told me she had a sturdy build, not tall and slender like I thought he'd be attracted to. She had solid blonde hair with blunt bangs, which gave her a kind of contemporary Florida feel, coming from a beach community. Young. A free spirit. She was living with her fiancé at the time, and seemed to be experienced with people like Bill—married people, like Bill. And he said it probably wasn't her first time. I hated HER and her experienced sexuality. I could feel myself wanting to cry, but stifled it. He was a fixer, and any sign of a tear coming was his notice to take charge and offer suggestions on what and how to fix, in order to get it to stop immediately. I wanted someone who would let me cry.

Time passed like sludge as we sat in the parlor. Occasionally, I'd get up and walk to the master bedroom and pace back and forth. He would follow me in, studying my every move, cautiously waiting to address any details I demanded. He pleaded that he knew he made a mistake and every time she reached out to meet again, he declined.

This bitch was reaching out?

I was furious. I wanted him out of my life. I left the room and headed to our upstairs library.

"You've been talking to her? What the fuck?!" I yelled as I stomped up the stairs. "Do *not* follow me," I demanded, as I noticed him approach.

Unable to follow my directions, he kept a cautious distance behind me. Somehow, I heard every step he took, even over the thick Berber-carpeted runner.

Why couldn't I hear every step he'd taken towards infidelity? I may have been able to leave him beforehand, or stop him. Maybe weekends away or a new therapist here in North Carolina would have helped. After all the fucking books we'd read? I wasn't in tune enough to see this happening? *Pathetic*, I thought.

I was about to descend for an escape down the other split set of staircases leading me to our kitchen and family room, but instead kept climbing to the second-floor library.

"Stop. Stop following me everywhere. Please. Just go away."

He stood there frozen, "Judy. I can't lose you."

I turned to him and quietly responded, "Oh, Bill. You fool. You've already lost me. I may not have consciously known this information until today, but my soul knew and *MY BODY KNEW!* You lost me the night you spent fucking that chick. The blood work will come back soon, and we will know what disease this bitch has. And I want you to get a fucking AIDS test immediately!"

His agreeable nod frightened the hypochondriac in me. It was like he, too, was fearful he risked not only our marriage but our lives, as well.

I don't know why, but, while at the top of the stairs, I noticed his hand wrapped around the wood carved banister. I looked out the huge 'A' frame window, curiously focusing on random details right in the middle of all of this. Our perfectly manicured hilly yard was lined with 100-foot tall, long-leaf needled trees. The enormous wood deck reached from the house to a hand-carved gazebo.

A perfect spot for a happy family; not ours, I thought.

For some reason, his hand kept drawing me back in, but it felt different than the first time I studied his hands at Panther Lounge. This time, I could see HER. I could see her naked ass and thighs in his hands. I could see him rolling her around in a hotel bed, wanting her and pulling her close into his naked body. Jealousy continued to floor me as I imagined her breasts may have been too big for his hands. The hands that pulled phone books apart, pulled her legs apart. His hands touched her bleached-blonde hair. He may have even expertly held her hands down on the bed with his, while on top of her. His fingers may have touched her full lips before he passionately kissed her. I hated HER, but I hated him more. His hands explored HER. Every part of her. The hands that held my babies fresh from my womb. *My womb!*

And I paused, stifling a cry wanting to break free: "AGHHHHHHHH!"

I heard myself scream in a way I never had before. I dropped to my knees so fast his reach couldn't catch me. I pushed him away. From the corner of my eye, I saw the collection of books on marriage, relationships... all alphabetically organized. Tapes of past sessions with our Chicago marriage therapist, Nathan, were stacked next to them. We'd read all the books, and now it felt like an enormous joke, as I sat on the floor, soaking in the truth of us. Not one of them prevented this from happening, nor would any of them be able to fix us. *We studied all of this to end up here?* I'm sure some author from one of these books would remind me, "It's the journey, not the destination." Well, right now I'd say, "FUCK this journey and FUCK him, he's flawed!"

I continued to sit on the floor, staring at the titles and recalling some of the contents. My first thought was to end the marriage in the most expedient way possible. He should go to Florida and explore a relationship with HER. All of the sudden, I liked the idea of him doing that. Just go, I thought. *Make it easy; tear us permanently apart and then I don't have to think this through. It becomes super simple—Divorce.*

"I'm sorry, Judy. I'm so sorry."

I could see by the look in his eyes that he may have discovered the same truth I had, *he never deserved me.*

I leaned into him quietly so the kids, who had just re-entered the house and were now playing in the playroom, would not hear, "You think you're sorry now? Wait until you're alone on *your* weekend without the kids and you realize what you destroyed. I will be sure to try to have forgiven you by then, as I live happily ever after, with a *stronger* man than you."

Over the next few weeks, Bill traveled often. When home, he honored my requests and kept his distance. While he was away, I started paying attention to how I had let myself go, physically and mentally. It had been years since I thought like a stand alone woman. If I was to be single again and decided to seek a new partner, how was that really going to work out? I was 33 years old and had three small kids. Even though I kept in fair shape with walks and yoga, I wasn't as attractive these days. And I wasn't happy either... even before HER. I hardly ever wore makeup and my hair was pretty much in a ponytail daily, and I honestly could not remember the last time I'd gone out in high heels or a dress. Even though our collection of books on marriage were not helping, I had uncovered a deep understanding that in order to move on and leave this marriage behind, I was going to have to find forgiveness for Bill somehow so we could set up a peaceful existence for our individual selves and for the kids.

I finally agreed to see a psychotherapist. It was Enmei, the one who Claire introduced us too. He was nothing like Nathan, our therapist from Chicago, and he took some getting used to. He never asked us about our sex life, maybe because he knew it was non-existent. Even though Bill had been sleeping in our bed, we did everything we could to not even touch each other's hand. I think privately, he had hoped I'd cave and fall into his arms, and as lustful as I was becoming over the last few months, I'm surprised I hadn't. It was a strange phenomenon to actually desire sex now when it was inappropriate for us to have it.

In the days following, I found myself spending more time in the playroom. There was a desire to see them in action under one roof. One afternoon, after entering their space, I found them: Nicole, age 2, searching for a purple crayon; Clint, age 4, building an elaborate racetrack for his hot wheel cars: and Marcus, age 6, carefully concentrating on shooting hoops into a Little Tike's plastic basketball hoop. Cartoons quietly played in the background. Clint was humming engine noises, Nicole was singing some nursery rhyme, and the thump of the basketball hitting the backboard made it all come together, like a symphony. *Music to my ears.* I felt calm. It certainly was a place *where troubles melt like lemon drops, up high above the garage top, that's where you'll find me.*

ANGELS EXIST

Our initial appointment with Enmei felt like it went on forever. For the first time during counseling, I wanted to leave the office while Bill wanted to stay and talk. As the many sessions continued over the months, I did like to see Bill engaged and tackling his issues like a warrior. He assertively tackled the secrets stored inside that allowed him permission to sleep with HER. It was interesting to watch that unfold. I remember thinking: *he may make someone very happy someday.*

At one point, Enmei turned to me and asked if I had any input into what Bill was expressing. Bill's eyes were filled with tears, and that startled me. I'd only seen him like that once—the day his father died.

I responded with stifled frustration, "Um... no... no input at this time," as I turned to look down at my lap.

Then Enmei said, "Bill, would you excuse us for a moment. I want to talk privately with Judy."

The peaceful and poised Enmei turned to close the door and stared me down. Being used to his peaceful Buddhist vibe, I silently flipped on a dime and stared back, secretly thinking, *What's your problem?*

But he was so gentle and kind that I restrained myself from saying it aloud.

"Judy, I'm going to come straight out and ask you something. Do I have your permission to do so?"

I reluctantly nodded.

His head tilted, and with a sincere look on his face, he asked, "What's your role in this?"

I could feel heat rising up my neck and flushing into my cheeks. I stood up, grabbed my coat and the car keys on the table in front of me and walked out, slamming the door behind me. I walked past Bill without saying a word. I headed out to the parking lot, jumped into our car, hit the accelerator, and fish-tailed it out of the parking lot.

I was furious. I wasn't anxious. I wasn't sad. I wasn't anything except fucking mad. I drove for about 20 minutes, unaware of my speed. I don't recall stopping for any lights; in fact, I don't even remember passing any of the familiar places I shopped. The outside world was a blur.

The one thing that did get my attention were the flashing lights and sirens coming up from behind me.

"FUCK! ME!"

I slammed on my brakes and erratically swerved off to the right of the road. I sat still, but in a rage of fury, waiting for the officer to come up to my window. His slow approach to my vehicle was pissing me off, so I stuck my hand out the window and waved for him to come faster. *What the hell am I doing?* I thought.

"Registration and license please, ma'am," he politely asked.

I opened the glove compartment and looked in the usual orderly place for the registration but couldn't find it. I looked for my license in my purse, so I could at least give him that while I continued the search for the registration. Then I realized: I'd left my purse at Enmei's office. The officer was watching my every move, offering suggestions about where things might be located.

I blew up, "Okay. Here!"

Unreasonably frustrated, I grabbed everything out of the glove box and handed it off to him—the owner's manual, a small flashlight, an old pair of sunglasses, a first aid kit, an old granola bar, receipts for oil changes and new tires—and said, "It's somewhere in there!"

Papers from the glove box were landing and blowing around like confetti on the busy highway behind him. I tried to open my door to get out, and he pressed it shut, so I exited from the passenger side. Standing on the shoulder of the highway, I waited for him to join me. He seemed shocked I was out of the car, and he said, "Ma'am, stand still and tell me how can I help you?"

"OH, OKAY! HERE'S HOW YOU CAN HELP ME. GIVE ME THE GOD DAMN TICKET ALREADY. How 'bout that? Can you do that? It's your pleasure, I'm sure. I JUST NEED TO GET THE FUCK OUTTA HERE!"

Through my rage, I started to notice his ability to not be taking my conduct personally at all. It was as if he decided to deal with me as you might a drunk, to "*not* argue with a drunk."

I continued on, but with a sorrowful shift: "I can't believe I'm behaving this way. I'm not even *like* this. This isn't me. I'm nice. Generally a people pleaser. I obey laws. Follow rules. I have God in my life. I do the right things. I help people. I'm a good mother. I was a good wife."

I turned to face him, "I was there for him. I did everything for him... E-V-E-R-Y FUCKING T-H-I-N-G. But it wasn't enough. He fucked her anyway. And somehow I'm supposed to take some responsibility for it? He went out and did that, not me."

He consoled me, "Now, now."

"I was a good wife," I whispered.

Then it hit me: I felt there was something stopping me from repeating the mantra I'd adopted since learning about HER. The one my sister and a girlfriend kept lovingly supporting and reinforcing for me, "I was a good wife." But in this instant, I wasn't buying it. I cautiously toyed with the idea, that if I did have a part in it, then what was it?

I felt myself calm down.

"I'm sorry, sir," looking at his badge that read: Officer Gabriel.

In a sweet North Carolina accent, he responded, "I don't have to tell y'all how dangerous it is to drive in this state, now do I?"

I shook my head in agreement.

"I've a feelin' Ma'am, that everythang's gonna be all right."

His black skin glistened in the North Carolina sun now starting to set. I hadn't let myself notice how beautiful he was. His dark brown eyes twinkled kindness below long, thick lashes. He was a large man, maybe 6'3 and 260 pounds. He looked like a fighter, yet was dripping with love.

My rant could not continue in his presence.

"Y'all have some sortin' out to do, that's all that is. So, I ain't writing no ticket. Consider it a 'warnin'. Ya'll take good care now, and Ma'am, one lass thang, when thangs *fall apart*, leave room for the almighty so he can help things fall into place, ya hear?"

Later that month, I wrote a letter to the chief of police. In three pages, I explained in detail how this officer truly had protected and served. I received a personal phone call from the chief's secretary asking for the officer's name again so they could recognize him appropriately.

Two weeks later, I received a call from the Chief, "We don't have an Officer Gabriel here Ma'am. I even checked the counties on either side of us. Are you sure his name plate said, Gabriel?"

"Yes."

I was sure.

DAVID

Shortly after Enmei's session, I was relieved when Bill went out of town again. I needed more time alone. I was listening to one of "our songs," Foreigner's "I Want To Know What Love Is," and I felt an old familiar rise in anxiousness. I figured it had to do with that last session on "responsibility" with Enmei. It hit me hard, and, as the kids played outside, I started to pace the kitchen floor like a caged tiger. I prayed and tried to meditate; nothing seemed to calm me. I walked in my bare feet on the humid grass outside to get grounded and felt no relief. Claire had introduced me to an energy healer, David Cree, and since he had such an immediate calming effect on me, I decided to call him for an appointment. He remembered meeting me and told me to come right away, as he had a cancellation. Claire watched the kids and off I went.

After my arrival, he admitted that he actually canceled his previous appointment because he could feel a healing crisis in my energy field and felt he could be of help. He had to duck his head as he moved through the old wooden doorways of his home, leading me to the back of his house, where a room full of windows looked out onto a heavily wooded yard filled with a variety of vocal birds. I didn't realize he was so tall and slim when we had first met because he was seated at the time. He had a look like Jesus, and his light brown eyes emanated love and kindness.

Our connection was instant, and it was easy for me to lie on the massage table he had covered with an old colorful blanket from India. Strong scents of incense and herbal tea lingered in the air. He had rented this old house in the woods and made the entire back of it his office, where he saw many clients daily. People traveled from all over the country to see him. He had studied many modalities of healing in India and also Tibet over the last 10 years, and had just arrived here after spending three years in silence. He carried peace and quiet confidence with him, and I desperately welcomed his company.

As he hovered his hands slightly above my body, occasionally he would say, "hmmm" or "um-hm" or whisper, "yes."

With his fingers spread, held above my crown chakra, my head, he slowly moved them all the way down to my feet, and whispered, "I'm happy for you and your husband."

His eyes were closed, and I had opened mine as I watched him closely. I didn't know what to say, so I remained silent. *He obviously didn't know about our marriage and Bill's deception.*

He found areas to place his finger on my wrist, heart, throat, forehead and the bottoms of my feet. I liked the way he would gently pull his hair behind one ear as he bent over me. He clearly was healing in a way specific to him and not in the way I had been learning over the years. But I trusted him. He was the kind of person who seemed to instantly love others; not the outside of a person or personality, but their soul. No judgment was felt in his presence. He focused on one's soulful work only and wherever you were, was exactly where you should be.

"Enough is enough," he whispered.

He continued to hover above me with two hands stroking the air as if he was cleansing my aura. I felt no anxiety so I had the courage to cautiously ask, "Why are you happy for us?"

He smiled and kept at his work.

His reputation for doing some miraculous things had swept through the grapevine in North Carolina, and I was wondering if maybe he was just "simply off" with Bill and me because we weren't showing signs of being able to make it through this. I was preparing for a departure from this marriage now, not a resurrection.

"Suffering is a gift that drives us deep into ourselves. This too shall pass, and you have choices of direction, but, when embraced, it can be explosive in the most glorious of ways."

He took a deep breath, and exhaled and then continued, "The anxiety you felt swarm inside and build up in you today is good. It's alerting you. Heed the call it makes. 'The way' is calling you. When you continue to listen to your inner voice, you will hear the truth, you will uncover understanding, and that will let Love in. Love will grow, and all of this will allow anxiety to lessen and then leave you. When you are trapped in confusion, anger, busy-ness, regret, resentment, judgment, blame, and embarrassment... your anxiousness will gain momentum and will grow. And in that place, truth you will not know."

He left me on the table, "Rest," he said, as softly as a breeze.

I drifted off to sleep and gently awoke to his hand laying on my chest over my heart. He let me rest awhile and then clasped my hand to pull me up to a seated position on the massage table. I sat cross-legged as I talked about nonsense, which he politely let me do even though he had no interest. He remained present in his task of making me tea, which I didn't want at first, but made up my mind to accept anyway. The tea was like nothing I had ever consumed. It was a delicious combination of earthy and sweet flavors. I asked him what was in it, and he said, "Love. *It's all you need.* I infused your tea with love."

He went on, "My intention is for you to love yourself more deeply than you ever have before. Once you do, any healing you need in your life will come."

As he slowly walked me to the door, I felt immense peace. I wondered if he stayed in this state all the time. *Does he do his laundry in this state? What if he washed his car? Does he hover around the vehicle slowly, as he hovered over me?*

I'd seen many healers in Chicago and had met plenty of intuitives, but David was striking a chord inside me. As I stepped off his small cement porch and was heading to my car, he asked, "What's your connection to Brooklyn? Brooklyn, New York."

I stopped dead in my tracks looking straight ahead with my back still to him.

He continued, "I saw a young man standing next to you while you were on the table. He shows concern. In his mid-30s. There's a magnetic pull between you. He recently passed? He's saying something about "getting your house in order.""

It took every ounce of courage I had to turn and face him.

He studied my face to see if any of this resonated with me. It took only a second for him to realize another chord had been struck. He swiftly walked toward me, grabbed me and hugged me tight. I buried my head into his chest and cried. It felt good to finally let myself cry... about HIM.

Enmei's question about my role in the current state of our marriage came to mind, and David's gentle nudge pushed me face to face with the loss living deep inside; a loss needing to be unleashed and felt. It was, after all; doing damage.

THE BOOK OF PAUL

From the age of 3 or 4, I remember being whisked away from Paul's naked side. Somehow, during every family gathering, we'd find ourselves glued to each other. We attracted like magnets. We were second cousins and even at that young age, we knew "it wasn't right," but something *was* right.

At first, we were counseled, "Judy, your father, and Paul's mother are first cousins because their parents are siblings."

As the years went by, I learned that a second-cousin relationship can exist, even in the eyes of the law, but it still felt like taboo, as our family members had never traveled down a path like this before. While growing up, we continued to secretly hold hands under picnic tables, and disappeared from holiday parties, funerals, weddings and family reunions. During our teen years, while some of our cousins used our family get-together's to party, we stayed alert and sober, to cherish the precious time we had. We created our own world, free from them. We snuck away behind sand dunes in Indiana, ran off at Lincoln Park Zoo in Chicago and found hidden areas throughout SanBar Beach in South Haven, Michigan, to just be alone. The ferryboat my Dad rented out every summer on Lake Geneva was trickier. On one particular occasion, we secretly jumped off the boat before it launched onto the lake, leaving us with three hours of walking, hand-in-hand, along the waters edge.

———

One early August day in South Haven, Michigan, our Uncle Klindt decided to take all the cousins in his van for an outing. The older ones all piled in first, leaving Paul and me disappointed we weren't sitting side-by-side. He tried to act cool about it because he was 17, but I knew he wanted me next to him. I slid into the benched seat behind him. He kept sliding his hand through the back of his seat, to hold mine. There was no air-conditioning, and the windows were down on this humid 90-degree, summer day. We were on our way to pick the blueberries, famous in that area, and I just couldn't think of any other place I'd rather be. My long hair kept blowing in all directions, so I pulled it back, using my hand as a temporary ponytail holder. I remember him turning to look at me as I did. I felt pretty this day. I looked older than my 15 years. Thanks to having older siblings,

I had matured faster than most girls my age, which may have given me an edge of quiet confidence.

We arrived at the farm, and all quickly jumped out of the van, grabbing our bushels. Paul and I did what we always did... we disappeared. It was easy to do that here. The fields went on and on, and if you took a sharp left, a quick right and squatted down, you were gone in no time. No one chased after us; they were done trying to pull us apart. At one point, I drifted away by myself in the bushes of blueberries. Paul was nowhere around. The air smelled sweet as it circled around me in a gentle breeze. I set my bushel down and lost myself in the beauty of the day.

Somehow, at 15, I had tapped into bliss. It probably had something to do with Paul; he had that affect on me. The sun shone on my face, and the air was moist. I stood there for a while with my eyes closed, head lifted to the sun. I didn't hear him walk up. Without saying a word, I felt his lips press against mine. They were soft, and we had never kissed like that. Even though I already had experienced my first French kiss, somehow this one, without tongue, was a thousand times better. I felt butterflies and faint, and the entire world melted away. It was my first experience of recalling being absolutely present, in the presence of another. I didn't want it to end. I didn't care if Uncle Klindt or the other cousins found us this time. All was well in my blissful world, and I wondered where this would go as we got older.

I sensed that it would have to go somewhere. We never said a word about the kiss, as he took my hand and put a peach in it. "Keep your eyes closed," he said.

I laughed, "Where'd that come from?"

He laughed, "There's a farmers' market up there, in the front of the property. They gave this to me because it's too ripe to sell." He repeated, "Keep your eyes closed. Man... you're so pretty."

He cradled my hand in his and lifted it to my mouth. I giggled.

I loved this game, whatever it was. I guessed it had something to do with art.

As a teenager, Paul was already painting and drawing like a seasoned artist. He was also into taking bikes and other complex machines apart, and rebuilding them in better or more artistic ways. The summer previous, Uncle Klindt had a truckload of old lumber dumped in the middle of all the cabins. Paul was given nails and a hammer, and he ended up building a small house out of it. His family was filled with working artists and musicians, and I loved how different their family was compared to mine.

As I held the warm, soft peach in my hand, he said, "Let's say you want to paint or draw a peach. If you eat it, you become so familiar and close to it that you're able to paint things about it you couldn't otherwise."

It was delicious, and the juice trickled through my fingers, down my hand and dripped off my elbow. I couldn't remember ever loving a peach as much as I did this one. I wasn't an artist, but I understood what he said, and so I wanted to try to someday paint it.

In the distance, we heard, "Hey Paul!"

Uncle Klindt was ready to go.

Our Uncle was a patient man, and I imagined his art students would greatly benefit from that. He was a University art professor who had become the director of the College of Art and Design at the University of Illinois-Chicago Circle campus. On the side, his creativity dove into enormous rehab projects, where he turned old buildings into hip loft condos. He was a cool Uncle even without that resume, though. In group settings, I always wanted to hear what he'd have to say. You had to listen carefully because he didn't say a lot. He was a man of few words, intelligent, with a heart of gold and very introspective. He was handsome and always seemed to have a sophisticated, educated, attractive woman with him at almost every function. He had the most interesting cabin on the lake for the summers and a cool city loft in downtown Chicago, both of which were art-magazine worthy.

Aunt Barbara, Paul's mom, was his sister. Aunt Barbara had a cabin as well, a couple doors down. She was hip and cool. When she asked you a question, she had intention behind it and seemed to be interested and intrigued in your answer. If she didn't care for your answer, she could slice you to the core, if she chose. She had a way of highlighting one's truth before they could see it. She was the epitome of a strong woman, never needing a man to clarify a damn thing. She divorced and remarried and divorced again, but never seemed rattled by it. Her house was always full of unique art—her own metal-relief prints, or the works of her other friends. Her dark hair offset her blue eyes and tanned skin, she was very attractive, but her beauty combined with her intelligence made her a knockout. Her hearty laugh and comfortable nature poured through our conversations, and I was always interested in spending time with her. She was a teacher at The Chicago Art Institute. Paul was her only child. His respect and love for his mother was not surprising, and I was sure he would be good to his wife someday. He called her Barb or Barbara. I never once heard him call her Mom or Mommy in the earlier years. I loved this about him. He was the typical only child, raised by brilliant adults. She took him everywhere, and he was exposed to mostly adult conversations, which may have explained his great depth at young ages. When I asked him why he called her Barbara, he innocently said, "That's her name." He was an old soul, and I felt like I'd known him many lifetimes if that was possible.

Most of the family saw the connection that Paul and I shared, and strangely never questioned it. It was like a knowing that seemed to have a power no one wanted to mess with. We belonged to each other in some strange way. Throughout our high school and college years, while I dated others, we would randomly check in, asking if the other was free. We went years where it didn't line up. I toyed with the idea of cheating on the boyfriends. After all, this connection with Paul was intense, unlike what I had with any of them. But there was a part of me that held back. Maybe I was afraid to fall that deeply in love.

And then one day, when I was 18, it happened: divine timing.

"Hey," is all Paul said.

Even though we didn't talk often, we never had to explain who we were. It was like we just talked that morning. I was beyond thrilled to hear from him. He had just completed an adventure, where he rode his bike clear across the United States, from New York to California. He had a tent but had shacked up with various strangers along the way. When he wrote me, he mentioned staying with some flight attendants in Colorado, and I was flat-out jealous. I wondered if he experienced his first threesome, but I didn't dare ask. He was private that way. Although we had this deep connection, a strange unconditional love and natural comfort with one another, he had a way of looking at me that gently reminded me to think, before I spoke. I never let anyone get away with that, but I appreciated it in him.

Paul studied art at the University of Wisconsin-Milwaukee, and he wanted to visit his old professors downtown. They missed him and wanted to discuss some of the new work he'd been creating.

"Wanna go with me to Milwaukee? We could stay in their brownstone and walk around, maybe have dinner at this Italian place I like."

"Absolutely yes," I replied.

I lay in bed that night after packing a bag. I didn't put too much effort into my daily or evening attire because I knew I'd be better dressed than him and he was always pleased anyway. He studied me differently than other males. He made me feel like I was a piece of art he was going to paint or sculpt. And the more raw and real I was with him, the better. He was going to pick me up the following after-noon. Unable to sleep, I stared out of my window through open blinds, a typical ritual to see the stars from bed. Paul studied them zealously and would at many times discuss his findings of the stars and planets.

That next day, my parent's condominium buzzer went off, and I rushed to the door, pushing the button that would let him in. I heard the heavy door at the end of the hallway open, then clang shut. My heart raced as I leaned into the peep-hole and waited for him to appear. Finally, he was standing there on the other side of the door, looking down to the floor. *Why wasn't he knocking?* He looked beautiful. His medium-length, sandy brown hair was naturally highlighted from his cross-country bike ride; it was a gorgeous combination, with his tan skin. He looked related to Matt Damon, with similar height and a lean build, wearing his typical white T-shirt under a weathered black leather coat and jeans. He looked up as if he knew I was there studying him. His deep-blue gray eyes looked intense even when looking from the other side of this door. His lips parted, and I saw his straight white teeth. He gently swung his head to the right, sliding his long bangs away to uncover his eyes.

I swung open the door and jumped right into his arms. "Hi!" I said, and he laughed and said, "Hey."

He was stronger than I remembered; it must have been the bike ride that built muscle. I could feel he didn't want to let go. I didn't want him to either. He gently let me down, stroked my hair, holding the ends against the middle of my back and he slowly leaned in and our lips met. The blueberries, the sun on my face, the twirl, the peach, it all came back to me. *I loved him. I always loved him. And he still loves me.*

We hopped into his mother's old, beat-up station wagon, and I wondered if the car would even make it to Milwaukee; it was a two-hour trip, and the weather was getting cold and snowy.

"Does this have snow tires?" I asked.

He laughed, "Hmm, not sure." He patted the hood, covered with a light dust-ing of snow, and said, "She'll be fine."

I looked forward to the 2-hour drive; I wanted to find out every detail of what he was painting, sculpting, building and what he was reading. Or had he been taking pictures with his grandfather's camera? I never knew what to predict when it came to him. As always, I wanted time to slow down, it went too fast in his presence. We only had one night. And I wanted to know everything about the bike ride (with the exception of the potential threesome), and we hadn't even gotten to his current art projects yet. Weather reports announced a potential winter storm on its way, so I prayed for a blizzard to hit Milwaukee.

My seatbelt didn't work, which became the perfect excuse to move closer to him, and I slid into the middle of the benched seat. I could smell raw gasoline. *Probably a gas leak,* I thought to myself. I didn't care, because I was with him. Just as I moved closer, he put his hand on top of mine. I'd forgotten gloves, so the warmth was quite a sensation.

When we arrived in Milwaukee, he pointed out a bar and the little hole-in-the-wall restaurants he loved, "Oh, and there's my favorite coffee shop. You drink coffee?"

I thought *no, I hate coffee,* but replied, "Sure."

I wanted to go to every place he ever traveled.

Now that I was 18, I was starting to pick up on something new. As I got to know him over this long period of time, I started to learn more of who I was, each time we got together. And I loved who I was when I was with him. He pushed me like some of my books had. I may be reading the same words a second or third time, but with each year of wisdom, the words became more profound, more clear. Voltaire's quote explained it well: We only hear that which we understand. After knowing Paul all of my life, it was interesting to observe myself with this growing understanding of self. Each year seemed to bring more enlightenment of all things (self, life, people, art…), allowing me to be ready to hear more, feel more, see more, be more.

We had many discussions about religion and theology. The topic fascinated us both even from an early age. After Paul had read extensively about the function of the brain, he encouraged me to read a 650-page book about it, and I encouraged him to give me the Cliffs Note version instead. I had just met a group of people claiming they had passed on and returned so that became the highlight of our discussion. In a matter-of-fact way, he explained the light that people reportedly see at death may be a chemical reaction in the brain while dying. Although I agreed there was probably a scientific process happening, I also believed there were people actually coming back with genuine and authentic healing experiences, consisting of more than just a story about seeing the light. Besides, my own personal experiences after prayer had always led me in the direction of a bigger spiritual world than the eye can see.

Refusing to say I was 'certain' about anything, I'd stand firm and say, "Paul, I only know what I've experienced, and it's led me to the belief that we're not alone. I believe we can reach out when suffering, there are no guarantees we'll be spared, but we can lean on, trust and be grateful for this divine current of support." He would end the conversation respectfully by saying, "I love that you have this in your heart. All I can be certain of is that I know you are overall happier than me and people believing the way you do, seem to be as well. So, you have that."

We pulled up to a beautiful brownstone, and he insisted on getting my door and bag for me. We slowly walked up while reminding me of their names, Martin and Mary Richards. It didn't take long for me to figure out, they were an amazing couple, and I instantly knew why he wanted to stay in touch with these two. Their good nature and deep love and respect for one another emanated from them. When they laid eyes on Paul, pure joy and love poured out. They knew he was special; we had that in common.

They showed us our room. It was a tiny space containing a single bed. She apologized profusely, but when we were settling in and putting our bags away, we both laughed and said "Nice." We couldn't wait to be forced to sleep that close. We grew up having spent many nights sharing one sleeping bag on the beach at SanBar Beach, where we always restrained ourselves from getting too intimate and going all the way. Now that I was 18, I felt like tonight, finally, might go differently.

As we sat in their family room, Professor Mary Richards' interest turned to me, "So, Paul says you attend Eastern Illinois? What are you studying?"

"Oh, yeah, I'm undecided," I replied.

She asked, "Well, what are your loves? Paul said you're a singer and songwriter?"

"Uh, well, not exactly," I said, with a nervous laugh.

Paul interrupted, "Yeah, yes she is. She sings and, yeah, she's an artist and a songwriter. She just hasn't picked up a paintbrush yet or a ball of clay to see what she comes up with," he winked.

"Oh. Well, great. We have an enclosed porch in back that we made into a comfy studio. There are canvases, clay, and a wheel. You kids should go explore in there."

Soon after our talk, he took my hand and led me back to their studio. The wood floor of the hallway creaked as we made our way to the bright room. The studio jutted out from the building over a community courtyard below where an enormous fountain was frozen over. The snow was lightly falling outside the three walls of windows while the space heater warmed the room. White paint peeled from some areas, and it reminded me of the cabins in South Haven. I had a scarf around my neck, and he slowly pulled one end, slipping it off to drop onto the floor. At the same time, he closed the door with his foot.

The room was artfully decorated, like a tiny gallery. The minimal wall space was covered with huge paintings, and the tables displayed carvings and sculptures. There were blank canvases of various sizes leaning on an easel. Next to that, two large stacked crates, full of unique textures of handmade paper, sat recycled glasses and jars filled with various brushes, well-used colored pencils, chalk and tubes of paint. It looked like a productive room, and I loved the energy. This was Paul's element. I adored him outside of this space, but when I saw him among his other loves—his paints, brushes, and canvases—I fell deeper into him. This is where he belonged, and these professors agreed with me that he'd be well known and acknowledged for his gifts someday.

I pulled a brush from a canister and handed it to him, saying, "Paint me something."

He barely took his eyes off me. He placed the brush in water and reached for orange, yellow, gold and some muted red watercolor paints. I studied him as he moved the brush around, gathering color and absorbing water. As the brush hit the canvas, it made its own sound, which shifted in tone as he added more paint or more water. I tried to sneak a peek, but he twirled me away. "No, not yet," he smiled.

I felt myself melt, from the way he locked into me visually. He finally stopped abruptly and announced, "And it is done." He swung the canvas around to show me… it was a peach. Realistic, with imperfect shape, distinct life-like coloring, and fuzzy texture. *A perfect painting for me*, I thought to myself, *how did he do that while barely looking?*

I begged for him to sign it and give it to me. But, in Paul's eyes, it wasn't signable. He humbly thought I was simply being polite, and tossed it into the trash.

I playfully leaped for it, "No! I want that."

As he chased me to the garbage, we tripped and fell to the floor. The professors must have been shoveling the sidewalk out front because no one entered to find what the ruckus was about. While on the floor, we found ourselves in a deep kiss. He pressed his soft cheek against mine, pulled me close and whispered, "I can't remember ever not loving you. It's like I was born and then you showed up…" and I stopped him with another kiss.

We already had gone over all of this. Yet, neither of us could understand this pull to one another. And we were not about to figure it out here. I moved his hand that I was holding in mine up to my breast, and I said, "I want you to paint me someday."

Smiling, he kissed me again.

The next morning, on our drive home, we quietly held hands. No prayers were answered on the arrival of a blizzard. I studied him as he swept his bangs from his eyes, licked his lips, changed the radio station or stared ahead. From his profile, his blue eyes reflected the light. There was little that did not interest me when it came to him. The wall that always stopped us from taking this to the next level sexually had yet again, appeared last night. Instead of talking about it, I silently pondered while studying him. *Not sure what holds us back, while at the same time keeps us deeply connected.*

When we got to my parent's condo building in Glenview, Illinois, I insisted we just say goodbye right there in the parking lot. He wanted to be polite and come say hi to my mom and stepfather, but I didn't want them to potentially read me, or us. I wanted to keep him private, leaving them no room to judge or give advice. He was heading to Germany to show some of his art, and then he had made plans for a permanent move to Brooklyn, NY. He held me close to his chest for a long time in the car. He turned the engine off, and the interior turned private as the windows fogged over. After a while, I gently pulled away from his embrace and grabbed my purse and bag from the backseat.

"You smell good," he said. *Ditto* I thought.

He reached into the backseat for something in his backpack. It was a miniature art kit he had toted along on his cross-country bike ride. The 3" by 3" box was filled with small pieces of paper and a little tray of watercolors. He rolled his window down, and with his finger, scooped a small amount of snow from the ledge. He placed it into a tiny container made to hold water. He stirred it, allowing the snow to melt from the heat of his finger. He stared at me, studying my eyes. "You said you wanted me to paint you a picture." He was smiling. "The color of your eye shadow, the dusty blue with midnight blue… it may become a theme for my next paintings."

He kept the picture hidden from me, as he worked. When he was finished, he blew on it and waved it in the air to get it to dry.

Handing it to me, he said, "There, I painted you a *pitcher*."

I laughed and said, "Clever."

It was a 1.5" by 1.5" watercolor paper with a tiny water pitcher surrounded by dusty blue and greens, sitting on a table next to two peaches. As tiny as it was, it was fit for a gallery. *Who paints like this on a whim?* He did it as a joke, but it was so beautiful that if it had been a regular-sized painting, it could be mounted to any gallery wall. I wasn't sure who wouldn't have appreciated it.

"Okay. Well, can I at least keep this one?" I asked while hugging him.

He nodded.

I was reluctant to be the first one to say goodbye, but I did. We shared one last kiss, and I said it first, but slowly: "Bye Paul."

"I'm gonna paint you tonight," he said before I closed the car door.

I leaned into his window. "I love you, Paul," I said as I looked down into his gray-blue eyes.

"Love you, too."

I didn't turn around, but I know he watched me walk through the doors.

I wasn't sure why, but saying goodbye felt different today.

———

I didn't hear or see much of Paul over the next 10 years. As scheduled, within weeks of the Milwaukee trip, Paul went to Germany to paint and show his art in galleries and, of course, to study more. He could never get enough. We wrote to each other once in a while. He didn't make it home, as he was always too broke. I heard through the grapevine that he had met a girl in Germany, an amazing artist, born and raised there and that she wasn't terribly interested in him, but he was into her. In the back of my mind, it didn't matter because I knew what we had was unique. I often wondered about him, but kept recalling one conversation we had shortly after the Milwaukee trip when I had said, "If we were ever able to knock down this wall, I'd marry you."

He gently replied, "Judy, you don't want to share this life I'm livin'. You want a family and all the stuff I can't give you."

"What 'stuff' Paul?"

"The big house, walk-in-closets, clothes to fill it, three-car garages, you know... Not gonna happen on artist's wages," he explained.

At that time, I knew enough to trust the universe and God's plan, but that plan battled with what lived buried beneath, which was the unanswered, "What if" we had taken it to the next level.

WHAT IF

After 10 years had passed, when I was in my 30's, I had heard enough criticism and complaints from Bill, from family and even from complete strangers, who felt compelled to correct me on how I should operate in this life of mine. Sleep deprivation and caring for 3 small children under the age of 4 preoccupied me, and I was seeking to uncover myself, buried under the roles of wife and mommy.

During this time, I reached out to Paul in his loft warehouse in Brooklyn. It was dangerous to invite him and the "What if" question back into my life, while Bill and I were in the thick of what I called, the "when bored, beware" stage of our eight-year marriage. Nathan, our marriage therapist, specifically told me not to do it, but I did it anyway.

Just as Paul's art was always about "the process" of things, he too, applied that to me. Any process I was in was always enough. Not only that, he believed the process was mandatory in order to move in the one unique way that served you, and only you. These days, I craved feeling like I was enough.

He picked up the phone right before I was about to lose my courage and hang-up. Reggae music played in the background, and his voice was just as I remembered. He was happy to hear from me. I asked a million questions, like usual, and he asked only a few, as usual.

"Are you happy?" he asked.

I replied with a breezy, "Sure."

We talked for months by phone. I told him about Nicole being such a darling baby, but feisty; about Clint being so quiet but sincere; and about Marcus being huge on the growth chart, sure to be a future football player, but also showing signs of being a quiet thinker who may be better suited for being an engineer or philosopher. We laughed about all my predictions. We were astonished to uncover that he had adopted a male Shepherd-husky-wolf mix puppy about the same time I gave birth to Marcus. He coincidently had named his puppy, Marcus, after the Reggae singer-musician, Marcus Garvey, the Jamaican political leader and the subject of many reggae songs.

He asked, "Are you playin' guitar, singing, painting, writing lyrics?"

I answered, "Nope."

Bill had just bought me a very expensive guitar, but I hadn't really even touched it yet. I couldn't feel the music in me these days. He even purchased a glossy black Yamaha baby grand piano that collected dust in the living room. That piano was waiting for the piano lessons I kept blowing off. I wasn't even sure where the guitar was, so I didn't mention any of this to Paul.

He commented about getting my Christmas card the previous year. It was a family photo of Bill, me, Marcus and Clint all standing in front of a huge oak tree. I wrote "Merry Christmas from Bill, Judy, Marcus, Clint and (?)." The question mark was an announcement of my pregnancy with Nicole. That was the first photo of my family I had sent to him. Over the years, I had not seen the point in sending pictures of my family to Paul, but last Christmas, I just felt drawn to reconnect. Deep down, I had this feeling he'd be happy for me and that his life was probably settled, stable and thriving, enough so that when we talked we might have closure on our chemistry and connection. I wondered if it was just simply something from our youth. We were in totally different places, but they were individually the right places, I hoped. It was different today, though. This attempt to connect now was about desperately searching for that part of me that was lost.

We talked about his art, and the kinds of paintings and sculptures he was working on. Presently, he was experimenting with mercury, salt and sugar which made his art shift and change, based on lighting and temperature of the room. He mentioned that some of his pieces were a mix of sculpture and painting. I was eager to see them, so I talked him into sending me slides through the mail. Blown away by his slides, I commented about how striking some were and how they seemed to trigger me. There was one, though, I had to have.

During this conversation, he laughed out loud and said, "What? That's funny that a suburban housewife would want that one! My artist friends like that piece. And I can't let you buy a piece of art off a slide."

"Oh, yes you can! Bring me that piece the next time you come to town. You need the money, and I want to pay for it."

"I can't charge you!"

"Yes, you can! And you will. How the hell are you going to make a living doing this if you don't charge?"

Within a couple months, he brought the painting to my house out in the suburbs. It was a good thing Bill wasn't home when he came by to deliver his art because the chemistry we shared was still there. I couldn't pretend to fool myself any longer. The years had hardly aged him; in fact, he was even more handsome. Engaging him while in the "when bored, beware" stage of life weighed heavily on me. But at the same time, having him around gave me a spring in my step again.

After having never been to my house, he walked in the door as if he'd been there a hundred times. He set the piece on the kitchen table and started to unwrap it. It was even better in real life, and I said, "It needs to go there!" as I pointed to a place over the fireplace; it unquestionably belonged there. The size and scale were perfect, and even the grain in the wood around the fireplace matched it in a finished design way. The heavy, 2-inch-depth square wood piece was 32" by 32", and he had used industrial staples to adhere a square piece of canvas on top. He'd roughly cut a small square in the middle of the canvas and tacked it back with black industrial tacks. The top flap was an ocean teal-blue, and the interior flap below was a bright summer green, surrounded by creams, tans, and grays. These were my Pisceanean colors, and the piece simply made me feel joy. When I told him that, the look on his face appeared to be a mix of approval and surprise. He nodded his head, shrugged his shoulders and said, "Let's go with that."

He was an artist that spent little time explaining the meanings and interpretation of his work; he was more dedicated to being present in his process. I think the painting-sculpture was done during a darker time for him, and the brightness I saw reflected my own perspective. He respected that and refused to share what the creation of this piece was about for him. I pried for a few minutes and then knew to give up.

As I slid a kitchen chair across the floor toward the fireplace, I announced, "I need a hook and hammer. I want to put it up now."

He turned and went to a kitchen drawer and opened it to where we kept a small hammer and picture nails. We both locked eyes and laughed as he said, "How'd I know that was in there?"

We continued our contact over the phone, and our conversations gradually returned to the "What If" question—what if we had gotten together? My marriage was disconnecting rapidly now, largely as a result of these phone calls in combination with Bill's extensive travel. I was exhausted by raising three kids so close in age, and I was lonely. I wasn't doing anything creative except scrapbooks, and that just wasn't feeding me. At this point, it was clear I wasn't fooling myself. I simply went to the first place where my heart was filled, and to a person who unconditionally loved me... that was Paul. The "What If" started demanding an answer.

I strategically plotted a trip to see him, using the excuse that I would be going on an art tour in Brooklyn with him, to see all of these amazing new artists, most of which were his friends. This was going to be fun. I'd be back in the world I so loved, one that made me feel alive. But unbeknownst to Paul, I had a plan. If that wall came down, I planned to finally sleep with him. I'd held back all those years with him that my driving thought was, *maybe that's why I feel incomplete.*

The rightness of making this move was confirmed for me when I received a call from a very close, recently divorced girlfriend of mine. She shared that Bill had recently hit on her. I combined this new information, with no question, along with an on-going suspicion about him and his co-worker at Motorola. It was the illusion of an excuse I longed for.

Paul and I agreed on the dates and times, and I was excited to call him with the details.

"Hey. I'm going to come in three weeks. Can you pick me up at the airport?"

Dead silence.

"Hey. Paul? What's up?"

He said, "I want," pausing with a sigh, "I want you to think about this."

Oh, okay, I guess he's figured out that I'm not just coming for the art walk. I'm coming for him.

"Listen, Paul, I'm a big girl. Making big decisions, yes. But I'm making them, not you. So any guilt you're ready to take on, you need to just let it go. Okay? Are we good?"

"Look, I want you to come, and I want you to come for me."

"Okay, then it's settled. I'm bookin' this flight.

"Okay. Hold on..." Paul said.

And then he said it.

"You can't come, Judy. Don't do this. What you and Bill have with the kids and everything, you just can't. You'll resent me later. I'm not gonna live with that. I won't share and expose this life with you. You need to trust me. I can't give you what you want. For me, looking from the outside in, you have a house that needs order, and I'm not willing to disrupt that. And most importantly," he paused, "Judy, I can't fix you."

Silence set in for a couple minutes, but it felt like 20.

"You need to talk to Bill," he said.

I could hear some hipster kind of music playing in the background, some band out of Brooklyn that had just recorded their first CD. I loved the raw, edgy sound of them, and I made a mental "note to self" that I had completely gotten so far from the things I loved that I needed to find a way back to me while being a wife and mommy. The next time I turn on the radio to just have something on, I was going to rethink that and try to find a station with new up-and-coming artists. I need to listen to lyrics that mean something… music that moves me.

I knew he was right about talking to Bill, but I continued to gently push and argue my case for a few days; we even went into our oldest argument about faith and Jesus. Eventually, we let the wall work *for* us and miraculously found our way back to platonic emotions while we discussed astronomy. He talked of the peace he found while laying on the rooftop of his warehouse apartment as he studied the stars. In time, I recognized why I was seeking and reaching out and started working on myself as far as getting more emotionally sound. His support was welcomed, and we continued to talk, but less frequently.

I never saw that warehouse apartment in Brooklyn or his friend's art. I had let go of trying to fit him back into my life. I called Nathan, our dutiful therapist, who I think secretly, made us his favorite clients. If not, he sure was good at making us feel that way. We made some efforts to see him every Saturday but quickly got sidetracked with our up-and-coming move to North Carolina, where Bill had landed a whopper Vice President of Sales position. I was actually relieved to not do the work the marriage called for, as I wasn't interested in fixing my marriage yet, and I could tell Bill wasn't either. We carried on. "When bored, beware" shifted into "parallel and pretty." We kept busy, busy, busy, with Bill's work and travel, as well as, with my crazy schedule with the kids, house management, play dates, sports, school and one errand after another. Packing for the move to North Carolina became my new hiding place.

ROUND HOUSE

While still living in the suburbs of Illinois, my brother Johnny showed up at the house. He sat at our kitchen table, surrounded by partially-filled boxes scattered about for our North Carolina move. He mentioned that he randomly decided to write Paul the following letter:

7 MAR '97

Cousin Paul,

Shocked to hear from me... or just mildly surprised? Life is packed with "firsts", but since I did little more than inhale and exhale today (not firsts), I guess writing to you will be it for today. How are things in New York? Your name came up over at Judy's the other day. We were speculating as to how certain people would adjust to different environments and one of the subjects was you in New York. I said that I couldn't imagine you living in Shawano, WI, for example... it'd be like an eagle in an attic (I'll have to work on my metaphors!). Anyway, I was thinking about you prior to my conversation with Judy. I just finished Irving Stone's biography on Vincent van Gogh* and it struck me harder, in many ways, than I had imagined. I attribute some of it to my general ignorance of art. It's a bit like a child looking at the moon... in a complete state of wonder and awe. But as soon as some of the facts are realized... what it's made of, how it moves, the effect it has on the earth, it becomes a bit more clinical. There is still the wonder and romance, but it's a bit more fettered in the fact-absorbed mind. It's always a little dangerous for me to read biographies, because there's invariably an explosive offshoot of expanded interests that I dive into. Now I want to know everything about the Impressionists... and the other painters during this period. Emile Zola was also acquainted with van Gogh and I want to know more about that, etc, etc... you get the idea. Aside from that, the book struck me in another way. Personal suffering. Internal... which is mostly speculative even in the most perceptive and fair biographer, and External, which is a bit easier to calibrate. And when I read about the suffering endured as a missionary for the coal miners in Belgium as he gave them his food and clothing, and how he walked on blistered feet 40 or 50 kilometers to meet a master painter just to get a bit of advice and encouragement (he didn't have train fare) and the many times that his money ran out and he ate nothing but black bread and then often went days on nothing, until he became sick and fevered, and how his passion for painting drove him into exhaustion and illness and his eventual breakdown and stay in an asylum, and finally at the age of thirty-seven... when I think all those things and the numerous others too great to mention, and when I realize there is so much more that we don't, and never will know... this is what struck me the deepest. I want to know, but certainty is not a possibility. When all the facts are in, the only thing that can be done is take "educated guesses." This novel also compelled me to reflect on some of my own suffering, and this was somewhat humbling in comparison. Vincent van Gogh hungered many times to the point of delirium and would rather pay two francs for a model to pose, than eat that day. I have never gone hungry with the feeling that another meal may not ever come. I recall having nothing but 2 or 3 dollars several times and buying a five-pound bag of potatoes and eating nothing but those for days... (hardly falls into the category of abject poverty). Now whether suffering is noble, and whether it's a prerequisite for creating great art is a subject that I'm sure has been debated over coffee tables and absinthe bars since Hannibal mounted his first elephant. Did Toulouse-Lautrec, Gauguin and Seurat need to follow such tortuous paths to carve their names more visibly in the history books? Would they have been any less artists with less suffering? I would certainly say to anyone across the coffee table that, with no shame, I can't answer that question. Now if it were the absinthe bar...of course I'd have all the answers, even to questions that weren't asked... (ah, the good(?) ole days ...)

O.K. ...now to Hemingway style. How are you? I'm fine. Working as a court clerk to put potatoes in the pot. Judy's well. Everyone's good. I haven't talked to your ma since I left S. Haven. I hope she's well. The sun also rises over the old man and the sea as he says farewell to his arms... (oops... that's a little too 'Hemingwayesque?)

Paul, I'm really not sure why I tapped this all out at this time, but it was necessary, and I appreciate having you there to receive it.

Take good care of yourself. Hope to see you this summer... in S. Haven? Chicago? N.Y? Paris? Jakarta? Best Always, John

* 'Lust for life'

At the bottom of the page, Johnny had sketched crows in a wheat field on a starry, starry night. My brother hadn't sent it yet because he didn't have an envelope or stamp, so I started up the stairs to get those. I had just left Paul a message a few days earlier and hadn't received a callback, which I thought was weird and unlike him. I thought this letter would arrive at the perfect time. Since we were handling ourselves platonically, I felt it was inappropriate to ask intimate questions about the sadness and withdrawal I started to notice. I knew something was off. I figured it had something to do with advancing in the world of art. Johnny, no stranger to darker days, came from a highly creative place as well, which might be why he reached out.

In the conversation Paul and I had two weeks previous to this, he expressed how pleased he was with how I was trying to *get my shit together,* and he described my family as a *roundhouse.* He mentioned that he saw it as a *well-rounded person or a house in order.* I loved that he shared that because I found the timing was simply divine.

As I headed up the stairs, with the letter in my hand, on the hunt for a stamp and envelope, the phone rang. Bill answered it, and we happened to be passing each other on the landing, so he handed me the phone as he brushed by me to go downstairs to say hi to Johnny in the kitchen.

"It's your Aunt," he said.

I put the phone up to my ear. I don't know why I didn't say "Hello."

"Judy, you there?" she asked.

"M-hm," I hesitated, sensing an overwhelming desire to brace myself, but hoped my intuition was wrong.

"Honey," she said, followed by a pause. "Paul is dead."

We shared a long chunk of silence.

"Um, no. Impossible. Wait. Who? Paul? No," I objected.

"Oh honey, it's Paul, he's gone. He hung himself. Your Uncle Klindt flew out to check on him and found him in his warehouse in Brooklyn. His dog, Marcus, lying under his feet."

Her voice trailed off into instruction, saying something about the funeral being in South Haven and for me to call other family members. I didn't realize it, but I hung up in the middle of her sentence, dropped the phone and sat down on the landing of our staircase. Stunned by this news and nearly paralyzed, I slowly rose and walked into the kitchen.

I put the letter I had clutched in my hand down in front of Johnny, "Not gonna send this."

"Why?" Johnny asked.

"Paul is dead."

I pointed out that Johnny had written that letter on March 7th and Paul had passed on March 9th. I walked directly upstairs and into my walk-in-closet, closed the door behind me, dropped to my knees and sobbed, quietly. I prayed Bill and the kids would not follow me or find me here.

I sobbed with guilt, *How could I have not known the severity of his suffering?* I sobbed for the loneliness he must have felt, the hopelessness, despair, and *Oh my God,* for the rope that probably tore or dented his beautiful skin. The neck I kissed. The arms that dangled, once pulled me close to him in a sleeping bag on SanBar beach and his cold finger that once melted snow in order for him to paint the pitcher. I sobbed for his blue lips, the ones stained from blueberries we picked as kids in South Haven. I sobbed that we never figured us out, and if we had, maybe he'd still be alive. *I should have gone to Brooklyn.*

The "What If" I had lived with now returned in full force. I stood up in the walk-in-closet and cried, remembering how he very clearly had told me that he "would not be able to provide on artist wages." I started studying the collection of shoes and the perfectly hanging wardrobe, and wondered when I had agreed to all of this? I wanted an artist's life. A deeper life. A connection to life with purpose. *What the fuck happened to me?* And then I noticed, there it was, behind all the long dresses: ALVAREZ, the guitar Bill bought me. Covered in dust.

The funeral took place weeks after his death because red tape delayed the transfer of his body over the state lines. The drive to South Haven for the funeral was emotional, to say the least. I brought my pillow, explaining to Bill that I would sleep the whole way. He knew I hadn't slept well for a few weeks, so he bought my story. He thought it was because of our upcoming move to North Carolina and all the organizing, packing and planning of our going-away party. I brought it to pretend I was sleeping, knowing full well that no sleep, nor peace, was going to be in my near future. I turned my face to the window and silently cried. Tears rolled out, soaking my pillow as I watched the cold, dreary Midwest scenery speed by.

Even though my relationship with Paul had been strictly platonic of late, that changed when I heard he was gone. Like an inferno, his death reignited my connection and desire for him. At the same time, it drastically drove more distance between Bill and me.

Of all the times I'd traveled these roads to South Haven, I never thought it would be for Paul's funeral. The minute I entered the church, eyes were on me to see *how I was going to react*. Each person, one by one, embraced me and whispered their sweet comments and acknowledgments of how special our connection was. So swept up in all of this, I lost track of Bill and his feelings, and of what he was overhearing. I couldn't find a way to manage my sorrow and Bill's too, so I stayed close to Aunt Barbara and she to me.

Some family continued to treat me like the widow, and it wasn't long before I noticed that Bill had seen enough. Our therapy hadn't prepared us for this, and we were nowhere near finished working out our "When bored, beware" stage. This whole scene was pushing us over the edge. The chemistry Paul and I shared all those years was now obvious to Bill; he had no idea it ran that deep. I had never told him. But here it was, in our faces. And for Bill, my traditionally protective warrior of a husband, it was too much.

Paul's stepbrother, Luke, walked in a trance-like state around the church with one of his sculptures clutched to his chest. It was two "one-way" metal signs that Paul had bent and entwined together. One had a curve with a slightly skewed opening and the other bent and closed into itself. Recalling our conversation on the phone, he mentioned finding these old one-way signs and was working them into a sculpture. He also mentioned finding a sign with me in mind, as well, but said he would share more on that later.

When talking about the one-way sculpture, he said, "This one-way thing is cool, cause it challenges the idea of something only being one way. What if you were to look at the process of it rather than the actual flat sign?"

I effortlessly agreed and spun it into a spiritual and ethereal place, suggesting, "We create our own unique journeys to Source: our own *one ways*. And with courage, our one-ways should bend and mold to be flexible for our individual paths, as we follow the lights' lead."

He responded with a "Hmm. Okay. I like it."

And here it was, part of Paul's essence, maybe one of his last pieces, clutched to Luke's chest. I resonated with the piece right away. That sculpture was a reminder and reawakening; we have the power to shape, to change, to create, to bend or not bend our own one way... Yet today, I could barely move out of my paralyzed state.

Author, Chuck Bowden, Aunt Barbara's dear friend, delivered the eulogy, and I did not hear one word. Whether I was sitting, standing, or walking, I could only describe myself as aimless. I sensed Uncle Klindt watching me move from one family member to the next. I wasn't sure why he was doing that, but because of his quiet nature, I wasn't totally surprised. Towards the end of the night, he approached me with an envelope in his hand, "Hey kid, not sure if you want to open this here." He may have sensed Bill ready to explode. "I can't quite figure out what this is all about, but I'm guessing you'll know. I found it, propped up on Paul's desk, with your name on it, next to his will and a letter to Barbara."

He didn't ask me to call him later to explain what it was and what it meant, so I could tell it was something I would "know" about and it would be private between Paul and myself. I slid it into my purse and couldn't wait to be alone to see it.

The ceremony was grueling. I just wanted to leave. I had never been to this cemetery before, and it seemed close to the blueberry patches, which was breaking my heart.

Barbara had told me that Uncle Klindt explained that his warehouse apartment had been double-bolted from the inside, and it had taken a long time for the police to enter. Even the janitor didn't have all the correct keys. Uncle Klindt mentioned that he noticed a doormat nailed to the wall, where Paul painted his own creation on it: GET HOME. I found that interesting because I knew he wasn't much of a believer of heaven as his Faith was hard to pinpoint. Nobody could answer my question about how long it had been nailed to the wall. Was it created the night before, as a part of his departure? Had he had it there for a year? If so, did he manifest a way home because it subconsciously burned into him every time he stepped inside and outside of his warehouse? This is the doormat he wouldn't let me see. His HOME was Chicago. All I could think of was *why didn't he come back home? And reach out... for his family... for me.*

Paul's Shepherd mix, Marcus, was allowed to come to the funeral. Barbara acquired and gratefully adopted him, and I immediately worried how awful it would be when Marcus passes on. But, for now, she needed him, and it kept a piece of Paul close to her. He lay down in the grass right next to the casket while the minister spoke. I pulled my purse close to my side, knowing I had a piece of something he left behind, just for me. Something I may cherish forever and would remind me of him. I studied Marcus and wondered what he was feeling. Had he seen Paul strategically position the rope on the beam above? Did he watch him move the ladder over? Was there a ladder? What was this dog thinking? The natural role and nature of this Shepherd was "to protect." Did he feel like he failed Paul? Like we all felt, and Barbara felt? He was the last one to see him alive and the only one to see him take his last breath. I wanted to lie down on the grass next to him, to comfort him... to comfort me. I was lost in my thoughts, and then abruptly, yanked out. At that very moment, I heard a light whine and then he went on, howling, yelping and whining. He paced and charged back and forth around the front of the casket. We all stood stunned in deeper silence, while the pastor ceased talking, to let Marcus have his say. I hadn't shed a tear since I stepped foot in this cemetery. Initially, I couldn't feel Paul here. He didn't believe in any of this anyway. But these howls were connected to Paul. I watched him pace back and forth, changing from howl to yelp to whine, and I sensed and felt Paul, just as he did.

After the funeral, I returned home and waited for all to turn in for the night. I went to the basement, where my makeshift studio was in a large utility closet with laundry machines, our furnace, and a water heater. Letting the hum of all the machines soothe me, I opened the envelope Uncle Klindt gave me. It had one photo in it. It apparently was a photo Paul had taken of our 1995 Cochrane family Christmas picture a couple years back. It was the photo he mentioned to me on the phone. Next to the picture was the metal street sign that he had also mentioned finding, with us in mind. His reflection illuminated in his window startled me, but also brought me great comfort at the same time.

It's strange how death can actually make the rest of us left behind feel more alive. So alive, in fact, that you temporarily wish you were dead. This stream of consciousness became exaggerated in my vulnerable emotional state, and it overwhelmed me.

While in North Carolina, during the processing of HER, and heeding David's call in regards to Paul, I felt as if a shimmery light had been cast on my truer self, allowing me to see where the energetic twist of connection to Paul had choked me off, leaving me unavailable to Bill. I could now see my part of the disconnect in our marriage. *My responsibility. My part... in HER.* The challenge I had going through this, is that while the black and white of it was, he cheated, it seemed fair for me to go right to blame, which threw me into a defensive victim mode. But that mode didn't allow all the truth in. As a defensive victim, I was going *around* the messy marriage rather than *through* it.

Going through, taking my fair share, took more energy and work. When I found out about HER, I eventually allowed myself to feel every emotion I needed to feel. But it wasn't until Enmei stretched me to think about the role I played. My mourning, and also romancing the idea of Paul before I even got to North Carolina, simply made my heart unavailable to Bill. His violent departure startled me, and I dropped into an illusion where I was submerged in "What If" again. The hero in me, wanted to know, *what if,* I could have saved him? The lover in me wanted romance and wanted to know, *what if,* the love would've been deeper with him? The joy in me, wanted to know, *what if,* I would've been happier with him? Fair questions, but if pondered under anything other than truth... became dangerous.

Turns out, I had entered dangerous territory without realizing it, but Paul had. He saw the house out of order. After this realization, I learned to cherish what Paul and I actually had, and found peace in the parts I didn't understand, all in a healthy way, and simply let it be. Without extra romanticizing, I let it just be what it was, with no illusionary energetic strings attached to the "What If" it could have been.

All in all, watching me at the funeral and my longing for Paul afterward, was a jarring surprise to Bill. It left him wondering if he truly ever had my love. That disconnect created a gap between us, distracting us from doing the work our marriage desperately needed at the time. Paul was right about a lot of things, but the one thing I value most and could clearly see, was that *a house in order is one that must be processed from the inside out.* It's definitely an ongoing process, and it will be unique to each person to find their one way to navigate through it.

As the months rolled by, Bill and I carried on with counseling. I took responsibility for my own fixing as I focused on falling in love with myself so I could, in turn, love another more deeply. My search and rescue started for this mother of three, lover of music, design, art, reading, and nature. The girl I sought, was the joyful one who, in the past, had the depth to love, while also having the ability to be light and laugh at herself again. So, the hunt was on. *Take me to Church.*

THY WILL BE DONE

rolled my sleeves up and worked even harder on the processing of HER and Paul. Being such a special energy healer and now becoming a dear friend, David and I often shared afternoons sipping his delicious tea. At one point, he casually mentioned that he felt Paul was content with all that was evolving between Bill and me, but that he may need a little help detaching from this world. I was concerned and asked, "What are you saying here exactly?"

He explained that sometimes we can energetically hold on to people after they have passed, and they can sense that from the other side, so they feel like they should stick around. He suggested I meditate and pray and see if that resonated with me. He added, "Paul is grieving alongside his mother, Barbara, and it may not be serving them any longer."

I went to Church and talked with our minister about David's comment. He shared a similar notion, suggesting prayer was the answer. We sat together for about 30 minutes and silently prayed. We prayed for Paul, and we prayed for Aunt Barbara too, as she was grieving so deeply. She currently was going through all his art and was trying to figure out what direction to take all of it. There were not only costs to consider, but also great reflection on what he would have wanted. His profound writings were becoming even more intense with his passing, while she poured herself into those. As she studied his philosophies, she kept uncovering his brilliance in it all. It would have been an enjoyable process if Paul were alive, but the heavy truth weighed on her heart now as it was so clear, that real brilliance had left this earth.

After the prayers, I moved my car from the front parking lot around the back, where I pulled under some beautiful oak trees for added privacy. Nobody was around. I'd been here the night before, for a Bible study class I had started months prior so my folder from the class, with all my notes, sat on the passenger seat next to me. The ladies in the group were a bit nerdy, and I still wasn't sure if I would stay for the duration. They started to push harder on the idea of "accepting Jesus into my heart." For me, they were starting to sound too preachy, which was beginning to turn me off.

The church ladies cringed when I asked them a few months ago if they ever had experienced hearing songs on the radio or signs of any kind that felt like messages about exactly what they were going through at the time. I explained I was having books fall off shelves in my library, which ended up perfect for me to read based on something I was specifically struggling with. I even told them that I'd stand with the Bible in my hand, pray, ask a question and randomly open the book to what seemed to be exactly what I needed to hear.

Somehow they believed the idea of doing that with the Bible, but they would not agree that a message could be delivered in any other way.

They said, "Signs coming from anything other than the Bible were most certainly the Devil, and you should protect yourself with the light of the Holy Spirit." *Maybe they're right. Maybe they're wrong.*

I battled and debated for a couple classes and then let it go. It was always 12 against one—me. At one point, we all became heated, and I told the whole group, "I've just decided. I'm not quitting this bible study group tonight because we disagree. I'm staying to study the Bible, you and myself. But I will say this. If you think your delivery of this information in the Bible will bring people closer to Jesus, you *may* be wrong. I *may* bring more people to think about Jesus than you ever will, and it's *certainty* that will set us apart. Each and every one of you in here can recite this Bible better than I, but your desperation to have me see it your way, rather than having any allowance in letting me get there, make you seem far from living it."

I eased up sharing every *coincidence* I was having and stopped making it a goal to convince them to be open to my perception and experiences. I figured I had possibly planted some seeds, and they had in me as well. If the seeds were to grow, they would. The bottom line for me was their certainty was sometimes aggressive. It most definitely turned me off, but instead of judging it, I started to let it go… into the arms of an angel. They are entitled to believe in the *one way* they want to, as am I. We'll have the answers when we depart.

Since age 7, I never felt anything other than connected to God, Jesus, my Angels, Saints, Guides, and Ancestors of the light… so the need to say "exactly" what they are telling me to say, off a piece of paper to Jesus, wasn't easy for me to buy. I remained in the van and twirled the small piece of paper through my fingers that had the exact wording to accept Jesus into my life. Strangely, I felt a pull to just do it for Paul. If there is an in-between place, and he feels like he needs to be released, then I will intentionally say these words to support him spiritually in that way. If this acceptance of Jesus brings clarification that a prayer of mine will connect, be understood, heard, louder… than, so be it.

And then I felt inspired to say this out loud:

"Dear Heavenly Father, Mother Mary, Holy Spirit, and Jesus. To all of my Angels, Guides, Saints, Fairies, Ancestors, Archangels and of course Paul and anyone else I may have left out; I'm going to read what they gave me to read. You know my heart, though. You already know me. But just to be safe, I'll say it like they want me to."

I took a deep breath and exhaled.

"Lord, Jesus, I come before You, just as I am. I am sorry for I repent of my sins, please forgive me. In Your name, I forgive all others for what they have done against me. I renounce Satan. I give You my entire self. I invite You into my life, Jesus. I accept You as my Lord and Savior. Heal me, change me, and strengthen me in body, soul, and spirit. Come, Lord Jesus, cover me with Your precious blood, and fill me with Your Holy Spirit, I love You, Jesus, in the name of the Father, Son, & Holy Spirit."

I went on with my own prayer, "If there was something I was supposed to do to help Paul and did not, please God forgive me. And if you have not already, please take him in your arms, Lord… and thank you for watching over me and guiding me during this trying time with Bill. Please forgive me for any hurts I have caused to anyone. I feel you all present in my life. I am so grateful for this. Thank you for our three healthy children. I love them more deeply than I could have ever known… And if I am right on track here, please give me some signs. You know how I like signs."

I sat silent for a while. No tears. I was surprised because the ladies in my group assured me to be ready for a gush of emotions and, yet, there was nothing. *Was it because I had already made this connection?*

I turned the keys in the ignition and started up my mini-van. The crisp Bose speakers blasted the recent new single by Sarah McLachlan "Angel." Instead of pulling out of the parking lot, I paused, recognizing that perhaps this song might have been the sign I had asked for because I did feel pulled from wreckage and comfortable in the arms of my Angels. Even though I had been hesitant to follow the North Carolina church ladies' rules, a strange peace did come over me in the van. It's not that I hadn't felt something similar before, but it felt like a different connection tonight. Maybe my faith was deepening or maybe because I summoned for every Angel, Saint, Spirit Guide, Fairy, Ancestor, Archangel, and Paul, to show up… they may have.

I trusted Paul's revelation about our *roundhouse* in and out of order. I believed my experiences with him may have potentially been a part of holding him to this earth, and I was not okay with that. I intentionally, lovingly, traditionally, officially, uniquely and prayerfully released him. With love and great honor and grace. Not from inside the Church, but from outside.

That same evening, in the middle of the night, Bill was sharply awakened. He sprung out of the bed, knocking his bedside light from the nightstand and hit the floor running. Like a linebacker, he ran right into our dresser, dropped to his knees and turned back to look at me with a shocked expression.

I shot up out of a dead sleep and said, "Oh my God! What's up?"

He stuttered and finally said, as he pointed up to the ceiling, "I don't know if I was dreaming or if my eyes were open. I just saw Paul. From the beams!"

We had thick hand-carved contemporary wooden beams in our 13-foot tall master bedroom ceiling, and, on our first night when we first lay in bed in our new house, we both agreed it reminded us of the three crosses.

On this night, Bill saw Paul hanging, as if crucified, on the middle beam.

I always wondered if it was Paul's jarring, raw artistic way of displaying closure by accepting my invitation to release him. And, making it even a bit twisted that it was Bill who saw him, rather than me, made it even more possible to believe. Paul wasn't a believer in the traditional sense, or perhaps he was telling us he was now. I don't know. I had spent a lot of time contemplating Paul's departure from this earth and where he would end up. After this experience, I stopped asking if Paul was able to GET HOME.

TRULY AND DEEPLY

A few weeks after my realization of *my part in this*, Bill cautiously entered the kitchen area where I was cooking dinner. I noticed him shuffling the kids off to the playroom a few minutes earlier.

"Hey," he said.

I liked how he snuck up on me these days. Since HER, he seemed to enjoy my presence. We had new chemistry, and I could sense our sexual abstinence was creating a mountainous yearning, but we were still unsure if this was a marriage we could commit to. He leaned on the island counter with his elbows.

With his hands clasped, as if in prayer, he said, "You haven't mentioned anything about how you're feeling, like physically, your cervix... Are you better now?"

I was rinsing lettuce in a colander with my back facing him. I turned around with a smile, "Yeah. I'm good. Kate took another look. Kind of a mystery. All tests came back negative for everything, and it seems all is in good working order." Playfully, I said, "Why, do you want to have another baby?"

"You know I do."

"Well, like I said before, surely you and your next wife will live happily ever after with all those kids." I laughed.

I sensed he had something important to say. Enmei and David had retrained us to seek the truth and hold each other accountable, so I let the lettuce dry on a paper towel and gave him my full attention.

"What's up?" I asked, sincerely.

"I have a huge meeting in a week. All my employees will be there. My boss will be there ..."

"Will *all* employees from all over the country be there?" I asked.

He paused and hesitantly said, "Yes. *She* will be there."

Our therapists had spent many hours preparing us for this moment.

SHE would be there. I had studied all her past emails suggesting why they should hook back up. She had recently called him too, which he had been honest about. I knew he was going to eventually have to see HER, and I wasn't sure I could trust him. I wanted to, but my doubt kept creeping in. And when I let the doubt in, really let it in, it drove me to truth, and I remembered anything happening around me, is just that, and it has nothing to do with what's inside me. I'm in charge of how I react. *I'm not the deer. I'm the headlight.* I'm strong, and if he chooses HER, I'll be okay, eventually.

I responded, "Feels a little like a test we're about to take. We're not solid right now, we probably have a lot more work to do, and we don't even really know each other that well anymore. We've both grown in some similar and also different ways. Maybe we'll have the tools we need to keep this marriage together. I don't know. I think we'll be okay. I'm willing to keep working on it, let's just say that."

"I don't want to go," Bill responded.

"Because you don't trust yourself?" I asked.

"No. Not that. Just doesn't feel right."

About a week later, I noticed his travel bag sitting at the front door. I entered the master bedroom with a pile of laundry in my arms, which he took from me and put on a chair.

He reached out for my hands and pulled me to him, "Listen, I've been think-ing, I thank you for taking some responsibility in all this with the Paul thing. You're doing your work. I'm doing mine. I don't know exactly where your head's at, but I want you to hold on and wait a bit longer before you make a decision to leave this marriage if that's what it's going to come too. Fact is, I'm not whole right now, but I'm close. When I'm whole and *if* you find I'm not enough, then leave me. I'll help you leave me emotionally and financially, and we'll break up with some peace, keep the kids solid, but just don't leave me too soon."

After hearing him speak, I had this overwhelming desire to climb into bed with him, but knew it would complicate things. I wasn't sure how to respond, so I said nothing and hugged him. I felt like if I said something too hopeful, I might regret it. Our silence felt right. With all the therapy sessions we'd been having, we were all talked out anyway.

The transformation that took place—where Bill had begun with his shameful tail between his legs, to today, where he quietly and confidently told his truth with-out desperation of what my answer would be—was enlightening. I felt a partner pulling his weight. He was looking at the man in the mirror. Our love, not our marriage, felt deeper now. Deep, where no words live. I could rest assured that together we will forever be capable of that love, and I was deeply grateful to share three unbreakable bonds between us: Marcus, Clint & Nicole.

Bill stepped out of the shower, and because we hadn't even stood naked in front of each other for quite some time, I gave him his space and waited for him to leave the bathroom before I hung the clean towels I just laundered. This master bath was my favorite to date. An enormous shower equipped with two shower heads, surrounded by walls of clear glass, was a pain to keep clean and squeegeed. But it was so worth the look of it. I purposely took my time in this bathroom because it was a true showpiece. Travertine tiled floors, the high 'A' framed ceiling with exposed beams, along with the custom his and hers huge walk-in closets, filled with floor-to-ceiling cabinets and drawers, made me feel spacious and abundant. Special touches like the recessed medicine cabinets, hidden in the huge glass mirror, thick granite countertops, and a luxurious hot tub nestled under two gigantic windows, created a spa-like setting always reminding me to unwind.

The steam-covered shower glass wall appeared to have a smear on it, so I got closer to take another look. At first, I thought it was a favorite quote of his. And then I saw, Bill had used a bar of soap to write, "est. 8.21.88."

That's it. Nothing more. *Our wedding date.*

Clint entered the room, just as I was making it out and he asked, "What's that? What's that mean, Momma?"

Smiling, "That's the date that Daddy and I got married..."

Then Bill walked in, picked Clint up and whisked him in a circle and into his arms, while holding him close to his chest, "That is the day you were actually established."

Clint asked, "What's that mean?"

"The day Mom and I got married, is the day our family really started. God only knows, but we think you were waiting in heaven to come to Mommy and me."

"You knew about me coming then?"

Bill looked at me, and I at him.

"We think the Heavens above did," he said, as he kissed the side of Clint's face.

Bill seemed in touch with a sensitive and real part of himself these days. It gave me the first glimpse of a silver lining in regards to HER, and I let myself embrace the tender moment.

We agreed to stay strong, and not become dependent on constant contact with each other, since this would be the first time he traveled to Atlanta, since HER. We decided to talk about the details after he returned, just in case we got thrown off with a weird tone on the phone that may be taken wrong. I could feel I was going to have to stay very present and centered and not let my mind and emotions get carried away with thoughts of him and HER reconnecting on this trip.

Bill and I then noticed Clint, lying on his back, on Bill's closet floor. He had a pair of Bill's Allen Edmond shoes on top of his little boy Michael Jordan's and was banging the insides of the soles together. His arms were bent over his face and eyes, and I could see his lip quivering. I knew that quiver from anywhere—he was losing the battle to hold back tears. We both leaned in.

While Bill was down on his knees, hovered over him, he asked, "Hey Peanut. What's going on?"

Bill was so tender when he needed to be. Clint's muffled sobs and words collided, and it took us a couple minutes to figure out he was crying, upset about Bill's constant traveling. Bill had traveled 335 days in one year, and apparently, this was not just hard on the marriage. The perfectly polished $500 shoes were now anxiously banging together as Clint lay there explaining, "I don't like it when you always go away."

I tried my best to buffer with an explanation about the way of the world, and how parents sometimes have to travel for work, while Bill cradled him in his arms and assured him that he would call him more while away and that someday he would have a better job, one that kept him at home more often. Clint asked if he could keep Bill's shoes in his room when he was gone, so Bill flung Clint up and put him up on his shoulders. With the big shoes dangling over his chest, and with an exaggerated playful walk up the staircase, he took Clint up to his bunk bed, where the shoes would stay while Daddy was away.

The next day, while I was finishing laundry, belting out songs at the top of my lungs, I made my way into the master bathroom. While brushing my teeth, I noticed the est. 8.21.88 and I smiled. The establishment of this family and any other establishment of any family warmed my heart. I'd spent so many years concentrating on my own personal growth that it was delightful to see us as one unit with the love and growth potential we offered each other. We actually are going to make it through this because whatever direction we go in with this marriage, the bond in the five of us will never break. If God's hand was in it to bring us together, then I could trust His sacred will to see us through, no matter how we end up.

Bill left town, and because of my lifted mood these days, I turned the stereo on and danced with the kids, at eye level, while they danced on top the coffee table. We danced and sang along to the song by Savage Garden "Truly Madly Deeply."

I sang right to their little faces. This song had meaning because it reminded me of how I truly loved them. That they make me want to stay strong and faithful. And that their lives are new beginnings for us, and the bottom line is that they give their dad and I a real reason for living. And in the end, I want to have fully participated in this life with them… standing on every mountain and bathing in every sea. And then, because we had made this our new family song, the kids had memorized segments, and they sang it right back to me.

My master teachers at work.

Anne, my dear friend, and her husband, Mike Anderson, had a dinner party planned that evening. They never expected Bill to come because they knew of his extensive travel schedule. So when I showed up, they weren't surprised to see me alone, but they were pleasantly surprised to see me all dressed up, with makeup, hair and nails done. They had gotten used to my puffy red eyes, a dirty ponytail, holey jeans, white T-shirt, and flip-flops or actually barefoot. During some of these trying days, there had been a few times I had absent-mindedly, picked the kids up at school with no shoes on. Anne gently pointed this out while she was there picking her kids up.

Mike was a guy who loved and appreciated women. He was respectful, but also flattering. He picked a perfect occupation; an obstetrician/gynecologist. In the beginning, I was hesitant to tell him about HER, but he was cool when I finally did.

He said, "Oh my God, Judy, relax. This is not so uncommon."

I loved that he didn't judge us. He'd seen enough of this type of thing that he wasn't in a place of judgment, just a fan of seeing people come through it.

Since Greensboro was known as the furniture capital of the world, our neighbors' and friends' homes seemed to all be beautifully and professionally decorated. I sat in their living room, admiring how everything just seemed to have a place and come together with elegance, but also comfort. It wasn't as contemporary as I liked to live in, but I loved how it had a vibe staying true through the whole house. It screamed expensive, but in a comfortable, classic way. I loved how their home always smelled new, even though they had lived in it for a while. Everything was in perfect order and spotless. High-end art and accessories were found throughout each room, including the playroom and kid's bedrooms. They were well-traveled, as you could see in their family photos; images of skiing, boating, sledding, beaching, and hiking were scattered beautifully over many tables and walls. I loved how Mike took Anne on private vacations, just the two of them. That seemed healthy, and I imagined and hoped they would never have a HER because of it.

Anne displayed her china and crystal on their enormous dining room table like a Thanksgiving dinner was about to take place.

"Ohhh, it's beautiful. What's the occasion?" I asked.

"Every day is a special occasion," Anne explained with a smile.

"Well, yay for us," I said.

We all took our seats as she pointed to where we should sit.

I was the odd man out, as usual, but this group of eight was awesome, and they understood. We had all gotten used to it anyway. Their husbands had similar work ethics and were master providers, so they understood Bill's passion for work and drive to succeed, so no judgment here on their part.

"Bill's traveling, right? Have you heard from him?" Mike asked.

Anne didn't dare ask because she knew I might be uneasy about it. She'd seen quite a few of my ups and downs through this. She was such a gentle and dear friend. I so needed her at this time in my life.

I thanked God for her and answered his question, "Yes, he's in Atlanta."

Anne and I locked eyes, "And no, haven't heard from him, but I don't expect to."

"Well, I'm sure he's swamped busy," said Steve, one of our friends that did not know our whole backstory, but knew Bill traveled extensively.

I thought it was sweet that he was trying to ease me. I, all the sudden, was appreciating males for their natural desire to protect women. I wanted to stop taking it as a personal attack against me, assuming they thought I was a weak female. It was natural, and if I was to watch, with no judgment, it became real clear there are times when the intention to protect was coming from a genuine place. I love an authentic man.

In the distance, I could have sworn I heard Bill's car. It had a unique exhaust system. And then I heard it again and caught myself wishing he was there.

Somebody sparked a conversation about religion, and I quietly engaged as I observed the Baptist battle the Catholic. The topic of religion rarely escaped a dinner party here in North Carolina. I liked the deep belief systems and the Faith that ran through all of the different religions. It generally ended in a heated conversation with educated people reciting Biblical passages that would effortlessly roll off their tongues. At times, it felt natural to question their real connection to a verse when it was so perfectly memorized as a young child. And did they as a child, really ever understand the verse or did the task of memorizing it mask their growing love and growing understanding of God?

During the more heated times, I couldn't help to think about how ridiculous they all sounded. I often pictured Jesus sitting at the end of our table, quietly listening in and thought, *What would Jesus do or say right now?*

Would he say, *I'm not turning the water into wine for these boneheads!*

I'm all in when God is concerned, but I'm out when that *absolute* certainty folds into the conversation, and Love for one another exits the room and is replaced with anger, ending in a fight to be right. But, on this evening, it was still productive, amusing and had captured my attention.

In mid-conversation, the front door opened. We were in the dining room, which was close to the door, but a wall separated us. I heard footsteps, and Mike started towards the door to see who it was. He said a couple words and then reentered the room, with Bill! All of us were stunned, seated at the table. With the exception of the one guy at the table, everybody else knew of HER and our attempts in healing HER aftermath. We waited impatiently for his explanation.

I stood up and said, "My God, Bill! What happened? Why are you here? You should be in Atlanta!"

In a stare down, I waited for his answer, and I braced myself like the therapists taught me.

Choked up, he responded, "I resigned."

"What? Why?" asked Mike. A natural response from an expert provider.

Bill pointed at me, "I want to get to know my wife."

His entrance into the room that evening was like a permission slip. It dawned on me, since I was doing "my work" and falling back in love and newly interested in myself, he too, was falling for me. I gave myself instant permission to let him get to know me even more and, in addition, I gave myself permission to receive his love and also to know him even more, without assumption of who I already thought he was. Neither of us felt fear about showing the whole truth of ourselves and being rejected any more. Being rejected would mean to simply just let it be, let it go and move on. It wasn't a personal attack or a declaration that we should be a different person.

Over the years, I'd been a busy mommy telling him and the rest of the world, what he and they mostly wanted to hear and I temporarily lost touch with who I really was and who I wanted to become. I also somehow decided how and what I wanted him to be, without taking the reigns off of him to become exactly what he needed to be. The therapy and processing helped me stop blaming myself for Paul and stop blaming him for HER. I also stopped blaming US for being stuck, bored, parallel and pretty and for not doing the work on US. I forgave myself for not taking loving care of myself the way I had used to. It was time for our love to unfold and to grow… together.

Within seconds of returning home, the Foreigner song "Feels Like the First Time" came on. Again, music seemed to follow and find us. The lyrics sunk in when describing the declared passion of lovers who will climb any mountain and will swim across stormy seas. This night was our "first" all right. We let our old marriage die, and we began again. The song played on as Bill's hands rolled over me with ease. I was so grateful for his strong hands and arms wrapped around me. He always dripped of experience, and as I thought that, for a sliver of a moment, I saw HER in his hands. But I let it go, and I started feeling gratitude for his vast experiences, making him such an expert lover. Although, I wasn't quite ready to accept full gratitude for "HER" yet. I could not deny that I had a smidge of hope that someday I might.

Occasionally, on that evening, SHE would creep in and then out of my mind, and I would feel self-conscious. He probably enjoyed having a new lover with HER experience. I had to honestly ask myself, who wouldn't? When I would look into his eyes and feel his hand on my abdomen, the hand that rested on my belly during three pregnancies, waiting to feel the kick of creation, it made it all feel right again.

I briefly recalled a therapy session where he explained the drunken vapors from her that early morning in the hotel room in Atlanta, making him vomit. The smell of her all over his hands and face made him wretch more. The torture he felt afterward was enough for me to fear experiencing that shame and guilt for myself. During therapy, it was excruciating to watch him release the raw truths of his night with HER. I was grateful that I didn't have to process the same with

Paul. In the back of my mind were our therapist's words, "Do the work," which fit perfectly with Paul's message of getting our house in order... a round house.

And so the intersection of us began.

That night reminded me of and reintroduced me to a deeper power of love ... and that a HER could not touch what we had. And if someone wanted to argue that she did, then I would say, perhaps. But only to crack us wide open so the light could filter in.

A poem from Hafiz (translation by Daniel Ladinsky)

> Nothing can shatter this love,
> For even if you took another
> Into your arms, the truth is,
> My sweetheart, you would
> Still
> Be kissing
> Me.

CHICKS IN THE NEST

Back in Tucson, I awoke with North Carolina on my mind, just as I felt Bill roll out of bed. I must have dreamt about it all night long... HER, Paul, Bill's surprise visit to Mike and Anne's dinner party... those memories filled with grit and grace flooded my mind as I ran my hand over to his warm spot, wondering if he ever thought about the 'us' from those days. Eventually, I let the sound of the kids and cartoons blasting in the background encourage me to get moving.

This was it. The day of departure. Santa Barbara was calling my name.

I attended to the daily chores and to-dos. We ate cereal together as a family, and afterward, I stood behind Nicole, loosely braiding her hair while she watched "Sponge Bob Square Pants." The boys sat beside her. Their laughter made me smile. *The kids seem okay with me going.* I headed into the kitchen, where the still-grosser-than-ever white tiles triggered me, making me want to neurotically scrub them with bleach. I couldn't wait to leave those behind. The Formica kitchen cabinets were permanently stained by the many renters before us, and the hinges were all bent, leaving the cabinets crooked. *Aw Horehole, I can't say I'm gonna miss ya.*

I tried to ignore the crooked doors and stains while I put carrots in snack baggies for the kids' future floor-hockey camps and scooped peanut butter into tiny Tupperware's for their celery stalks I had cut earlier that morning.

"You're running late. You should go. So you don't hit LA at rush hour," Bill suggested, again.

He was always so stressed about getting stuck in traffic. He often calculated the exact time to depart in order to make sure he could navigate around a stampede of rushed drivers.

I nodded yes, but not in agreement. It seemed stressful for him to think this way and I looked forward to not having him in the car with me because of it. I didn't mind sitting in traffic because I was more a people watcher anyway. I was going to be on my own, and I could care less about traffic. All I would have to worry about was getting gas and finding a bathroom once in a while. This was going to be easy breezy, traveling alone.

Just in the last week, I felt Bill grow more distant from me. He didn't seem impressed by my last-minute gestures to show how much I cared about leaving him ready to take care of the kids. I placed the snacks in the fridge and headed out to the garage as they walked out in single-file. Marcus gave me a hug and a goodbye first.

"Mom, I will miss you," Marcus said, with a big hug lasting longer than expected.

Clint gave me a quick hug and kiss. "Bye, Momma," he said, with a skate-board under his arm. He then quickly took off to the front yard to try out the new ramp he made, even higher than the one that had chipped his front tooth a couple months before.

Nicole quietly sobbed and slowly worked herself into hysterics: "Mommy, please, ummm, pweeeease don't go."

I reached down to pick her up. "Awww honey, it's okay, Mommy won't be gone long."

Bill gently pulled her from my arms, knowing what was coming next, impressive for a dad that hadn't been hands on.

Bill continued to take charge, "Mommy's going to be gone 11 days, and we can make a calendar on the chalkboard in the kitchen, and you can be the one to mark the days off. Just like we do with the 12 days before Christmas, okay?"

Her buried head pressed against Bill's chest in full sobs as tears streamed down her cheeks. Her head popped up from his embrace, and she was looking directly at me as she cried out. "You said..." before catching her breath and starting over. "...you said you would never weave me again, like at the food stamp pwace... 'member? 'member when you left me, and I got sweaty in the car?"

Bill's face turned to confusion and then disgust. I had never shared the details of that horrific day with him and hoped it would never come up. Never had I been more ashamed of anything, ever. I gently kissed her while I patted and rubbed her back.

Keep it together. If you cry, you'll make it worse.

He nodded to me to insinuate, *hurry... get in the truck... and go.*

Clint had switched to his bike, and he'd taken a few jumps. He looked so cute with his bright blond hair poking through parts of the bike helmet he wore. He was waiting for me to pull out now. I waved to him, and he didn't wave back. His lips looked puckered, and I guessed he might start to cry.

Oh shit, what am I doing?

Well, at least my little Marcus, who'd just turned 11, was okay. He seemed good with all of this, and since he was the oldest, the other two might follow his lead. He even ran into the house for a toy or something after he said goodbye, so at least he appeared solid. Bill seemed fine, besides the fact, he'd practically said nothing directly to me all morning. He walked up to my lowered driver's window. I wanted to hear him hint about something deep and profound, assuring me everything was somehow, going to be all right. But his silence screamed: "Just go, leave me alone, divorce me. Whatever you gotta do, do it."

I felt like I was leaving him in the dark with our circumstances, but it was a place I knew, no longer served me, and I no longer could serve it.

I wanted to say, *Sorry I couldn't get to you. Sorry I can't wait around for the man you wanted to be. And I'm sorry that I can't light anymore of your darkness. I have to seek some sense in all of this alone, as I seek my own light.*

His left hand rested on the window while he held Nicole in his right arm. While fixating on his hand, our whole relationship flashed in front of me. From that first night at Panther Lounge, to today. The good, the bad, the happy, the sad. *We're dying.*

Nicole's sobbing turned to soft gasps as she tried to catch her breath. She stared at me with her big brown eyes as her head lay on Bill's chest. His T-shirt was soaked from her tears. I turned to check on Clint again. I attempted another wave, finally getting a half one back, down low by his waist. Just a little wave, but it was something.

"The kids have been coloring, and stuff and they gave you some of their favorite toys, and wrote letters. I put them in the back of the truck last night after reorganizing your guitar, your bags, and stuff," he explained.

Oh my God. He had seen all the crap I was taking! I was embarrassed I brought so much. I felt more guilt. I was about to burst out crying. Was it for my chicks in the nest? Or is this the art of leaving him for good? Was this the trip where clarity would come, and I would finally say goodbye to him? *Kiss me then. One last time.* I leaned my head towards him, and he followed cue, gently kissing my lips.

Bill placed his hand on top of mine, which rested on the steering wheel, "Jude, I don't know if you're running away from something or running to something. Whatever it is, I hope you find it."

He gently patted the top of my hand and stepped back, away from the truck. *I had an eight-hour drive to ponder that one.*

I started the car, scanned everybody again, and put it into drive. I could see them all in my rearview mirror. I noticed Marc was back in the garage, watching my truck pull out. I waved my hand out the window, and off I went.

I turned the corner and made it past a few houses, driving slowly, partly for my heavy guilt and partly because many kids played in the street here. I heard an urgent, panicked yell from behind the car, a familiar "Momma. Momma! Wait! Wait!"

I looked in the rear view mirror, and I saw him… *Awww Marcus….*

He was a solid kid with natural thick blonde hair and beautiful blue eyes that contrasted with his gorgeous tan skin and pink cheeks. He had a look of a young Leonardo DiCaprio. Because of his big body, and the relentless 90-degree temperatures this morning, he was sweating profusely. I stopped the car and got out. He ran so hard into my arms, I nearly fell backwards. He was like a little linebacker, built just like Bill.

Marcus was my quiet one, so to hear his yell, his voice, and see him chase my truck down both horrified me and brought some relief. He pulled my heartstrings in a unique way. During his elementary years, he'd been bullied by many kids, teachers, and a bus driver—this had silenced him. But he was using his voice this morning, to tell me what he needed, and that was a good thing.

"I'm going to miss you, a lot. I made a snack for you. Here you go."

He reached into his pocket and handed me a plastic snack bag with warm, slightly crushed goldfish crackers, "You might want these for your car ride."

He gave me a big hug, sprinted back to Bill, and stood at the end of the driveway. Nicole's face was still buried in his chest. Clint was holding Marc's bike, wanting him to join him on his new dirt ramp.

"Bye, Momma!" Marcus said as he waved from the driveway.

I pulled out of the neighborhood feeling emotionally paralyzed. My chicks were in the nest, but I wasn't there. I knew it wasn't safe to drive numb like this, but I didn't want to risk letting the floodgates open if I pulled over. I needed to get out of here. I needed to go to a place where it was safe to cry.

———

"Welcome to California." I had seen that sign many times in the past, but today, in this pouring rain, it caught my attention as if it had neon lights. I was floored that I had driven a couple hours outside of Phoenix with no recollection of the drive so far. Just like a medicine bottle would read: "Do not operate heavy machinery." I too, needed to wake up and be present while driving. I was dangerously operating not only this vehicle but also my life, in a hypnotic trance.

My main thoughts circled around my relationship with Bill, who was heavy on my heart, and saying goodbye to the kids was excruciating. I may have done severe damage to both by leaving.

I realized, I'd driven through and past Yuma, the one spot marked on my map to stop for gas. Bill had printed a map with pre-calculated stops marked in red pen. It's something he always did for me... for us. If I were to separate from him, I would probably not do that for myself. I winged things more than he did. I wondered if that would change if I divorced him. Maybe I was able to wing things because he always took charge of the order in our lives.

My low fuel light flashed as I turned into a small gas station. I was the only customer. Undisturbed by the pouring rain, I began pumping the gas as I listened to it fill the hollow tank. I thought about making a call to see if everyone was okay, but worried it would leave them worse off. About halfway through filling the tank, a friendly gas station employee came by to empty the garbage can next to me. He looked at my Arizona plates.

"Where ya headin?" he asked in a friendly tone.

Instead of answering, "Santa Barbara," I froze and said nothing. It was an awkward moment, but an anxiety attack, one like I had never experienced, silenced me. The pump shut off, the tank was full, I didn't wait for the receipt. I just screwed on the gas cap, gave him a half wave and drove off.

Bill had asked the same question earlier. And I still had the same answer. *I don't know where I'm heading to or running from.* And it hit me like a truck. While in Tucson, I could hide behind the busyness, noise and chaos of my daily life. Here, the silence was already deafening. It scared me.

LET IT RAIN HERE

Anxiety started to move into my throat, and a sudden shortness of breath alarmed me. I quickly pounced on the thought behind Bill's fair question. It reminded me of something Dr. Wayne Dyer had taught: "Remain open to every-thing and attached to nothing." I was going to have to find a way to apply that to our marriage and to my life. I didn't want to just stay locked into staying married just because we had spent so long together and we had three kids. I wanted to stay together for the right reasons. And I didn't want to commit to a divorce be-fore reviewing my exact role in this life of ours. If, after doing my "work," then I could leave, but not before. I felt myself leaning in this direction, but I knew it was too soon to tell. *I'm not done thinking and feeling this through.*

All I knew was that the labels I placed on myself had to go. Those labels had too many desired outcomes attached. I needed to clearly see the space in be-tween myself and the exterior roles I agreed to over the years. Because I had not understood this space previously, I suspected that this anxiety had been hiding behind an actual nervous breakdown that needed to unfold. *Is this what one feels like? What would a psychiatrist diagnose me with today? Do I need professional help and maybe even some meds?*

I quickly threw the thoughts aside because I knew my insurance would not cover the specialist I'd want to see anyway.

My mind was locked into "seek and find," "search and rescue" and "lost and found." Those thoughts fed my anxiety, so I did what I often had done in the past: I reached out for help.

I dialed his number and got his voice mail.

"This is John Wilson. I'm not here right now, feel free to leave a message."

I started to cry. Just hearing his voice made me cry. I dialed again, not be-cause I thought he'd answer, but just to hear his voice.

My Dad. My sweet father, who stood almost 6-feet-tall and rounded, with light blue eyes that often filled with tears because his heart was so easily touched. He wore a navy suit and sneakers often, even in the Arizona heat, not because he cared about what he wore, but because it's what he had. Sometimes the hint of cigar would follow him. His white-gray, uncombed wavy hair was usually covered with an off-white rimmed hat that made him look like he was taking off for vacation. The finger smudged glasses that loosely lay on top his nose remained smudged because he was too distracted to notice. He was usually buried in developing genius computer programs that Bill Gates would probably want to know about.

Dad had a gentle way of talking me off cliffs, reminding me of my own strength. He generously and courageously showed his own weaknesses in order for me to better understand my own. He may not have been able to provide financial riches for me, my brother and sister, but he was rich in spirit, kindness, and pure genuine unconditional love. He called every man and woman, of every race, his cousin, and truly believed it. He set no conditions on anyone. But did have a side that was so mentally sharp and honest that if he needed to stab one with truth, he could. My Aunt Corinne, his sister, would say, "I love ya, and there's not a damn thing you can do about it." My Dad may have never said these exact words, but he lived it.

I needed him now… to talk me off the cliff.

The radio hadn't been working because of poor reception. The combination of the unfamiliar silence and now not being able to talk this through with my dad sent me scrambling for any random station. I hit SEEK. A Christian radio station started a 7-minute song called "Let it Rain."

I began chiming in with the simple lyrics that repeated over and over. It talked of opening the floodgates of heaven. And of feeling the rains of God's love, the winds of spirit and the heartbeat of Heaven. All of this because we want to see your glory, God, and because we just want to know you.

My wipers were on their highest setting, and I embraced it, belting it out like I'd written it myself. Christian rock was not a favorite of mine, but it felt good to hear it today. With both hands on the wheel, I realized my speed of 90-m.p.h. matching my accelerated emotions, so I took my foot off the gas and turned my blinker on. I was alone on the highway and made a jarring stop on the side of the road. I opened the sunroof and laid my head back on the driver's seat and let the rain pour down on this dried-up desert girl. I was soaked and should have been cold, but I remained meshed into that song.

Flashing in front of me, I could see Marc's sweaty face chasing my car down the street as I left. I could see Clint taking jumps on his bike in the front yard, trying to act like he was okay with everything because he wouldn't want me to know he was upset. I revisited Nicole's face buried in Bill's chest as I drove off, her muffled sweet baby voice with a lisp, pointing out, 'You said you would never weave me again…,'" while her body convulsed with deep sobs. And I saw Bill's hand rested on my window. He seemed genuine about hoping I'd find what I was looking for. And he seemed quietly confident that if my answer were to leave this marriage, he'd be okay with that. He had always fought for me in the past, and the fight was gone.

I cried so hard, I had to concentrate on taking my next breath. I finally let myself go and let the last few years in. Friends would comment on how strong I was to be able to have risen that high and to fall so low. Sometimes I agreed, but my predominantly positive nature could no longer hold. It probably would have held if we'd only been suffering for six months to a year, but I knew now I was going to have to dig deeper to get through all of this. I could clearly observe my self-talk, and when I told myself the truth, I felt I was an overly sensitive woman who was apparently too weak to just deal with what is. I was embarrassed to be sad and dramatic about losing anything material. There was worldwide hunger and starvation going on. 9-11 happened! There were families in other countries dropping their kids off at orphanages because they could no longer afford to feed them. I was so disappointed in myself. Not only that, I wished I weren't so physically weak in times of stress. This, coupled with my weak emotions, just made me feel pathetic. I was ashamed of my mental health; I always thought I was stronger than this. My spirituality and soul looked flawed, and I considered that I had manifested it all and that I did deserve anything bad that happened. Maybe this was proof of Karma. A "serves you right" kind of thing... maybe I was answering to a higher power than me. I could clearly see that I remained in a busy survivor mode through it all, but I could feel that *shit* was getting real now.

I took a deep breath, and from my gut I screamed something... not a word but a guttural yell. The scream was unrecognizable.

Who was that?

I don't know how long I stayed there on the side of the road. It felt like five minutes, but it could have been an hour. Then I felt a welcomed, massive release of sadness that was not gradual but was immediate, and it literally snapped me out of the anxiety I was wrapped up in. The tears started to slow their pace, and my thoughts stopped racing. It was as if the scream and the bottled-up tears transformed into a physical release to a spiritual peace. Finally, the cliff I thought I was standing on was now somehow feeling more like a curb.

Over the next few hours, I imagined this trip might be showing itself to me. It could be powerful, or if I don't embrace it, it may just simply be an 11-day vacation. That's okay, too. I immediately thought of the kids and hoped I could calm them down in the next couple days so they could actually enjoy having their dad to themselves.

I thought of the few family and friends who rejected the idea of me taking this time. I was surprised and pleased to have a new thought process sink in: I cannot expect others to understand *my* journey; I don't even understand it. Also, it's not their responsibility to make sense of my journey; it's mine. These raw thoughts delivered a clear message: I would need to work on accepting who I was. With intense clarity, I realized that I might need to work on being kinder to myself, to begin with. I pulled it together, closed the sunroof and enjoyed turning the heat on in the car. After what had been a brutally hot Tucson summer, it felt good to be chilled to the bone and then warmed up. I couldn't tell if my hands were shaking because of the potential nervous breakdown or because I was freezing. Maybe it was both. But it felt good. I felt alive.

The rain stopped.

The gray clouds started to break up as I made my way through Palm Springs and then the sunshiny City of "The Angels," Los Angeles, welcomed me. The sun was bright but didn't seem as jarring as Arizona. I took in the rich green vegetation around me. The palm trees, bushes, trees and flowering vines covering parts of the hillsides along the highway were more satiated here. It was a welcomed relief to the dry cracking desert I left behind.

The honking cars reminded me that the traffic might have been bothersome for others, but I was comfortable to be in the thick of it. And for someone who just experienced the worst anxiety attack ever, you'd think I'd be scared to have another in this jammed traffic, but I wasn't. Somehow, I felt a bit free.

After the traffic, while pulling onto U.S. Highway 101, I paid attention to how foreign everything felt, inside and outside of myself. Since this was our primary kid transporter, silence was rarely experienced. With only six hours into the trip, I was missing them terribly. I forced myself not to look at the clock and figure out where and what everyone was doing. When I turned the radio on, the hit song by Uncle Kracker "Drift Away" dominated the stations. I always loved the original version by Dobie Gray but enjoyed the remake. I knew every word but restrained myself from singing it. It was like I was holding out, maybe waiting for permission to get lost in rock 'n' roll and drift away. The song reminded me of my deep love for music, and I wasn't sure if even bringing ALVAREZ, my guitar, was worth it. I thought: *I probably wouldn't even play it and why should I?* It's not something I could make a living at. And even if I were involved in a Church band, I surely couldn't afford the time to participate, as it would potentially take me away from the family. I was guessing I'd spend more time doing yoga, meditating and walking on the beach.

My thoughts drifted back to the fact, I'm all alone in the car and I won't sing "Drift Away" out loud. I grew up singing in variety and talent shows since the age of 7. I had bands in 6th and 8th grade, as well as in high school and college. *I loved to sing, so why wasn't I now?* It then dawned on me. When singing in the car numerous times with Bill and the kids, I was asked to stop. At first, it was more like a joke, but over the years I slowly restrained myself because they seemed legitimately annoyed. Bill would actually turn the music up when I started singing. I eventually honored their requests and apparently at some point stopped singing alone as well. *Hmmm, I'm gonna have to pick up that guitar.*

I was excited about the easy tasks I'd have in Santa Barbara. The kind I could effortlessly complete, unlike at home where most tasks were not made to be completed. They just went on and on, or immediately started over after finishing.

As I continued to drive, thoughts of North Carolina and Bill brought up emotions about the woman from California offering him a position. I had clarity; if he strayed again, I was done. At this point in my life, I didn't feel the need to experience that again. *I can leave if I've learned all the crap I needed from this relationship.* I found it kind of interesting: whether to stay or go had been a major theme throughout life. Should I go to college or not, should I take this job or not, should I start a family or not, should I move or not, should I date him, marry him, love him… or not.

Continuing down Highway 101, I lowered the window to feel the cool California air. After dreaming about what our marriage endured in North Carolina, I was floored by the new, yet again, parallel and pretty gap between Bill and me. We worked so hard to create a deepened marriage. I felt like so many steps forward had been taken, and now I was so disappointed in what felt like, fifty steps back. My thoughts moved back to Paul, and I imagined he might be bummed for me. His honest and truthful words, "I can't fix you" still lingered on my mind.

Then it hit me! I was waiting for Bill to get the right job that would fix our finances, which I thought would, in turn, fix me and fix us. All of these thoughts about how we courageously took fair shares of responsibility for HER and for PAUL made me aware I may want to take a look at my fair share in our finances, our past decisions and obviously, in our marriage today.

Paul's attention to our *roundhouse* inspired me to speak out loud to him in the car. "Paul, Bill and I made it through that broken land. We pushed each other to get to the mountaintops, and we swam through some stormy seas. Yet, today, all of the hard work has ended in despair. That road didn't take us there, Paul. And the little love we have left for each other, may not be enough to see us through." I could tell we not only had slipped away again from this *roundhouse* but perhaps our own individual houses were now needing to be individually attended to, again.

Damn it.

In my head, I went over the risk in leaving, even if it was only for 11 days. It's been written when there's trouble in a marriage and the two separate for any length of time, there is a higher percentage of not being able to make it work. The divorce rate today was higher than 60 percent, and since both sets of our parents divorced, the odds were greatly stacked against us. On the other hand, stories of second, stronger marriages were on the rise, and I was starting to contemplate how both Bill and I might benefit from those. We had been through so much at this point, I played make-believe and imagined we would have the potential to eventually become good friends and raise the kids apart. We could probably be sane enough to deal with our new partners. He would say I'd end up with some yoga dude, which was highly unlikely. And I could see him with a younger, more career-minded version of myself, with big boobs, which was probably more likely.

I rounded a curve on Highway 101, and the breathtaking view of the Pacific coast drew me in and right out of these thoughts. Desire to re-hash where we came from started to drift away. The question now, while watching the deep blue ocean crashing onto the sandy shore was, "Where do I go from here?"

Leaving the heat of the desert behind, I was starting to cautiously feel optimistic, like I might find an answer or two here. I was ready for this.

PART THREE

THE LAND OF PLENTY

MEETING ARROYO

After 8 hours of driving, I was feeling a bit drained, but not anywhere as tired as I thought I'd be. Besides, I counted on the crisp ocean air to rejuvenate me while I slept soundly tonight.

Throughout the drive, I kept noticing mile marker 111, or 11 more miles to my next exit, or I would randomly glance at the clock, and it would say 10:01, 11:01, and 1:01. In numerology, numbers with one in them usually meant new beginnings. I wondered if the universe was supporting these 11 days and if so, great. Maybe a prayer is being answered.

I was sure that if I talked to Bill tonight, his first question would be, "Did you hit traffic, and if so, how much time did you lose?" It was strange how time meant something different to me here. After I touched base and got my housesitting instructions from Tracy and Ed Martin, my time would be my own.

Tracy and Ed expected me at 6 P.M., and it was only 5 o'clock now. At the last gas station stop, I realized that I might be running an hour ahead of schedule, so, before taking off, I took a quick look at the map Bill printed out for me and traced with my finger from their house to the nearest beach. I made a mental note to go west at their exit, rather than east, if I wanted to say hi to the ocean first and maybe catch the sunset. I couldn't think of a better place to launch my 11 days.

After I saw the sign "BEACH," a wave of excitement shot through me. My entire life had circled around the dream of living in a beach house. This was now a chance to play "make believe." I followed the winding road, lowering the windows so I could take in the cool seventy degrees and the abundant earthy scents. At this point, I couldn't see the ocean, but the smell of beach was in the air. I took a deep breath in. It seemed easier to breathe here. *What a difference from how I was feeling this morning!* And I could have sworn my wrinkles were smoothing out as I crossed the state line. *Is that even possible?* I felt welcomed by the tall beach grass that lined the road. As I drove past, it waved to me, as it gently swayed in the late afternoon breeze. The chaos in me, the busyness, the war I had been fighting like a mad dog, wanted to know that peace in the sway of that grass.

Upon arrival, the entrance sign read, "WELCOME to ARROYO BEACH".

I pulled into the full parking lot and drank in the ocean view from up close. I couldn't help but smile as I turned into a spot, hearing the sand squish under my tires. Without hesitation, I hopped out of the truck and headed toward the beach, scanning the surroundings of what I knew would be my new home for the next 11 days. I saw a snack bar and a restaurant called The Brown Pelican, off to the north of me. Mounds of seaweed were scattered across the neatly raked sand. I liked this beach. Not too fancy, just a beach where you could relax. It didn't seem to have a lot of tourists, which I appreciated, because I didn't want to have to see happy couples and families on vacation, or worse, meet new people.

I used to be a people person, but as of late, people seemed to have ruined that for me. Funny, how over the years, I'd been highly criticized for being too nice to certain people in Tucson, North Carolina, and Chicago. I was told that I was too open and vulnerable and needed to stand my ground more with those who appeared to be taking advantage of me. I understood what they meant, but I was always drawn to see and find the good in others, and it wasn't hard for me to feel hopeful for them, no matter how skewed their intentions and agendas may have been. In the past, I'd never felt like they had the power to hurt me or take anything away from me, so maybe it's true that I trusted too many people over the years. Until now. These days, I was starting to agree with those who had occasionally warned me. This, "No More Mrs. Nice Girl," was probably a safer place for me to be now. I get it. It's a cutthroat world, and we got our asses handed to us. Time to grow up. *I guess.*

Over the years, I'd always found some significance in my astrological sign. Based on all the readings I had received, I was usually described as a typical watery Pisces. I could be strong, by being flexible, just like water can flow in and out of everything and everywhere. As a Pisces, I could sometimes be described as elusive and sometimes mysterious, and if people unfairly wanted something from me, I could slip away when cornered, just as water will do if you try to hold on too tight. *Where was that part of me today?* Everyone seemed to have access to and a hold on me in a negative way. *I must be closer to being ice, rather than water.*

As I reflected on my next stop, the house I'd be staying in for the next 11 days, I recalled the street name: Los Pinos Street. With my limited knowledge of Spanish, it hit me: Los Pinos meant The Pines.

Hmmm. Weird.

THE PINES

As a child, the Pines was a regular vacation spot in Wisconsin. My family, and about ten others would visit there every other summer. The cabins were broken down and musty. Lake Michigan was choppy and cold, and if you dared to swim, you'd have to wade through schools of monster carp. Even in my mother's arms, I was horrified to enter the water because they behaved starved as their mouths opened and closed perpetually while bumping up into our calves. Other than when my sister and the older kids occasionally went water-skiing, we all pretty much stayed away from that lake and spent most of our time in the big pool. Night and day activities consisted of campfires, horseshoes, Jarts, and hide-and-seek, most of which I only observed, being too little to engage in the fun of it all.

The Beatles' hit song, "Hey Jude" played on the jukebox in the kids clubhouse. The older kids teased me, while they act convincingly that the song was written for me. As a toddler, I sat on a stool next to my brother, who was deeply entranced in breaking another pinball record. He paused, looking away from his game, and said, "Don't worry, your name is Judrick, not Judy."

He always teased me, but I didn't mind. He was funny to me. On rainy days, we played cards like Go Fish and Old Maid, or the lady behind the desk would pull out well-worn board games like Candyland, or Monopoly for the older kids. Her book collections were just as used, and I loved pretending to read them before I was able to read. It would crack my brother and sister up.

The most impactful memory for me, happened when I was three. The dads were off in the deep end playing a competitive game of water volleyball. The splashes were huge, coming from some of the heavyset dads, hurling themselves through water and air, like breaching whales, to get to the ball. These were competitive men, all athletes in their day, so even a horseshoe competition became a serious affair. I adored my dad, and because he worked so often and I never saw him, I wanted to be closer to him. So, I carefully sat on the metal stairs that entered the deep end, wearing a navy blue bikini with a white embroidered anchor on the top.

"Uh-uh, Judy! Back up on the cement," my mother said, pointing to me with her lit cigarette in hand, while my dad was deeply consumed in the game, competing like an Olympian.

I could tell, even at my young age, that he adored me. I felt joy when I was with him. He made me feel like I mattered. I knew that gaining his attention while he was focused on his friends was not going to happen, so I waited patiently. And I waited and waited some more. I realized that the game might never end, and so I experimented with the ladder. I flipped around with my back towards him and took a step down to the next stair and then to the next one. With my mouth closed and nose under water, I started to make bubbles, just like I had learned in swimming lessons at the YMCA months before. I bobbed up and down like a frog in water, while one hand held onto the ladder's railing.

I had full view of my mom, now smoking her next cigarette and smoothing Hawaiian tropic oil, which smelled like coconuts, on her already-shiny, dark tanned legs. I stared at her to see if she was going to catch me and order me out of the pool. I knew she surely would be mad if she saw where I was now. *I don't belong here.* I had just started swimming lessons and had never even been to the deep end. I leaned back a bit, so my ears were under water. I liked the underwater noise: the laughter, the muffled screams for the ball, the other kids giggling in the shallow end, the mom's laughing at each other's jokes. The next thing I remember is sitting on the bottom of the pool, cross-legged. Complete peace. Eyes wide open and studying the dads' hairy legs above me. I saw the ball hit the water and a dad plunge for it. His eyes met mine. IT WAS MY DAD! *Hi, Didderdee!* I thought with joy.

I was startled to see his blue eyes staring back at me in horror; I had never seen him look at me like that before. It scared me. He grasped my arm so roughly that it felt like my shoulder had popped out of its socket. The underwater muffled laughter turned into screams, and within moments I was looking at the same hairy legs, except now they were all standing over me on the concrete pool deck. Moms were crying and yelling at their kids. "Stand back! Call for HELP!"

People were punching my chest and abruptly turning me over and pounding my back. There were shouts of, "We need help, she's not responding!" I wanted to say words, like, "I'm okay," but it was like a dream where you try to scream, and nothing comes out. Once on my side, I was able to see my brother and sister. They were standing on the other side of the pool, shivering, even though it was a hot, muggy July day. They stared at me with the same shocked look as my dad. I knew they were scared, and I wished they'd hold hands to comfort one another. But they just didn't seem to like each other that much. I tried to smile at them, but I couldn't move my mouth. Something was stopping me from taking a breath in and I thought it might just be okay if I didn't breathe. It didn't hurt at all. I had thought that same thing at the bottom of the pool: *It doesn't hurt.* It was so peaceful, and something felt okay about it.

My mom and dad continued to move me into various positions to see if they could expel the water in my lungs, I guess. I vomited the water and was gifted a breath. After the resort doctor arrived, my dad's horror started to subside. My dad insisted that I lay on his lap while the doctor checked me out, "But sir, it would be better if you laid her on the ground," the resort doctor explained.

"No, don't move her. She's all right here," my dad demanded.

I remembered sitting on his lap, curled up into his chest, both of us soaking wet, both of us shivering in the heat of the day. Everybody had a collective sigh of relief, and I heard my parents say, "We'll all catch up later for dinner in the rec hall. We're gonna let little Judy rest."

Our family of five solemnly walked back to our musty cabin. I sat tall on my dad's shoulders, which was my favorite place to be. He walked close to a tree line, knowing I would reach for the branches, as I always liked to do in our own yard at home. I had been sleeping on my own little cot next to my brother's and sister's beds, and when we entered, my mom and dad announced new sleeping arrangements. I would now spend the rest of the vacation in their bed. *I couldn't be more thrilled!*

———

Los Pinos, (aka The Pines), was the street where I'd stay for the next 11 days in Santa Barbara, and it dawned on me, Arroyo Beach may need to be the place where I finally face my fear of water. I could swim in pools, but lakes and oceans were greatly feared. Bill always said, "You need to face this, so we can have our beach house someday."

And then my regular negativity popped in: *We're so far from ever having a beach house, why waste time facing that fear?* I instantly resented the reality of my situation, which slapped me so hard in this beautiful setting. I tried to shake it off by deeply breathing in the crisp saltwater air.

I closed my eyes and listened to the waves fold into the shore while shifting my thoughts: *Beach house or no beach house, it's irrelevant. I'm 38. It's time to do this.*

MEET & GREET

Interesting people congregated on this beach. They looked like "regulars" rather than tourists. I hoped I'd just blend in, unnoticed. A 70-something year old man walked with a cane and an oxygen tank. He wore a fishing cap with many different lures pinned to it. The last of the day's sunshine caught some of the shinier ones, and the light ricocheted from his hat. *What a colorful character.* He noticed me too, and I started to feel that I might not be blending in. He stopped walking and stared me down.

It was getting close to 6 P.M., and I didn't want to keep Tracy and Ed waiting. I didn't want to miss the sunset, either, but reminded myself there were nine sunsets and ten sunrises left. I felt I needed to see them all. I always felt that a sunset gave us permission for closure so that we can begin again tomorrow with the sunrise.

I made my way back to the Denali, and before getting in, dusted the sand off one foot while balancing on the other. Clumsily, I slid one shoe on, lost balance and gently fell against the car.

"Evening."

Looking up, I saw a striking young man, about 25 years old. I was immediately stunned by his good looks; he looked like the actor, Paul Walker, from "The Fast and Furious." His light brown-blonde hair had been highlighted by the sun, and his smooth, tanned chest led down to chiseled abs. He'd unfolded his black wet suit from his torso to below his navel. Quickly, I forced my eyes up because they were naturally leading to where I was afraid to look.

I was stunned that I had walked right past without even noticing him. *How dead am I? Am I a shut-down 38-year-old biddy? What the hell happened to me? I don't ever recall being this awkward.*

Bill had called me frigid one time in our marriage, and I practically divorced him in a state of rage. Today, I was disgusted because I might have to agree.

"Hi," I responded, awkwardly.

I watched him effortlessly place his surfboard on the roof-rack of his Jeep, thinking he could do it in his sleep. His triceps and traps rippled and shifted as he adjusted the board on the roof. His thighs and butt were in perfect proportion, round, and firm. While looking at his strong-jawed profile, I noticed the transparency of his blue eyes as they reflected the last light of this day. The only visual flaw I noticed were his feet. His bare feet looked like they had taken a beating. He walked on pavement, pebbles and assorted rocks with ease like a barefooted American Indian might do on our unforgiving desert floor. I imagined his battered feet were the result of constant surfing, skateboarding, running barefoot on beaches and maybe scraped on coral while scuba diving. They just didn't fit the rest of him. I was happy that he wasn't totally perfect, though, because that would just be too much. God must have known this when he created this man.

This was a water boy for sure, Cali-born-and-raised. He probably spent every waking minute on a scanner for news of waves and weather conditions for surfing. "Arizona, huh?" he asked.

"What? How'd you know that?" I answered, thinking, *oh my God, he may be psychic. Let's just hope he can't read my awkward mind.*

"The plates," he nodded with a smile while whipping his hair to the right to keep it out of his eyes—the way Paul used to. It was just as natural for him, as it was for Paul.

My face flushed, "Oh. Yeah right, the plates."

Clearly, I was in touch with the part of me who spent too much time asking if everyone's hands were washed, beds were made, teeth were brushed and if toilets were flushed. *I'm such a dork.* And on top of that, this is a 25-year-old kid who could have anyone he wants, and I'm worrying about how *I'm* coming off to him? *I'm embarrassing myself.*

It's been one hour since arrival, and I'm already not liking the person I'm traveling with. I thought.

"Here for vacation?" he asked.

"You could say that," I said, feeling a tiny bit more in control.

The old man with the oxygen tank was looking at us both now.

"Hey, who is that guy?" I asked.

The young man turned to look over his shoulder and waved to the old man. He waved back.

"Oh, that dude is Bayard Stockton. He's a writing professor at the UCSB, the University of California-Santa Barbara. Walks here every day, sometimes, three times a day. Cool dude. Ex-CIA. Really freakin' smart. World traveled. Every fishing hook and item pinned to his hat are from the beaches he has walked. Loves the ladies. He's pretty ill. Poor dude."

He turned back to me, "How long will you be here?"

"Eleven days," still watching Bayard watch us.

He held his hand out, "I'm Sean, by the way."

While shaking his hand, I silently renamed him *Hottie* as I responded, "I'm Judy."

"Where you stayin'?"

"You sure have a lot of questions for having just met a stranger."

Looking into the back window of my Denali, he said, "A L V A R E Z. Nice guitar."

Nodding yes, "My husband bought it for me."

I realized that might be news to him because I hadn't been wearing my wedding ring. The ring was in the car, but I wasn't planning on wearing it. I hadn't put it on for many months but felt weird just leaving it in Tucson. Bill hadn't been wearing his either, but I didn't know for how long. It had been months as well.

It occurred to me: what if I hadn't mentioned that I had a husband? What if this was my opportunity for payback for the new assertive and inquisitive HER from Bill's old company, or for him saying, "Fine. Go," when I first told him about the trip. Technically, I was in a space where I could say I'm in a midlife crisis. If this marriage is over, I could literally go out with a bang.

Hottie was talking a lot, but my mind was already deep into a dreamland filled with logistics of how this could even get started. What would it feel like to flirt and then take it to the next level? Maybe I should see this as the universe giving me a gift—the chance to feel this gorgeous young man's naked abs against my body. To feel his lean, ripped arms wrapped around my waist. His lips on mine. Nobody would ever have to know I did this. There may be another HER, so what's the difference to our marriage? *He deserves this. I really deserve this.*

But who was I kidding? He probably guessed my age, noticed my wrinkles, saw the SUV's juice box stains and the cracker crumbs crushed into the crevices of the seats, and thought, *She may have had some looks in her younger days, but today this is a totally broken and wrecked housewife.* He might've even described me, as he'd described Bayard, with a dismissive "poor thing."

I was poor all right.

Yep, it appeared this trip was going to be a *Judy-bashing trip.* Eleven days to rip her to shreds. I needed to get away from this perfect young specimen, which was highlighting each and every flaw of my own.

"So, you stayin' at a hotel in town?"

He sure was a curious one.

"Nope. Housesitting."

"Oh cool. Frugal."

Laughing, "If you only knew. I'm staying on a street called Los Pinos."

"Hmm. Whose house?"

"Tracy and Ed Martin," I answered.

Whipping his bangs to the side again, "Hmm, cool."

He stared at me like he knew exactly what he was doing.

At one of his past workshops, Tony Robbins' taught people how to master the way they *looked* at a partner. This guy had it down. During that workshop, we had to partner up with a stranger and practice "our look." My male partner, an overweight, balding accountant, awkwardly stared into my eyes, while we laughed hysterically at first. But he soon nailed his "look," and I screamed, "Oh MY GOD, that's it!"

He was shocked that the successful look that "got" me was on his face. I don't know if that was "the look" his wife was going to fall for, but he had my number, for sure. I grabbed the accountants round face and told him to freeze what that felt like and try it on her.

I couldn't recall the last time I saw Bill's "look" and felt that same "got me" feeling. Maybe he was all "looked" out as far as I was concerned. *I was betting the HER from his old company had seen it.*

Sean's look not only "got" me, it stunned me and then flipped me inside out. Did he know it got me? If so, I may be in trouble. After a bit more small talk, he suddenly shifted gears, acting as if he was in a hurry to leave. He hopped in his Jeep and gave me a wave. "See ya aroun' then."

As I pulled out, I saw the Professor from out of the corner of my eye. Still staring in my direction, he raised his right hand with his cane in it, as if to say, "See you soon." Hesitantly, I waved back, not sure if he had been waving to someone other than me. After I had turned to look behind and around me, I turned back to him. He pointed his cane towards me, as if to say, "Yeah, I'm talkin' to you."

That was strange.

You do realize, Judy, that your friends are just me in disguise? Pulling out all the stops and starts to reach you, love you, and see you. The Universe – Mike Dooley

While in the car, I dialed our home number to tell Bill I arrived, but there was no answer. *Thank God*, I thought, I didn't want to talk to him. I heard two beeps after the recorded voicemail's outgoing message, notifying me that we had a message to be heard. I hesitated because it was probably our lawyer with more bad news. But I had a feeling I had to hear it, so I entered the password and listened.

Nicole's lisping baby voice came on: "Mommy? HI. It's me... Nicole. I hope you are having... fun. I wuv you... and I will talk to you, waiter. Okay?"

Then I heard her say to her dad, "Okay, do I hang up now or," and then he sharply cut her off and said, "Yeah. Hang-up."

Apparently, he probably had enough of her asking to call me that he side-tracked her and let her leave a message on our home phone rather than on my cell where I would have answered. She would never know the difference because you can't hear those voicemail messages unless you type in the code like I had just done. *Wow, who was he protecting? Nicole? Me? Himself? Or was this something he would punish me with later for leaving?*

While on the drive to Los Pinos, I calculated the time difference and started to obsess about what all four of them would be doing at that exact moment. They're probably at football practice, I decided. But it felt good not being in charge of knowing those details right now.

The house was 2.9 miles away, and I drove about 7 minutes to Los Pinos. I drove through a family neighborhood and past the front of the house; it was a charming 1920's Craftsman bungalow. The pale sage, gray-and-tan exterior matched the 7-foot hedges around the property. The yard had 18-foot oak trees that shaded both the back brick patio and the huge, grassy front yard. I went around to the back driveway leading to the garage. Noticing an apartment above the garage sent a sense of panic that I may not be alone. I hoped it was empty.

A quick glance at all the crap in the backseat and cargo area left me embarrassed. The plan was to figure out what to bring in and what not to. Bill was right; it looked like I might be moving here for good. Carefully, I opened the back door of the Denali, studying the brilliant way Bill had repacked all my belongings. I hadn't seen it until now. He had bungee corded everything in place like he always did on our road trips. Being an ex-paramedic, he knew that people died in accidents when unsecured items flew around inside of the vehicle. This made him hyper-vigilant, and we were always under a complete lockdown when we traveled.

"Wow, you are locked up tight."

Noticing a familiar voice, I turned around.

It was the Hottie.

What is he doing here?

"You live here?" I asked.

He whipped his hair to the right with a nod to the apartment above the garage.

'Why didn't you mention that?"

"I wanted to surprise you. You're fun to catch off guard. I'm gettn' a kick out of ya."

Tracy came out the back door with her two dogs trailing behind her. Sean knew them well, and they obviously liked him. She was short with a medium build and had warm brown eyes. Her shiny brown bob bounced and swayed as she walked towards us.

"Hey, Tracy," he said. She was perfectly comfortable with him and replied, "Hey, Sean."

Ed followed them out, and we all were formally introduced. Ed was the same size and similar height of Tracy. They were a cute couple with similar coloring and features. I wasn't sure what he did for a living, but I got the feeling he'd done all the remodeling of the bungalow and the apartment above the garage, so he was handy for sure.

"How do you two know each other?" Tracy asked, perplexed.

"We just met at the beach," he explained, laughing, "Bayard had an eye on her."

"Oh, geez, well be careful. He's on his last legs, but he's still a little dangerous with the ladies."

Feeling a little more at ease, I could imagine blending in like a "regular" eventually. I'd already met a few people who called that beach their home, and I had ten more days to call it mine.

Hottie turned toward me, now wearing faded jeans and a well-worn, long sleeved white-cotton T-shirt that smelled freshly laundered. "Well, lemme know if I can give ya a hand while you're here. I have school and work, but I'm aroun'. If surf's up, I'll be getting' wet. And oh," pointing to ALVAREZ in the back of my truck, "if you wanna jam, I'm hosting an open mic night next week; my boys and I are playin' at a place off State." He leaned into me and gave me a polite half hug.

It felt good to feel that hug, even though it was just friendly in nature.

After he walked away, Tracy chimed, "He's studying music at UCSB. Really talented guitar player. His band is awesome. You should take him up on that open mic. Well, c'mon in, let me show you 'round. By the way," pointing to a short, stocky, black-and-white Tibetan terrier, "this is our baby boy, Maximilian."

I bent over to pet his long soft fur, and his tail wagged with great excitement. I knew we'd get along well.

"And this is our other fur baby, a mixed terrier and mixed personality to match, Titus," she said, laughing.

As I bent to pet him, his short, stubby tail stayed still. He reminded me of a schnauzer, but even more serious. I guessed he'd eventually warm up to me.

"Sam I Am, our cat, dislikes most, so he's hiding. Don't take it personally. You may *never* see him. But please keep feeding him," she giggled.

All of the sudden, I felt ill and panic set in. There was only one bathroom. *What if they haven't left for the airport yet and I need to use it?* My stomach was so fragile, and I was really growing tired of this at my age. As we stepped inside, I was temporarily distracted to see the beautiful fir hardwood floors, floated ceilings and original windows complemented by a new kitchen & bath. The new wood floor and paint scents proved a recent rehab project. Both bedrooms had been updated, as well, with retextured walls and ceilings, and cool contemporary lighting throughout. To me, it felt like a Crate and Barrel floor room, with touches of original art tastefully placed. I could not be more pleased. *This was no Horehole.*

Naturally, Tracy and Ed wanted to know who was going to be staying in their house and taking care of their adored pets, and so they asked great questions about my family, my work and my life in general. I was disgusted that I wasn't able to share anything positive, except in regards to my children. If I had shared the whole truth, I would've had to include the financial crash, the weak marriage, the dumpy rentals, Bill's dead-end jobs, my shitty support system, and my hypnotherapy practice that I couldn't personally stomach... It was all frankly embarrassing that we fell from that high. And then there's the fact that I was such a weak-ass, whining bitch about it all. Giving them a watered-down version, to avoid setting off any alarms, seemed like the safest plan.

I also found it necessary to mention nothing about acid reflux, ulcers, and irritable bowel becoming a constant in my life. I had already practiced keeping that to myself because Bill's agitation and annoyance of any ill condition would literally take my symptoms to a whole new level. I mostly directed blame to our circumstances and to him. At times, I literally felt my insides clench as they tried to survive him, his depression and aggression. Lying about symptoms became mandatory. Getting away from him and our situation felt to be the key to recovery from these ailments, so I was surprised to feel ill. Among my packed items were some things that helped me physically in the past, and I was looking forward to getting my hands on the homeopathics, herbs, green drink powders, probiotics, B12, ginger, kombucha green tea, chamomile tea, and charcoal tablets I had brought.

Tracy showed me to my room: simple, comfortable and elegant. Almost everything in it was white. *Heaven.* The puffy cotton comforter looked inviting, and I planned on the best of sleep here. Two huge windows allowed natural filtered light into the room from the oak trees outdoors. I imagined myself reading, and for the first time in my life, taking afternoon naps. Tracy showed me some empty dresser drawers I could put my clothes in. She tucked her bangs behind one ear as she bent over and opened each drawer. She moved slowly and seemed more present than most. The drawers were lined with contact paper and had lavender satchels in each of them. Her attention to detail and organization made me think she must be an amazing middle-school teacher. Her organization reminded me of myself back in the North Carolina days. Since stepping foot in Tucson, it had been like our hair was on fire. We'd been in GO, GO, GO, and move, move, move mode so long, I hadn't taken the time to pay attention to details like this.

Tracy offered her beach hat and the bulky sweater that hung on a hook at the back door, for the beach walks I looked forward to. She thoughtfully had fanned out tourist flyers on a large dining room table of all the places in Santa Barbara, so I could completely fill my days and nights with activities if I so chose. I scanned the places, some of which I already scoped on the internet before coming. It wasn't like trying to jam everything into one weekend away, so I was sure I had plenty of time to fit it all in.

As we made our way back to the family room area, I pointed to a quartz crystal and her gardenia scented soy candles, "Seems we have a lot in common."

She nodded with a sincere smile.

My physical condition was getting worse, and dizziness started in. Bending over to pet the dog, I almost toppled over. Was it the drive? *Maybe I'm carsick for the first time?* I just wanted them to leave. I needed the bathroom to myself.

"Hey, Tracy, I know we had planned on possibly grabbing a bite before ya left. I may need to pass on dinner. I'm just so tired that I'd like to rest."

"No worries, hun, we're runnin' late anyway. We'll just grab somethin' on the way to the airport. That sure is a long drive, and you should rest."

She added excitedly, "You have 11 days to rejuvenate!"

Ed packed the trunk with their suitcases. They packed much lighter than me, and there were two of them. Knowing my digestive track had not been behaving, I had brought some bland foods, but the thought of food actually made me more nauseous. I worried that something was really wrong with me and wondered if I had made a mistake by coming.

"All set?" Ed yelled from the back patio. Tracy threw her purse over her shoulder, gave me a hug like we were old friends and yelled "Ready, Eddie!"

She turned to me, "See ya soon. Our contact info and vet info is on the sheet on the fridge. Call for whatever you need and e n j o y Judy!"

disEASE

Seconds after the back door closed, I raced to the bathroom, dropped to my knees and vomited. I was convinced that this had to be food poisoning, not stress. *Surely, I could not make myself this sick over stress.* Mulling over everything I had eaten for the last few days, nothing came to mind. Vomiting and diarrhea had their way with me, and I immediately closed the small window above the shower, so Hottie wouldn't hear me.

About 1 A.M. I awoke on the floor next to the bathtub. The damp, lukewarm washcloth I had pressed against my forehead became annoying.

"Cold cold. Oh my God. I need this cold," whispering to myself. My head throbbed, and my limbs were weak. I rinsed the washcloth in the kitchen sink with Tracy's lavender hand soap, then placed it in the freezer for a bit. I was desperate to get my toothbrush from the Denali but feared I'd be seen by Hottie. It would be just my luck. He's probably up studying or playing guitar or entertaining some hot Santa Barbara student. By now, I was wearing only underwear and the T-shirt I'd worn on the drive. I thought about sliding my jeans on but was too weak and exhausted. I decided I would only throw them on if I saw any of his lights on in the garage apartment.

Peeking out back, the coast looked clear. No lights on anywhere. With keys in hand, the mission was to get one thing: my toothbrush. But then I remembered what I was wearing, and added my pajamas, too. *Where did I put those? The top, bottom or middle of the suitcase.* I knew I didn't have the strength to grab the whole bag right now.

As I left the house, the screen door, slammed loudly behind me. I was halfway to the car, first tiptoeing and now sprinting because the dogs had started barking when they heard the screen door slam shut. At the top of his stairs leading to his apartment, I saw Hottie sitting in a chair on his small, square porch. I could see another guy sitting on a step next to him. They were looking down on me. Hottie had a joint in hand and was taking a drag. After stepping onto the driveway, the automatic motion-detector floodlights lit the place up like a freakin' carnival. He stayed cool as a cucumber and gestured, "Wanna hit?"

I grabbed my toiletry bag and gave a quick half wave. "No thanks. Night." With as much muster as I could manage, I rushed back into the house to quiet the dogs down. They seemed to forget that they had just met me, and they were still barking like I was an intruder. Hottie yelled, "HEY! Max! Titus! Stop!" And they stopped.

I closed and locked the door, and leaned my back against it while my body shook from the short, panicked sprint. *Can you make things any more awkward, Judy? Holy shit, Girl, you really need to get a grip.*

The rest of the evening was spent married to my washcloth, which smelled like lavender half the time and vomit the rest. Maximilian lay with me as I slept on the cold ceramic-tiled floor. We liked each other. I missed having a dog in my life. I had never not had one, until now. Our financial reality stung, which highlighted that having a pet would be a stupid and an irresponsible addition for us. It would be a long time before we could do that, according to Katie, the intuitive.

Titus was feisty with a quirky personality. His ears lay flat as he backed away every time I vomited, while Maximilian wasn't alarmed at all. Sam I Am, still had not made his presence known. I wasn't surprised, though. Due to the intuitive nature of most cats allowing them to sense whether they like your energy right away. I didn't blame him for not introducing himself tonight.

Whatever this dis-ease in my body was, it was not letting up, and I needed a healthcare strategy to act on. Calling Bill was absolutely out. He would be so annoyed that I took this trip and put everyone out, and then wasn't even able to embrace it. We obviously weren't in a place where he would be able to comfort me. I made a mental note to call Katie first thing in the morning and have her pull cards on this.

I hoped a reading could give me insight.

DAY 2
FAR FROM GOOD

My cell phone ring woke me up at 5:30 A.M. My face was pressed against the washcloth that lay on the floor. I wasn't feeling much better but managed to not throw up.

"Hello," I answered.

"Momma?"

"Oh, Marcus. Hi, honey. Whatcha doin?"

"Watchin' cartoons."

"Where's Dad?"

"Sleeping," he answered.

"What cartoons are you watchin'?"

He changed subjects, "Momma, I made a calendar, and I scratched one day off. Only ten more days."

"Yep, that's right. I really look forward to seeing that calendar, Marcus. How are Clint and Nicole? Okay?" I asked.

"Clint built a new ramp in Huey's yard. Oh, and Nicole cried herself to sleep after you left. She woke up after a couple hours, and when she went to scratch a day off, we told her she hadn't slept through a whole night yet, so she cried herself to sleep again."

"Oh, my. That's sad."

This was building a case of how huge of a mistake I made by coming here. Eleven days away is too long for them.

"Uh-huh. Dad says we're gonna get ice cream when the truck comes around. Maybe that will make her happy. Oh! And I tried to teach her that thing you taught me about *dolphins in... pain out...* 'member that time I had Lyme disease, and they had to stick needles in me, and you taught me to say that... cause it is a happy chemical or somethin'?"

"Um, yes... but it's *'endorphins in and pain out'*..." I corrected him and couldn't resist smiling.

"Oh... maybe that's why it didn't work," he said.

"Oh, and Dad yelled at someone on the phone named Frank. He told Frank 'to go to hell' and then he said, 'Never mind, you're already there,' and Frank hung up on him. What does that even mean? Is he like the devil or what? And is Frank Jake's dad? I hope that wasn't Jake's dad!" He said with worry.

"Oh, honey, no. He isn't the devil. How about when Daddy's on business calls, you stay as far away as possible because, for your age, those calls are just too confusing to explain. And, as far as Jake goes, don't discuss your Dads right now. They will talk things out eventually. You know it's been hard for Dad, and I'm so sorry that you are exposed to all of this."

"It's fine. So, how's Momma? Did you eat my goldfish?"

OH, the goldfish. That actually sounded like a good idea. I need to get those from the truck soon.

"I'm good honey, and I ate some goldfish during the drive. That was a perfect snack. Thank you, and I'll eat the rest today. I'm going to rest a little bit, but call me anytime okay?"

"Okay. Bye, Momma."

"Bye. Honey. I love you."

I was beyond exhausted and wanted to feel a bed underneath my body, so I took a warm shower, dried myself off with their thick, white, fluffy towel and crawled into the guest bed, naked. I brushed my teeth, but didn't bother with lotion, or even brushing my hair. It felt so good to not care at all about how I looked or to even bother dressing. If I were home, I would tidy up enough so that I wouldn't worry the kids or annoy Bill. The bed was mushy and comfy, unlike ours at home. I appreciated the white cotton fluffy down comforter, which felt cool to the touch and heavy, in a good way, as it lay on top of me. All the nice things we used to have, had either been sold with the house in The Canyons or let go in garage sales. Sadly, all that was left was trashed by now just because of the numerous moves.

Tracy had left the window cracked, and the cool, damp air blew across my body. It felt refreshing having this down comforter draped over part of me, giving me both the coolness and warmth I was seeking.

Because of the stomach acting like another brain, when in distress, it seems to wreak havoc on the nervous system. I started to feel terribly uneasy and fragile as another anxiety attack hit me hard. I threw the covers over my head and prayed to God, *Please God, wake me up when this is fucking over.* I had plenty of people who would talk me off the ledge of these "spells," and now that I had made this commitment to stay clear of all of them, there was no one to come to my rescue. I just finally started to notice that all of those I was leaning on, over the past years, had messages that were not totally resonating with me. I started to see their agendas, and the sometimes misguided intentions to serve their own stories and belief systems, not my own. I struggled with my tendency to be a doormat and not speak up about this. Instead, I either withdrew from them or worse, just agreed, by going along with it. I'd surrounded myself with others to feel safe because they told me what I wanted to hear. I wasn't sure if anyone was telling me the truth because I hadn't slowed down enough to know what the truth was anymore. I obviously had to break out of this and attempt a new way to heal. I have tools here to help. *No more excuses. I have to do this on my own.*

For the last three years, my thoughts could not have been more clouded with negativity, doubt and hopelessness. Today, I was feeling the deep pockets of just that, and it was gaining momentum. I had a feeling that if the Tucson turbulence were to continue another year, I'd be in dangerous shape. Once in a while, something like the crisp fresh airflow through the window would pull me out of a negative thought and I'd slip into a purer thought. This thinking rekindled memories of my first recollections, as a little girl.

Over the years, family members often shared stories of me and the effortless joy I had as a child. I loved those stories. I sat on the edges of their laps always entertained by them sharing the details again. Apparently, as an infant, I often awoke in the middle of the night, but not to cry. They would describe my high-pitched laughter, babbling and giggles, waking those that were asleep. When approached, I would stare around their faces and coo as if I were talking to someone else. My grandma would squeeze me tight in her lap, laughing while she shared the story of when she watched me for a long weekend and had to put my crib in the hallway because it kept her and my grandpa up. But today, I was far from that little girl and I couldn't seem to manage to stay steady in the more positive mental and emotional places for any length of time.

I drifted off to sleep and awoke to more vomiting. Dragging myself into the shower, I hoped I was nearing the end of this. I was heartbroken I had now spent DAY TWO entirely inside, with the exception of letting the dogs out and feeding them. No beach. No yoga class. No food. No sightseeing. Just dehydrated and not seeing any relief.

I broke down and called Bill.

No answer. *Was he not answering on purpose now?*

Somehow, I slept through it.

DAY 4
KEEP THE FAITH

Anxiously, I shot up and out of bed so fast, and bolted into the kitchen to look at the dog bowls filled with half-eaten dried dog food. The startled dogs began barking and tearing through the house.

"What happened here… what the hell day is it?" I said, as if my furry friends understood.

I sprinkled more dry food into their bowls, but they declined. Feeling relief that they seemed somehow satiated, I started investigating.

It was just past noon, and, according to the date on my cell phone, I had completely slept through an entire day! Still feeling sick, I scrambled to look at my phone to check for missed calls from Marcus, Clint or Nicole. *No missed messages.* Suddenly overwhelmed with homesickness, I scrambled to find the TV remote in the family room and scanned through the channels until I came to a cartoon. I set the volume low and let the playful sounds fill the house to comfort me. I wished they were here to lay in my bed, or for me to lay in theirs. My chicks, all in the nest, comforted me many times in the past, and it actually hurt not to have them here. Energetically spent after my sprint to the kitchen and back, I crawled back into bed, lying on my side as I rechecked the date on my phone. *Did I pass out? But the dogs seem happy and fed. What in the hell?*

Most everything was still packed in the car. I was horrified I'd run into Hottie again while retrieving my belongings, so I opted to wait until I was sure I heard his car leave. Exhausted, I pulled the comforter over half of my body and realized my frailty. *I may need urgent care and an IV drip.* But before I figured out how to manage that outing, I decided to check in with Katie to get a brief reading to see what was going on with my body. As I began searching for Katie's number in my cell phone, my phone rang. Figuring it was a call from Marc or maybe Nicole now, I answered by saying, "Hi, sweetie."

"Hi, Judy, it's Katie Campano. Welcome to Santa Barbara girl!" she said, cheerfully.

"Oh my God! I was just looking for your number and wondered if it was okay to call you. I need a reading."

"Oh goodness, you sound horrible, what's goin' on?"

"I'm sooo sick. I literally just missed an entire day with no recollection of it. I've had dis-ease issues with digestion and stress, but this is over the top, Katie. I don't even know if I can stay here by myself. I'm contemplating going to see a doctor and getting IV fluids."

"Okay, okay, let's see what the cards say here, 'cause they were outstanding in regards to this trip when we last checked. Let's see if they shifted."

OMG. Shifted??? Just kill me now.

"Ok, hon, same great cards are comin' up and then some."

Thank God, I thought as I braced myself before hearing more.

"I don't see dis-ease due to stress. I see it as a Kundalini awakening."

This was disturbing information because the unprepared people I knew that had gone through this in the past suffered greatly, and even the prepared seemed to get hit hard as well. In the past, I had read about how Kundalini energy centers attached to chakra centers can awaken spontaneously, for no obvious reason, or be triggered by intense personal experiences such as accidents, near-death experiences, childbirth, emotional trauma or extreme mental stress. Some sources attribute spontaneous awakenings to the "grace of God," or possibly to spiritual practice in past lives.

I continued to silently recall all of the information I read on this and the download was making me worse. A spontaneous awakening in one who is unprepared, or without the assistance of a good teacher, can result in an experience that has been called a "Kundalini crisis," "spiritual emergency" or "Kundalini syndrome." The symptoms are said to resemble those of a Kundalini awakening but are experienced as unpleasant, overwhelming or out of control. Unpleasant side effects are said to occur when the practitioner has not approached Kundalini with due respect or in a narrow, egotistical manner. Kundalini has been described as a highly creative intelligence, which dwarfs our own. This awakening, therefore, requires surrender; it's not energy that can be manipulated by the ego.

Katie interrupted my silent recollection, "I should have known when I first saw the cards. The only way to get these outcomes is to go through a significant awakening. So, yes, it's definitely a Kundalini awakening. You know what that is?"

"Yes, unfortunately, I do. Fuck!"

She wasn't used to my foul mouth.

"Now, now," she soothed, "it's all right. Do yoga and meditation to open yourself up. You may want to consider some self-hypnosis. You're a hypnotherapist, right? Have you even tried that? And, knock off the judgment of self. I can see that's strong right now. Be kind to yourself. And, Judy, the blame on others sucking up your light is something to consider. It's you who's having trouble lighting your own darkness."

After the call, while lying on the floor with Maximilian sprawled out by my head, I felt his warm breath on the side of my face and neck. Since I was too weak to get my guitar, I just lay there on my back and sang the one song I seemed always to be attracted to during some of my darker married days, except today it wasn't about the marriage. It was about the inability to light my own darkness. For the first time, I sang Elton John's "Don't Let The Sun Go Down on Me," to myself. I was stuck and tired. Losing everything: money, marriage, self, and now faith… felt like the sun going down on me.

Maximilian plopped one paw on my shoulder as I sang. I continued to deliver the lyrics directly to the part of myself I was clearly having trouble with. Katie was right when she mentioned on the phone: I was unable to light my own darkness, and I was too late to catch myself from falling. This left me knowing I was no longer able to turn back and pretend that I didn't have work to do here. And then it dawned on me: This had nothing to do with Bill or the dis-ease I had been blaming him for: "I get sick because he stresses me out." I was no longer able to hide behind that any longer.

Sitting up, I made myself as comfortable as possible on the floor. While I sat cross-legged on top of a floor pillow, the dogs circled and settled into their positions, pressing against each side of me. As I petted them, I took a breath in through my nose and out through my mouth, focusing on the flow, by first following their breathing pattern. I practiced some familiar self-hypnosis I'd often taught others and hoped I'd begin to calm down. Unfortunately, these initial relaxation steps weren't effective. I tried and tried again. No relief. I shot up from the floor, recognizing that I was going to need to roll my sleeves up more, utilize the many years of teachings, and implement all the tools I had waiting in the truck. *Let's start over.* To begin, I took a hot shower while standing in baking soda, Epsom salt and lavender essential oil, just to clear my energy.

After the shower, standing in front of the steamed mirror allowed me to only to see my silhouette. I noticed how easily I pulled the brush through my hair, thanks to the soft water in their house. Smoothing lotion onto my face, neck, arms and legs became trance-like.I didn't let myself become distracted by the dark circles under my eyes. With my index finger, I wrote BEGIN WITHIN on the steamed-up mirror while watching the tiny beads of water fall from the words. Catching a glimpse of myself, I said, "Come on now, you got this."

I slid my faded jeans on and pulled a loose white low V-neck tee over my head. While layering some more sweet lavender and bergamot body lotion, I took a deep breath from my cupped hands, letting the scent in. I was dizzy from dehydration, so I filled a glass with tap water, which I prayed would be well received by my body. My wet hair drenched the back of my tee, leaving me chilled as I briskly walked outside to get the tools I had collected throughout the years of studies.

Silently, I carried my bag in, convincing myself that these were the right tools to push me out of a Kundalini awakening like no other. I thought, *I'll get grounded, aligned and I'll feel better soon.* I knew exactly what to do and say and think and pray. I had everything I needed to heal. With good intention I thought, *everything is going to be all right.*

Displayed like a gift shop on top of the dining table were my journal, tarot cards, angel cards, and my special soy candle; the one that may have waited to be a part of this needed healing ritual. Also, there were spirit and animal guide cards, purchased and home-made affirmation cards, meditation CDs, a yoga mat, my Bible, the Tao, hypnotherapy CDs, books by my favorite authors, alternative health books, Reiki and hands-on healing books, and, of course, some sheet music with lonely ALVAREZ, leaning against the table.

Holding the Bible in my two hands, I opened it to a random page: **ROMANS 15:13: "May the God of hope fill you with all the joy and peace in believing so that by the power of the Holy Spirit you may abound in hope."**

"Amen," I whispered.

I went from one item to the next, expecting relief from the anxiety billowing inside me. But my unease continued to grow like a snowball rolling downhill. After a couple hours of dabbling with the tools, relief had not emerged. It was as if, I were making myself worse. I ate one goldfish cracker and threw it up. Took one sip of kombucha tea, which had always offered some relief, but not now! Not today! Apparently, I had spent years on workshops, certifications, and healing methods only to find that today they were ineffective. My mind spun in circles of disappointment in all those days and hours lost learning and practicing those modalities of spiritual, emotional and mental practices.

I suffered through the early afternoon and then broke down and reached out to Bill.

"Hello?"

It was Day Four, and, for a second, I forgot about the present "us" and remembered how I felt with the past "us." Maybe the desperation of the dis-ease made me that way. My throat tightened to try to cover up my cry, which came from just hearing his voice.

He heard it in me right away, "Oh God, you okay?"

"I'm so sick, Bill. I think I need to be seen by a doctor. Katie, that intuitive, said it's a Kundalini awakening, but I don't know. It's getting worse, too. I haven't even been to the beach, except for a short time when I first arrived. I've missed sunrises and sunsets. I haven't left the house or eaten, barely even drank water..."

The anxiety was gaining momentum as I continued to ramble on: "And, I heard Nicole's heartbreaking voicemail message. Marc is missing me, and simply I probably screwed up here by coming. Clint's probably messed up because of it."

I was crying, which he always wanted to fix with immediacy.

"Hey, hey, hey, you need to calm down. You're just getting yourself more worked up."

Knowing my past dis-eases and his belief that I tend to "overreact" to them, I expected him to come down strong and hard saying, "Suck it up."

Instead, he came off as more gentle and said, "Aw, not again. Well, maybe you should be seen. But you know how you have worked through these trying times before."

"Yes, but this feels worse. It's scaring the shit out of me."

Instead of arguing that it probably was not a Kundalini awakening, or that it was not the worst I've ever felt, he just listened to me talk it through. It's not that he didn't believe in the possibility of a Kundalini awakening, but because of the fires burning in his world, he didn't have time or energy to dissect that. It was easier for him to believe this was stress or just regular old food poisoning. Plus, he looked at imbalance in the body in a different way. He didn't have a fear of it like I did.

Once, when we were in Key West on vacation, his appendix burst in a surgeon's hand. Just hours before the emergency surgery, he had tried to have sex with me, and he also had eaten an enormous tray of breakfast foods from the hotel buffet. After he had thrown that up, he ate some more, thinking it would fix his "stomach ache." After repeated demands from me to take him to a doctor, he succumbed, but only after I let him take down the convertible top on the Mustang we'd rented. "If I'm goin' to the hospital, I at least, want to enjoy the drive with the Gulf on one side and the ocean on the other," he negotiated.

I obliged and handed him a barf bag.

An hour after we arrived at the pink hospital—where real pelicans lived on the grounds—I watched orderlies roll him through big metal doors for emergency surgery.

Jolting back into my present pain, I rambled, stuttered, paused and rambled on: "Maybe this was a mistake, and maybe I shouldn't have done this. I'm sorry. It's punishment, maybe. Serving me right. Like Karma or something. Maybe I can call Tracy and Ed and arrange for someone else to be here, or what about you coming here to get me and drive me home? This is bad. It's not letting up. I'm a freakin' wreck."

And then he said the wisest thing: nothing.

My mind raced to interpret the meaning behind his silence. We sat there a long time without saying a word. A thought came to mind, and I couldn't connect where I had read or heard it, or if I had just made it up: "Silence is mandatory in order to hear God."

"You there?" I asked. Wondering if his silence was simply because he was already gone and done with this marriage.

"Always," he replied, and I could tell he was sincere.

So, I am wrong about that. He's not *totally* gone. And then it hit me.

"I'm gonna regret it, or resent you if I let you come rescue me, won't I?"

He remained silent.

He's brilliant, I thought.

Simply being out of the habit, I didn't say "I love you" before I hung up. But I felt like I wanted to say it, and that was interesting to me. Maybe I'm desperate and reaching out because I'm falling apart. Maybe it was because our marriage may die, but not our family bond. Since I was nauseated and preoccupied with the bathroom, I decided I'd think more on that later.

Returning to the table with my tools, I noticed my scribbled note, "Silence; mandatory in order to hear God."

This makes sense. After all, when I met Arroyo Beach, I prayed that over the next 11 days, I was going to *pray less and listen more.*

Time to walk my walk then.

This could be the key that unlocks the busyness and anxiousness in me, untangling both, so they no longer make me ill.

In the middle of the family room, I sat down again, crossed-legged, now on my yoga mat. Each dog circled, taking their position on each side of me, again. The light gardenia fragrance of my candle filled the room. The cool, damp breeze coming through the cracked open window gently moved through the living area. Vocal birds outdoors briefly caught my attention, but I decided not to let myself spend time there. I hadn't truly dove into silence since living in North Carolina. It was eerily strange to observe the race I'd been running in, and I felt the pull of the course wanting to correct and slow me down. Clarity of my busyness was crystal clear. Like a blanket being pulled off my naked body. The anxiety, the chaos and the busy years of going, going and going and more, more, more was coming to a welcomed screeching halt as I realized I was becoming calmer, stronger and clearer.

It was as if this dis-ease allowed my body to scream so loud, it yanked me into the present, pushing me off the train tracks of chaotic despair created by our exterior lives falling apart. I could now see how preoccupied I had become by being bombarded with financial drama tied to fights with lawsuits, old business acquaintances, collection companies and landlords. Everywhere I looked, I fixated on the material illusion of what I thought I wanted. TV and the Internet had repeatedly reinforced my fairytale desires to have the false lives of others. The disconnect and distance from Bill had busied and exhausted me, as well. My body screamed, *NO MORE! You can run Judy, but you cannot hide,* and I finally listened—for real now.

Some moments deserve solitude, and this was one of them. Continuing to follow the dogs breathing patterns, I felt an energetic current pull me into relaxation. I allowed my brain to downshift and my thoughts to ease up, while past chaotic reasoning gently fell away. I moved into self-hypnosis. Traveling from a relaxed meditative state to a deeper self-hypnotic space, I stuck with it. My conscious mind moved aside. It was as if my brain was a circle; the top half, the conscious mind that allowed me to talk and the quiet bottom part was the unconscious mind that held my true beliefs. I rested in that bottom space now. I had explained this process to many clients in the past but needed to spoon feed and nurture myself with this same information. Like an arcade Pac-Man character's mouth opening up, the goal was to get relaxed enough to where the top conscious part flips over and out of the way. Then the unconscious mind (the true beliefs) can be heard and also accessed—where you can realize, re-program or re-empower them. It's necessary to address this part because the unconscious mind rules. *I know this but hadn't been doing any of it*. It's the part that negatively keeps us stuck while being addicted, sad, hopeless, nervous, hateful, angry, fearful. It can also store the opposites in positive form: loving, hopeful, empathetic, motivated, joyful, calm and kind… I began to see and feel and better understand the good, bad and ugly of myself here. As I processed, each time I recognized a negative belief, I would gently suggest the positive to step up and replace it.

After spending way too much time fighting and negatively preparing for the future, expecting the worst in everything, always bracing myself for what was coming at me next, I had literally programmed myself to brace and expect the negative. Today, I finally tapped into a silent reservoir of the help I needed. Right here! Right now!

With each obstacle Bill and I came across, I could see where we became trapped in the conscious heady parts: the bills, the bill collectors, the tone of his voice, the tone of mine, the paperwork for food stamps, the incorrect and correct accusations, the unchecked goal sheets, the opinions of others and more. We aimlessly drifted around these topics day after day after day. It was like we were on an endless racetrack, in a race, we would never win or be able to exit. We were so busy navigating *around* things; we drifted far away from just simply loving ourselves *through* things. It was every man for himself, and it wasn't working for us. Married or divorced, this was not the right *way* for us as a family.

Continuing to let my troubled body demand my focus, I used it as a tool to practice awareness. I saw moments needing solitude by connecting to the quiet place inside me, no matter how tempting it might be to let the future outside demands pull me back in.

I could recognize the soon-to-be climbs I would make, and how they would need to be free of fear, loss, and regret so I'm not desperately rattled in the search to find my way. Like a veil being lifted, more parts of me became exposed. That old familiar, amplified, fully present sensation I had been longing for returned. I could see the tracks of my tears where I'd given up on positive outcomes for us due to the distractions where both my exhaustion and busyness reigned. Belief in good people turning bad lived in me. I could plainly see the escalated trust issue between Bill and me because blame was an easier place for us to stay. I was able to observe the loss of hope that hid in our bad news and what seemed to be bad luck that hunted us down daily. I saw us having our own version of post-traumatic stress disorder due to the constant negativity, and feeling no end in sight. The veil had very well hidden that dis-trust, fear, and hopelessness, but no longer. They were an illusion. A distraction from truth—my truth. This *way* didn't feel like a fit any more.

Abby's words ran through my head. "We'll see how their faith sees them through." As far as my spirituality went, my faith had been temporarily lost because I had cornered it into showing me proof first. Only doubt could grow here if I so chose. And that's what I kept choosing over and over again. My suffering was unique from Bill's. But I could see this was a choice both of us were making. Dr. Wayne Dyer once said, "Change the way you look at things, and those things will change."

I recalled wishing Dr. Dyer could move in with us for a while and observe our obstacles, bad luck, happenstance, the piling law suits, the moves, the aggressive bill collectors and more. I would ask him, "HOW DO YOU CHANGE THE WAY YOU LOOK AT THAT!? WHEN IT'S IN YOUR FACE 24/7."

But today, I felt the shift, knowing, I have to detach from seeing a conditional outcome. And I let go of the idea that I needed to see actual and immediate things change. I grew more comfortable with telling myself that I may see change immediately, which is sometimes called a Satori moment, or possibly in the future or maybe not at all. The point was to carry on, as if, anyway.

The phrase *Fear not, Want not,* stuck in my head and I decided it would be a good mantra for me, for now. Being attached to outcomes had to go.

Surprisingly, not one tear was shed. These kinds of clarifications of "what is" would normally leave me sobbing. This silence thing was a good place to be, and in it, I felt God. I finally captured one thing I set out to do in these 11 days: To reconnect to Source. And it was mandatory I be quiet enough to begin within and listen. The truth was, I had to completely lose myself here in order to find myself.

After sitting in the same position for more than two hours, my laptop chime alerted me of the arrival of a new email. This was such a quiet and productive place to be. *Don't ruin it by going back to your old ways, Judy!* But I trusted my gut and felt a strange pull to check it. Besides, I was in perfect view to see it from where I sat.

So I simply needed to just open my eyes.

There in bold, huge print, taking up my whole screen,

KEEP THE FAITH – PAUL.

What? I immediately got up to see where it came from.

Aunt Barbara had sent it. I hadn't spoken to her in a long time. Not only was she unaware of my meltdown, she didn't even know I was in Santa Barbara. She wrote: "I found this in Paul's things today. He wrote this to a fellow artist who was having trouble in the art world getting his collection into a gallery. Thought you'd appreciate. Love B."

Appreciate it? I was in love with this message. I closed my eyes as I held a vision of him and whispered, "Hello Paul," gratefully taking in the awe of divine timing. I let the clarity sink in, even more, noticing that those are the same words Bill wrote on his office window, in times of trouble.

Keep the Faith. Regardless of outcomes, this was going to be key for me. When I was little, I remembered the minister explaining, "God does not cause bad things to happen, Judy. He doesn't sit up there and decide one family is more deserving of happiness, ease and grace than another. He isn't up there to punish people. He is however, there for us afterward, if we call on him. So, keep your Faith in him."

Until now, I had kept tight reins on the signs of relief I prayed for: Bill's fabulous new job, I depended on; the house we would eventually own again; the savings accounts we could lean on; and the relaxing vacations where we could rejuvenate. They all interfered with the idea of *Keeping The Faith* with a looser grip. Up until now, I had little Faith *in* Faith. By having it in this moment (being the right moment, not a wrong one), I could simply admit the truth of how things were in our lives. And that having awareness of this, allowed me to move through it, rather than around it. This marriage and our finances were exactly where they were. And, based on the free will of others, there are things that will be out of our control. Period. And loosening my grip on these things in my life would let faith fly through me and sweep me off my feet.

I was unaware of when I misaligned with those beliefs, but I resigned to the fact that things may happen to us here on this earth that we may never understand until we pass. I needed to plant myself in a place where suffering didn't look the same; If I could convince myself to have faith in my personal growth, to become stronger, or do something good afterward, then it started to make sense. And having faith that we have universal love and support to help us do all of this during our suffering is where I needed to plant myself.

I didn't on this day have full ownership of that faith yet, but I did know one thing. I was going to not only, keep the faith in God, but I was going to have to keep the faith in myself, my life and in others, and this meant to keep the faith in *e v e r y t h i n g*. Believing that everything is and has been right in my world may take me some time to digest, but it was a direction I would decidedly move in. To believe, *it's all right here* was not an effortless thought.

I started testing myself as less-graceful thoughts crept into question. Can I really have complete faith that all things, are all right? Rape, murder, hate, loss of a child… is everything *really* serving us right? *Please God, no. How could it?* It dawned on me that it would not be the act of these things that would serve us right, but it might be one of many entries, and then allowance of this universal current—God's love—that comes in afterward that would serve us right by helping us to heal from the potential horrors like these. This kind of faith was the kind I couldn't hold captive to specific outcomes. *To have Faith in Faith.* I could rest assured that somehow with *not* fully understanding, or even finding peace in the *ways* of the universe, or the *horrors* on this earth—that would be faith in itself.

Just then, I noticed Titus tearing around in circles, chasing his tail, something I hadn't seen him do yet. Maximilian's tail wagged as he pounced in front of me in the downward dog position, engaging me to play, which he hadn't done yet either. I could feel the energy shift too.

Moving outdoors, I sat down on the brick patio getting the dogs all riled up with play. Then I looked up and saw Hottie heading our direction. It looked like a summer school day for him. He was dressed in jeans that loosely hung off his trim hips and a T-shirt that lightly hugged his biceps and triceps perfectly. It was a dusty orange color, and he looked dreamy. His hair wasn't perfectly combed, matching his look of being relaxed in his own skin. This reminded me of Bill's vibe, back in the day. *What will become of this young stud if he gets his ass handed to him like Bill has?* He looked like nothing bad was ever going to happen to him, and today I found that refreshing. I kicked back and welcomed the idea of finally forgetting about myself and learning more about him.

We sat outside, petting the dogs. He comfortably plopped himself down on a lounge chair looking like he'd be staying a while. I don't know why it was so easy to talk to him. It could have been his fresh, youthful perspective on life. He had a way of keeping things light, and I found information just effortlessly rolled out of me in his presence. He asked good questions, and he spent time listening to the detail in my answers. This was new to me because Bill was known for asking for the condensed version of everything. Explaining how I came to be here in Santa Barbara was easy, and he got it better than the average 25-year-old might. He was a deep thinker, a musical artist who wrote his own moving lyrics coming from past experience.

He was open about himself and eager to share his hopes and dreams, which I found delightful and intriguing. He had a million questions. Which helped my awkwardness dissipate as our friendship and connection quickly unfolded. Without question, I knew why I had met someone like this. While being both a sounding board for him and a sponge, he healthfully distracted me from my own world. This allowed me to actually begin to not only remember who I was, but I found I also liked who I was, with him.

He started throwing a tennis ball to the dogs as I watered the plants, part of my glorious and minimal daily to-dos. I couldn't help but appreciate the way the California clouds and sun danced together on this beautiful day. The cloud coverage was a welcomed treat, as I wasn't used to being outdoors without sunglasses. After mentioning that I still had not brought in all of my things yet, he politely offered to grab my suitcase from the Denali.

While standing at the backdoor with the bags, he asked, "What bed are you sleeping in? Master or guest?"

I said, "Yours. Put them upstairs," as I nodded to his apartment.

The look of shock on his face broke my poker face, and we became hysterical laughing.

"Ahhh, she's coming around," he said with a wink.

I did it. I flirted. Hopefully, I wasn't flirting with disaster. I didn't need any more of that.

Hottie had plans to meet up with his friends at Arroyo, and so he took off.

After playing with the dogs some more and exploring the rest of their yard, I went back in. I noticed the candle I had lit earlier was burning fiercely out of the top of the glass jar. The wax was now liquefied.

I know better than to light a candle and turn my back on it.

"Oh damn, that's stupid," I whispered to myself as it brought me back to the material loss endured when I was a little girl, age 9.

THE FIRE

After sitting down at the dining room table, I wrapped my hands around the warm glass candle. The burning flame threw me into another trance-like state, bringing me back to the time when I was in 4th grade. It had been decades since I'd thought of that time in my life.

It was Saturday night, and I had planned a sleepover at my house with my best friend, Karen. I lived in the northwest suburbs of Chicago on Sussex Court in Buffalo Grove, Illinois. It was a freezing night in January, and we made a plan to stay indoors, creating candles from a kit I received on Christmas. We moved the second TV in our home from my parents' bedroom to my room so we could watch "Charlie's Angels" and then cartoons in the morning. Even though it had a fuzzy black-and-white picture, a television in my own room was luxury living for me.

Karen and her three other siblings lived in the same cul-de-sac, all having their own color TV in each of their bedrooms. Their house was the envy of all. They had soft black leather chairs and couches, soft shag carpeting, colorful wall art, dramatic fabric window coverings and shiny, well-running cars parked in the organized garage. The backyard was a playland built for kids and also used for entertaining their country club friends. Her beautifully decorated room and bedding was a place I always dreamt about. I recalled my longing for a house that was not blazing hot in the summer (due to no air conditioning) or too cold in the winter (because of drafty windows and the heat being "too expensive" to turn up). We slept at her house in the summer more often because her parents kept it ice-cold.

Karen didn't mind my house, but she often questioned why I only had two pairs of shoes, one coat, one pair of jeans and some hand me down shirts from my brother and sister. The shelves in my room were lined with books that literally taught me to read. There were illustrated stories of Pinocchio, Goldilocks and the Three Bears and others, each with a 45-rpm read-along record slipped into a plastic pocket in the back. They were my prized possessions, along with the wooden butterfly wall sculpture my grandpa, the ex-engineer, skillfully hand-built with great detail. It had perfectly curved wood wings, while inside there were a thousand multicolored strings filling out the color in her wings. He delicately hand painted it, and I cherished it as it hung over my bed like a headboard.

My grandmother, using the same color scheme, had hand-quilted three long pink flowers with bright green stems and leaves on a white quilted comforter. It had a thin layer of polyester filling and wasn't warm, but I loved this blanket more than anything. On the very bottom corner, she stitched her name, ALID. I loved her and her unique name. These were my treasures.

We raced down the tri-level stairs to the basement where we set all the supplies up on the ping-pong table, and we stayed busy running from the kitchen to melt the wax and back down to the basement to add coloring and wicks. They needed to set overnight, according to the instructions, which we carefully read. That evening, we played some board games on the floor of my room, played with my shepherd-husky mix, Gaza, and coaxed our Calico cat, Luv, out with cat treats. As usual, my brother, age 16 and sister, age 17, were out and about with their friends. My Dad made us his famous buttery, salted popcorn and we ate the entire bowl, asking for another, which he gladly made. He retired to bed early, as he was planning on going downtown to his office at 5 o'clock Sunday morning. Towards the end of the night, Karen and I practiced our new dance in my room. We had just made it up and planned to show our neighborhood friends the following day. We turned in for the night with our tummies full of buttered popcorn and excited about the new dawn of day, where according to those instructions, the candles would be ready to light.

It was about 5 A.M. when Karen woke me. She slept in the trundle bed below. Even though we had mounds of blankets, we were still freezing. The frost half-covered the window, and with our fingernail, we scraped "HI", a heart and a smiley face.

"Lookit, I can see my breath," as I exhaled into the air. Karen laughed and did the same.

"Let's get the candles!" I said, jumping out and over the trundle bed to the floor.

Karen raced behind me downstairs. We were wearing flannel footie pajama bottoms and long-sleeved sweatshirts. The plastic bottoms on our footie PJs, no longer had a grip, which made it fun to round the slippery linoleum floors in the kitchen on our way down to the basement. We raced down the stairs. Gaza was sleeping on the family room couch, made of hard vinyl. She probably would have been more comfortable on the floor. It was like outdoor furniture, and I hated it but liked the fact I could clean it with Windex as I was a clean freak.

We tested the candles by jiggling the containers they were in. "Looks good!" Karen said.

"Yep," I agreed, "Let's take them upstairs."

When we reached my room, we turned on the TV, planning to be in cartoon heaven for hours.

"Hey let's get a bowl of cereal and eat up here while we watch TV and burn our candle," Karen suggested.

"No. No food in my room," I said.

Gently placing my candle on the TV, with a pack of matches, which I had practiced with earlier, I struck the match and ignited the wick. It was exciting to be able to do this. The fact my mom bought me this kit was so empowering. *I'm a grown up.* We stood in awe of our beautiful creation. As we watched it, we talked about the other color designs we could combine with the unused wax, and that maybe Karen's mom would buy her a kit for her birthday so we could make more. I noticed the flame jet up and wondered if there may have been a pocket of wax inside opening up and before having a chance to think another thought, the candle immediately disintegrated into liquid. It was dripping down the front, back and sides of the TV. The electrical wires started to pop and sizzle as they cooked and then melted. The picture on the TV started to flicker, then shut off. A crackling followed by a sharp pop made Karen and me leap to our feet, wanting to bolt from the room.

Just last week in school, we had a visit from some firemen who taught us about electrical fires. There was something specific that you should not do, but I couldn't remember what it was.

Oh my God! I thought. Recalling everyone's whereabouts: my brother sound asleep in a downstairs bedroom; Mom in her bed; Dad had taken my sister, Cary, to her car wash job at 4:30 A.M.; after that, he went downtown to work. I thought of Luv and Gaza and remembered not seeing Gaza on that awful couch when we came back upstairs with the candles. Panicked, I ran to our bathroom and grabbed a Dixie cup of water and returned to my room. Karen had been trying to put the flames out with my grandma's quilt, and I ripped it from her hands throwing the water on top of the flames. Suddenly, I remembered what the fireman said, and it was to do exactly what Karen was doing and not what I had done. I noticed Karen's footie pajamas were on fire, and I told her to drop and roll. Another botched memory. She stayed collected and stamped it out against her blanket on the bottom trundle bed. I told her to run and get Johnny as I went screaming into my mom's room.

"FIRE! FIRE! FIRE! Mom! Wake up!!!"

She jumped out of bed, noticing the billowing smoke coming from my room and screamed *"JOHNNY"* as she bolted out the room. I didn't have to remind her that dad and Cary were gone. She went into stealth mode while she flew down the split-level stairs, grabbing the kitchen phone in full sprint and dialed 911, with the phone in hand stretching the cord all the way to Johnny's room. He was a deep sleeper, but Karen had done a good job screaming, and he was on his feet.

"What the fuck!?" he screamed, as he saw the house filling with smoke. The crackling and whooshing sounds of things going up in flames or melting was sickening. Karen had already bolted out the front door and had headed to her house.

My mom screamed, "GET OUT, JUDY! JOHNNY, GET OUT! NOW!"

I could hear the fire engine sirens from far away, and her pleading screams to coax Luv and Gaza to come to her. Johnny chimed in as he rounded corners of each room, tempting them with their favorite treat, "C h e e s e? C h e e s e?"

She kept telling Johnny to go to the porch, but he wouldn't. I found myself with my arms wrapped around my legs sitting in a fetal position, out on the cul-de-sac curb staring at the enormous flames of fire escaping from the top floor of our home. It was probably 35 degrees, so it was understandable, but for the first time, I felt my body shaking out of control. I backed up off the curb onto a railroad tie that squared off a pine tree that sat in the middle of the cul-de-sac. I threw up at the base of the tree as I listened to the sirens getting louder... closer. Hopelessness overwhelmed me. *I killed Gaza, my dog and Luv, Cary's cat. Cary was going to run away again, for sure. My mom might burn and Johnny, too.*

Squeezing my eyes shut, I screamed from the cul-de-sac, "Pleeeease M o m, Johnnyyyyyyy, GET OUT GET OUT GET OUT!" My eyes were closed, and I felt someone grab me.

With a quick embrace from Johnny, "What happened? How did this happen?"

Answering him, "It was the candle I made last night... something went wrong."

And instead of the normal teasing, he was known for, he tousled my hair and patted me on the back.

"It's all right, Judrick, we're alive. We're all okay. Gaza and Luv are okay. It's gonna be all right."

My mom stood in the driveway now with our neighbors, watching the hungry flames devour and rise above the rooftop. Boards were breaking free and crashing to the ground as the fire tore through its structure.

The fire truck rolled down the street and whipped around the cul-de-sac, coming to a screeching halt. An ambulance and three police cars followed. Seeing the fire truck in the parking lot at school last week was completely different from today. The once pleasant, smiling firemen were now barking orders, as the seriousness of this fire was obvious. The Chief continued directing the others on what to do and where to start. Orders were understood and followed accordingly; it was like watching an orchestra. Halfway through the fire, they had to change strategy because the smoke was worse than expected. The Chief had entered our house and started up the stairs, but ended up running back out to throw up in our front bushes.

The paramedics started jumping out of the ambulance. They were looking for someone. The Chief yelled to one of them and then pointed to me. The paramedic started heading my way and with a whistle, he got the other two to follow. I liked him immediately. He wasn't sprinting to me; he was calmly walking towards me with a gray, thick wool blanket in his hands. He had a smile on his face, and he waved before saying anything. He knelt down in front of me, draping the big heavy thick blanket around me and I instantly felt warm but was till shaking. He was tall and looked strong under his heavy coat and pants. He had soft blue eyes and dark brown hair. His skin was olive colored. "Hi, li'l lady. How you doin?"

Noticing my throw up in the pine trees behind me, "Did you spend a lot of time in the house when it was smoky?"

"No, just when the fire started. I started it." Crying, I continued, "I burnt my whole house down. It was an accident. I didn't mean for this to happen. I made a candle, and it melted on top of the TV. It happened soooo fast."

He signaled the other two paramedics to kneel down with him. They created a barrier around me. The four of us were now huddled in the cul-de-sac. One by one, they expressed their opinions, offering advice on the situation. "Can't be that hard on yourself, kiddo. It was just an accident. Everything will be all right. Bet your family is happy that nobody got hurt, huh?"

Their comments made sense, but I was fixated on the flames and smoke, pouring out from our house. Parts of the roof were now gone. The front door was off the hinges and lying in the driveway. I heard windows shattering on the backside of the house. I could see my mom still standing, with her perfect posture, in the driveway while being hugged by our neighbor. Her back was to me. She was not a "hugger", but she seemed to welcome one from the nieghbor. Her body was shaking, and I could tell she was crying. I had never seen her cry before.

"I'm so sorry," I continued.

The paramedic whispered something to one of the others and off he ran. He came back about five minutes later with Gaza and Luv. They had been safely kept at the neighbor's and felt so warm. I pulled Luv closer to my chest under the blanket, and she purred. Gaza sat on top of my feet, like she always did, while she continually tried to lick my hands when I let them peek out of the warm blanket.

The paramedics had been told I would be staying at Karen's house, and once they thought I was calm enough, they walked me over there. Karen and her siblings were thrilled that these guys were at their doorstep. I felt their importance too, as they delivered me to my temporary housing. Their dark blue suits that clanked when they walked from all their dangling tools made them look like huge, armed angels.

Hours later, under layers of clothes from Karen's closet, I went with the firemen so they could explain how the fire took on its own life. When we entered the house, I could feel the wind whip through, and I lost my balance but recovered quickly. I didn't want to draw any more attention to myself. Most of the windows were gone either because the scorching heat had shattered them, or from an axe the firemen used to enter or exit through them. Sleet and rain had come down after they put the fire out, and so the floors looked like the dirty slush of a downtown Chicago side street in March. We had quite a mess on our hands. I thought we were going to be able to continue to live in parts of the house, but after seeing it now, it felt like it might be many months away. Black soot covered every single thing on all three levels. The fireman mentioned that the smoke damage was the worst they'd seen. A pitch-black soot dust covered everything. The smell was lodged into my nostrils, making me feel ill. Furniture was destroyed. The living-room drapes my mom made were ashes on the floor. Melted linoleum met up with the burnt carpet, which had melted off the stairs, and the sleet made them dangerously slippery as we made our way up to my room.

The windows, with frost that morning, had been smashed out. Every belonging of mine had exited that opening and was now piled in a heap in the backyard, covered in wet, freezing soot. Looking down from my bedroom window, I was unable to make anything out in the pile below. Half of my ceiling was gone, leaving the room completely open to the elements, and water still dripped from what was left of the fireman's hoses. The closet door was burned off, and there was nothing left inside but ashes. The shelves holding my books were gone along with all the books. My favorite Beatles album was melted onto what was left of my practically unrecognizable record player, and the new guitar I'd gotten for Christmas was in ashes. The butterfly was gone, and so was the bedspread. The backyard, which backed up to Dundee Road, a four-lane highway, displayed all that was mine. It was as if I stood naked in my backyard where all drivers and passengers going by could take a good look. Guilt weighed heavy on me, and an unrecognizable sadness was settling deeper and deeper as the day went on.

This was a brutal confirmation of my first awakening of sorts. Within an hour, I went from being a happy little girl, with no cares in the world, to one drowning in an ocean of hopelessness, shame, guilt and regret. It was the first time that I couldn't just effortlessly tap into my natural, joyful state. I felt like I said goodbye to the little girl in me as I stepped into this new dark place where I now had trouble even seeing the remnant of a yellow brick road—the one I used to skip along on.

I returned to Karen's house, where her parents were cautious and kind toward me. They encouraged me to play a board game. After declining, they had a list of options for me to try: watch TV, read books, listen to the stereo, or eat a snack. I couldn't say yes to any of them. Nobody had punished me, so I was going to take care of that myself. Karen knew me well and disappeared into her pantry, coming out with a box of Cap'n Crunch. "Mom, can you get us some milk?" she asked.

"Of course," she cheerfully responded. She welcomed Karen's idea with relief. She remembered that our family never had sugar cereal at our house and, as a result, I often raided their pantry for cereal and Pop-Tarts. These would never be found in our kitchen unless my brother had snuck them in.

Her mom added, "How about a strawberry Pop-Tart too, Judy? They're plain, with no frosting, just like you like."

"Yes, please," I said. Finally finding something to say yes to.

I had specifically been warned not to enter the house or backyard. But, about a week later I got my courage up, snuck through the cul-de-sac, hopped our bolted backyard fence and landed on two feet in an enormous pile of mud. *That's going to be hard to explain later;* I thought as I looked at the mud splashed up all over the front of the clothes Karen's parents had given me. I cautiously approached the pile.

Noticing the back exterior of our house, where pieces of wall and wires dangled, it seemed dead with no electricity pumping life into it. It was quiet, but in a deafening way, even with the cars and trucks whipping by on the highway behind me. The burnt smell in the air from my cherished contents on the ground seemed to be even more pronounced because the once-frozen snow was becoming slush as the temperatures were on the rise. From the highway, any car passing by could see the brutality of the fire that had ripped through our home. Some kids from school made special trips to drive past with their parents and later made remarks about how stupid I was.

"I'm sorry," I whispered to my house, the only home I had known.

Carefully using my muddy shoe, a hand-me-down from Karen, I started moving items around. My hands were bare and cold, and it started to drizzle. But I stayed. Work gloves would've been a good idea, but I knew those wouldn't be hanging in our garage. As my shoe moved some things over, I saw something bright yellow underneath. I used my hands to dig closer to it. It was a dandelion, smooshed, but still bright yellow. "How did you make it through the winter and this fire?" I asked.

Wiping and rubbing my cold hands on my pants, I picked up the first layer of something melted into a large plastic sheet. Chunks of wet snow broke free and slid off of it as I pulled it out to get a better look. What was once my Barbie camper was now a solid sheet of pink plastic. I started moving the pieces around and decided to make two piles: a *garbage* pile and *keep* pile. My cautious optimism passed after a half hour, as I still hadn't found one item worth keeping.

Mr. Daniel, our next-door neighbor, apparently had been watching me rummage through the pile and appeared with two sets of work gloves. One for one for him and me. He was usually one of our sterner disciplinarian dads on the cul-de-sac, but today he was gentle and just handed me a pair of gloves.

"I just want to find one thing, just one, ya know," I squeaked from my tight throat.

His eyes squinted as he studied the pile, "Now, now, keep the faith child, keep the faith."

His family were regular churchgoers. I watched them all on Sunday mornings, dressed nicely, all six of them, piling into their station wagon. So I wasn't surprised to hear him fold faith into our conversation. I was kind of hoping he'd say more.

We continued for another hour and had basically given up hope that anything would be found. Our fingers were freezing inside our soaking wet gloves, now filled with mud and soot.

I held my hands out to him, "I'm sorry, 'bout your gloves."

"Don't be sorry," he consoled.

At the bottom of the pile I had been working on, I felt a book. As I pulled it from the rubble, Mr. Daniel yelled, "Well, looky there! Is that a Bible?"

Wiping it off, I exclaimed, "Yep, it's mine!" I clutched it to my chest while smiling.

I opened it to show him my name inside. "This is the Bible the minister gave me when I was 7. Pretty weird that all the other books burned and this didn't, huh?"

"Yes, indeed it is," he agreed.

Still working hard on his pile and not showing any signs of giving up, he inquired, "Hmm, what's this?"

Just then, I saw my grandma's hand stitched name on the corner of the quilt she made; the one Karen tried to put the fire out with.

"Oh my God. My blanket! Is it... is it all there?" I cautiously asked as I watched him carefully pull it out of the rubble. There were burn marks, but it kept coming out in one big piece.

While inspecting, I shrieked, "OhmyGodohmyGodohmyGod! My blanket! In *one* piece!"

I continued to examine, "It's real dirty and has a few pieces burnt off on the edges, but maybe..."

He chimed in, "Well, that can be hemmed up and cleaned for sure!"

And then he bent over and pulled another item out, "What's this?"

"Oh wow, that's my baby blanket! My mom wrapped me in this after I was born."

It was originally powder-puff pink in color, with a nylon trim border. The nylon trim had disappeared, but most of the square blanket was intact.

"How about we go show these to Mrs. Daniel and see if she can clean these for you?"

"Yes, yes, Mr. Daniel, I am so happy to see these," I replied as I skipped away from the pile with all items clutched to my chest, "I found *three* things!"

I wished we had found the butterfly too, but decided to imagine that it didn't burn, it *flew away.* I experienced a pocket of deep gratitude that day, for my good neighbors, my family that refused to punish me, and that at least, materially, I had the blankets and this Bible.

ALL IS NOT LOST

The Santa Barbara day passed while the dogs lay at my feet. Sitting with my hands still wrapped around the gardenia candle, it hit me. The skip in my step when going to Mr. Daniel's house was about realizing all was *not* lost. My family, neighbors and those items had been in my life and backyard the whole time, yet I suffered so dearly anyway. It seemed clear that sometimes you might have to dig deeper into what is right in front of you, whether they're people or things to find the treasures or the silver linings.

The similarity of loss in the fire and the loss of today was feeling like two puzzle pieces snapping together. It also reminded me of how unsafe and unpredictable the world can be. While at the same time, there's always room to see your fair responsibility in it all. Most important, when faced with a challenge and learned the hard way, that it's best to move through it, not around it. Because of my hypnotherapy background, I had already been hypnotized to deal with the fire, and I thought I'd processed it enough. Turns out, I had moved around it and past it, but didn't move through it, like I had today. The hopelessness, guilt, regret, feelings of bad luck, and the false mantra of deserved punishment, "You deserved it stupid, you made the candle," mirrored "You deserved it stupid. You wanted to build or be a part of building an empire."

The fire and the turbulence today shared the same out-of-control, hopeless feeling where a rebound or recovery seemed impossible. It's that feeling that comes when you face an overwhelming obstacle that makes you feel like you have been hit so hard that you can't and don't want to get back up. I had never unlocked my paralyzed emotions that came from that material loss.

Over the years, I held onto my *things* as if my life depended on it. I packed way too much when I left home for college and I similarly over-packed just for these 11 days here. It had always been nearly impossible for me to clean out a closet and give away items because of the scarcity grip I had learned back then, which had clung to me throughout the years. I recognized the illusion of security that some of the material items gave me—the home, the cars, the clothes, the jewelry, the prized possessions and the 401K. This left me feeling the same fear and helplessness I had experienced as a 9-year-old girl. It was now time to feel it as a 38-year-old woman.

In hypnotherapy sessions, it's common to ask the client to see their older self sit down with their younger self to help explain things and reassure them: "Don't worry, everything will turn out all right. You're gonna be okay." With the luxury of being older and wiser today, I realized it was unnecessary to carry the heaviness of the fire and its material loss into today.

Some might say that the fire was meant to prepare me, years later, for *this* loss. Perhaps it was meant for that, but it was also an unwrapped gift that lay dormant for three decades, waiting for me to open it...Make it serve me right. I could now embrace the idea that I carried this heaviness unnecessarily. Separating and not combining the two losses made the financial losses today easier to grasp.

As I let this soak in and processed the connection to loss, a memory emerged, piggybacking on that of the fire. This event came a year after the fire, on December 23, 1975. I could see where this second memory reinforced a strong case in my young mind that this world was an unsafe place, full of surprising tragedy.

Off and on throughout my life, I felt I had an Angel watching over me, and he came to mind immediately after processing the fire. His name was Monty Klemmer. Monty was my grade school friend from Kindergarten through 5th grade. He tragically hung himself from a cloth towel dispenser in a school bathroom. I'd always thought it was an attention-getting move rather than a full-on choice because I had seen him do it in our school bathroom before, as a joke. He was a vibrant embracer of life, even at this young age, and when he no longer walked our hallways, it was painfully obvious that life can be quite tragic and full of a lot of pain. I recalled the fear that rushed through me as I held the phone to my ear while hearing the news. It was *unbelievable*, and I thought the person was lying or mistaken. "No," is all I said, and I refused to go to the funeral, choosing to spend most of my Christmas break behind a closed door in my bedroom.

In school, Monty had spent a lot of time getting sent to the hallway for time-outs, and occasionally to the principal's office. We all found his prank jokes and side comments hilarious, and most of the time, I could see reluctant twinkles in the eyes of the disciplinarians, as well. He was, by far, the cutest boy at school. He had an outgoing personality, but never had to try too hard to get our attention. He was naturally witty and playful and was the first kid my age who seemed to have no fear of jumping from high walls, sliding down two-story staircases or eating a bug. I never saw him decline any dare, and if he was in a race of any kind, he was sure to come in first. Even at his age, he found joy in making others laugh. He was the only reason I looked forward to going to school. I recalled the feeling I had while locked in my room during that freezing Christmas break. It was my freshly painted new room, after the FIRE, and I couldn't even feel grateful for that. The room with the fire was burning, yet again.

This day in sunny Santa Barbara was exposing loss in a new light. I could now see how losses could pile one on another—first the fire, and then Monty. The compounding losses that had been building during the last few years were also clear. Bill had once said, "Thanks for everything, I couldn't do it without you," and he was absolutely right. What part I played in this current financial crisis was what I could fairly question now. There was no question that my mistake caused the fire, but the gift of hindsight showed itself today. I could really let go now, and I couldn't believe I hadn't already.

The tragic and sudden loss of Monty had left me with a great feeling of uncertainty, leaving me scared for what might come my way next. I could see now that the loss and pain in losing Monty was connected to the departure of Paul. Those unprocessed fears of loss, compounded while shaking me to the same core when I heard of Paul's passing.

I could see a glimpse of myself without the layers of beliefs, and what I saw was a more peaceful woman. My suffering today became clearer; I understood how it was coming down to whether I wanted to keep stacking experiences on top of one another while letting the fears grow, or not.

As I unpacked the bag Hottie put on my bed, I scanned the many items I had insisted on bringing here. It occurred to me that all the gut issues I had read about in books confirmed this very thing. I could trace my digestive issues and link them to feelings of scarcity, of feeling attacked, unsafe and unstable in the world due to having a lack of financial security, a lack of trust of others and finally a lack of trust in the universe. So, as for the recent losses in our life, our money, our home, and our possessions, I was able to break it down into compartments and consider my fair share of responsibility. I could see where I was consumed with my disappointment in Bill, especially for ignoring my intuitive instincts about a couple of his business associates. I now understood my resentment that I had been right about them, and if he would have trusted me more, maybe we would not have been in this situation. But I couldn't know that for sure. Reaching down into faith on this one, I could consider everything that happened was now going to eventually be made right, it didn't have to stay wrong and heavy.

It was a perfect time to let it all go, as a wiser woman could. I allowed my hands to loosen its grip wrapped around the burning candle. Feeling its warmth, I said out loud, "I *forgive* myself for the fire and for any and all parts I played in all the fires of my life. I truly, gratefully and finally forgive myself."

I dipped each of my fingertips into the wax while waiting for them to cool so I could gently tap my fingers together, just like I did as a kid… before the FIRE. Placing my hands, with fingertips of cooled wax, back around the candle, I wondered what it would feel like to forgive a lot of things. Forgiveness was setting me free, and I added *more forgiveness* to my list of things to do in Santa Barbara.

The reflection and the awareness of the LOSS that had buried itself inside me lifted. As I tapped into the past, it felt unchained from my present. Many hours had passed since seeing Paul's note, but at the same time, it felt like a few decades of therapy came together.

Earlier that day, I loved the way the jets from the showerhead felt on my head and body, so I decided to take another shower. While adding conditioner to my hair, I opened the small window over the shower, so I could hear the birds outside. I made a point of paying attention to the sensation of water cascading down my back, front and sides. I could feel a shift, of a physical nature and smiled under the water. Mentally, I felt a bit spent, but at the same time invigorated. Emotionally and spiritually, I was starting to feel solid ground again. Although I was alone, I felt a large crowd of invisible love and support, and I dropped to my knees and said: "Thank you."

The plan now was to play some guitar and then hit the beach.

I dried myself off and threw on some shorts and a T-shirt. I put a tea kettle on the gas stove and pulled out a kombucha green tea bag, setting it by a mug with a 'double happiness' Chinese symbol. Marc's little bag of half-eaten goldfish crackers was on the counter, and I raised it to my lips, letting them spill into my mouth. I poured the tea, stirred it and blew across the top to cool it. I raised the cup saying, "Cheers" to Maximilian who was studying my every move, hoping a goldfish would hit the floor. I sat down on the couch and picked up ALVAREZ. I had printed the lyrics and chords to "I Shall Be Released" by Bob Dylan. Wrapped up in the message of this song, I recalled every person that had come into my life and out, but instead of feeling dreadful, it felt purposeful. I sensed being able to shed any victim beliefs I had been holding onto. I wanted nothing more than to see my own light shine and there was a knowing that when it does, I would be released.

Noticing smooth rocks displayed on their coffee table, I wondered where they came from because I saw a different kind of rock predominantly at Arroyo. Our family was known for rock collecting. I couldn't remember when it had started, but we had a way of always finding heart-shaped rocks. Before leaving Tucson, I made a mental note to find all of the kids their own special rock.

Just then, Sam, the cat, appeared. I don't know where he even came from. He just hopped up on the back of the couch, with only a couple feet of distance between us, and stared me down.

"Hi. I'm Judy. And you are Sam I Am. Nice to meet you, sir."

He seemed serious. It's no wonder he hadn't come out until now. Puking, crying and talking to myself made his absence understandable.

"Maybe you can sit in my lap sometime," I suggested.

His ears twitched back as he continued to stare.

The recent reflection of The Pines, and the near-drowning inspired me to go to the beach, but before I plunged into that fear, I needed some facts on riptides. I planned on talking to someone local at the beach about that when I got there.

I threw my bathing suit on and slid a long-sleeve white-cotton blouse over it, and then slipped on my frayed jean shorts and flip flops. My hair was pulled in a ponytail, and I applied no sunscreen as I was determined to get a California glow on this trip. An Arizona desert tan had a deeper brown skin tone versus the California tan, which had some golden tones to it. I was on a mission to see the glow that might separate myself from the same-tanned Tucson folks. I needed a new tribe now.

Nurturing myself became easier as the hours passed; I ate a couple saltine crackers, a banana, Ed and Tracy had left in the fruit bowl, sipped the last of my tea and drank a green-protein powdered drink. I grabbed my keys and a towel and headed out. The animals were happy, and I'd had no emergency calls from kids. Feeling *even* better now, I was ready to go. Today would be a decent day to face this fear of the ocean, and with success, I'll be able to swim every other day while I'm here. On the drive over, I turned the volume up on the radio, and Uncle Kracker's song, "Drift Away" came on. This may have been the 10th time so far on this trip. Elated, I sang it at the top of my lungs with the sunroof open, sun beaming, feeling stronger, happier and more solid. Knowing it will only get better.

WHAT'S YOUR STORY

Letting myself feel like a local, I pulled into the same parking space I had the other day. On the beach, I found a spot tucked away up against Arroyo's cliff. The Pacific scent of vegetation, salt water, and various floras filled the beach. I laid my towel down, hiding my keys underneath. *Surfers are out there, so the waves must be right.* I scanned the parking lot to see if Hottie's Jeep was there. *Nope, no sign.*

While pressing my feet through the soft, warm sand down low to where I felt the cool, damp, gritty sand beneath, I practiced deep breaths while getting my courage up. I studied the waves and their patterns. Being a neophyte, as far as the ocean's ways were concerned, I studied the surfers and measured their demeanor and faces, the same way I would watch the calm, unflustered flight attendant on a turbulent flight. My heart was racing, and I started to rethink this whole idea. Maybe if I walked closer to the shore and just felt the water, made friends with it, start off super slow… *for crying out loud, there are kids in over their head, and they are both peaceful and playful in the ocean. I could be that! I'm doing this!*

Just as I was about to get up from my towel, I saw the guy that Hottie had mentioned, Bayard Stockton, walking by. He hadn't noticed me sitting here tucked away, up against the cliff. He was much closer in proximity to me now, and I could see better detail of his hat with the pinned lures attached. He wasn't wearing sunglasses, so I noticed his weathered skin with deep crow's feet around his light blue eyes. He had blunt handsome features and long hair for an older guy. With his oxygen tank and cane, he walked slowly along the shore, but with purpose. Strangely, he emanated sexuality, and I could see his free spirit in his gait, which could not be disguised by his cane or tank.

Although concentrating deeply on his walk, he suddenly turned to me as if I had screamed his name. He stopped dead in his tracks and stared. I stared back and smiled. Instantly, I sensed he was an interesting character. Immediately, I wanted to read the books he had read, or at least hear of them, and I was ready for his sage advice. He started heading my direction, and I got up to meet him halfway.

He said, "Glad you like my beach. Good enough for a second look, huh?"

Remembering him from the first day, I said, "Oh yeah. It does draw one back."

With eyes that commit, he said, "Pleased to meet you. I'm Bayard Stockton. And you are?"

"Judy Cochrane, nice to meet you Bayard," I said as we shook hands.

"j u d y c o c h r a n e," slowly rolled off his tongue as he paused and looked into my eyes, but it felt like he was looking into my soul, "What's your story dear?"

He caught me off guard. I wasn't sure what to say, how to answer, or where to start.

He took the lead by sharing a brief version of his story. "This isn't a private beach, but to me it is. The locals call it Hendry's Beach because the Hendry family owned it in the late 1800s. It's my living room, my sanctuary, my temple, my church, and it's my hospital; it's the love of my life, besides my family. I love my work as a professor, I've traveled worldwide, I'm a veteran for peace, and I have embraced life fiercely without *too much fear.* I'm in my 70s. I'm sick. And I am dying. That is my story."

"Okay. Wow," I said as I joined in his robust contagious laughter.

"Well, Bayard, let me start with this: I don't want to be my story anymore. I'm thinking—I need to dream a dream I haven't dreamt before and start moving in that direction."

He let out a hearty "HA!" and he held his right elbow out for me to latch onto where we locked arms, and he said, "I need to spend more time with you, my darling."

We walked to a park bench near the entrance of the beach and sat for two hours downloading details of our lives. It was as if we were long-lost friends. He had a strong personality, was extremely intelligent and had keen street-smart awareness as well. He read me perfectly and guessed things about me before I told him. It was as if he was asking me to show him the parts of me I did not love so he would somehow know where to begin. When he asked about Bill, I got real serious. I flat out said, "I don't know if this marriage will last." I was about to cry in front of this stranger, and he said, "Will you marry me then?"

He let out a big belly laugh, and I joined in. He was a beautiful and vibrant man, and I was now looking forward to seeing him every day on this beach.

I discussed the last few days of processing: the near drowning at the Pines, the Fire, our marital and financial struggles, beliefs, keeping the faith... He had a way of casting a light on it all while he embraced and enjoyed all of these stories.

Naturally, he was a perfect person to ask about riptides. Just as he was about to answer, Hottie appeared with his surfboard under his arm. He was soaking wet and apparently had been out there for a while. I hadn't even seen him enter the beach.

"Well, well, well, you two are in your own little world over here. Hey Dude," he said as he shook Bayard's hand.

Bayard was happy to see Hottie, and he told him that I had just asked about how to deal with a potential riptide. These two were experts as far as I was concerned, so I hung onto their every word. They pointed out what I noticed before, that there were a lot of children out there having no difficulties, and they strongly encouraged me to face my fears, especially while the tide was where it was right now. Like a couple of football coaches, they cheered me on and pumped me up. Slipping off my blouse and shorts, I headed in.

The cold sand beneath my feet and toes shifted as the waves rolled up over my ankles and splashed my calves. I felt uneasy with this ocean's power just standing on her shore.

Deep in thought, I reflected, *what a productive wonder full day.* Suddenly, I felt something move under my feet and jumped. An 8-year-old boy standing nearby saw me jump and he laughed.

He started jogging towards me, "Hey lady, did you think that was a crab or somethin'?" While laughing, "You don't look like yer from aroun' here."

Ugh. He figured me out—I'm not a local.

He bent over and picked up what was under my foot and handed it to me, smiling. "It's just a rock."

Smirking, I took a look.

Just as I exclaimed, "Hey, it's heart-shaped," he said, "Hey lady! What the heck, look all around your feet! Did you bring those and drop them here?"

I stood stunned as we both saw the many heart-shaped rocks surrounding me. We went around picking them up and showing each other as if we both needed proof. We started recognizing their differences.

"This one is a broken heart," if it had a line or a crack through it.

Or, "This one is a full heart," because it was well rounded.

Or, "This is an ugly heart" because of ridges or pieces missing.

I suggested we whip them back into the ocean, so the sand could smooth the ugly ones, and someone else could discover the beautiful ones later. He loved the idea and so we started throwing them back into the ocean, one by one, yelling our plans for each rock. I kept three for the kids. He took a few too, but first, I told him we have to ask the ocean if it was okay to do so. He responded, "Lady, you're weird, but I like you."

His parents came to take him home, and he explained to them how strange it was to find me in the ocean field of heart-shaped rocks. I didn't tell him I had set the intention of finding heart-shaped rocks earlier. That would have put him and his parents over the edge.

My heart raced, and I wasn't going to be able to procrastinate the swim anymore.

"Hope there are no riptides," I said to the little boy, who was still hanging out, trying to delay his departure from the beach.

"Oh, riptides are cool! Hopefully, you get in one and get pulled way, way, way out. That happened to me once. Not here, but in Del Mar. It's so fun! It's like a ride at Disneyland!"

"I don't like rides at Disneyland." I turned to the boy's parents and asked, "What are you supposed to do with a riptide?"

The father began explaining, "Well, if you start getting pulled out, don't fight it, go with it. You can swim parallel to the shore for a while and then work your way back in. But..." and then he got a call on his cell phone and walked away.

But what? OH God. I scanned the beach for Bayard and Hottie, but they were nowhere to be seen. So much for them being my lifeguards on duty.

Ankle-deep waves still lapped at my feet, and the little boy pointed and screamed, "Uh-Oh! WATCH IT LADY! A STING RAY!"

I jumped so high, I practically broke my ankle with the landing. He was doubled over laughing, as I chased him out of the water. The next 20 minutes were spent going over all their instructions in my head, just in case. After studying a few more kids body surfing, I thought *enough is enough. I'm going in.* My young friend left after his prank, so there were no more excuses to wait any longer.

Relieved to see Bayard and Hottie now sitting on a park bench, I thought to myself, if nothing else, if I get swallowed up in a rip tide, he could send Hottie in for me.

I slowly waded out as the chilled waves slapped against my stomach, holding my arms out for balance to combat the ocean's pull. While letting the water slowly rush up over my arms, I tried to imagine it was welcomed like a baptism of sorts. My toes had a shaky grip on the sandy bottom. I waded deeper. *Sharks. What about Sharks? Ugh. I didn't clear it with anyone... about sharks. Stingrays are their best eating. I read that somewhere. Had that kid seen one today, or on any other day?* The water came up and over my shoulders and up to my chin. Leaning my head back, I heard the muffled ocean fill my submerged ears. It freaked me out, so I concentrated on my feet planted in the sand. I would need to just lift them and swim out a little further, but it terrified me as I considered just how deep this ocean floor went. And how many unknowns of the currents that flow through. And how many creatures will I attract as I wiggle about. I looked up to the sky, hoping for some calming peace, but thought the same... *How far does the sky go?* It was a bad idea to consider that now. The vast nature of how deep and how high, panicked me more.

Flashing back: Even on the back of a jet ski, in Key West, Florida, where I could clearly see the bottom of the ocean, I was uneasy. Bill had taken me out there after he completed flips on a jet ski reassuringly saying, "OK, see, now look down, doesn't that make you feel better to see the bottom? Do you want to drive this and I sit..."

Cutting him off, with hardly any breath left in my body, "OhmyGodOhmyGodohmyGod! I can see it. The bottom! I'm freakin' out, get me back to shore!"

"Judy, calm down. Stay seated," he instructed.

I was ready to jump off, which would have only made matters worse. It was his first example of how irrationally freaked I was with large bodies of water. It didn't help to be able to see the bottom or not.

The waves looked more intense from this level and I could feel my shortness of breath. *Breathe, Judy, Breathe.* I can't pass out here; I was light-headed because of lack of food for a few days. Turning to see if I could get a glimpse of Bayard or Hottie, I thought, *what the hell was I thinking? I should go back!* But the shore seemed so far. Just then, a wave crashed over the back of my head and sent me flying down to the ocean floor. Coming back up, gasping for air while looking toward the shore, I saw Bayard now standing up and leaning against his cane. I couldn't make out whom he was talking to, but it wasn't Hottie. Bayard couldn't get out here fast enough. I was counting on Hottie for the rescue. But his face was still turned in my direction, so he still had an eye on me at least. And since he isn't running for help, maybe I'm fine. I'm just going to start heading back. But the ocean pull from behind was obvious, and I had this sinking feeling that I was in the rip tide they'd warned me about. Pure panic started to settle in. Another wave crashed into the back of me. This time, instead of hitting the ocean floor, I swallowed what felt like a gallon of salt water while spinning in circles like my laundry machine at home.

Oh, how I wished I were doing laundry at home right now.

This was so unnecessarily stupid. And where are the surfers I originally saw when I entered the ocean? I could have at least yelled for help and hung onto a surfboard for a safe trip back to shore.

Feeling the ocean's pull, I let myself pretend that I was in my bath at home. I leaned back into the water letting the waves gently push up underneath me as I started floating up and over each one. I was way out there, and the surfers had left. I started swimming parallel like the kid's dad explained. I seemed to be making some good progress, but when I started to turn inwards toward the shore, I realized I might have to go further in the parallel direction, swimming south. I kept at it, breathing and going with it, rather than against it. Bayard was right. Going with the flow of his life was going to bring him more peace than fighting what was coming. He was embracing his life today rather than becoming heavy and hardened and fearful of it. "We all have a death sentence," he said as he explained his rationale. "Some of us know it's coming sooner than others, that's all. Besides, there's no future in the past. We're born to leave."

If he could live the rest of his life like that, well then, I could potentially live the rest of my life like that too. Finally, I returned to shore far down the beach from where I started. I walked for a while before coming up to Bayard and Hottie. I was thoroughly exhausted and elated that I had not only faced my fear but attacked it with *some* grace, even while caught in a riptide.

They had shit-eating grins on their faces.

"Need a lifeguard?" Hottie asked.

"Verrry funny. I just faced a *huge* fear of mine—swimming in the ocean and on top of that, I worked through a riptide," I said while toweling myself off.

Hottie looked at Bayard, and Bayard looked back at him. I was sure they were impressed with my courage and victorious conquering, as I was. This was just adding to my already powerful day. Hottie had a night class and was off and running. But as he left, he said with a wink, "Good job, Jude. Maybe you can learn to surf now."

Bayard clearly had thought a lot about what we had spoken of earlier, and we dove into two more hours of conversation. We watched the sunset together in silence, not because we didn't have more to say to each other, but because that's how he does sunsets.

The ladies' man they all described him to be—I never saw it. He was a perfect gentleman, and we were instant friends. We had an understanding that was rare between two people. He didn't talk much about the silver tank strapped to his back, the cords in his nose or his cane. He said he had no regrets. I sensed he had a lot of fun in this lifetime, and his fascinating stories backed that up. He was a free spirit and an intellectual. He ran a radio show, sharing his bold and sometimes controversial opinions of our world today and his deep love for Santa Barbara. He was well-recognized and an awarded writer of quite a few books and spoke like a poet. I thoroughly enjoyed his comments and questions, and most of all his brilliant and intuitive observations of who he thought I was, agreeing with most and arguing others. He let me sharpen my teeth on him, and he made me want to think before I spoke.

In these few hours, he understood what this trip meant; he challenged me to continue to face fears while I was here. After asking him if he was worried about me out there, he said, "No, I don't have doubt in relation to you, only *you* do. I was honored to see you work through that. Keep up the good work. And you do realize that someday these 11 days of yours may need to be written. Just in the last few days, you have enough material for a book."

"Oh, I'm not a writer, as far as the arts go. I used to sing, but I wasn't good enough to do that. And I would rather be a painter. My brother and sister are writers, not me."

"You may not think so, but your story, the one you don't want to be, wants and may need to be heard someday. Just stay open to the idea, dear. You only need to write how you speak. You're a good storyteller. You don't have to pretend you're Shakespeare. William Faulkner once made a claim stating, if you were to read a Hemingway piece, you would not need a dictionary. And Hemingway responded, **'Poor Faulkner, does he really think big emotions come from big words?'**

Just tell your truth, Judy. And when people read your work they'll say, I can't put my finger on it, but I get her, I resonate with her, I don't doubt her. And the part they like about you is really the part they like in themselves. Truth runs like a well of love through all our veins. We either embrace it or we do not. Those seeking their own truth and joy will see the light in others only because they recognize it in themselves. If you can shine your light onto others, so that they may see their own, then you simply must. Period."

Get it down, Take Chances, It may be bad, but it's the only way you can do anything really good.   William Faulkner.

Having worked up an appetite, I started to roll my towel and gather my belong-ings. "Will you be here tomorrow?" I asked.

"Absolutely, I plan on dying on this beach."

I placed my hand on top of his, which rested on his thigh, "Well, okay, I hope that is *NOT* how I find you here tomorrow. Stay with me a while, Bayard," I said, as we both laughed.

I'm not a hugger, but I wanted to hug him. As I hesitated, he reached out and pulled me into his arms, holding me tight. I could hear the escaping whiz of air that pumped through the oxygen tubes pressed between us, and it reminded me of his struggle for breath. That seemed so strange to me because he was clearly a man deeply and richly breathing life in and out in a way most don't. I hoped he was sticking around longer than my gut was telling me.

After hopping into the Denali, I was delighted that the sand had followed me onto the rubber floor mat. Bill's desire to have spotless cars, while having three small children constantly on the go, was always a stress for the kids and me. He would most certainly want to vacuum this sand out right away. I, on the other hand, was hoping to leave it in there for a very long time.

The plan was to stop at a grocery store I had seen earlier near the bungalow. Just entering a grocery store chain I was unfamiliar with, was refreshing. But the welcoming fragrance of fresh-cut California flowers plunged into plastic tubs that lined the sidewalk in front was a delightful greeting. Over time, I had become a hater of this task. With overwhelming clarity, I realized that because of the many years and many hours of visits to the grocery store, I was legitimately burned out. I never came right out and complained about it; I simply learned to slip into some trance-like state just to get it over with.

Last-minute, rushed visits to the grocery store were part of what ruined it for me. Before, during and after school; delivering forgotten lunches, snacks for the class, emergency art supplies and poster boards for projects... the stops before, during and after games for snacks, waters or a quick sandwich at the deli seemed to involve coaxing agitated and exhausted kids to join me. My inexperience about not knowing what to buy and then what to cook, made it frustrating as well. And the agony of our finances these days made it worse. I seemed to focus on what I could *not* afford, and I was consumed with coming up with generic explanations to the kids on why they couldn't have certain things. My mantra became "Next year, when Daddy has a job, we can get the food we want and maybe take a vacation or something."

But as the years went by, the kids rejected that rationalization by responding with annoyance, "You said that last year!"

Fact is, these days I had been leaving the grocery store with a feeling of scarcity, never abundance. I could now see why the kids would beg, to not go with me.

As I walked past the fresh-cut flower selection indoors, I wanted the stalks of gardenias in my basket so badly, but today instead of feeling scarcity, I was pleasantly distracted with being fully present. And in that present moment, I remembered an actual gardenia bush sat right outside my bedroom window at the bungalow. If there was a definition of Zen, I felt I might be in it. It was delightful to be all by myself and clear about what I wanted to eat, and not having to run it by Bill or the kids. Because of lack of food, I craved pasta with pesto, cooked broccoli and cauliflower and a fresh salad. It was a simple decision, no negotiations or changes to the menu, no tears, and no one was angry or felt left out. I walked slowly up and down the aisles enjoying, no list and no meal plan for the week ahead. Winging it, by eating whatever I wanted, when I wanted, within the garage-sale money budget, felt good. Passing the pastries, warm pies, sprinkled cupcakes and even my favorite, a chocolate cake donut seemed natural as I had no desire to put that in my body after how sick I had just been. Feeling like a restart button on my body had been pushed, I had a desire to be good to myself. I walked down the alcohol aisle with plans on putting beer in my cart; I hadn't let up on that at all while in Tucson. But I wasn't interested in the buzz tonight. I was starting to like, rather than fear, the clarity, and crispness in my thoughts, and I didn't want interference. Comfortable, knowing I could have a beer at some other time, I relaxed. Tonight, I planned on painting, reading and playing guitar.

While in line to check out, I heard someone mention that they loved a certain brand of coffee. I stood there silent, but in shock, as I realized I hadn't had any for four days! Being a regular coffee drinker and knowing it wasn't good for my acidic issues, always weighed heavy on me. It was nice to have let that go, without a fight.

This would now go down as my most enjoyable grocery store trip, thus far.

In the checkout aisle next to me, I studied the dynamics of other people's children. There were the typical siblings teasing one another, kids begging for anything at eye level in the check out line, and a crying baby in an infant seat. There was one mom that looked like she was gonna crack. She was annoyed and scattered. One of the kids had dumped her entire purse on the floor. I recognized this tribe right away. I was part of it. It made me wonder if I would ever really be able to continue this peace back in a Tucson grocery store. I wanted to reach out to the frazzled Mommy and remind her to stay strong. But who was I kidding? I was far from mastering that.

The literal distance between Bill and me combined with the years that had passed, gave me a little clearer perspective though. It was interesting to watch the mother and her kids in the grocery store, and now the parking lot. She might have just come out of weeks of puking kids, as we all have from time to time, or she might be worried about money, health or her marriage. This whole motherhood thing is hard, and marriage can at times be helpful, but it can also interfere with and get in the way of personal harmony and healthy space.

One thing was clear, though, I had no regrets about having kids. Where I fell short was how does one stay centered in the middle of the temporary chaos, while raising kids, being married, and dealing with the good, bad and ugly of family life and work life, all in full swing? I feared for my return, but at the same time felt gratitude for the peace in the next California days to come.

Returning to the bungalow, I received another warm welcome from the dogs and was so pleased to see Sam I Am perched on top of the back of the couch, as part of the greeting crew. He hopped down and brushed up against my leg when I entered this time. The temperature had dropped to around 75, with a perfect breeze, so I secured the screen door open, allowing the dogs to come and go from the back patio to the house. I filled a medium size pot with water and placed it on the stove for pasta, chopped up vegetables for a salad, and placed a pot on the burner for the veggies to boil. I lit candles on the kitchen table. Fiddling around with the stereo, trying to figure out how to just play the radio, I accidently turned it on maximum volume, and it blasted, startling us all. A radio announcer said, "An oldie, but a goodie, for all the 1970 disco bandits, get up and dance!" and "You Should Be Dancing" by the Bee Gees, blasted through the speakers. I turned to Maximilian, guessing he was the best participant as a dance partner. He was a short, stocky dog, but I had strong arms from holding three kids on my hip for 11 years now. As I spun him around and rocked him back and forth, Sam sat perched on the back of the couch, watching my every move. Like Garfield energy, I sensed him thinking, "What in the hell?" I put Maximilian down and went over to Sam to pick him up. This was my first time holding him. I spun around carefully and rocked him gently. I felt him purring against my neck. After setting him down, I spotted Titus, peeking out from behind a big chair, watching it all from afar. I continued dancing while recalling the Hustle, line-dance back when in eighth grade. In rejoicing mode, *I danced like no one was watching,* while moving across the wood floors and spinning around the furniture, miraculously keeping balance and rhythm.

My stomach growled with the welcome aroma of pasta filling the bungalow.

Having never felt confident on a dance floor, I surprised myself as I accepted my low-par dance moves. I'd always, until now, compared myself to Bill, who danced well, and to my college roommate, Shannon, who effortlessly could lock into a groove. She always got compliments when she came off the dance floor. But, tonight, I just let go.

Love for '70s music and past memories—the Fire, the Pines, Monty, Paul and other childhood growth opportunities—made me feel rich tonight. I could no longer fit under the title of "the have nots." I had a lot, and for the first time in a long time, I enjoyed my own company. The desperate hope for a bailout coming from a lottery win, a miraculous job opportunity, or the announcement of a whopper opportunity from a random stranger, vanished. In the last four days, I finally nurtured myself. Beginning within and then working its way out. It was like watching the crumbs come together that make the cake.

Having heard it so many times, I finally understood: *I was the one I was waiting for.*

Dancing over to stir the pasta, I stuck a piece of crisp lettuce in my mouth and embraced the crunch, noticing how good food and life tasted again. Continuing the groove back to the family room, I shed my sweater like a stripper might. It brought me to a full belly laugh. I was cracking myself up while singing to the dogs and seemingly keeping them entertained.

Somehow in between the thumping loud music and my hypnotic striptease, I heard, "Judy! HEY! JUDY!" Hottie shouted over the blasting music.

With my back to the door, I hadn't a clue he had walked in. Trying to look natural and play it off, I slowly, rather than abruptly, stopped dancing. We stood there staring at each other and then burst into laughter.

"W h a t i n t h e h e c k is goin' on in here?" he asked in a kidding nature.

Trying to quickly explain, "It was that epic swim through the riptides! The talks with Bayard, and you know how I've been locked up in the house… so, celebrating? I guess. I'm rarely alone, ya know. Gimme a break." I laughed as I threw the sweater back on over my head.

He continued laughing. "You're a trip. And ya, hey, about the riptide; there wasn't one."

He ducked backward, as if I was going to reach out and slap him in the face. His bent body lifted his faded orange T-shirt rode up just high enough to see the start of his abs and the top of his low-cut jeans. He was laughing so hard that I couldn't *not* join in.

I questioned, "But Bayard said…"

He cut me off with a time-out sign. "Bayard was playing along. He convinced me not to say anything because he wanted you to have the experience in your mind at least."

He trailed off into laughter again, and I couldn't help but smile.

Tears welled up in my eyes; I hadn't laughed that hard in so long. I couldn't remember the last time Bill and I had laughed like this. He would've found this hilarious. I wonder if we'll ever be in a place where I'll want to tell him. And if I do, will he think that it's funny? He was a different guy today.

Hottie continued: "He made me promise not to tell you until tonight, if ever. I couldn't wait to get back here after rehearsal to see you and to tell you," he said.

It got immediately quiet in the room, only the radio softly played. He picked up on the sudden silence right away.

"Did I say somethin'?" he asked

"No, no, it's okay. It just… it just hit me. I haven't had anybody say or show *'that they couldn't wait to see me'* in a long time. It feels good, that's all. Thanks."

He made his way over to my pasta and gave it a couple stirs. He looked into the pot of veggies. "So, are you known for your cookin' at home?"

"Um, absolutely not," I laughed. "Never quite mastered that one."

Relieved that divine timing played its card; Hottie's buddy was parked outside honking. They had plans to hit a bar together. Showing him my vulnerability, in regards to Bill not being excited to see me, was dangerous territory, and I knew better, to watch it from here on out.

Sitting at the table while the doors and windows were still open, I ate my dinner in silence. Listening to myself chew was something I had never tuned into before, and I let it pull me to the present moment. A moment I could welcome.

While looking at the items on the kitchen table, I saw Byron Katie's book, "Loving What Is." I had a lot of trouble with this book over the last three years. I would argue with some of her points out loud as if she were sitting in the room. Seeing her live and also on video, of her working through these steps and her process with other people, always left me with a feeling of, "Well I can see how that would apply to them, but for me, this doesn't work."

I decided to give it a try again.

I started with the statement/issue: *Bill never feels like he can't wait to see me.*

1. IS IT TRUE? Is it absolutely true that Bill is not happy, eager or joyful to see me when he comes home? *I feel like it is, because of how he acts towards me.*

2. CAN I ABSOLUTELY KNOW THAT IT'S TRUE? *No. Because I am not him. I have never spoken to him about this. And he has never actually said this. It is impossible for me to know if that is his absolute truth.*

3. HOW DO I REACT WHEN I THINK THAT THOUGHT? *Defensive: because I feel like I have to protect myself from my annoyed and angry husband. Sad: because he once seemed excited and happy to see me in the past. Broken: perhaps I'm not enough for him or anyone... Because I'm not being my genuine self. I had been having trouble liking myself as of late. Disappointed: that he doesn't feel that way. I had my heart set on him wanting to see me for many more years. Mad: that I invested myself into this marriage for so many years, and now this is where we ended up. With all the marriage therapy we've had? We should have known better than to get this far apart. Hopeless: I can't stay married to him when he's like "this." I need someone excited to see me.*

4. WHO WOULD I BE WITHOUT THE THOUGHT? *I would be Free to be ME. Void of all emotions above: defensiveness, sadness, brokenness, anger and disappointment toward Bill and myself. If I were not wrapped up in who was going to love me, and love seeing me and who was going to leave me, I would just BE.*

TURN AROUND THE ORIGINAL STATEMENT: *I'm not excited about seeing me...*

BAM. I realized in this hour that I had to look in the mirror and claim responsibility for actually feeling about myself the way I imagined Bill felt about me. This certainty of how I thought he was feeling about me was destructive, and it wasn't telling the whole truth about how things were between us. Our years of organized marriage therapy, in the past, worked for us. But I settled down and got comfortable with the truth, and that is, we don't have the financial wherewithal to pay for therapy. This 11 days was all we were given, and it was going to have to be all we would somehow need. *I'll keep working on getting whole and see what happens.*

Glancing at the clock, I noticed it was probably story time at home, before bed. Showers or baths may be in process, and books might be chosen. There may even be a spontaneous game of tag taking place where toothpaste drips off toothbrushes that were supposed to have brushed teeth. Bill may be starting with Nicole and ending with Marcus or maybe he had his own plans for them. So I picked up the phone and called the home line.

It rang and rang. No answer. No voicemail.

I hung up and tried again. Nothing.

I contemplated calling Bill's cell, but I really wanted to talk with the kids, not him. Not yet.

DAY 5
FRAME OF MIND

I woke up at 8:30 A.M. The bedroom window was still cracked open, allowing the cool morning air to gently fill the room. This morning felt peaceful and easy to wake up to. So many past mornings in Tucson, I awoke abruptly because of oversleeping, and on too many occasions, slightly hung-over leaving me fuzzy and unclear of my schedule for the day. Pulling the fluffy white comforter up to my chin, I reflected on how good and gracious I felt for this heaven on earth. It was easy here. Even their well-trained dogs politely waited for me to get up.

Busy parents quickly learn, starting during pregnancy, that sometimes the plans you make for your day can get derailed and also need to become that way in order to take care of these little beings in your life. My mother, friends with children and even random strangers, warned me of this. But until you go through it, it's difficult to comprehend. I missed the kids but allowed myself to embrace this peace. I knew it was good for me.

My sister, Cary, and brother, Johnny, both seven and six years older than I, were not experiencing marriage, and neither had children. So in times of trouble, when I looked for guidance or direction from them, I was able to get a complete outsider's perspective. Talking through things with them these days was more about me trying to get a glimpse of what life would be like as a single person. Walking into my sister's small neatly, organized townhouse was like walking inside a private indoor-outdoor garden, sanctuary/spa. Wouldn't matter if I dropped in for a surprise visit or a planned one, her incense lightly filled the room, and because she was a fresh-air girl, at times I could smell it gently escape through a cracked window as I walked up to her front door. Her little-rescued dog, Angelina, would always greet me with great gratitude upon arrival. There was almost always classical music playing softly in the background, and you might hear a teakettle rumbling, getting ready to whistle. Her furniture was mostly items she thoughtfully collected over the years from our past grandparents, a generous acupuncture client or a friend. But beautifully it all came together, so perfectly. I felt so comfortable at her place that many times, I would simply plop myself down on her couch and collapse, in a good way. When she left the room to water her lush flower garden outside, I imagined myself living like this.

As I lay in bed this morning, I was aware that I captured a bit of that feeling here. But then I allowed reality to sink in, realizing that I'd better check my phone and make sure there were no urgent needs from home. Upon observation, my cell phone had four missed calls, and I couldn't believe I had slept through them. For the last 11 years, I had been immediately awakened often by the slightest of sounds. It wasn't like me to sleep so deeply. Apparently, I'd put a halt to the starving of myself, in various ways, guessing all the processing, the swim, and the pasta were partly responsible.

Noticing the first call came in at 5:30 A.M., I hit "call back." *That was probably Marcus.* The phone rang for a while, and I was about to hang up when an out-of-breath Clint answered the phone: "Cochrane residence."

"Wow, that's formal. Hey, buddy, it's Mommy. How are you?"

I held steady to my calm, chilled-out place of being while lying on my back on top of my comfy cloud of a comforter. The birds were chirping in the background on my end, and on the other side of the phone, I heard blasting cartoons, Nicole crying, and Marcus half-yelling, half-laughing about something. I heard Bill barking orders to Marcus, but I couldn't make it out.

I don't want to make it out either.

Clint gently answered, "Well, I guess fine? Nobody's letting me mark off the days you are gone, and I think that's mean."

"Well, how about you make your own calendar?" I suggested.

Without giving Clint a chance to answer, Bill grabbed the phone away from him. Without asking me if I was feeling any better, he said, "Hey, um, okay, well, the bank called and said we're overdrawn! I thought you said you had transferred money to the account so I could pay the rent and well, it's not there. I wrote a check to Nick Mahoney (our attorney) last week, but I thought you said there was enough in there for that."

"Ok. Wait, for Mahoney? No, I said hold off on paying him until you have commissions come in on new mortgage loans."

"Shit!" he yelled.

"Look, calm down," I said.

I could tell by the noise in the background that he had moved to a more private room.

"Don't tell me to fucking calm down right now, while you're on vacation. Okay? I'm closin' up some gnarly loose ends at i360. I need to get Mahoney to take care of some stuff now, not later. This industry is crushed. I can't seem to get funding from anywhere. We may have two more fuckin' lawsuits coming. And there's no getting out of having to pay the unpaid lease payments on the old building. The amount is f'ing growing bigger everyday. I have no choice, but to let him just come at us full throttle."

I found myself sitting straight up on the bed, rather than on my back resting on my comforter cloud. I battled the old anger creeping in, and my past peaceful desire to not engage in this war was slipping away. Stepping back into it, I recalled how I hated our life as it was. Our desperation was sickening. The fact that we may have two more potential lawsuits waiting to strike infuriated me. They would draw swords with their mis use of power and resources to keep coming at us... *for what? To seek and destroy? They appeared ruthless, cruel and rotten to the core. How do they sleep at night? We have kids to feed and a house to pay for, for God's sake.*

Bill yelled something at the kids, but it was muffled by his hand held over the receiver. I didn't ask him what he said because I could tell he was at wit's end.

I've been there, done that, just last week.

I tried to switch to the positive, "So, football practice started. How did Clint and Marc do, and how does your team look? Good group of kids? And parents? They good too?"

"There is a frick'n waiting list to get on the team; I may have to coach two teams. The parents are pissed, and the kids are coming up to me cryin.' A new lady involved with the organization is psycho and had the parents of the kids all riled up over what kind of snacks they couldn't bring to practice. This one mom actually slapped another mom. I told Mahoney we might need to take action against this crazy shit too."

"What the hell? I said. "Everywhere we go, we just seem to attract battles and lawsuits. Even in the Pop Warner world of football?"

"Judy, don't start about how we manifest all this shit now, it's just happenstance, it's how it goes sometimes. People have free-will to be fucking assholes, and once in a while, you need to fight back. We've gone over this. You can't just "OM" it all away!"

I tried to stay calm and re-direct, "So you have loose ends at which office? Arizona or California?"

"Holy shit, Judy, really? I'm getting the feeling you want to start a fight about that girl again. Well, I don't have the luxury of time to address that right now. Not one box has been unpacked, the dishes are piling up, I have a shit ton of laundry, I'm gonna have to go grocery shopping..."

I switched gears again, recognizing this is one of those times where a critical approach was not going anywhere.

"How are the boys doing in floor hockey camp this week? Do they like it?"

He responded, "It's fine. I guess. It's a pain in the ass gettin' them there and back and snacks and shit."

"How did the interview go yesterday?"

We hadn't talked about it yet, and the first ones had seemed positive. I heard a big sigh, and I could feel my jaw tighten in response as I recalled Katie's take on the whole thing. *Abort the mission. Abort. Abort.* I thought to myself. I shouldn't have asked. I knew better!

"You don't wanna know. I'm so fucked. They saw our credit standing! It just kills me too; the fact you didn't stay on top of paying our bills on time, over the last seven years has fucked us. Jesus, Judy, we had all that money and a liquid 25K plus coming in a month, and this credit statement shows you couldn't seem to figure out how to pay the bills on time? Why didn't you just let me pay them!?"

I could see where my relaxed, not-attached-to-our-money-thing was biting me in the ass. I had been careless when it came to the bill paying, as it would have been easy to have put everything on direct debit pay. Usually, I would wait for it all to pile up and get a call from a utility company and then sit down for a couple hours, paying them at the same time. During that period our credit scores stayed high because we were free of debt and had so much in reserve.

This sounds like we would be, not only the nice but also stupid guys finishing last. Except my guy isn't what I would describe as nice anymore. He had a violent state of mind, and I had a hard time separating from it. I felt myself slipping back in. *Damn it!* I thought as I entered his energetic field of battle. I said, "We need Mahoney to grow a set of balls or break down and get an attorney from L.A. or Chicago who wants to do what's right. We need to fight *and* to win. We need to hit them so hard *they* don't fucking get back up."

There goes my peace. Although I said that to make him feel better, I could tell it wasn't my truth. It was something his dad would say in regards to football plays. *Who was I kidding. I've' never been a fighter.*

One positive from this conversation was that I was able to take the ownership on the overly relaxed bill paying today. Immediately, I saw my role in that, and I tried to comfort him by saying, "I will look for a job when I get back, so we have access to more money for attorneys. And I can take on more hypnotherapy clients. I'm feeling a little stronger after coming here."

"Well, we can't afford the day care we'd need for you to do that, but okay. Besides, you know our credit won't stand up for you to get a hypnotherapy office. You will have to keep borrowing other peoples' offices," he said.

It was classic fighting for us. One day he would take the stand *"get a job, Judy"* and I would say *"no, and here's why I can't..."* and then it would flip-flop the following week, and we would take each other's stands. It was the circle of fire and disorder we lived in. A round house spinning out of order, with no way out and never knowing where we would land. Trapped and stuck. Stuck and trapped.

But this house I was in now, the cloud comforter, the birds chirping, the beach calling my name, the future manicure I planned on getting this morning—all of this made me feel like things were right in the world. Everything was in order here.

After asking Bill to take over my role, with no preparation, I felt bad for him and sorrow for the kids. How could I have underestimated my role? I knew better. I'm the one, doing it all, by myself. I wished he could see it from this perspective I had now in Santa Barbara. It was like watching a movie with some emotional attachment, but it was more manageable from here as I could continually pull myself out of the negativity in Tucson. This space between us allowed me to think creatively. I noticed how effortlessly I saw solutions and healthier perspectives to everything Bill had brought up. I was just too scared to share revelations with him while he remained stuck in a violent frame of mind, fueled by his deep, relentless drive to provide. All I wanted from him was to stand up and tell me what he wanted. Take charge and tell me what he's going to do next. Maybe even fake it till he makes it by telling me everything was going to be all right. But as for the last few years, I saw a different man than the one I'd married. He was beaten, from a brutal fight, there was a lot of blood loss, and he had been left for dead. But the fight wasn't so much with others as it was with himself. Bills disappointment in himself far exceeded what any other could have felt for him. He had doubt, but, worse, he'd started to believe in the doubt others had in him. My warrior, my soldier, my *Superman*, my beloved, the one I knew back in the day, had checked out and showed strong signs of giving up. He'd dangerously distanced himself from his dreams, for himself and for me.

As much as I would have liked to be sharing my life with someone more pleasant, I now fully understood where he was coming from. The millions of years that have been burned into this male being a master hunter and provider was not something to be taken lightly. Having clarification, I realized he just might not work through this financial loss with grace, ever. And I can't make him do anything he doesn't want to do. I needed to prepare to dig deeper and walk through it for the two of us.

In the background, the kids were placing orders for eggs cooked a certain way.

Nicole cried out, "I don't like *freed* eggs! I only like scrambled!"

I chimed in to help Bill, "Does she mean fried eggs? Oh yeah, she doesn't like those. She may puke."

He replied, "Great. Thanks for tellin' me."

He turned his attention to Nicole," Honey, I don't want to waste food, how about you just give it a try?"

She continued to scream, "That looks like an eyeball! A gooey eyeball! I am going to frow up now!"

Then I heard Marc respond, and it sounded as if he was trying to lighten things up by slapping the fried egg on his forehead, imitating the third eye chakra. He then proceeded to chase her through the house. I guess he was listening when I talked about all the chakras. That was the 6th one, which sits in the middle of the forehead, called the third eye.

Marcus was yelling, "I can see you, I can see you!"

Clint's laughter made me want to laugh, but I kept it under wraps because Bill was seriously annoyed and was now chasing after Nicole, saying "Honey, throw up in this towel, not the floor."

At the same time, he yelled at Marcus to stop chasing her, and at Clint, to stop laughing. Nicole continued to threaten to "FROW up," and the boys' laughter escalated.

Listening in while the phone sat somewhere in the middle of it all, I was overcome with emotion. I could see what five days had done for me already. Somehow the space and time between us let me appreciate them differently. Bill was too close, and was too trapped in his angry frame of mind, to feel this, just as I had been.

Bill chased Marcus, who was chasing Nicole. Somehow Marc was able to avert Nicole throwing up. *Thank God.* I think that would have put Bill over the edge. I had purposefully been putting vitamin C and Zinc in their waters for a week before this trip, just to make sure, he wouldn't be battling sick kids, on top of just their regular care.

I realized the pissed off feelings I was having, based on the financially woeful information Bill just shared, had passed. My gratitude for those kids, and for their spontaneous laughter and cries, snapped me right out of it. Clearly, I still needed time to process what was left of Bill and me. Heaviness came from knowing this version of him was not going to be something I would keep enduring. I was sure of that.

Staying in a state of abundance was the goal for today. It might be a perfect day to treat myself with the garage sale money to a facial or manicure.

The phone still sat in the middle of it all when I heard Horehole's doorbell ring. The previously scheduled play dates had arrived. I could feel my mommy-self slipping back into tracking the busyness as the house filled with other kids and their parents. But my role was not needed, so I let go of all the daily details of their plans.

The call didn't unfold with ease and grace. Clearly, I needed practice. But I could tell I was getting there.

FREE THE MIND

Driving over to the spa, I made a quick call to a friend to share my concern for Bill amidst the chaos and asked her to keep an eye out for them at practice tonight. "Say Hi. Ya know, just check in."

Her son was playing football on a different team, and she could do that easy enough.

My plan for a facial or manicure was perfect timing this morning. The $100 from the garage sale, I brought specifically for making myself feel abundant, was going to be well worth the exhausting 100-degree Tucson day that it took to earn it. It felt good to not have an appointment and just to wing it.

I found a front parking spot and approached the gorgeous Mediterranean building that housed the spa I'd discovered advertised in a Santa Barbara magazine. Bright white walls with cheerful yellow trimmed the plantation shutters, which stuck out at an angle allowing, what I imagined, just the right amount of light to filter inside.

Across the street was a majestic looking church where I saw an actual minister watering flowers in huge pots at the entrance. *Surely, they had landscapers to do that?* He noticed me staring and nodded. His energy seemed kind, and I hoped he'd be out there when I left so I'd have an excuse to go up and talk to him. I wondered if he'd have time to discuss faith-kind of questions and maybe some newfound answers about my own. If I had the courage, I'd like to get his take on the faithful people we just did business with, who seemed to conveniently hide behind theirs. But I felt a lack of confidence to walk in cold without having more traditional knowledge under my belt. I wasn't sure if this church would be another one that would roll their eyes when I discussed the presence of spirit felt by someone less traditionally religious.

Stopping dead in my tracks after walking up to the spa, I noticed the princess soldiers. There they all sat, lined up next to one another either to be primped, plumped, plucked, painted, waxed, colored, conditioned, blow-dried or styled. I thought to myself, *Hello there, I'm back... I was once a member of this club.*

A woman caught my attention as she whisked by me and entered a door next to the spa. It was a yoga studio. As she opened the door, a waft of bergamot essential oil filled the air around me. It was my favorite scent and had been since first giving birth. It was expensive, and I hadn't had any for quite some time. The sidewalk to the spa and yoga studio was lined with potted trees in full bloom that smelled like orange blossoms. Enveloped in full fragrance, I stood in between both sets of doors and felt a pull to check out the yoga studio and before I had time to think about it, my feet led toward yoga. I felt myself pull away, confirming I wasn't a part of that tribe in the spa. It felt okay to feel relief knowing I may never belong there in the way I had before. A manicure, combined with all the beach sand and plans of finding rocks, was not the right fit for me, right now anyway. *Maybe later, maybe never.* I could see the ladies' eyes follow me from behind the salon counter, probably thinking, "Someone needs to fix that girl's roots." For the first time in a long time, I didn't care. I entered the yoga studio, where the woman behind the desk had no interest in my exposed natural hair color.

"Good Morning. Do you have weekly packages?" I asked.

A tall, lean woman, who had her back to me when I entered, turned around. "Here in Santa Barbara for a visit, or do you live here?"

Yes! Yay, I'm starting to look like a local again.

"Just a visit. Are you the owner?"

"Welcome, Dear. I trust your visit will be fruitful," and she handed me a week-long pass.

When I started reaching for my cash, she waved at me to put it away.

She was as ethereal as a human could be. She was the woman who had walked past me on the sidewalk, and it was her that smelled of Bergamot. That essential oil was known for having healing properties, and I felt it after first bathing in it. During pregnancy, after submerging in a bath of that oil, my melancholy mood changed, and I would feel emotionally lifted.

I wanted to see this woman come away from the counter because she looked like she was gliding around on ice back there. Her movements were so graceful. She never confirmed that she was the owner, and I could tell she found the question unimportant. She was in her 60s, maybe early 70s, but well-taken care of and healthy. The whites of her eyes were bright, and her light blue eyes shimmered. Her healthy, long gray hair was pulled back in a loose bun. She had bright white teeth and a pink tongue.

My sister, an acupuncturist, trained me to always look at that first with the kids in order to see if they were dehydrated, or running too hot or too cold. Clearly this woman regularly fasted and juiced daily. Her lean strong body stood tall, and she looked like she had done yoga her whole life. I imagined only organic fruits and vegetable entered her temple. She was stunning. And I couldn't take my eyes off of her. I hoped she would be attending or teaching this 10 A.M. class because

I always loved to watch masters of yoga. I was just a beginner compared to most. The class was starting in a few minutes, leaving me no time to talk with her. She was colorful like Bayard, but had a poise and dignity about her. Slipping my sandals off into an open closet, I laid my Denali keys and cell phone down on top of them. Technologically disconnecting from them, worried me. I entered the room and felt her slide a mat under my arm.

"Thank you," I said.

After walking in, I looked for a spot in the back. I knew I picked the right studio; these people were at home here. Being around those who knew what they were doing felt good. The people on these mats were advanced yogi's. You could always tell if you were in the presence of one by their present vibe, their lean legs and arms and Buddha bellies that came from mastering deep belly breaths. I overheard one of the people in the class say she had just done a 30-day juice fast and dropped 15 pounds. Her tiny frame was ripped to the bone. The whites of her eyes popped, and freaked me out when first looking at her. They were so white; I imagined a very happy liver operated inside.

It was a serious class—no music. Although I was used to music during yoga, I was okay with not having it. The silence had been working for me anyway. Most of the positions started just as they had for me in yoga classes in Tucson. I felt comfortable with the pace and wasn't spending any time judging myself. Release with tears was not uncommon in yoga. Personally, I had only experienced it once, but based on the last five days of emotions, it wouldn't surprise me. So, I got ready. *If I cry, I cry. What's one more day of crying?*

A young girl, whom I'd seen at the front counter was our teacher, and she had a slow, soft speaking voice. You could tell she was tapping into well-practiced intuition as she was sharing visions she had of the people in the room. Apparently, she knew everyone, which confirmed they were all regulars. I didn't think she'd say anything about or to me and I was hoping she wouldn't. I didn't want to be the sobbing idiot, disrupting the class.

As she shared information on others, you could sometimes hear them respond in a whisper with an, "uh huh," or "yes," or "thank you." It was serene and beautiful in this space. With filtering light streaming through the plantation shades, the summer breeze that gently crept in, and the silence mixed with her occasional voice tapped into her intuition, it wasn't like the classes taken in Tucson. And it was far different from my own private yoga, where I usually used curse words from pushing myself too far into a forced position. I compared my past classes to this one, realizing that the past classes were sometimes more for women wanting to wear the tight fitting clothes and just say, "I do yoga." And because it was centrally located in the business sector, I noticed that the studio had become a place of networking for business and social reasons. It's why I mostly did yoga on my own, at home. But I longed for a place like this.

At one point, I opened an eye to see if the instructor was touching people as she walked around the room. Her voice trailed off, and when I peeked to guess where she was, I was always wrong. The hour flew by, and at the end while laying in savasana, she slowly zigzagged around the bodies lying in the corpse position. I love when they do that. Catching a glimpse of her as she dabbed a drop of essential oil onto her slender finger, then lightly patting a dot onto the third eye of the person laying face up on the mat, I wondered, *was she a healer too?* I heard her footsteps near my head and thought for sure her message of being "freed" was not for me.

"Freed one" she first whispered, and then a little louder and then drawn out, "F R E E D O N E."

At first, I thought she simply sensed the freedom vibe in the room, and that's why she used those words. But after she moved closer, I quickly realized the message was intended for just me. I flashed back to that phone call this morning and recalled Nicole's mispronunciation of fried eggs, where Nicole's adorable lisp made it sound like freed eggs. The "gooey" eyeball comment, the threat to "frow up," the visual image of Marcus slapping the gooey egg on his third eye area and Clint's laughter just put it over the top. As she bent over to dab my third eye with the essential oil, I tried everything to hold back the laughter. I covered my face out of embarrassment for the now deep stifled hysterical laughter wanting to explode. She then compassionately knelt down by my side, laying her hands on my chest, as if to heal my broken heart. Finding that even more hilarious, I rolled to my side, unable to hold back the laughter. The people to either side of me started to rise from savasana to lovingly come to my aid, all laying hands on me now.

Besides feeling elation from the support and love of complete strangers, I came to the conclusion that I was so tired of crying. It felt so good to laugh. The crying had served me well enough. *Enough is enough.* It made its impact, opened me up and turned me inside out. The laughter was where I needed to go now. For so long, I hadn't felt the desire even to have fun or feel joy. I thought it was a luxury the poor me could not afford to experience. My mission now was to seek joy!

I never shared the reason why I was laughing, not crying. They wouldn't have cared anyway. What I loved about people like this was they didn't seem to judge

HOW you would process or transform something, they just encouraged you to get there, in whatever way you could.

After sliding my flip-flops on and grabbing my keys, I turned to see the ethereal 60-ish woman again. We had an interesting pull toward one another, and I wasn't sure where that was coming from. She asked me if I had time for tea and invited me to a café, "It's walking distance from here."

"I would love to," I answered.

It was 80-degrees and sunny. The trees lined the walkways on State Street. I loved it here. It felt rich, but not just in monetary ways. There was a good-size, high-end mall tucked away. But I was more drawn to the high-end boutiques, with one-of-a-kind pieces of clothing and jewelry. As I walked past one of them, a $350 light blue, deep V-neck cashmere sweater caught my eye. That establishment stood next to a funky, fun, artsy gift shop and as I walked past the open French doors, I was pulled to the flowery candle scents, ethereal music and an abstract hand-carved wood sculpture displayed in the glass window. I made a mental note to return later when I was by myself. The streets somehow stayed spotless even with all the traffic and foot traffic from locals and tourists. Every so often, a Ferrari would hum by. But, as if to add balance to the world, you would see a sweet homeless guy on the corner.

This street had it all. Formal restaurants, cafés, bistros and pizza places with inside seating and perfectly-shaded outdoor dining. These places might be situated next to a tattoo parlor or a high-end furniture store. It wasn't uncommon to see a bar tucked in between. Some of them looked modern and new, and some with original architecture, that reeked of spilled beers that saturated the cement floors over the years. Music pumped from a casual bar, where they were serving lunch now, and there were a few people having cocktails outside already. They looked like locals, not vacationers.

That world of "to have" seemed far away from me today, and yet it was only a few years ago when I was fully engaged and operating in it all. A small part of me recognized, *I wished I had been more grateful for it.* I could feel and imagine the soft light blue V-neck cashmere sweater in the window, on my body and my arms and I admitted to myself that I would most definitely like to experience that again.

Suddenly, the yellow Ferrari I had seen earlier roared by with mufflers rumbling, echoing down the street. Standing in silence, watching it pass, I recalled my happy Porsche and its custom Ferrari yellow paint. My yoga friend noticed and said, "Somebody you know?"

"I feel like I might," I said.

For a second, I let myself miss my happy face, Porsche. Oh, how I loved that car, and the idea of driving it down Hwy 101 was calling out to me. I wished I had embraced it more and had been more grateful for that too.

We sat in the back corner of the café, as she ordered what sounded like a delicious tea for herself.

"I'll have what she's having," I said.

I found myself wanting to mirror this woman's every move. Still Unclear on whether she was the owner of the yoga studio, all I knew, was her name was Violet Reed. I had always yearned for a name like that.

She said the tea was known to have healing properties, and I believed it. Feeling good after these past days, I wasn't sure what still needed healing, but whatever it was, I was feeling healed already. She and I were a lot like Bayard and myself. Without a lot of time or details, we knew where each other was coming from. She had been there, done that. I loved her *way*; she was calm, serene, not surprised by anything, never had children and didn't talk much about having a man or woman in her life. Although it was clear, there was no way she wasn't attracting them often. She was not attached to things like normal people; she had a freedom about her that I liked. She was world-traveled and had given back to orphanages, refugee camps, and churches. But, because she had a presence of humility, I practically had to drag that out of her. I never figured out how she manifested her wealth, but you could tell she had plenty. She mentioned owning an art gallery but didn't mention where. That was one of my dreams, so we discussed art for some time. I talked about Paul and his work. Based on stories she shared, I found out she rode horses on a property she owned, which she mentioned was on cliffs above the ocean. Presently, she owned more than three houses but wasn't specific about locations. Her neighbors were private and, I assumed, possibly famous, so she kept their names out of our conversation, and I appreciated her for doing that.

Name-droppers, trophy wives and trophy kids and the mis use of power had been all around Bill and me. We were inundated with people that would name drop. We hated it when we were on top when our names were dropped, and it became excruciatingly annoying when our names were later used in a negative way while we were at this financial low. It was freeing to be here where nobody had anything to say about me.

Like Bayard, she pushed and asked questions that surprised me, but more about the woman inside of me. Without getting into a bra-burning mode, she spoke of the female energy and female power: Goddess energy. We discussed Joseph Campbell's old lectures which showed his sensitivity for the uniqueness of the feminine form in mythology, and about what that could mean to women. Paraphrased from Goddesses-Mysteries of the Feminine Divine by Joseph Campbell /forward by Safron Rossi—Campbell understood and honored the vital importance of the female spirit and its creative potential to birth the meaning of women's experiences into mythic and creative form. He saw this as a gift, and the challenge of our age and he honored women in their visioning and forming of the journey. He explained that when women find themselves in a competitive relationship with men, they risked losing the sense of their own nature. The challenge of our time is to flower as individuals neither as biological archetypes nor as personalities imitative of the male. And since there are no direct mystical role models for either sex, we must seek compassion in each other to understand and love one another.

Violet shared a quote, coming from one of my favorites:

The eternal feminine draws us on. Goethe

"I LOVE THAT! And I can't believe I've never heard of it."

Without judgment, she said, "Perhaps you were meant to hear that for the first time today."

Violet suggested I see a healer named Skye Hawkins.

"Oh my God, I'm already scheduled to see her tomorrow!" I said.

"Lovely."

"Have you seen her yourself?"

"Yes."

"Well, is there anything I can prepare for?"

Violet lovingly smiled.

"What should I expect?" I prodded.

"Don't prepare, except for prayer. Remain open to letting all expectations subside, and I mean *all* of them."

What I liked about Violet was her ease and confidence with herself and the world. She reminded me how much I loved Joseph Campbell, and I couldn't wait to get back home and find the box with his books inside. Always feeling pockets of ease and grace in his teachings, I thought, *why did I let myself get away from studying his work?*

Earlier, I had decided to visit the Old Santa Barbara Mission, so I took off in that direction after tea. As I drove, I thought of the many times I was told I needed a teacher/guru/religious mentor. Some have said, "The teacher appears when the student is ready." I was shocked, with all the things I had been exposed to up until now, that I had never found one. Time and time again, when I would meet a powerful healer, gifted intuitive, regal priest or even a well-known inspirational author who I thought could be that person, the timing was always off. I always imagined that if I had found one, it would have been someone just like Violet.

ON A MISSION

Mission Santa Barbara was founded on December 4, 1786, by Father Fermin Lasuen. The mission was named Saint Barbara, after a girl who was beheaded by her father for following the Christian faith. Later, the Mission was named, "Queen of the Missions." It's a stunning structure and sits high on a hill overlooking the city of Santa Barbara *and* the Pacific Ocean. During the first few years, there were a total of three churches built, each larger than the previous one. The final and remaining church, which remains today, had two matching bell towers, each 87 feet tall. To me, it looked like a massive number 11. I was blown away by the interior of the church because it had not changed since 1820.

Back in the day, the Chumash Indians of the Santa Barbara area were friendly and willing to help the Padres with the construction of the new mission. The coast of California was home to many American Indian tribes. There were about 10,000 Chumash between San Buenaventura and Point Concepcion. They lived in reed huts in large, well-designed villages. The Chumash were expert boat builders and lived off the Pacific Ocean. They'd often travel to the Channel Islands in their 24-foot long boats to fish and gather food. Two hundred-fifty natives' homes were built next to the mission. They learned the skills and trades of the mission including how to get water. The Padres taught them how to build a water system for the mission for drinking, cooking, cleaning and irrigation. This water system was so well-built, a part of it is still used today by the City of Santa Barbara. In 1807, there were about 1,700 Chumash living at the mission. On the grounds, there is a cemetery where there are more than 4,000 Chumash buried.

Instantly, I wished I knew the details of the struggles when the Chumash and Padres started working together. I imagined some blessed friendships blossomed while some misunderstanding and power struggles slowed productivity as well. The rich history of faith, growth, and production captivated me.

The garden drew me in. I learned that the original flowers, vegetables and even trees eventually ended up reaching beyond the walls and are part of California's agricultural success today. The fig tree dominating the cemetery was fascinating. It felt like this tree was showing me it's most intimate aspects, pulling up parts of the soil around it, its exposed roots twisted and turned deep into the ground. The base of the trunk was enormous; it would take three or four of me to wrap my arms around it. It was perfectly shaded in some areas, but the grounds were also covered by streams of light that shined through its branches. The 4,000 unmarked graves of Chumash buried here, brought me peace; many people have tried to bring connection, cooperation, hope for the people and understanding for one another for quite some time. I could see how we were advancing in some small ways.

I left feeling fulfilled. History always made me feel that way. This history and my own history was helpful for reflection. Understanding where we as people had a way to go, I could see that very clearly for myself as well. It was as if, the more I began to understand, the more I could see how much further I had to grow. The quest for "enlightenment" felt more relaxed today, though. The urgency was dissipating, and I was starting to trust the process.

On my way out, I noticed a grape vine on display in the museum, and it looked to be as wide as the largest boa constrictor you could imagine. All I could think of was its fragility when it was first growing—the time, patience and nurturing needed to produce grapes and, lastly, the kind of grapes it produced in the later years of its life. And with those thoughts, I was able to project and see my future self. I imagined I would like her.

I headed back to the bungalow, and as I pulled into the driveway, there was Hottie with another guy standing by his side. He was excited to introduce me to his friend, and I wondered why. He was adorable, just like Hottie and I noticed he had drumsticks in his back pocket. One was peeking past his chiseled waist hiding under his fitted T-shirt.

"Oh, are you in the band with Sean?"

"Yeah, I hear you may rock the open mic. I'm Matt, the drummer. Let us know what music, and we'll have it ready for ya."

"Oh God," laughing and looking at Hottie, "I'm so *not* getting up on stage. I never outwardly agreed to that. It's been since college that I sang in front of an audience. I was below-average then and probably much worse now. Having a beer and watching you guy's play, though, sounds good. That, I'd be up for."

"What would you sing, if you did do it?" Hottie asked.

"Well, I'm not singing. But in the shower and the car, I like, "What's Up" by 4 Non Blondes. And I love all Tracy Chapman, Bob Dylan, Stevie Nicks-Fleetwood Mac, and Elton John. I don't know, and it doesn't matter. I'm not doing it. I have horrible stage fright now for some reason. I couldn't even get up at our last book club meeting to talk about my thoughts on a recent book we all read. It would be a disaster. And besides, if I go out, I want to have fun, not freak out and be nervous. I already faced fears here in Santa Barbara." I winked at Hottie.

"Oh yeah, Judy here, faced her monumental fear of getting into a riptide by swimming out 30 yards into the ocean."

His friend smiled at us both. Apparently, he knew the ways of the ocean, and knew in order to be in a riptide, or rip current, as they call it, I would have to be at least 50 to 90 yards out. I could tell by the smile plastered to his face, that he liked our friendship and chemistry.

Hottie went on to explain, "She swam and got rocked by two waves, came up for air, had pure panic on her face. Bayard was with me. Dude, it was hilarious."

I quietly went along with Hottie's version, but finally chimed in to explain my position to his friend. "I almost drowned as a kid. I felt there was a riptide, and went through the motions of working through that…"

Hottie interrupted. "Oh God, this story will never get old," he said, doubled over laughing. His friend and I joined in with the contagious laughter. Then Hottie spilled the beans: Apparently, when I got rocked by one of the waves, I was personally aware my bikini bottoms had slipped a bit, but now Hottie was sharing how he and Bayard saw that as well! So pretty much, everyone on shore potentially saw my self-rescue of a frantic swim through a fake riptide and my white ass!

Hottie went on, "Dude, her arms were flailing, we saw her feet, we thought she lost her bikini bottoms…"

I could not stop laughing. *They saw my ass?!* I can barely stand in a bra and panties in front of my closest girlfriends, but I showed my ass to a dying man and a gorgeous Hottie?

Bayard was right. Maybe I should be writing this down.

Bayard was so sweet never to question me, when I excitedly explained the details of the rip tide, the waves crashing down on me and how I pushed through the fear. He was like the yoga people who didn't care about correcting me or about being right. He just wanted me to have whatever experience was going to pull me through the fear.

Hottie's laughter continued to be contagious with periodic moments where one of us would get a grip, only to burst back out into laughter. After tea with Violet, the nonstop laughter practically made me pee my pants, so I dismissed myself quickly into the house.

While standing in the doorway, I said, "Hey, thanks for the laugh, you ass," With a wink, "Maybe I will see you guys later. Wait. When are you guys playing? And what day is today?"

"We are playing Tuesday night. It's Thursday," he answered while rolling his eyes.

It had been five days, and I had not kept track. This lapse in not knowing time and days was foreign to me but so enjoyable.

"Hey, I heard you sing 'Let It Be' the other day. I liked it. Kind of organic and edgy," he said.

"Uh huh, organic and edgy is the equivalent of raw and out of key, right?"

As I walked into the house, the dogs came barreling out the door.

I heard his friend say, "She's not."

As in "she's not going to sing."

I turned and responded, "You are right!" as I pointed my finger at him.

The look on both their faces was of surprise, but I firmly repeated, "I am *NOT*. You will just have to coax some other sucker to do it. You two have had your last laugh about me."

Hottie corrected me: "Judy, he said you're *"Hot"*, but okay, we will look for someone else." He smiled and shook his head to his friend.

Embarrassed, and now beyond awkward, I quickly disappeared into the house. I could hear them laugh off and on, and I wondered if my *"hot"* status dropped below to dork status. *Was I ever going to feel something other than awkward around this kid?*

SERVES YOU RIGHT

Before dinner, I decided to take a stroll on the beach, hoping Bayard would be there to swap stories. When I pulled up, he was sitting on the bench near the parking lot, with a shade of gray in his skin tone I hadn't seen the day before. I wondered if he had pushed himself too far on a beach walk.

"Hey, you all right?" I asked as I walked up.

He brightened up and replied, "Hellllllo there." He patted the park bench seat next to him. "Tell me about your day, dear."

"Well, hold on. You feelin' okay? Why are you sittin' here? You all right?"

"I'm having a tough day, doll."

My grandma used to call me that.

He continued: "Let's talk about being *all right*. What if everything that ever happened to us was *all right*? What if the things we needed to learn from served us right? Not in a punishment way, but in a way that supports our beings to flourish? What if having no money after having a lot became a catalyst to serve you and your family in a glorious way, and what would it feel like to not guess or question 'the way, or the why?'"

I looked at his oxygen tank, pretending to be a nurse. "Are you sure this is turned up enough?"

I responded with agreement because of my similar findings over the last five days. And also my realization when finding Nicole in the hot car at the courthouse becoming a wake-up call. We talked about the *Keep the Faith* message and the GET HOME message from Paul. I shared parts of what I learned from Paul's departure from this earth and our intentions to have or have not, a Round House in order. Bayard was deeply moved, and I knew when they met on the other side, they'd likely enjoy each other's company. Having not mentioned all of this to him yesterday, because I needed it to sink in deeper before I could talk about it, I found it interesting that we seemed to always be on the same track.

He chuckled without sound, and a smile was plastered on his face as he gazed out to the ocean and said, "I love that you are here with me tonight for this sunset."

He placed his hand over mine and gently squeezed. "I love the way I can look into your life and see what I need to see in my own. You are a gift."

I was catching on. "As you are to me, Bayard."

We turned to watch the sun drop to the ocean line, in silence, of course.

He walked me to the Denali, now parked alone in the lot. We had the entire beach at sunset to ourselves tonight.

"Bayard, on a lighter note, I'd like to apologize for overreacting to the non-existent riptide and," I paused, "and mostly for showing you my bare white ass."

He cracked up laughing, "Ohhhhh, I see the cat's out of the bag. You figured it out. Well, don't worry about me having a heart attack just because I've seen a woman's bare behind. I've seen plenty. It's my lungs that are suffocating me; my heart's never been stronger." He chuckled.

He continued, "Listen, dear, I was thinking, you do seem to have a tendency to be shy, and also hesitant, about your natural God-given gifts. I suggest you visit a friend of mine's private beach and bask in the sun all day, butt naked. Get comfortable with yourself. There are places all over the world with nude beaches where men, women, and even children gather and have no inhibitions. Practice feeling free like that. It's perfectly safe. He's out of the country for a couple more months. How does that sound?"

"It sounds stupid and also terrifying. So let me get this straight: You think I should go and strip down naked, lay my body in the sand, and that's somehow going to magically unleash something inside of me?"

He smiled at my sarcasm. "Yes, magically delicious."

"You are a dirty old man," I responded.

"Indeed. I am. I'm not dead yet, dear."

With that, he slowly stood up, adjusted his tank and cords, preparing his cane for his forward step.

"Go, doll. Go and fall in love with yourself."

He shared the address with some simple directions, and I decided right there, without hesitation, to do it. In a couple days.

THIS OR SOMETHING BETTER

After returning to the bungalow, I watered plants, slowly and mindfully devoured a Greek salad and then took the dogs for a long walk. Random neighbors waved to me as I strolled past their homes. Some who were near the sidewalk engaged me in conversation. Some recognized Titus and Maximilian and wondered who I was. Excited to meet and greet these people left me feeling relieved. I felt like myself again. So different from the last few years in hiding; moving from neighborhood to neighborhood, mostly after sundown to avoid embarrassing myself while using hefty bags for moving materials. *How divine to simply want to say Hi, again.*

The dogs and I returned from our walk, and for the first time since childhood, I actually had the sensation of feeling *bored!* Doing, hurrying and running out of time didn't exist here. I sat in a chair in the middle of the room petting Sam I Am. I focused on our synchronized breathing patterns as he was curled up on my lap. After some time, I glanced at the dining table with all my belongings and moved to the chair, toting Sam I Am along, where I flipped through a Metropolitan Home beach issue magazine.

I found a pair of scissors in Tracy's kitchen drawer and started cutting out pictures of things I liked. Grabbing a piece of poster board I'd brought from the kids' supply shelf, along with a few of their scented markers, I folded the poster in half and started placing pictures on it. I now had a book-like board and used the four spaces for LOVE/FAMILY; $/WORK/PLAY/TRAVEL; HOME/DESIGN and HEALTH/WELLNESS. The words I wrote and cut from the magazine all resonated with me. In one way or another, these were words I imagined already showing up in my life. I also cut out places I wanted to travel, flowers, fruits, vegetable gardens I wanted to plant and eat. Yoga and art studios, even guest houses found their spot in the book, my mind, and my heart. After they were all placed and ready to be glued in the appropriate areas, I went back to the kitchen drawer, looking for glue or tape.

She had a glue stick. *Perfect!* Shocked to see this in a house with no kids, I inhaled it like a junky might, and it made me miss my Marcus, Clint, and Nicole, more. To offset my homesickness, I focused on creating this "dream board/book," adding things with them in mind. I cut out a picture of a houseboat on Lake Powell. *Perfect, that's just north of Phoenix, that's kind of realistic.* Knowing we could probably manage that someday, I tried to keep everything possible and believable. And then I added a couple crazy things, like an actual beach house *on* the ocean, as well as a loft-like, edgy, cool Brownstone on Lake Shore Drive downtown in Chicago.

I cut a picture out of Jennifer Aniston because I resonated with her for some reason, and "Friends" had been the only show that could get a laugh out of me in the last few years. I had yearned for those kinds of friends in my life. Even though I knew it was make-believe for TV, I wanted to surround myself around those who allowed me just to be me, like the people I was meeting here.

Because I'd obsessively watched Oprah since college, when I would cut class to see certain episodes, I also cut a picture of her out, placing it near CAREER. I liked what she was producing in our world. I pasted contemporary lofts together creating a functional, but an architectural art piece for an office. This sat alongside the art gallery I would own. Next to that a recording studio where talented singers could explode with creativity. The interior office space would be alive and booming; it would start as an up-and-coming small business, turning into an empire I created while being mentored by Richard Branson or someone like him. I pasted the Virgin logo near it all. The green dollar sign in the corner represented the freedom of genius fundraising and simple, but unique, powerful giveback programs.

I imagined myself coming home from work. The interiors all designed with simplicity in mind, but surrounded in art that spoke to all of us. A negative-edge pool, reflecting ponds, waterfalls, fireplaces and outdoor living areas meant to relax and rejuvenate all found their way onto this page as well. With what I knew of Feng Shui, I balanced air, water, fire and earth elements throughout. This home had both a private art studio and private yoga studio. I found a picture of a contemporary yoga studio that was an outside structure made of wood, glass and metal beams. Thick foliage and flowers connected a bridge over a slow running stream on the land.

I whispered, "Ask and ye shall receive," while I used a marker to write on the top of all four sections: "THIS OR SOMETHING BETTER." I felt like that left enough room for God to intervene if needed. Using all the senses; to visualize, hear, feel, smell and even imagining the taste, I let myself reconnect to those things I had already experienced in my past to make it more real. Those things I hadn't experienced yet, I just imagined how all the senses might react. I closed the book with the intention to stay open to any of it while unattached to the particular outcomes.

I took a shower and went to bed early because I could. I had many nights when I wanted to do that in Tucson. But homework wasn't done, a tummy was hurting, a tummy was hungry, a nighttime story had not been read to the end, or the bills needed to strategically be organized for payment. So many recent nights ended feeling guilty that I should be having sex with Bill. *I've ignored him for too long.* Or the dishes needed to be washed and put away, or maybe I should just run one more load of laundry.

Here, I felt no guilt, or pressure to accomplish more. Here, I was enough, and I was doing enough. *Enough was really Enough.* I felt lighter than I had in years. I found myself wondering if it was that simple. Would I have remained strong if I had taken these 11 days before gritty obstacles arose? Would five days away work? Or two?

I started to drift off and think of the WHAT IF's. What if I carved out a small amount of time (1 day to 30 days) where the goal was to do nothing. No chores, no income producing, no planning of anything that might cause stress, no deadlines or goals, no talking, no networking, no responsibilities, no commitments of events to show up for. Would that not change my world? That perspective was changing me. If this works for me, would it work for others? Would it work for Bill?

Right after that train of thought, I considered my hypnotherapy background and my love for words, and started attacking the word "change." I loved breaking words down while exploring what the subconscious mind really believes about the word that's being used. Was change the right word? No. It wasn't exactly what I was experiencing. What was starting to unfold and unveil was *remember, recall, rejuvenate, and replenish*; not change.

All of the exposed weak and strong parts of me here in Santa Barbara were the same in Tucson. But shining a light on them here in this calm oceanside setting released me in a way, giving me a sense of feeling separated from the troubled me and less threatened by my own existence. I could see things better, from afar. I was getting comfortable with *all parts of me.* The good, the bad, the ugly, the weak and the strong. The word *remembering*, felt like a better fit. Truth is, I wasn't coming home a changed woman. I was going to come back more whole; I can *remember* more of who I am. The one God intended me to be.

Many visits to my sister's acupuncture office in Tucson always left me feeling better than when I'd arrived. I always knew my sister was a special healer because I had personally seen it happen in my own life as well as many others. My sister was notorious for the one mantra she always shared with me during our visits. "Judy, *remember* who you are." I thought I knew what she meant then, but today it started to really sink in.

It dawned on me that acupuncture worked in a similar way. It's a technique used for balancing the flow of energy or life force, known as qi or chi (pronounced "Chee"), which is believed to flow through pathways (meridians) in your body. By inserting needles into specific points along these meridians, practitioners believe your energy flow can re-balance. Based on how many personal symptoms disappeared over the years, I'm guessing the needles worked. Just as acupuncture reminds the body to re-balance, to go back to reminding the organs and system to do its thing... My sister's words ran deep. I was now seeing, feeling and re-*membering* my wholeness, my reconnection and how I was re-balancing in this world, while in the arms of Source, and I felt the current take me. Thank you. I thought as I recalled the quote from **C.S. Lewis - I gave in, and admitted that God was God.**

With comfort and joy, I drifted off to sleep with ease.

DAY 6
LEAP AND THE NET WILL APPEAR

As peacefully as I drifted off to sleep, I awakened in the same way. Another day of peaceful, easy living. It was 8:30 A.M., again. This was becoming a regular sleep pattern. My past cycle was up at 5:30 A.M. and to bed, if lucky, by midnight. Clearly, I was allowing my body to take what it needed. Maybe it was making up for lost time.

The new intentions of these days continued to hold pockets of ease and grace, where I remembered, recalled, rejuvenated and revived myself. I fully appreciated this break from the busyness as it allowed this kind of positive thought process to be the first thoughts of my day. Although I felt bad the kids and Bill were still struggling, I knew deep down I had to embrace this without guilt, or I was going to miss out on the 11-day potential benefits.

Excited to meet Skye Hawkins today, I wondered what I should wear; stretchy yoga pants, jeans or shorts? *Will I be lying on a table, Oh God, I hope she doesn't have me undress and lay under a sheet, or, worse, with bare-naked parts of me exposed? Or will we just sit in chairs? Will she lay hands on me? Or will this all be intuitive for her and for me?*

Up until now, I had been living out of my suitcase but remembered all the empty drawers Tracy had shown me. I began taking each item and placing it in a drawer, all neatly stacked and organized, making me aware of the numerous items I could choose from today. Just being present, and handling one at a time, made it easy to pull about eight different outfits together, out of a few different items. It felt like Jesus with the fish and bread loaves—where only a few morsels turned into an entire feast for many.

Heading out onto Highway 101 was a joy, except I did have a small hint of sadness that the next time I'd see that road I'd be leaving this beautiful place behind. It was a gorgeous day, again. And I had printed directions with a map. I made perfect time and arrived an hour early. It was weird how when I was carting kids around, no matter how hard I'd try, I was known for usually running late. But, when alone, no matter how hard I'd try to get there on time, I'd end up way too early.

I found the address of the house and drove around the neighborhood for about 10 minutes, noticing the enormous, high-security gates on surrounding properties. The foliage and trees were all blooming, and I could smell the different emerging scents from the mansions as I drove by. Each estate carried its own personality. Sometimes I was able to view the whole spread of the house as it begged to be seen, but, most often in this neighborhood, I saw only a small part of a residence—a home insisting on its privacy. I wished Bill were here with me. Studying homes *as if* we were about to make a purchase was something we loved to do, and hadn't done since Chicago.

Still having time to spend, I stopped at a small boutique, high-end strip mall. When I say strip mall, I don't mean the regular strip mall with chain stores. This one was made for successful celebrities. A small clothing boutique caught my eye, as I pulled into the parking lot. I studied the customers coming and going. I wasn't dressed to shop in this kind of place, but I found myself wanting to be able to. Just like on State Street, yearning for the cashmere sweater and the freedom money brings, so you can just do and buy whatever you want; all within some reason of course.

I got my courage up and expected them to treat me like the low-income person I was. I had become used to the way a few "kiss ass" people in Tucson were ignoring me these days, and over time I welcomed the solitude. Even though this shift in finances and our marital relationship was substantially rocking our world, the refreshing thing about it was I didn't have to be what others expected me to be anymore.

After walking in, the lady behind the desk surprised me by complimenting me on a leather strap with a string knot wrapped around my wrist. I'd been wearing this bracelet for almost two years and contemplated taking it off before the trip. I had used a black Sharpie marker to legibly scribble *leap and the net will appear* onto the leather. "It's a reminder," I smiled.

It looked as if I had worn it for a decade. The frayed leather edges explained a past in itself. This bracelet had taken a beating. It became a part of me after a lot of dish washing and hand laundering items. It had been exposed to blood from Clint's broken front tooth, puke after he ate a hotdog at his baseball game, sweat from the last moves into the rentals, moisturized with the desert rain, then dried to the bone from the desert heat, most likely some tears (a lot of them my own), soap suds from washing floors, cleaning house, washing cars, bathing kids, and now bathed in seawater. The marker had faded just right, making it look vintage. I decided not to take it off because I honestly didn't think I was *ready* to fully embrace and believe these words, so I left it on as a reminder to let it soak in.

Knowing it didn't match the tailored blazer I had on while at the lawyer's office last week, I kept it hidden under my sleeve. Since the message was privately needed, I wasn't wearing this to draw people's attention, or to create a conversation. When I first met Bayard, I slid it to the side, where he would only see the knotted string. I hadn't thought of it until today, but this bracelet essentially carried our family's DNA—our blood, our sweat and our tears.

"I needed that," she explained, pointing to the message on the bracelet. "You should sell those, just like they are, weathered and worn as it is. Did you make that?"

With a smile, I said, "Yes, I did."

She handed me her card and asked, "Do you live here in Cali?"

"No, Arizona. Tucson actually."

"Oh, nice. Well, so we would need to factor in shipping, but the sales tax would not be an issue. I'm the owner. If you can make me a couple dozen, we can see how they sell. What would your wholesale cost be?"

My wholesale cost? Shipping? Sales tax? What just happened here?

I took her card and slipped it into my purse.

"I'll be home in a week, and I'll give you a call shortly after," I finally responded after the shock wore off.

Stunned, I walked from one rack to the next, wondering what the hell just happened. *It's a dream come true, creating pieces like this on a regular basis.* The hypnotherapist in me always dabbled in words and the meanings of them. At home, I had over-flowing file cabinets and numerous boxes full of quotes I had collected over the years. My mind spun off on how I could create hundreds of bracelets with different messages on leather, silver, fabrics, even recycled materials.

She motioned for me to come to the back rack where she held up a pair of faded celery green, lightweight summer corduroys. I saw the designer tag and thought *Ugh*. Recognizing the designer, I knew that even on a clearance rack they would be way out of my budget. Besides the fact, I don't have a budget for clothes. She delightfully treated me like I had money to burn. I had $120 cash in my purse, and Skye was going to charge between $80 and $100. I still had a crisp brand new $100 bill at the house meant for the spa day I'd passed on. *Maybe I could come back with that money.*

"Try them on. With your figure, you could rock these."

I was too embarrassed to tell her I couldn't afford them. But, I so wanted to try them on anyway. *What could it hurt?*

I headed to the dressing room and slipped them on. They had spandex in them, so every part of my butt and thighs were hugged, but in the best of ways.

She was right, they felt like pajamas, and looked great. I walked out in them holding my T-shirt up.

"I knew it. They look amazing. They fit you like a glove. How do they feel?" She asked.

She was a good sales person.

"How much are they? I can't find a tag." I asked.

"On drastic sale, for $99. It's a one-of-a-kind. I only purchased one because the ladies around here never want to be seen in something their neighbor would also wear."

She saw my face and started explaining they were originally $245.

She paused and took another look at my face.

I smiled as I dipped back into the dressing room, taking them off as fast as I could. As I dropped them to the floor, I noticed how much I loved the way they looked with my worn leather bracelet.

Thank God I don't even have a credit card to charge them, I thought. I loved them that much. And I agreed with the one-of-a-kind thing; I'd want to be the only one with these pants. Having already decided the bracelets need to have their own uniqueness as well. Just as mine did. I was sold on them being one-of-a-kind with unique imperfections reminding us that we are just that—unique and imperfect.

After throwing the pants over the top of the dressing room door, I watched them disappear as she continued to talk to me from the hallway. I quickly applied lip-gloss and fixed my hair, as best I could, glancing into the mirror. Without being able to put my finger on it, I looked different. I'd lost weight from the Kundalini-thing, and some wrinkles disappeared, probably because of the humidity here, but it wasn't totally that. There was something I liked, something I hadn't seen before.

I came out to the front area of the store, ready to share a polite goodbye and confirm, "I'll be in touch soon on the bracelets."

The owner's blue-green eyes twinkled, and she stopped me and said, "I'll be looking forward to it," as she handed me a bag.

The soft green summer corduroys were inside and sticking out of the pocket was a thin stretchy headband with tiny crystals of light green, grays and browns.

I stood stunned. We shared a strange state of deep presence while standing there staring at each other. After telling her nothing about my background, it was as if she knew it all. Or, for the first time, I was seeing my story not get in the way of me.

"Oh goodness. I can't pay."

"Then you must accept," she answered. "You must. There is an art in accepting, receiving, leaving, falling and in leaping, of course," she smiled, "I want you to have these."

We embraced in a long hug and off I went. When I reached my car, I could not resist the pants. I needed them on. Having no business stepping foot in a boutique like that, to having a business plan rolling around in my head, reminded me of how I have mistaken mountains for curbs. *Now that is ease and grace.*

While in the truck, I silently thanked God as I proceeded to slide my jeans off and down to the floor. Distracted by the multi-colored headband, I began running it through my fingertips. The crystals were catching the vibrant sun, splashing the colors all over the dashboard and ceiling. My window was open because of the perfect 80-degree temperature. Startled by a noise, I looked up and out of the window.

"Ma'am, everything all right here?"

Oh geez. There he was, a very formal, no-nonsense officer of the law. Here I was, in my Denali, with no pants. Thank God, he can't see the thong part of my underwear. What if he asks me to get out? Oh my God.

"Sir, I can explain," I said.

Long story short, he was very nice. He became my lookout so I could put the summer green corduroys on. And I promised never to strip in a car again.

Pulling up to the winding driveway of the address Skye Hawkins gave me, I was surrounded by immense flowering trees and bushes. Both squatty and tall palms bordered the winding road up to the house, as well. This was lush living in the obvious Land of Plenty. Being used to my Tucson rental landscaping, which consisted of some gnarly cactus and dusty dirt, this was a literal breath of fresh air, smelling rich in a earthy tropical way.

I re-read her instructions a couple times before getting out of the car. I wanted to avoid creating any more awkwardness today. I had enough laughs; I assumed this lady would mean business.

Cautiously, I walked through the courtyard she mentioned while staying to the right as instructed. A guesthouse, her residence, sat in the near distance. It seemed to be a miniature version of the mansion I could see peeking out through the heavily landscaped yard. Her place looked like something you would see in a fairy tale. The flowering vines crawled out from huge ancient looking pots that surrounded the outside walls of the house. The vines climbed, over and around the entire home making it a multi-colored and multi-fragranced garden art piece. The soil, leaves, and flowers had recently been lightly misted by someone and were twinkling in some of the sunlight streaming through the larger trees nearby.

Skye stood in the doorway. Startled, I jumped back, because I had not even seen her standing behind the screen door. She slowly opened it, and all I noticed were the bright ruby-red lips around her smile. They popped off her pale white skin. Her white teeth sparkled, and pale blue eyes comforted me immediately. She reminded me of Glinda, the good witch in "The Wizard of Oz." I was then equally distracted by the beauty of her small house and didn't observe her other features until I sat down.

Inside, it was meticulously clean and possibly professionally designed, but by someone with a flair for expensive art. A life-size, enormous crystal was positioned perfectly for what appeared to potentially heal anyone who entered. Tucson was known for having the largest gem show in the world and after many hours of time spent there, I'd seen some unique ones. But today, I saw carefully placed crystals I'd never seen before. Bright, vibrant yellow and hot pink. All of them drawing me in. She noticed my interest, offering for me to touch them with a wave of her hand. I did. Lost in her crystals, I forgot why I was even there. *Why was I here?* I had never really discussed that with Katie or Skye on the phone. I wasn't feeling sick anymore, so I wasn't going to bring up health.

In the middle of her coffee table that separated us was a glass bowl filled with celery green smooth polished crystals. I had the sensation of wanting to put them in my mouth. I played with them, mesmerized by the sound of clinking against the crystal glass bowl.

"You're drawn to this green," she said, acknowledging my new summer cords.

"Love those," she added.

Of course, she does. She had great taste and was used to expensive things and, probably, one of a kind apparel. I was confused because she was unlike any other healer I'd met before.

David, back in North Carolina, sported ratty Birkenstocks over his bare feet in all four seasons while wearing torn T-shirts with well-worn jeans. Sometimes he would throw a colorful sarong on top, letting it drape over his jeans. Because of Skye's elegant chimes, I recalled the ones that lined David's front and back porch. The sounds were so masculine compared to hers. My chain of thoughts went to his healing teas. He grew herbs to create those, making me appreciate the intention of love he poured into each cup. I always felt exceptionally relaxed after drinking his teas, and after we had become closer friends, I teased him of lacing it with something else.

I couldn't help to think of another powerful masculine healer I met while living in Chicago, Tom Callahan. He was the first healer I ever met, and he was eating McDonald's when I showed up, while a lit cigarette sat in an ashtray next to him. He was probably 65 pounds overweight. I laid on a table while his hands hovered over me. The small room was dark, and it freaked me out that I wasn't able to see into its corners. There was no incense burning or chimes chiming. He had borrowed this office from a friend, and he couldn't care less about the room we were in. It was all about the space between us, and I could feel the power come from his clean intentions of just wanting to be of service to others. He shared stories about himself and then talked about me the entire session. I wondered if he did that with everyone, or if he sensed my anxiousness and thought it would keep me calm. We spent an hour together, and it was one of the best hours of my life. He was exceptionally kind, real, very funny and he was the first person who gave me 100 percent permission and encouragement to make mistakes.

Skye's crystals twinkled and sprinkled tiny dots and rays of light all over the place. Crystal-covered wires hung in her windows, which looked like $1,000 dollar necklaces. I noticed her light brown, naturally wavy hair, loose and relaxed on her shoulders. She may have been between 45 and 55 years old. She had obviously taken great care of herself and emanated good health.

She motioned for me to sit on a chair. *Thank God. Not going to lay naked on top of a table today.* Face to face, we sat looking into each other's eyes. She put her hands out, palms up, in front of me. I placed my hands on top of hers.

We remained silent for a couple minutes.

"Relax the muscles around your eyes dear," she said.

I had been told that I tended to have a sharp look about me when I was deep in thought, or intuitively trying to read someone's intentions.

I was trying to figure her out, so I imagined I held a sharp glare.

With my hypnotherapy as a background, I was able to easily focus on letting those muscles go.

"Good," she said, confirming I was relaxed enough to begin.

"Oh, goodness, I see great abundance for you and yours."

She paused, looking off to my right.

"Yes, abundance. But this will take some time."

SHIT! I thought. *That's the same as what Katie said.*

She placed my hands on my own thighs. She rubbed her hands together, letting them drop to her sides, palms facing me.

I rubbed my hands on my soft summer-green cords, reminding myself of the abundance that manifested just a short time ago.

She said, "I see layers of fears have compounded over the years. But like an onion, I also see you peeling them back. You do your work, and so it was important for you to find someone that could match that. Your husband."

I never mentioned I was married.

"Your husband," she continued, "is in great pain. Like a wounded soldier, he thinks you may leave him behind."

She paused, and her eyes filled with tears.

"He loves you enough to let you do that."

She glanced past me, off to my right again.

She continued, "You almost left him once before. He thinks you may this time, for good. He's preparing for your departure. In his mind, he's opening up to what *you* may need and is finding the courage to let you go if need be."

She continued, "I would pause before doing that right now. You have your own work to do to get whole. There is so much going on in your lives that to introduce a decision this big right now, under unclear circumstances such as these, will be trying. Your bond with him has been for many lifetimes; you are finally getting it right in this one. You're extreme task mates and will always be each other's student and master teacher. Makes it rough at times, but it also drives you deeper into yourselves and can create a beautiful bond. Your desire for him to be a certain way as a husband, father and provider has choked him off. When you allow yourself to fully BE, it is then that you will allow him to BE as well. You see, the annoyance, mistrust, betrayal, and hopelessness you feel about him, is actually about you, dear. Work on those first."

She paused and then continued, "He's gifted with children, particularly young men. I see him with a whistle. Does he coach?"

"Yes. He has a waiting list. He's amazing. Gives these speeches he can't remember because it appears they come from a different place," I explained quickly.

She nodded in agreement. "They do… come from a different place. He can give the same speeches to adults; he just prefers this age. He made a clear decision of what kind of a man he wanted to be at the pre-teen age and so he likes to plant that seed there. Also, he trusts the youth. He feels they'll tell him the truth whereas people his own age tend to leave him to navigate around lies and agendas. He has great walls. Formed early on, out of survival instincts needed while growing up. You're the only one that has broken them down, off and on. But right now, he is preparing to survive a separation and divorce from you. He isn't fighting for you anymore." She let out a big sigh. "This man has trouble reaching out and asking for help; he's not telling people what he needs because he feels he is not worthy of asking for it."

I was in awe of her natural knowing. She continued, "He's extremely intuitive and can read you from far away. And he is an artist, but has buried his love of music."

Wait what? My jock—is intuitive, an artist and a musician deep in his heart?

I recalled his mother's stories of how he would skip the half-times at his high school football games, when he started as a captain on the football team, in order to perform in the band with his trumpet. *And, oh my God, I had just sold both of his trumpets in the last garage sale!* I didn't pay attention to it at the time, but he was reluctant to let them go. And on that morning, I found that annoying. He was so quiet that day, and probably hurting, but I thought he was just being a jerk. **Hemingway's** quote came to mind, **You are so brave and quiet, I forget you are suffering.**

I made a mental note to add this to my list of things to fix or forgive in the spiral journal I started last night: *trumpets.*

She continued: "I see two male energies and one female. Your kids?"

I nodded.

"The oldest, how old is he?" she asked.

"Marcus, he's eleven, just turned it," I replied.

"Okay. His astrological sign is Cancer. He's the most sensitive of all signs. Aww, he's so dear. Still looking off to the right, like she was watching a movie of him, she went on to describe all three kids' personalities perfectly, and even the way they physically looked.

"Marcus is a stocky thing. I want to say athlete because of his stature, but he isn't drawn to team sports. He's brilliant and very creative. He could easily be in any kind of engineering of machines or even philosophy. He'll be an amazing husband and father. May have trouble with addiction. Watch that."

"The second one has a lean build."

"Yes, that's Clint."

"An athlete. Outdoorsman. You'll be watching him play sports all the way through college possibly. He's a natural in everything he tries. He loves to be alone, but also can be content in a crowd of people. Being the middle child, he's mastered flexibility. He'll need to pay attention to having and keeping a voice, just like you."

Next, she said, "Your girl."

"Yes, Nicole."

"Nicole is a perfect combo of the two of you. She won't do well scholastically until college, where she will take off. A social butterfly. Approachable by all types of people. Strong leader that will take her time figuring that out. A natural athlete, very strong physique, but won't just take a scholarship, nor a job, or a man for security. She'll want to travel abroad. If you can manage it financially, let her go. She'll take care of herself quite well. One last thing about you, the fear of getting sick makes you sick. Continue to peel back the layers of that onion. At this stage of your life, your fear comes from not wanting to leave your three kids."

Skye noticed the corner of my journal sticking out of my purse. I had brought it to take notes and forgot to do that. So, I made a mental note; I will go to the beach and write this all down while it's still fresh.

"Do you have questions?" She pointed to my spiral notebook.

Our one-hour session was going on three now.

It wasn't so much about questions. What I had brewing in my head was a big list of shame.

I explained, "Over the last five days, with forgiveness in mind, I'd been paying attention to potentially harmful words, acts and intentions from the past, to others and myself. I have to add 'trumpet' to the list because I sold the two Bill had."

Skye shared, "Your focus on what you don't have in your life has been holding you hostage. We cannot manifest anything different than what we direct our thoughts toward. That journal you have written in holds a lot of 'fix and forgives.' Remember, to forgive yourself, so you can invite all the good that wants to come to you. Go to the beach and focus on what you do want. And keep in mind you are already on your way. The reason Cali feels good and right to you is because you're in the right frame of mind here. Your thoughts have and always will become things," she said, pointing to my green corduroys.

She finished our session teaching me the Hawaiian ritual used for reconciliation and forgiveness called, Hoʻoponopono (ho-o-pono-pono.)

Modern versions are performed within the family by a family Elder, or by the individual alone. The purpose was 'to make right' broken family relations.

She explained that in 1976, Morrnah Simeona, regarded as a healing priest or kahuna lapaʻau, adapted the traditional hoʻoponopono of family mutual forgiveness to the social realities of the modern day. Simeona's version was influenced by her Christian (Protestant and Catholic) education, and by her philosophical studies about India, China, and Edgar Cayce, she emphasized prayer, confession, repentance, and mutual restitution and forgiveness. She didn't use mantras or conditioning exercises. Her teachings included: there is a Divine Creator who takes care of altruistic pleas of Men; when the phrase "And it is done" is used after a prayer, it means Man's work ends and God's begins.

After Simeona's passing in 1992, her former student Ihaleakala Hew Len, co-authored a book with Joe Vitale called Zero Limits referring to Simeona's ho'oponopono teachings. The book brings forward the new idea that the main objective of ho'oponopono is getting to "the state of Zero, where we would have zero limits. No memories. No identity." To reach this state, one has to constantly repeat the mantra: I love you. I'm sorry. Please forgive me. Thank you. This is based on Len's idea of 100 percent responsibility, which means taking responsibility for everyone's actions, not only for one's own. If one would take complete responsibility, then everything one sees, hears, tastes, touches or in any way experiences would be one's responsibility because it's in one's life. The problem would not be with our external reality; it would be with ourselves. To change our reality, we'd have to change ourselves. It views all consciousness as part of the whole, so using parts of the idea of holism: "any error that a person clears in their own consciousness should be cleared for everyone."

Over the years, I had heard of many modalities and healing methods, but the simple, yet deep nature of this was rocking me to the core. I looked forward to reading more about this, but for now, I was going to work with it by letting it kickstart my families ground zero. I found my hands rubbing the summer cords again. My bracelet caught my attention. "Leap and the net will appear."

Skye saw me look at it and asked, "What does that mean to you today? What could you do, during the rest of your stay that would allow you to leap? Don't tell me what it is. It's important to keep it private and do it for yourself. Whatever it is, Judy, keep the faith that the net will appear. Just remember, it might not be the net you expect."

Having already made up my mind to accept the dare Bayard proposed to open myself up to being naked on a private beach, I went to the place that scared me the most, the open mic night. It seemed silly, but for me, getting up on stage literally made my stomach ache. While standing in front of Skye, I silently confirmed to myself: *I'm doing it.* It would be good practice to leap in this way. Besides, I had no choice. Because now the fear of regret for *not* leaping far surpassed the fear of the actual leap.

EST. 8.21.88

I pulled into my space at Arroyo Beach. Opening the back door on the Denali, I grabbed my towel and yoga mat to sit on. Knowing Bill always stashed a few bottles of water in a hidden compartment where the tire iron was, I popped open the hard plastic door. Next to the water was a compartment with an elastic net holding a small bag of mysterious contents. I glanced inside, realizing it was filled with the items from the kids that Bill had mentioned the day I left. Excited about the hidden surprises, I placed the bag in my beach tote along with a spiral notebook and pen.

After hearing Skye tap into each kid today, I was deeply missing them. Going through the bag would be the first thing I'd do after sitting down on the beach. I went to my usual secluded carved-out space up against the mossy cliff, where the wind could not reach me. It was cooler today, so I was glad to have my soft summer corduroys on. Because of the brisk late afternoon temperature, there were only a few people with sweaters on walking the beach. With nobody planted in a beach chair or on a towel, I felt like I had the place to myself. Bayard was nowhere in sight, which kind of surprised me.

I started with Marcus's gifts, which consisted of a small stuffed Simba lion, a small yellow dump truck and a handwritten note from him. My mom and I had taken him to his first Broadway musical, "The Lion King," in Chicago, and we bought him that Simba afterward. Even as a little boy, he was so moved by the message of Lion King, that letting me have this Simba really got to me. One of his favorite things to play with, when he was little, was this dump truck. For years, he had filled it with Illinois snow, North Carolina red dirt and Tucson desert sand. I plowed it through the sand, and with a handful, I filled the back of it, before reading his note: **Dear Momma, HUSA. Love, Marcus**

"Husa" was part of a secret language we had developed and utilized until he was about four years old.

I flashed back to his pediatrician's growing concern about how he still hadn't started talking by the age of 31/2. The doctor warned me, "I don't know what to tell you, Mrs. Cochrane. He's in the 120th percentile as far as the growth chart goes. He's huge, healthy and seems alert, so I don't foresee a learning disability, but we'll need to keep an eye on this and run tests soon because it's strange that he isn't communicating."

I objected, "Well, he communicates, it just isn't with words. He uses a word he made up, 'HUSA,' (who sa) for everything. It means lots of different things depending on his inflection of the word."

I explained further, "When he's in his high chair and he's done eating, "HUSA" has the same tone as ALL DONE. And when he's in the high chair and wants more of something, his inflection sounds like MORE? And when you ask him if it's naptime, he would respond with a tone that matched, NOOO, Thank you."

The pediatrician already had some reservations about me. I always wanted to treat the kids alternatively before shoving antibiotics and immunizations into their bodies. Objections, questions or needed explanations were always a part of our visits. We had a lot of lengthy conversations and outright arguments, but, by the third kid, we ended up liking each other and learned to get along.

He, with annoyance, clarified, "If he doesn't start communicating with English words and sentences, Judy, we will need to take another look. Understand?"

At that time, I had to admit I was concerned, but on the flip side, I did like that we had a private language where, somehow, I understood him, and he was also heard.

I smiled, remembering the day when I told my Dad, who was visiting for the weekend, about the doctor's concern that Marcus wasn't talking yet. Being a member of Mensa, he was a "contemplator" of things, and he sat quietly for a while. Then, while staring with adoring eyes towards Marcus, he shared, "Maybe he doesn't think we've said anything important enough to respond to, yet."

I quickly decoded from the letter; Marcus was coming from a good place. The next item I pulled from the bag was from Clint. It was a small stuffed Dalmatian dog, a Hot Wheels racecar, and a note. This Dalmatian was the first stuffed animal I'd bought him. I recalled my naïve beliefs, as a new mother, thinking that these two would be so similar just because they were both boys. In some small ways they were, but now that they were 11 and 9, I could see the differences so well. All three would mirror back to me what I needed to see in myself, but occasionally Clint would mirror back with the feel of a lightening bolt. From birth, he had the ability to be present, calm and relaxed, which made him sharp as a tack. This gave him the ability to effortlessly slam open your door of darkness in the most loving and gentle way while letting the light shine in.

One day, while in North Carolina, before HER, I was frustrated, sleep deprived, and tired of mundane housewife roles. For no reason, I slammed shut a kitchen cabinet door. Clint was on the staircase landing, where he had full view of me. He was lying on his belly pushing a little racecar around, and he stopped to look at me right after he heard the bang. He rested his chin on one of his arms, and we stayed silent and still while staring at each other. Instantly, I felt bad because I didn't want him to think he was in trouble. As usual, he was playing by himself so beautifully and had done nothing wrong. And then this quiet, shy boy directly and genuinely asks, in a calm little 4-year-old voice, "What are you so mad at, Momma?" My canned answer, "nothing" wasn't the truth and I had to look at that.

It was a perfect question with perfect timing, and over the years, I have always appreciated his unconscious ability to pinpoint these thoughts for me.

His note was simple, and made perfect sense because not only was he able to shine the light; he seemed to stay in a place of gratefulness without asking for anything in return. This kid rarely had demands. Even as a baby, I had to offer feedings because he hardly ever cried out for them.

Momma, I love you. Thank you for taking care of me. Love, Clint.

Nicole's gift to me was the first doll I'd ever bought for her. The soft, powder-pink doll was the size of a large hand. She treasured this stuffed doll and slept with it every night, so there was a part of me that felt great guilt that she hadn't kept it to comfort her in those first few days I was gone. When I was pregnant with her, I prayed for a healthy child. Everyone around me flat out said they hoped I had a girl. Obviously, that would've been welcomed, but I was scared to put parameters around something as God-driven and miraculous as a baby. I received an ultrasound, and they told me they thought it was a boy, so I named the baby-on-the-way Luke. Upon arrival, she shocked all of us in the room. A day later, I found myself, like a seasoned birther of babies, with engorged breasts ready to explode and an ice pad between my legs, on a shopping trip, as I toted all three kids alongside me. We scrambled around town buying infant clothes in pink and this particular doll which the boys helped pick out.

When I think back, I could tell that, even as an infant, she would have so much to teach me. I was right. The female bond we already shared ran deep and pushed me to be better, stronger and more loving. Even at this young age of 7, I could see the things Skye brought to light. Nicole had a way of brightening a space and effortlessly drawing people in and commanding attention, yet she had a humbleness with no intentions to shine a light like that, and often when she recognized she was the center of attention, she'd humbly dip out of the room. Her genuine nature was seen by all ages, from infants to the elderly. I could see how one of my jobs would be to keep reminding her of that authentic nature at her core.

Her love of art, and the mixing of mediums emanated through her note, which was a multi-colored heart made with marker, crayons, paint, and some glitter, signed by her: *I love you, mommy. xoxox Nicole*

All the toys and letters surrounded me on top of my yoga mat. Using my camera, I started taking pictures of the three heart-shaped rocks I had found earlier, positioning them next to each of the kid's gifts. I planned on framing the photos to be given as presents for them. As I was about to put the items back in the bag, I saw a note at the very bottom of the bag. It was from Bill:

> *Dear Judy,*
> *I want to say something profound but can't find the words. Maybe I'm not supposed to. I don't know. I can only tell you this. I love you. Always have. And in all ways, will. These kids that we brought into this world are the greatest treasures. I hope Santa Barbara gives you the space you need right now to be YOU. I've too, noticed your smile diminish over the last few years. It's the opposite of what I wanted for you. If you feel like you need to fly and can't with me anymore, then I can and will move aside. Forever, 82188 – B.*

The note didn't make me cry, and it didn't provide answers to where this marriage would go. That wedding date, 8.21.88, the one he first wrote in the steam on our shower door in North Carolina, might just be numbers to most, but it was comforting to see him write it. No matter what happens or in what direction we go, we will always share that date as it was the invisible start of our family of five. *So gratefull for that.*

Bill, at times, had been good at encouraging me to be my best self over the years, so his desire to see me soar, even without him, wasn't surprising. What I did pay more attention to, is what Skye had confirmed: He wasn't fighting for me anymore. He was going to find a way to let me go *if I said so.* He had lost his voice.

Just then I heard, "What in the hell? Okay, you may have legit lost your mind girl. Is this a make-shift kindergarten classroom, with a nap mat and all?" Hottie laughed as he stood in front of me and my yoga mat, surrounded by all the kid's toys.

While I explained what I was working through, he sat next to me on the mat. He took the Hot Wheels racecar and ran it up and down his surfboard just like a little boy. I couldn't help to think how much fun the boys would have learning how to surf. In my curious and imaginary mind, I was picturing them, not meeting Hottie, but someone older, and what it would be like to introduce a new boy-friend. I fast-forwarded to their teen years. Would they even be able to relate to a new man, and could this new man relate to them? And then I fast-forwarded to when the kids were getting married and having their first babies. What would it be like to have the new guy attend all of those functions? I pictured myself, annoyed because Bill and his girlfriend, or second wife, could potentially be allowed to visit one of our kid's first babies, before me. We'd have to navigate around all of those details for the rest of our divorced lives. I pictured still enjoying Bill's company, but the idea of introducing new players to our world looked complicated. I mean, it could be done. I hadn't had much proof where I'd seen it done very well yet, but I figured because of the way Bill and I operate, we could eventually make it work. But I let myself feel the deep sadness creep in. After all these years of talking about spending our future years as engaged grandparents, I realized they might be memories we would not create in this lifetime.

NO REGRETS

Hottie was curious about marriage and kids in general. He had an interest in how and when that would unfold in his life. Having him up to speed on where I was at with Bill, he felt comfortable asking, "Now that you've been married for 15 years, what would you say is most important in a marriage? Besides finding someone super-sexy and smokin' hot?" He smiled.

I answered, "Yeah, well chemistry has to be there. And finding someone who's able to do the work on themselves and the marriage, to keep it rich and also, on the flip side, to make sure you and they are courageous enough to move on if needed."

He asked, "So where are you at with Bill today then?"

"Not sure. Maybe I want it to work. But I know one thing for sure, I don't want to tell him *how* to make it work. He needs to come to the table having done his own work on himself. Like he did in North Carolina."

He nodded. "I think I get that."

He continued, "And what about the kids? Was having them harder than you thought? I'm not so sure I'd be any good at that."

Laughing out loud, I said, "Aw, you'd be great. I can tell you've been raised by some cool parents. Just do all the good stuff they did and work on not repeating any of the bad. Listen, you have a big heart, you're patient, you're funny, which your wife will appreciate when the shit hits the fan, and I mean literally. When you have your first weekend where they are all puking and have the runs at the same time, including you and your wife… you just have to laugh. There is no predicting of when they will be sick, hurt, mad or sad. You just have to roll with it. You'll be good at that. Besides, you'll be the best at teaching them about the ocean, music and all that you love. We need some more spawning in that direction, right?"

"Absolutely."

"There's no way to prepare, so don't bother worrying about it. I can only shed so much light for you as it's a unique experience for each parent. I can say the love I have for these children is explainable to a small extent, and then it's something in the heavens that knows the real depth. I can't fully articulate that love, but I am, at the same time, sure I can *feel* it. Deep."

I continued: "So far, having these three children came with surprises, tests, lessons, challenges, obstacles and gifts, and then more gifts. They're supposed to. We switch the roles of student and teacher routinely, day-by-day and, sometimes, hour-by-hour. I found that when I was open, they became my master teachers. At times, they were vibrant and sometimes gnawing, painful mirrors that let me peek inside myself and then there were times of full, glorious exposures of truth.

My connection to the kids is often of awe. Here's an example of the mirroring; I could see the ties that bound us, highlighted by recent events in Tucson. If I happened to be anxious, I saw that sometimes play out in them. If I were at peace, they most likely would be too. When I noticed they might need to have a voice to stand up to a bully, I saw that for myself in my own life as well. I study them like I've never studied anything before. Now that I'm a little more experienced, I know better than to make them a mini-me, or worse, overly highlight their unique abilities and make them trophy kids. We can create too much discomfort for our kids by going in either of those directions. They have to just be supported and loved… no matter what.

Having always had this feeling they were on loan from God, I felt it was mandatory to honor them as they were here specifically with Bill and me, for reasons I may or may not discover until I'm on the other side."

We paused our chat for a bit and then I continued, "The teen years frighten me because I could envision them at 18, 16 and 14. God help me."

We both laughed.

"I can only hope that they will love me as much as I love them, but I have a feeling that's impossible. I've never loved any beings more."

"So, do you feel the same love for Bill then?"

"My love for Bill is different. With the kids, it began at my core. For nine months they were connected to my umbilical cord, feeling like it came straight from Source and worked its way out. My love for Bill appeared to start more on the outside, I believe with support from Source, but worked its way in. Bill's DNA inside each child may mean the same core connection for him. And for our friends that had adopted, or the Aunts, Uncles and Grandparents that also feel that same core connection, *without* an umbilical cord, it would be the intention to connect to a child and then, when found, it comes as a divine gift that answers the seeking intention or prayer connected to the same Source."

Laughing, he said, "Geez, that's some deep stuff, Jude. You're so fuckin' weird. I love it!"

I nodded and laughed along.

"It's just, I can see where the kids pushed and pulled us in directions we were unable first to prepare for, and I imagined that would carry on throughout the years. But I rest assured today that there is one thing I would never find with them, and that is regret. Up until them, I'd never known that feeling in regards to another.

There may have been one wise elderly lady who said it best in our local grocery store back in Illinois. After she randomly asked me if I would have more children after having just Marcus and Clint, I replied, "Probably done."

And she said, "Well, I can assure you of this, my dear, if you decide to have another, you'll never regret it."

"That resonated with me, and a few months later, I ended up pregnant with Nicole."

"Ya jumped right on that one, didn't ya?"

We both laughed.

"But, seriously, it's about love, love, love. Love is endless. I found that it drives deep into your soul. But it isn't something foreign or new; it's more of a reminder. It reminds you of the love you have to give. And these little beings give you silent permission and a nudge to give more than you ever thought you could. While at the same time, they open you up to how much you are loved and also expose you to how much you are willing and able to receive.

It's funny how sometimes wishes do come true. Because one of our 'family songs' is from Foreigner "I Want To Know What Love Is." It would echo, as I sang from a second-floor banister in the first house Bill and I owned. It's the same house we brought all three kids home to after they were born... it's where we were established, on earth anyway. If you want to know what love is, children, *all* children, are clear answers to that question."

"Well, I know I'm only 24, so I don't have all the answers, but I can say this, I feel sorry for any new guy who comes into your life to try to sweep you off your feet."

Laughing, I asked, "Why?"

He stood up and grabbed his surfboard, and scanned all the items around me. With his finger, in the air, he drew an imaginary circle around me, the yoga mat, the kids' toys and letters, he said, "As an outsider looking in, just seems like, what you're looking for, *is all right here.*"

In awe of his youthful, yet wise wisdom, I returned his sweet smile, which lingered. *A Hottie, inside and out.*

I watched him walk away, and sat on the mat for quite some time, thinking of his words. Pulling the spiral notebook out, I read the notes I took on the ho'oponopono mantra. The mentioning of a family in repair and ground zero resonated with me. It made me want to fight for them, but without an end result in mind, as in a reconciliation of this marriage. Just a good fight, the one with intention for the good of all, no matter where we land.

GROUND ZERO

After Hottie had taken off, I had a desire to feel as much of the ground as possible, so I laid on my stomach, feeling the bumpy sand beneath my belly and thighs. I held a vision of Bill in my mind while I spoke these words that Skye shared earlier:

I LOVE YOU. I'M SORRY. PLEASE FORGIVE ME. THANK YOU.

I repeated the mantra over and over again while I visualized all of our past issues and walls dissolving until it felt like it resonated truth. I imagined a white light around him and love, without conditions, reaching him.

Bill's kiss and the words he spoke to me right after the merger, popped into my head: "Thank you. I couldn't have done it without you." With that, I felt a confirmation of the earlier release in taking the fair amount of responsibility in our family's rise and our fall. It was clear to me, where I had pushed and/or supported Bill to go after this life of wealth. I even pushed for living in certain parts of the country. He would have been perfectly happy staying in the Chicago area, but I insisted on warmer climates, and I insisted on Tucson. I became a partner in the gamble to come out on top. I let him lose himself in the race, knowing full well, as his best friend, that he wasn't happy. Sure, he's a big boy, and should be "finding his own way towards happiness," but our agreement to marry united us, and I had bailed on parts of our relationship that I could take responsibility for now.

Some truths took longer than others. All of them relating to the kids came easy. Focusing on Nicole and my leaving her in tears that morning, I could see where this whole trip was going to be positive for her. She was finally spending time with her Dad, which was probably both good and also hard... but it is the "place" we are in presently and the process we are going through. We aren't going to be happy people and a happy family every single minute of every day. And, as a grown woman, taking this time for myself would be like a lifelong permission slip for her, in her later years, to do the same, as well as for the boys.

Deeply inspired by the natural release I was feeling by doing this, I began scribbling new people down in the spiral notebook I hadn't thought of before. I could no longer be mad at Cami, the friend "greatly opposed to me taking this trip." I had given her silent permission when we became friends to voice her opinions, and she was only offering her thoughts because she thought she was helping my world to be more like hers. And, to her, that was a good thing. Even if she even had negative intention in regards to our friendship, it was powerless, as long as I remained clear and had a voice. *I love the gift of honesty.*

I moved on to thoughts about Abby, 'the bitch' at La Paloma Country Club. I couldn't take her attacks personally after saying this mantra. I recalled meeting her sisters and mother at an event, and it all made sense. She wasn't raised to support other women. She was born into a family who submerged themselves in jealousy and judgment; she and her sisters had scratched their way to the top to be the enviable one in their tribe. I couldn't take her points about me personally after realizing this, and I slipped into gratitude for the exposure to her and the other women. I could forgive myself and thank her for being a mirror to me for my own growth.

The lawsuits that ruined every weekend for the last few years... their greed in wanting and taking more and more and more now looked more like desperate survival to me. So often I wanted to scream, "Go to hell," but maybe they were already there. It became clear that their desperate fight to stay "on the top" as a businessman, a provider, and a powerhouse was a literal living hell for them and their families. I'd been there. I get it. This was looking more like a personal attack, but on themselves, not me, not Bill and not on our kids. Any move they had and will make would serve them right in a good way. Just as I believed my moves had and will.

Any and all friends and family who had their opinions of us, good and bad, was never any of my business and no longer served me, so I was able to bless and release. I found myself in a beautiful groove and carried on.

I LOVE YOU.   I'M SORRY.   PLEASE FORGIVE ME.   THANK YOU.

Thoughts of the judge, who questioned my need for food stamps, came to mind. Wasn't he just doing his job? The rude woman behind the glass who wouldn't let me in... well, if it hadn't been for her, I wouldn't have been back to check on Nicole in the hot car so quickly. Sure, she may not have consciously known what she was doing for our family, but did a higher power intervene and possibly lead and direct her to kick me out of there?

God only knows.

It struck me, that the original lady who seemed annoyed when I first got my food-stamp card had become nicer with each return visit. *Maybe I had become nicer with each visit as well.* I could see clearly now how her background of beliefs and experiences had created a possible suffering from discrimination. I understood how she might not have been able to be color blind in my presence at first because of it. But I was feeling real peace and elation in the fact that over this short time of many appointments, we ended up getting to know one another. She and I created a different connection, a bond.

I recalled it was her kids' photos tacked to her cubicle wall that first broke the ice for us. She was a young, single, full-time-working mom, and the minute I genuinely recognized her children, their ages, and her obvious struggle to hold it together, things shifted for us. We may have broken through a barrier because we let go of our past sufferings by being present with one another, and as we did, it released us into a space where understanding allowed love to unfold.

I repeated the mantra over and over for her, for myself and—why not?— Any other person who may have held onto that at one time or another. I could now visualize myself arm-in-arm with them, entering battlefields.

I flipped my body over and let the first sign of sun today shower me. In one way or another, all of the people I thought of had their own set of complicated sufferings. I always thought, and had been told I was a compassionate person, but this took it to a whole other level. I let myself feel even more compassion for them, and I let go of anger, and God forbid, Karmic revenge, as I became more comfortable in a belief that whatever happens… if necessary, they will answer to a higher power than me someday. I could stay out of it now. Peacefully and lovingly. I don't have to take any of it personally, and if I do, that suffering was my choice. I remained with the desire to protect myself, if needed, from unfair, harmful free will, but the foundation of understanding and love poured through, drowning my past belief systems. I dropped my head back to feel the warm sun on my face.

I was finally feeling great LOVE for all again.

I was deeply sorry.

I clearly wanted forgiveness for any and all parts I played in any of it. And I trusted there were parts I couldn't see. I had to start by forgiving the part of me that was once unforgiving and then go from there. The tears flushed out of me. It had been days now. The feeling of gratefulness flooded, flooring me as I sunk into the sand. In joy, I sat there embracing this mantra, in all its parts. Silently repeating… I LOVE YOU. I AM SORRY. PLEASE FORGIVE ME. THANK YOU…

TRY TO UNDERSTAND MEN. IF YOU UNDERSTAND EACH OTHER, YOU WILL BE KIND TO EACH OTHER. KNOWING A MAN WELL

NEVER LEADS TO HATE AND ALMOST ALWAYS LEADS TO LOVE.
JOHN STEINBECK

The hum and whiz of the oxygen tank grabbed my attention.

"Ahhhhh, keep your face to the sun like a flower."

"Hi Bayard," I was so pleased to see him.

"Update please."

The download began on all the new information gracing my presence today; the boutique owner, Skye Hawkins, 82188 and the Ho'oponopono. He pushed the whole book idea thing again, and I politely ignored him. He enjoyed the corduroy story, so I explained the details about the bracelet and that I would be in contact with the boutique owner next week about pricing.

He just laughed out loud, as he got a kick out of it, "It could answer all financial problems."

"Well, hold on there Bayard," I explained, "Don't get too excited. It's gonna be a small home business. I'm excited, but also realistic that I may not be able to make this profitable. Plus there's no space in the rental to even create these. Bill will be opposed and pissed that I chose a crafty business rather than a traditional job with a salary and needed benefits, like dental and health insurance. It's practically impossible for me to start this with no money for tools, supplies, and materials."

"Your use of the word impossible is interesting, Doll. Since you love to dissect words so much, you may want to start with that one. It actually says *I'm possible.*"

We both laughed.

After a nice long walk and talk on the beach, we watched the sunset in silence. Hottie had returned from surfing and joined up with us. He brought up the open mic night again, and I told him, I made a decision. "I'm doing it."

"Oh Doll, I'll be there," Bayard confirmed.

He looked beat, so I said, "Don't push yourself if you're tired."

He reached out for me, and we walked hand in hand down the beach towards the parking lot.

"Ya know, Doll, Arroyo is Spanish for a dry creek that seasonally fills and flows with rain water and, on top of that, flash floods are common in arroyos. It's as if it seasonally finds itself over and over again."

I stopped, turning toward him.

He continued, as he pulled me in for a hug, "You've been waiting for the flash flood, only to become a body that continually flows after running dry. And you got there, Doll. You listen to me, the relationships you have had and lost in your life, have tested you—run you dry—but they've taught you something about yourself. Agree?"

I nodded.

He continued, "The failures we face in life may create a setback from time to time, but we emerge wiser, stronger and with a deeper understanding and some relief that we have the ability to survive things. I'm proud of you Doll. You do good work. Keep it up."

He let me stay in his arms for a while. With the side of my face gently pressed against his cold air tubes. While memorizing this moment, I watched the waves roll in.

Before getting in my car, Bayard made sure I was still scheduled to visit the private beach the following day.

Hottie overheard us and made fun saying, "Bayard gave me the address, so I'll be joining you! So, see ya tomorrow Jude! And hey, may want to wear some sunscreen, its gonna be hot."

I playfully flipped Hottie off and stared Bayard down with a look of: *you better not have given him that address.*

Bayard was doing his quiet bellowing laugh thing, while agreeing, "Sunscreen *will* be important. And remember, there's no truth without a dare."

DAY 7
GROUNDED

While driving to the yoga studio, "Drift Away" by Uncle Kracker, blasted over the speakers… again. This song was just not getting old.

I gently visualized a front parking place, without trying to manhandle the details and strategize around what traffic would be like. As gracefully as possible, I visualized pulling into a front spot with no strings attached to the how it was going to happen, just as if it was *already* happening. And, like magic, a lady started to pull out of the first spot for me.

After greeting the women behind the yoga studio counter, all by their first names now, I headed for a private spot in the back of the room. I knew ahead of time this class was specifically going to focus on getting the root chakra grounded into the earth, and I was thrilled it was perfect timing for me to do this before I headed to the private beach. This class would also be good for someone who may not be directly in touch with having open sexual centers, which Hottie innocently and unknowingly made me well aware of. I imagined the class being jam-packed with back bends and spread-eagle positions where all can have full view. I was desperately hoping it wasn't going to make me run for more cover. I knew it was something I should force myself to do, but I sure was apprehensive about it.

Violet was there, ready for class. Our favorite yoga girl would lead the class today. *Oh how I hoped that her dab of essential oil was not going to have to go where I thought it might.*

I'm leaving, if that is the case. No savasana for me.

Class started at a quick pace, and we were all soon dripping sweat. I couldn't help but notice that it mimicked a very hot sex scene where ravenous making out (rapid forward folds and backbends) would lead down to the intertwined extremities (straddling, twisting and spreading) and end in pure ecstasy and exhaustion (savasana).

The root chakra class was, as I expected. We spent a lot of our time on our backs; knees bent and dropping open into butterfly wings. And then flopping both knees to the right with a twist in the waist and then flipping to the opposite side. We ended with air-splits, lying on our backs while applying gentle pressure, with our hands, on the insides of our thighs. At one point, she asked us to visualize all of our sexual organs relaxing. I couldn't do it. I tried to visualize my ovaries, fallopian tubes, vagina, and cervix, as all relaxing, but I just felt myself growing tenser. I think our teacher recognized my struggle. *Damn my non-poker face*; I thought as she knelt next to me. She put her warm, small hand on my abdomen and her other hand, not touching, but right outside my root chakra, which was basically between my legs, allowing me to feel the heat of her hand. I was working on getting comfortable with this, as I understood the whole idea here. Eventually, I did settle down. I was proud of myself for not allowing my awkwardness to take over and produce unnecessary laughter. She hovered there a short while and then decided my sacrum didn't look aligned. She then took her two hands and slid them, so quickly that I couldn't react, under my butt cheeks. She pulled them apart and said "There" in a satisfied tone.

So, I lay there, warmed up and spread eagle with my butt cheeks spread. *I did it.* No laughter, not too awkward. And I was able to dive deeper into the position bringing me to a feeling of being more free and open.

While she stood in front of the room, she went into a deep visual meditation, encouraging us to stay open. She asked us to focus on the colors of the chakras. Red for the root chakra, orange for the sacrum, yellow for the solar plexus, green for the heart chakra, blue for the throat, violet for the third eye and white for the crown.

I reached back on my beginning studies of the seven chakras.* I contemplated all the others that were presently being discovered and spoken of today but stayed focused on the original seven energy centers in our body in which energy flows through. Specifically, the root and sacral chakra, as I wondered if I had blocked energy in this area.

I had read a lot about how blocked chakras can often lead to dis-ease emotionally, mentally and physically, and how each chakra represents what we can do to keep this energy flowing freely. The root chakra represents our foundation and feeling of being grounded. The location is the base of the tailbone area. It made sense that the emotional issues connected to this chakra are having to do with survival issues such as financial independence, money, and food.

I ended up falling asleep in savasana, and when I awoke, it was time to go to the beach and test myself on whether I'd be able to stay grounded, while naked. Not being sure of being able to make it back the next day, I announced to all, "If I can't fit this in tomorrow, I may not see you all again. Thank you for sharing these beautiful classes with me."

On my way out to my car, I encouraged Violet to join me at the open mic night.

"This is going to be fabulous. I wouldn't miss it for the world," she said as she squeezed my hand in hers.

*THE SEVEN CHAKRA'S

1. Root Chakra – RED.
    Represents our foundation and feeling of being grounded.
    Location: Base of spine in tailbone area.
    Emotional issues: Survival issues such as financial independence, money, and food.

2. Sacral Chakra – ORANGE.
    Our connection and ability to accept others and new experiences.
    Location: Lower abdomen, about 2 inches below the navel and 2 inches in.
    Emotional issues: Sense of abundance, well-being, pleasure, and sexuality.

3. Solar Plexus Chakra – YELLOW.
    Our ability to be confident and in-control of our lives.
    Location: Upper abdomen in the stomach area.
    Emotional issues: Self-worth, self-confidence, self-esteem.

4. Heart Chakra – GREEN.
    Our ability to love.
    Location: Center of chest just above heart.
    Emotional issues: Love, joy, inner peace.

5. Throat Chakra – BLUE.
    Our ability to communicate.
    Location: Throat.
    Emotional issues: Communication, self-expression of feelings, the truth.

6. Third Eye Chakra – INDIGO.
    Our ability to focus on and see the big picture.
    Location: Forehead between the eyes. (Also called the Brow Chakra)
    Emotional issues: Intuition, imagination, wisdom, ability to think and make decisions.

7. Crown Chakra – VIOLET or WHITE.
    The highest Chakra represents our ability to be fully connected spiritually.
    Location: The very top of the head.
    Emotional issues: Inner and outer beauty, our connection to spirituality, pure bliss

AS I AM

I'd seen it in travel magazines: large groups of naked bodies lying exposed on a beach somewhere far away in another land. Legs spread without a care about saggy boobs and wrinkles folding off into the sand. I had spent my whole life often being described by some, as a bit of a prude. I never desired to see random naked strangers, and I did everything I could not to be seen, as well. I wasn't surprised that Bayard felt the need to point out my timid nature, in regards to this.

Years ago, Bill and I stayed at a Marriott in Key West, Florida where they hosted a topless beach, and not once did I venture down that sandy path. I didn't know for sure, but I thought I could see in Bill's face that he wished I was more comfortable with myself and that I would have been the wild one to let go on that trip. It was one of the many times in our marriage when I wondered if I really was the best choice in a wife for him.

I followed Bayard's directions and found myself in one of the most serene and beautiful spots I had yet to see in Santa Barbara. *Who was this guy that lived on this property?* This place dripped of wealth, and it showed an obvious desire for privacy. The house was not at all visible from the road. Without even fully seeing this home, I wanted it. If for nothing else, I yearned for that kind of privacy. This is what I envisioned as a dream beach house. Even the entrance to his private street was secluded. I practically missed it.

Feeling like I was going off the grid, tranquility started to settle over the nerves of potentially being caught. I parked where Bayard told me to park and slowly got out of the car. After quietly shutting the door, I took a quick look around in all directions. I probably could have screamed, and no one would have heard me. *Bayard was right; I needed this.* I'd lived so many years in the presence of others 24/7, that by letting this solitude in, it surprisingly centered me in a way I hadn't felt since college. My root, sacral and solar plexus were open and engaged. I was ready for this. Courageously, I thought, *I'm even going swimming. Not too far out, but enough to feel the power of her.*

A metal railing sat at the top of the cliff, and I started heading towards it. I thought I'd heard two people laughing, but assured myself I was just paranoid.

Walking down the steep, sandy steps toward the beach, reminded me of the steps at SanBar Beach in South Haven. As a little kid and also today, a breathtaking moment always arose from the first glimpse of the sparkling glorious blue body of water seen from the top of the stairs. My black yoga pants soaked in the warm sun, and I felt my thighs baking underneath. I could actually look forward to taking them off. Arriving at the bottom, I yelped after sliding and missing the last few steps. It was for no one, but myself.

I wasn't going to draw this out too long. I need to just do this. First, I kicked my flip-flops off, feeling like a personal game of strip poker had begun. *Oh God, the flip-flops first and then what? The bottoms, or the top?* Feeling less secure about my top, I slipped the yoga pants off first.

The insecurity with my top half began long before the effects of breast-feeding. I was always the girl who didn't want to change in front of my roommates. *Yep, Bayard was right. Hottie was right.* I needed to "be a tad more free."

Stalling, I slowly laid my towel out, carefully straightening all the edges while folding my keys into the top corner. Before sitting on my towel, I looked out to the vast ocean and the absence of people, for as far as I could see. I looked down the beach to the left and right as far into the distance as possible. After taking a deep breath and glancing in all directions again, I slid my thong underwear off and then went for the quick removal of the shirt and bra. Cautiously, I sat down, noticing my hands gripping the edges of the towel, just in case I needed to use it for a quick cover. *Awww Jude, relax.*

Behind me, I was surrounded by a slight horseshoe shaped area carved out by the mountainside. *The exact definition of a private beach.* The cliff behind protected me from the wind while the sun warmed my skin. I had never felt sun shine on my naked breast, and as much as I wanted that to be comforting, it wasn't.

Mimicking the French sunbathers, I laid fully back, just like I'd seen in magazines. I didn't lay spread eagle but slightly parted my legs hoping any work I had done on the root chakra would stay open. Letting the warmth on my skin be my focus, I relaxed a bit, and before I knew it, I woke up after an hour or so, on my stomach.

Feeling sunburned, I turned over and sat up while beads of sweat dripped down the front of me. *Time for a swim.* Cautiously, I rose, glancing in either direction to make sure the coast was still clear while walking to the water's edge. I scanned the water all around to make sure I wouldn't step on a stingray or a sand shark. Slowly, I entered and kept moving, letting the cool ocean water submerge my feet, calves, thighs, waist, breasts, arms, shoulders and then my hands.

While getting my courage up, I waded in the shallow area for a while. I continued to scan the area for sea life, wading a little deeper, until I finally found the courage to float on my back. My ears and the back of my head were underwater so that I could hear the muffled sounds of the ocean. It felt more peaceful than swimming the other day, and I was able to let go in this ocean's embrace. Looking up at the blue sky and puffy clouds, I felt my breasts soaking in the sun. The waves became a bit more active, and I could feel a light wind pick up. Lifting my head and ears out of the water, I saw a gust of wind hit the beach and carry my towel and all my belongings off. *Oh, Shit!*

After floating out further than I thought, I wondered if the pull I was feeling was a real riptide this time. Slightly starting to panic, I quickly recalled the advice. I couldn't take my eyes off my clothes, which were blowing like tumbleweeds during a summer monsoon in our Arizona desert. I wondered where my keys were now. Not taking my eyes off the shore, I followed my wind-blown clothes and towel. When they seemed to have landed safely, I started towards the sand. Even though I had great concern about finding my bra, panties, and keys, I was proud of myself for getting relaxed enough to fall asleep and then also go swimming.

With each step, I planted my foot in the sand while getting closer to shore. The rush of water pounded against the front of my thighs while the waves rose and receded with a strong force. Wearing nothing but the ocean, I noticed a feeling of confidence with my body and my whole being. It made me question whether it was the yoga and the grounded root chakra leaving me feeling more solid. I just felt like I belong to this earth more.

As I continued to make my way out of the ocean, I noticed the top of my firm tan thighs. *How come I hadn't noticed them before?* Sure they could benefit from a professional trainer, but somehow they were okay to me. My skin was tanned that beautiful California shade, with the exception of my faint bikini lines. I guessed it had to be the beach walks, pumping green drinks, eating vegetables, taking in less sugar and no snacks in between meals only because it was just easier to live that way.

While knee-deep in water, a sharp stabbing pain hit my ankle area, and I heard myself scream out loud, "OW!"

I felt it again against the other ankle and screamed again, "What the fuck!" I screamed.

While quickly making my way to shore, I noticed welts blistering on my ankles and feet.

"Jellyfish," a woman commented, from a distance.

Startled to hear a voice, I looked up to find an entirely naked, tattooed couple, lying in the sand. Apparently, I'd interrupted a session of lovemaking and stood paralyzed in pain and now in awkward embarrassment. They did not completely stop their lovemaking, which nearly floored me, and I found myself overwhelmed in laughter.

While he lie on his back, with her straddled on top of him, I was surprised to see her whip her head my way and start up this conversation. I could see every part of him inside her, and it literally stopped me in my tracks. Besides a few episodes of horrible porn with unemotional, unattractive tired body parts, I'd never seen a live exchange.

This guy's triceps and biceps shifted and moved as he helped her to dismount. As he pushed himself off the ground, I couldn't help but notice the definition of his abs unfolding as he lifted himself up. These chiseled muscles had obviously seen a lot of sit-ups, surfing or something. He had a lean build and stood approximately 6'1". While standing, he was comfortable with hips relaxed and his right foot outwards. His left hand was rested on his left hip. He stood looking in my direction as if he was now evaluating me. His light brown, medium-length hair was blowing in the breeze, so I couldn't see his eyes. He was tanned perfectly all over so this whole naked thing today was not his first rodeo. He was heavily tattooed with vibrant colors, some skeleton looking things and a lot of florals mixed with tribal lines. There was a tattoo on the top of his hand. I saw it, when he pushed his hair away, but couldn't make it out from this far. He had thin lips with a beautiful smile and perfect white teeth. This was a man comfortable in his own skin.

The stinging was increasing, and I wondered if I was still being stung. I jumped and leaped as if that was going to help. I got myself on the sand and could see remnants of clear jelly like substances on my feet. The tattooed girl was right, whoever she was.

"I'm so sorry, please excuse me, I didn't realize you two… holy shit this hurts."

My towel and T-shirt sat next to them. It had blown from my beach to theirs.

"May I… could you…", I stuttered while motioning to her to bring me my clothes.

She meandered over, grabbed my T-shirt and handed it to me. Unfortunately, I was wet. So when I stretched the bottom of the T-shirt to cover my root chakra, I basically looked like I was in a wet T-shirt contest.

She was stunning. Her dismount was graceful, and I was actually impressed, as I know, I probably never looked like that to Bill. She stood about 5'5" and completely toned from head to toe while having not one ounce of cellulite on her. No plastic enhancements necessary here; this was the body everyone seemed to pay for. She was perfectly tanned all over as well, and her long light-brown hair was silky, and with a tapered cut, it dropped all the way down to the middle of her back. She had natural sun streaks on the tips of her hair, and I assumed she spent a lot of time on the beach. She was colorfully tattooed, same as him but with more floral designs. She had no hesitation when she came right for me offering assistance. I noticed her golden hazel-brown eyes right away. Her lashes were black, and for a second, I thought she was wearing heavy mascara, and then realized, those too, were natural.

Watching me squirm, he stood there confidently like an expert lover, fully erect. I wasn't sure if there was a full smile on his face, but I imagined there was by his demeanor. A desert girl being stung like this is a big deal, just as if he were stung by one of our scorpions.

"I'm gonna have to do what a man *can* do," he said, laughing as he walked towards me. Still comfortably naked and standing next to me trying to attend to my emergency, she interjected, "He needs to pee on you."

"What? No. Why?" I questioned.

I had read about that a long time ago but wasn't even sure if it was true.

"Yep, golden shower, baby. Here we go," he said, laughing.

Standing in front of me and still erect as ever, he said, "You ready?" His quiet confidence, instilled with amusement, made it clear he was really going to enjoy doing this. I could see the tattoo on the top of his hand as he aimed. In tiny words, it was a quote: "Don't let those miracles that have not transpired, blind you to those that have."

The quote hypnotized me for a moment, and I instantly wondered what would have made him tattoo that on himself. It was a story or future story in the making, and I wanted to hear it. He tried to pee. His eyes squinted as if that would help ease his erection. I tried not to stare, but I wanted to know when I'd be hit with a stream of warm urine.

"You're fuckin' hot," he blurted.

His girlfriend standing next to him, slapped him to see if she could break the erection, and he yelled, "OW! What was that for?"

"I'm trying to help," she explained, giggling.

I had to laugh at this point.

Laughing, he said, "Well, it's a little kinky, and you know how I like that, but it isn't helpin', it's hurting. There's a hot, half-naked MILF, standing in front of me, and you're slappin' my johnson."

He turned to me, "You're like a fuckin' mermaid, coming up out of the water like that. Not a good combo for relaxing an erection."

We waited a couple minutes and filled the space with laughter and "oh God's."
"Hold still," he said.

Finally, the urine flowed and without one bit of relief, I said, "*THAT* is not working at all, OW. It may be worse!" I ran from him to gather my blown belongings.

Glancing in the direction of my original spot, I could see in the distance, my shiny key ring catching the sunlight, letting me know I had a ride home later. *Oh thank God*, I said while shaking the sand off and kissing them.

It actually struck us all as funny, and the three of us were hysterical. Holding my T-shirt over all private parts, I ran, skipped and jumped because of the pain, to the area where they had their towels. My yoga pants were nowhere to be found, so I quickly slid my panties on, stretching my T-shirt even lower. Reasoning with myself, I thought, *relax, they're kinda like a bathing suit bottom*. I couldn't touch my blistering skin, so I just flailed my legs bent at the knee, back and forth to get a cooling effect. He walked straight up to me with his girlfriend by his side, still comfortably naked, but then casually slid his shorts on. She threw a towel over herself as she slid on her bikini bottoms.

"So, what's your deal?" he asked.

I briefly explained this crazy idea to explore the prude part of myself and just BE naked today. And it was kind of a "dare" from a friend who thought I needed to lighten up.

"Nice," with the look and tone of the Joey Tribbiani character on the show "Friends."

"Is there an ointment or a lotion I should apply for jellyfish stings?" I asked as I squirmed in place.

"You're fine," he said, laughing.

"Well, if you got bit by a scorpion in Arizona, you would need to get a tetanus shot. So, are you sure there's nothing I should do for this?"

I was going into Mommy mode and looking for life's safety manual. These two had no interest in getting caught up in that. They were the opposite of cautious. He folded back his towel, and lit a half-smoked joint and handed it to me. "It's strong, be careful."

"No thanks," I said. He took a hit and handed it to his girl.

"My name is Jenna, and this is Jessie," she said.

"Judy," I replied, as I shook both of their hands.

Jenna asked, "You want a drink? It's Tanqueray and tonic, with some fresh lime from our tree."

She swirled it in a clear bottle while the last of some ice chips mixed with lime slices hit the sides of the glass.

"Sure," I said.

It was delicious. Bill and I drank our fair share of these in college and had to stop because we tended to fight when we indulged in gin. Apparently, gin is not the depressant that the rest of alcohol is, and it got us in a lot of unnecessary feuds. The fresh lime juice slivers penetrated the mixture, making it the best gin and tonic I ever had.

"Your tattoos are gorgeous. I mean that is art I would purchase and invest in if it were on a canvas. Did you design these yourself? I asked.

"Yep. Thanks, girl," she responded proudly in agreement.

They both shared the stories that belonged to each tattoo. In a way, they allowed me to read them like a book. A deep, profound, painful and hopeful, powerful book.

This spontaneous picnic between the three of us didn't come equipped with cups, so we all took turns drinking out of the bottle. It reminded me of high school and college.

Oh, if Bayard and Hottie could see me now. Would they not be doubled over in laughter? I literally could dive into a threesome if I wanted to right now.

Jenna stayed partially naked with a towel draped over her. Occasionally, the towel slipped off, but she wasn't bothered by it. He was super sexual, root chakra wide open probably and most likely could have made love to both of us, all day long. He had similar sexual energy to Bill, and I was all the sudden appreciating having a husband who had never once, turned me down.

We became fast friends and shared life stories. We talked politics, war, disease, world hunger, religion, miracles, sex, family relationships, marriage, wealth, poverty and a lot about dreams. The gin kept us laughing and open to telling more secrets. After deciding to share a joint, I was relieved to leave behind the paranoia I'd experienced with pot in the past.

They got a kick out of why I was there, so all day long they dared me to lose the T-shirt. I teased them with the beginning of a strip tease I had no intentions of following through with, and we playfully laughed about it. *Is it possible to have a crush that is so sexy, but so sweet and pure?*

They both admitted they were attracted to me, and I agreed how tempting the idea of being with them would be. They encouraged the positive aspect that it could be part of *my* story, and yet, I would never have to tell a single soul. They were excited I had minimal partners, and genuinely thought I should explore this. I talked about Bill and HER and how I understood the pull to dive into something new and how natural that would be to feel that. But I could feel my free will empowering me to stay more aligned with what was true for me, and I was just simply a one-man woman as boring as that is to them. I was open to the idea that I might shift and change beliefs on this, but right now, right here, for the first time, I was getting comfortable with this part of me. The part I called prude and the part Bill once called frigid.

They'd had their share of threesomes, for sure, and I was entertained by the details of those stories. I loved how they sat with their quiet confidence in being found naked. And, I had to admit, it was refreshing to see another man's naked body. What I found interesting about looking at this hot young male was I had surprisingly still preferred Bill's body to his. I suspected it was because I embraced being fully free with Bill, and I just could not see myself truly being free with this guy, or her, for that matter. I realized, that in a marriage, there is the amazing potential to lower walls between lovers, and sex can't get any better than when you feel that free. I could see where I had closed him off, and maybe sometimes for good reason. But I could see the freedom in the kind of lover Bill was and he, of all people, always encouraged me to be me.

Over the years, my curiosity about their kind of sexuality often left me wondering if I lacked something. But I could see now that mandatory foreplay for me had to do with a lot of mental and emotional comfort taking place first. This trip had confirmed that my heart and head are a bit high maintenance. I started to gently settle with the idea... I am who I am.

Our conversation continued, and I told my new friends I was planning on singing at an open mic in a bar near State Street the next night. Jenna excitedly shared that their shop was nearby, and they always attended those open mics. She reached for a pouch from under her towel and said, "Want one?"

"What is it?" I asked.

"I can give you a henna tattoo. I can give you a real one tomorrow if you want, or..."

Laughing, I said, "I would love a henna tattoo. But you decide what to do, design-wise."

I had already raved over their artistic talent, and as it turned out, they designed each other's tattoos.

She shared the history of a henna tattoo: The ritual traces back 9,000 years. Apparently, henna has natural cooling properties and people of the desert, for centuries, have been using henna to cool down their bodies. They make a paste of henna and soak their palms and soles of the feet in it to get an air-conditioning affect. The cooling sensation is felt throughout the body for as long as the henna stain remained on their skin. Initially, as the stain faded away, it left patterns on the skin surface, which led to ideas to make designs for decorative purposes.

"Cleopatra herself used henna for decorative purposes," Jenna explained.

"Henna was not only a popular adornment for the rich. It was for the poor, who could not afford jewelry, by using it to decorate their bodies, as well. It was used for self-expression, celebration of special occasions like weddings, holidays and birthdays, inspiration, reminders, beauty, cosmetic treatments, medicinal uses, blessings and well-being, to be part of an ancient tradition and an alternative or precursor to a tattoo."

A Henna tattoo was a divine match for me.

It might have been the gin-and-tonics or maybe the pot, but I was shocked at how much I adored this young couple and this new friendship. Jessie, Jenna, Bayard, Hottie, Skye and Violet reminded me of the importance of having friends I actually deserved. It was easy for me to see the dark hole I'd fallen into in regards to friendships. I had given up on people in Tucson, and those I kept around, I didn't fully trust. That belief system built a wall around me, and I continued to manifest unstable and unfulfilling relationships. I hadn't realized it until now, but Santa Barbara was a safe place for me to drop the wall of beliefs I had been clutching onto.

With the exception of wanting to roll in the hay with me, Jesse and Jenna didn't *want* anything from me. And once I voiced being comfortable with being myself, they immediately honored it. It was also refreshing that they were not interested in whether I had money or not. Jenna had grown up in wealth, was well-traveled, growing up with the beach house and the fancy ski trips. She went to a prestigious college, and had the adoring parents and such, while still "living her truth." She still did her work. Her personal work on herself. Sure, her parents had arranged a studio for her to work in off the beaten path of State Street, but she utilized her trust fund well while building a thriving business. I encouraged her to dip into the trust fund and open a gallery where her art would be sold on canvas, metal, and wood. Since Paul and his whole family of artists had exposed me to this love, I had learned enough over the years, and I was finally comfortable saying I had a knack for recognizing things like good art and music. I wasn't just a sheltered suburbanite, unexposed and unaware of the creative art world. Her eyes lit up as if she somehow received permission and she said, "I'd been thinking about a gallery! I have always wanted to do that!"

I untied the strings on my bracelet and handed it to her. "Then do it."

Jenna read out loud: "'Leap and the net will appear.' Love it! Thank you, Judy," as she gave me a slippery, sweaty hug, where her breasts let loose from her draped towel, brushing against my arm.

While I lay there on my back, Jenna started working on my hand, the one that would hold the microphone tomorrow night. She said, "You'll understand later when I tell you the meaning."

With my face to the sun, I gave her full reins to my right hand. Jessie had fallen asleep. When she needed to do the other side, she gently tapped me to turn over. I don't know if I was wrapped up in her creative energy, or just simply high, but I loved the way she held my hand in hers. And whatever her intention behind the carefully chosen tattoo was, I could feel the love. She and Jessie were genuine, and I completely adored my new colorful friends.

While lying there, she did her work, and it was as if a sexual switch inside me turned on. I couldn't remember the last time I felt like this. *Was it the yoga practice that opened my root chakra, the gin, the pot, being naked. Was it them being naked. Was it the space between Bill and me. Was it a combination of all of it, or just an illusion?*

I felt a desire to hold this day secretly close to my heart. Being known for exposing too many details of experiences, and Bill's constant requests for condensed versions of stories had shut me down quite a bit over the last few years. I could feel a shift inside of me, though. I wasn't coming from a place of anger towards him about that realization today. In a way, I appreciated that it might be his unconscious way of trying to help stop me from existing anxiously rather than existing in a calmer, more peaceful vibe. So far, on this trip, I lost the desire to need to explain and seek approval on everything, to not needing it at all.

My thoughts kept turning to Bill. For the first time in a long time, I fantasized about having mine and Bill's songs play on a private beach excursion of our own. I could hear the music in my head: "I Want To Know What Love Is," "Can't Fight This Feeling" and "Truly Madly Deeply." This trip was sinking in, and I was feeling whole again. While I had been *getting by with a little help from my friends,* a lot had happened within me that I might decide, to keep to myself upon return. And I was comfortable with that.

As I lie there, closely studying the grains of sand that sifted through my fingers of the free-hand she wasn't working on, I felt a massive, overwhelming peace and ownership of this *wonderfull* life of mine.

I manifested this. Presently, this is my land of plenty. I am rich here.

The sun was about to set. After Jenna and Jessie got dressed, we exchanged long hugs.

"Thank you," I whispered to each one of them. I felt so blessed to have run into them, while in such a vulnerable place. In a way, I could plainly see how they'd squeezed me so I could see what was inside.

While climbing the steep steps back to my car, I stopped in the middle to turn and gaze at the vast, blue, shimmering ocean. I watched the sunset in silence, and after watching it drop and disappear, I thought intimately of Bill, his body, his lips… and his hands.

THE PRIVILEGE OF A LIFETIME IS BEING WHO YOU ARE. Joseph Campbell

DAY 8
FOR RICHER & FOR POORER

Massive waves of hope swelled inside me, matching the sunrise coming up over the horizon this morning on Arroyo Beach. While each evenings sunset was feeling like daily finish lines, this sunrise felt like a new starting line. It was a new day. Another chance. A clean slate.

Carefully sitting down because of my new sunburned rear and scorched thighs, I let the thoughts wanting to pop up, pop. I had noticed, in the last few days, the need for less sleep. My body felt differently. It was more vibrant and alive, and my mind was sharp. I didn't have the feeling of exhaustion in the late afternoons; my digestion was working normally and any negative thoughts that may have found their way in seemed to make their way out just as quickly. It was easy living here. And to make it even better, I had discovered a heavily-treed park in the neighborhood, where the dogs and I spent hours over the last few days with what felt like a magical forest all to ourselves. Maximilian was so well trained that he stayed close to me, and I loved how he emanated no stress. And I appreciated Titus and his elation just nearing the park. It's amazing how subtle peace, outright joy, pure love, and adoration can emanate from animals reminding us of staying aligned to all of those things.

Today, the beach was serene as I listened to the gentle waves lapse against the shore. If my kids were in town, Clint and Nicole would be asleep, and Marcus would be up at the crack of dawn with me. Watching our kids on the beach was pure joy. *I can't wait to take them here someday.* Bayard was nowhere in sight, so I laid my blanket out on the sand. Off in the distance, a young couple were entangled in each other's arms, quietly talking. There was also a woman, propped on a beach chair with a big beach hat, immersed in a book. I felt alone enough to open the journal I'd been writing in since I got here. With all the self-help, healing, meditation, hypnotherapy classes and workshops taken over the years, the one thing I never learned to love was journaling. I actually hated it. But I sure took it seriously here.

After laying my towel in a private, tucked-away area, I studied the blooming white and purple morning glories sprawled up and around the rocky mountain behind me. The flowers trailed all the way up to the grassy cliff. *How many years did it take to attach and climb that mountain of rock? Did someone plant them here? Was it the Hendry family back in the day?* I pressed my feet into just the top layer of the sand, warming them like a blanket.

I re-read what I had written the first night in Santa Barbara, and barely recognized myself. Not only that, I barely recognized my own handwriting. My anxiousness and fear of the unknown were understood now. Making it feel as if I was reading about a complete stranger. My journal from last night was light and fun to re-read because it was about Jenna and Jessie. I couldn't wait for Bayard to show up this morning. I had decided to share the jellyfish story.

As I was briefly looking over some lyrics I'd scribbled down a few days before, I heard his voice.

"Praise God. She's started the book!"

Laughing, I replied, "Um, No, I have not. Listen Bayard, Can't *YOU* just write it? You're the writer."

He grinned, "This is your song, Judy. Sing it."

I threw a tiny pebble against his oxygen tank just to hear the little "ding."

Laughing, he said, "That's never going to get old for you, is it?"

I had made a habit over the last seven days of always making his oxygen tank "ding" like that. On the first day of us meeting, I accidentally kicked up a shell, and after hearing the ding, I announced, while throwing my arms up and out, "The Angels are amongst us."

It threw him into a hearty laugh, and because he's so much fun to watch laugh, I couldn't resist making it a regular thing.

I changed the subject on *writing*, to the private beach and filled him in with a brief, but packed version. He beamed with pride, knowing it was his idea.

"Ahhhh, now, if I can get you to listen to me about the book."

Writing a book was not resonating with me, and I didn't want to keep talking about it, besides it started to seem like he was getting annoyed with my rejection. He was losing a little bit of patience, which is all he had for me since first meeting.

I wondered if this was going to be our first fight.

Knowing there was a yoga class at 10 A.M., I decided to head that direction. Making last-minute decisions, to do spontaneous things, simply because I felt like it, reminded me to make a mental note, to do that once in a while when back in Tucson. I would add that to my *homework* list.

Since I knew the parking lot would be full this morning, I set an intention to locate a front spot again.

When I pulled up, I noticed, NOT ONE spot was open.

What? Dang. It didn't work! I thought.

I drove past the Santa Barbara Yoga Center, toward the church, and across the street, and found a spot. A front parking spot, but right in front of the church. Seeing that it was just opposite the studio, it was a great spot, so I took it. I grabbed my mat and headed past the church, toward the class. The minister wasn't watering at this time, but the two church doors were wide open. They were majestic and reminded me of our house in The Canyons. I remembered seeing him standing there after a service. Quiet confidence in his faith emanated from him as it seemed he earned the right to stand in that door. Like he belonged nowhere else, but there. I heard music and wondered if there was a weekly service of some kind, but there were no people around. I stood in the doorway for a while but worried I'd miss the yoga class. As I started to turn and head for the studio, an angelic voice echoed from the balcony in the main church area. I wanted to see this person, but couldn't place her.

The minister greeted me at the door, holding his arm out to enter like he was expecting me. "Heavenly, isn't it?"

Backed up by an acoustic guitar, a woman's voice cascaded down from the ceiling, but I couldn't see a banister anywhere. He encouraged me to sit in the pew. As he disappeared through a door off to the side, I finally saw her, way up high, in the corner of the church. It was as if her voice lived up in the rafters. I always wanted to be able to sing like that. It was a formal Episcopalian church, and yet it felt current and hip. Her voice was raw and real. Trained, but not overly trained. She believed what she sang and today she was singing Mindy Smith's "Come to Jesus." I agreed with the lyrics that summed up how we have angels that dance around our shoulders and that sometimes in our lives we need a helping hand.

She finished the song, and I watched her collect the sheet music and set her guitar down. I wanted to clap or tell her how much I loved her singing. But she wasn't seeking a compliment like that. The minister reentered and sat down next to me on the pew. I felt so honored. He didn't have to do that as I wasn't a member, I hadn't tithed his church or attended services, or become a part of his community by donating and volunteering my time.

"Would you like to pray?" he asked.

I nodded yes.

He held his Bible out for me to lay my hand on top of it. His hand covered mine. It felt big, but light. It was like I could feel the years of faith pouring out of his hand. *How many times did his hands fold in prayer, up until now? Surely, God listened to him.*

His quiet confidence encouraged me to believe so.

"Dear Heavenly Father and Mother Mary, bless this child as you did before time began. Protect her and her family from harm. Where there has been suffering, allow her to be released. Thank you, Heavenly Father, for the gifts that are on their way to this blessed woman and family. And thank you, Father, for those gifts that have already arrived. Father, thank you for allowing her to see the light, your creation of her in herself and to remember, recall, and unveil the love in her heart and the light that lives inside her through you. Heavenly Father, I pray this in your son Jesus's name and with the Holy Spirit. Amen." Turning to me he said, "Bless you." And he kissed the top of my head.

With Angelic help, I easily explained past suffering, doubts, and hopelessness over the years. We talked for quite some time, and he came off similar to the yogis. He continued to intuitively pick up on things that surprised me. The most startling of all was my doubt still lingering about this marriage to Bill.

I asked him, "What are your thoughts and beliefs on divorce?"

He shared 1 Corinthians 7:15: "If the husband or wife who isn't a believer insists on leaving, let them go. In such cases the Christian husband or wife is no longer bound to the other, for God has called you to live in peace."

I explained Bill's belief in faith mirrored mine. "We may just not believe in this marriage. Isn't it possible that we may just simply have hit our limit to grow together, and it's time to part ways?"

He nodded, and he pointed to my finger, "You don't seem like the kind of woman afraid to ask herself some hard questions. Can you start by telling me why you don't wear your wedding ring?"

I sat there quietly searching his eyes to see if the answer would come from him.

"You mentioned financial troubles. Did you have to sell the ring?"

I don't know why, but I couldn't speak.

"Where is the ring, dear?"

"Please wait. I'll be right back."

I shot up from the pew and ran out the doors to the Denali and opened the arm counsel, where it sat. I rushed back to the Church, joining him on the pew while showing him the ring as it sat on the tip of my finger.

"What vows or verse did you share with him? Do you recall?"

I could feel my throat tighten, and I was holding the tears back.

Reluctantly, I shared, "I, I actually asked the minister of our church *not* to say, 'and the two will become one,' during the candle lighting ceremony.' I also made it clear to him and Bill that I would not go for the word 'obey,' and Bill would have no rights over my body, as well. I can't recall the actual vows. But we did request 1 Corinthians 13:1-13.

And he opened his Bible and read it to me:

> *1 Corinthians 13*
>
> *13 If I speak in the tongues[a] of men or of angels, but do not have love, I am only a resounding gong or a clanging cymbal. 2 If I have the gift of prophecy and can fathom all mysteries and all knowledge, and if I have a faith that can move mountains, but do not have love, I am nothing. 3 If I give all I possess to the poor and give over my body to hardship that I may boast,[b] but do not have love, I gain nothing. 4 Love is patient, love is kind. It does not envy, it does not boast, it is not proud. 5 It does not dishonor others, it is not self-seeking, it is not easily angered, it keeps no record of wrongs. 6 Love does not delight in evil but rejoices with the truth. 7 It always protects, always trusts, always hopes, always perseveres. 8 Love never fails. But where there are prophecies, they will cease; where there are tongues, they will be stilled; where there is knowledge, it will pass away. 9 For we know in part and we prophesy in part,10 but when completeness comes, what is in part disappears.11 When I was a child, I talked like a child, I thought like a child, I reasoned like a child. When I became a man, I put the ways of childhood behind me.12 For now we see only a reflection as in a mirror; then we shall see face to face. Now I know in part; then I shall know fully, even as I am fully known.13 And now these three remain: faith, hope, and love. But the greatest of these is love.*

While holding my ring, he took my left hand in his, and he looked into my eyes. *Silently, as if he were asking my permission.*

I nodded.

"Judy, will you say, 'I take you, Bill...' "

Then pausing and nodding for me to repeat what he said, I repeated after him: "I take you, Bill..."

"to be my lawfully wedded husband,"

"to have and to hold,"

"from this day forward,"

"for better and for worse,"

"in sickness and in health,"

"for richer and for poorer?"

And I paused and said, "I Do."

And then he slid the ring onto my finger.

"Beautiful. One other thing. Not wanting certain words because of certain reasons is understandable. But you need to make sure you understand your certain reasons fully. Perhaps the ideas of a young woman would be perceived differently by a more life-enriched woman today."

That resonated with me.

On my way out the church doors I saw Violet, "Hey, what in the world are you doing over there?" she asked.

"I was going to take the 10 A.M. class, but a *plan B* came up," I responded.

With complete understanding, she said, "Well, good, you're following the universal process then."

I smiled and nodded yes, and asked, "Are you attending the 11 A.M.?"

"Sure am."

On the quick walk over, I wanted to tell her about Skye, Jenna, Jessie, the minister, his prayer, the vows and the angelic singer, but silence won over as I kept it to myself. I truly felt blessed and was having trouble finding words for the experiences.

The hour and a half class somehow whirled by and I found myself laying in savasana, beside Violet. I had no recollection of the pace, the positions or if a dash of essential oil had touched my forehead.

My cleared mind allowed me to recall with great detail my 23-year-old self, soon-to-be-bride. With good intentions, before marriage, while trying to make things clear to all males present, I saw how I had adopted ideas from the elder women in and around my life: some family, neighbors, and teachers. I listened to stories of their divorces that carried a monster message of having to "fight, demand and claim your independence," not in always loving ways, but in a more fearful, aggressive way. Their perception was that most men were there to take away from them, and these women ferociously stayed in defense mode. They were intelligent and had sharp tongues, so I found them exciting. This behavior is exactly what Joseph Campbell described in his Goddess book; where women may sometimes lose their pure nature when falsely in competition with men. I could see where some men had, and would, take advantage of women, and defense was a good plan of action. But I noticed a generalization around this way of thinking that represented a prejudice of sorts. There was risk of good men being overlooked because of poor snap judgments.

After my mom divorced my dad, her co-workers—all psychologists and social workers who were well read on feminism and the psychological and emotional welfare of one taking care of themselves—attended a "divorce" party at our house.

I recalled being 15 and sitting in the front yard while my parents were inside with mostly my mom's peers. As much as I liked my parents' commitment to stay kind and on good terms, I was feeling the typical 15-year-old emotions. I was nervous; my stomach hurt and I wanted to scream and cry. Plus, I had just been told I'd be moving and starting high school in a town far away from the one I had spent 15 years growing up in. I watched my mom as she glided through the party. It appeared she had carved out a great future with her new cool hip friends, while my Dad was quiet, and his plans were to be temporarily living in his mother's apartment downtown until he found his own place. While sitting cross-legged in the grass, under a big oak tree I had loved all my life, one of my mom's friends joined me. He knew I was suffering. He hadn't had kids yet, but he seemed to understand them pretty well.

He said, "Judy, I know you're upset, but it's time for your mom to have her own life, and a voice all her own."

I could see all of this, but didn't want to. It was obviously a time for women to have a stronger voice in the household and workplace, and quite honestly, I liked the "rah rah" of all of it. I never got the occasional aggression or even burning of bras, but it sounded to me like we were fighting for an underdog and that was a fight I could easily engage in. So I bought into all the feminism without questioning most of it.

Today, I realized I was in support of feminism as long as I wasn't looking to pull power from men or any others in order to get it. I'm not claiming that my mom did that to my dad in the divorce, but I could, all of a sudden, see how I may have done that to Bill.

The equality I was seeking at 23 was already there. God created us all equal, no matter what the free will of others in a home or workplace would say. What I overlooked is that I had a husband who was absolutely supportive of me stepping up in any and all ways I so chose, at home and in workplaces. I saw how I might have stomped my foot down on Bill's throat with our vows while he was on my side the whole time. It was as if, by taking that stand, I had one foot out the door and one foot in. My dramatic demands didn't get me anything or anywhere because the truth was I didn't have to give up a part of me to become one with him. I could remain solid and whole while making this spiritual commitment of marriage.

I felt the fear of ever "losing myself" begin to diminish. I vowed to spend more time knowing my true voice and only to use that one. It was obvious my voice had been lost and found my whole life in many regards, and I knew that would continue. I rested in savasana and asked for forgiveness, for any intentional and unintentional hurt I may or may not have done to Bill, and also to the foundation of our marriage.

Clearing that up in my mind felt better. Since the minister specifically prayed for us and our family and even had me recite our vows, I was sure if Bill was meant to feel it, he would. We were no strangers to the power of prayer in our past, and today, I could feel this minister's words penetrating me immediately. When I said, "I do," I said it because it became clear to me that if I ever divorced Bill, I would have to have already exhausted every measure to reconcile this marriage. I had not. The woman I was feeling like today had a different handle on things than the woman I'd been in Tucson. As his wife, or even potentially his ex-wife, my new plan for him was to bring awareness to his lost voice and let things unfold from there.

WHEN TWO PEOPLE MEET, EACH ONE IS CHANGED BY THE OTHER SO YOU'VE GOT TWO NEW PEOPLE. JOHN STEINBECK

After class, over tea with Violet, I shared my new "F" word:
FEMINISM/ noun/ 'femen nizem/

1. Is for everyone; colorblind & gender blind;
2. A warrior for fair equality in politics, social & economic arenas;
3. One who shares truth without agenda, punishment, or intention to pull power from any other;
4. A human undeterred by others' opinions or one's own excuses to become anything that they want to be;
   Encourages *all* to have a voice.

DAY 9
3RD CALL WITH BILL
A HOUSE IN ORDER

My phone rang this morning. Noticing the caller ID, I just picked up, "HI."
"You sound good," said Bill.

"I am. How 'bout you?" *Sounded like a house in order*, as I didn't hear any kids in the background.

He answered, "A little tired, didn't sleep much. Made some progress with learning all the new mortgage stuff. Have to take some tests in the next couple days. Hopefully, I pass. I have a few loans, but they aren't going through this month. Been looking these lawsuits over again, so I've been on the phone with Mahoney. Spent time on conference calls with potential investors the last few days, and it's keeping me up at night, but 'this too shall pass', right? I can sleep later."

I was relieved to hear him less stressed. He hadn't used that quote in I don't know how long. After the day I had on the beach, I was a bit sexually revved up and wished we were in a place where we could just naturally crawl into bed together when I got home. But because we hadn't talked, he may be feeling exactly the way he was when I left, which was disconnected from me. Truth is, I may be fantasizing about something that will never be.

The reality of me going back to Tucson with all the bad news, bad luck and many to-dos to be buried by, trickled in and I immediately began feeling ill. Oh my God. *How am I going to manage it all again? I can't bring Santa Barbara and all my new friends home with me.*

And that reminded me that tonight if I see them, I need all their contact information so we can all stay in touch.

"Hey I'm doin' an open mic tonight," I said.

"Wow. Really? Where?"

"A bar, in town."

He wasn't used to my lack of detail. At this point, back in the day, I probably would have overly explained Hottie, and how he is Tracy and Ed's tenant, how the dogs know Hottie, how I met his friend, and how he's a drummer...

"That's cool, Judy. I remember the first time I ever heard ya sing."

I interrupted, "Yeah, me too." Remembering the college days, like it was yesterday, "I invited you over to my upstairs apartment at Eastern, in that old white house and I sang "Landslide."

"No. That wasn't the first time I heard you. I had arrived early and when I entered the front screened porch and started up the stairs to your apartment. I heard music, and you were singing, "Help Me Make it Through the Night" but I thought it was the radio. When I got to the top of the stairs, I saw you sitting on the floor with your guitar, strumming away. I waited on the top stair, 'till you finished."

"Why didn't you ever tell me that?"

"Don't know," he said.

"You thought it was the radio?"

"Yeah. I like to hear you sing. It sucks when you get shy and stop every time I turn the volume up in the car."

WHAT!? So, he was turning the volume up to encourage me to sing louder and bolder? Sigh.

Marcus picked up the extension in our bedroom, "Hi, Momma!"

"Hi, Marcus! What are you guys all up to?"

"Well, Dad and me and Clint built an even bigger ramp this morning."

He was building ramps in 105-degree heat with the kids?

Marcus started laughing hysterically and said, "Dad, is this one mine?"

I heard pots clanking, so I could tell they were all in the kitchen now. While Bill and I had been talking, he had been making custom pancakes with no "freed eggs," just scrambled. He customized each pancake to match the kid. Marc had a pickup truck with big tires, Clint had a racecar with big wheels, and Nicole had a big heart. My mom had brought him fresh oranges and lemons from her trees, and he had, with the kids, squeezed a ton of them earlier that morning.

"Okay, guys, do these dishes, then we're outta here," he said.

He told them to do the dishes? This was sounding like a house in order... without me.

"Where you guys headed?" I asked.

"They have floor hockey camp today, and Nicole's goin' to Haley's. By the way, spending time with Nicole has been blowing my mind. Our girl has a sense of humor! At seven years old, she's crackin' jokes that even I think are funny."

He continued, "Football's been goin' well. They just started hittin' with pads and helmets, so Clint has a smile plastered to his face every night at practice. Marcus is killin' it, but I'm seeing he doesn't have the love for it. We should talk more about that when you get back. As for my team, I'm spendin' hours on strategizing plays, based on each individual player's strengths. I think some of my players are going to be pleasantly surprised by their performance and the impact they'll be making to this team. Because of our last 1 and 9 season, I'm inspired to find a way to a championship, and a lot of new strengths are showing up on this field that might make that a reality," he explained.

Compared to how he sounded a few days before, I was cautiously optimistic with his attitude today.

So I shared, "I saw a tattoo recently about miracles that said, 'Don't let those miracles that have not transpired, blind you to those that have.' Even though I heard it before, holy cow, it just rang true. It's hard to see the good when wrapped up and distracted."

He said, "Yeah, that's a good one. The last few nights, I've been listening to music while unpacking. I watched our wedding video, and videos of the kids being born, and I noticed how disconnected I've been. I've been watching them sleep. Haven't done that since they were babies. It's been cool to get to know details of who they really are, what they need, what they don't need."

I was now looking forward to the details of his 11 days. But I planned on not sharing every single detail of mine, especially the golden shower. *Yep, the golden shower was definitely out.*

I heard a box being ripped in the background.

"What was that?"

Bill answered, "It's Clint, he's making a front door."

Marc was still on the line and heard Clint's name mentioned, so he handed the phone to Clint.

"Hi?" said Clint.

"Hi Clint, it's Mommy."

"Hi, Momma!" In an excited tone, he said, "Momma! Dad built a fort for us, and we woke up, and there it was, and it has windows, and he taped stuff to it and…"

"Wow, wow, wow, sounds amazing," I replied.

He continued: "and we all have our own rooms and…"

"Wow, did you do this *with* Dad?"

"No, no. He did it when we slept. We woke up and there it was!"

"Hey Bill, you still on the line?" I asked.

"Yep." I could hear him putting dishes into the dishwasher.

"So this is what you did all night, last night?" I was laughing now. I winced at the thought of ALL the contents of the boxes needing to be put away.

"Sounds like you went through a lot of boxes. Do I have stacks of 'things' in the corners of the rooms I need to find places for now?" I was kind of kidding, but sincerely wanting to know.

I could tell that since I was closer to the return day, I needed a little preparation. There was no denying the to-dos were going to be there especially with the start of school, practice every night and games starting up. I just hoped I'd find some graceful way to do them now.

But I was a bit relieved with his answer, "No, I got through them. Pretty much everything is in place."

Wait. What? This is not the Bill I left. My husband, who hates packing and unpacking even more? The guy who's left all those details of our lives up to me?

Skye had said something about us being task mates. I so appreciated the task part of him right now. What a relief I wouldn't come home to that!

He cautiously asked, "So, about this trip, are you finding what you're looking for? What would you say you've gained?"

My bad habit of assuming this was one of his typical series of questions filled with criticism almost made me defensive, but I caught myself and didn't take it personally. I reminded myself that he was a guy who loved results that birthed from well-thought out, set goals. He was a football player and a businessman, so his life had revolved around playbooks, and Excel spreadsheets with clear gains and losses. Those became a compass for him to evaluate, and in the past, when it became necessary he would usually courageously, and fearlessly try to fix things by changing direction while course correcting in order to find a victorious result.

"Hmmm, good question. Can't think of what I'm gaining. I can only think of what I'm losing."

I could tell by his silence that he thought I might be talking about our marriage.

I continued, "Listen, it's hard to believe, and even I'm surprised, this trip is so independent of you. The work I'm doing on myself here is not going to hurt you. What I'm finding here is not about gains. It's most definitely about loss. Loss of fears, regret, anger, anxiousness, envy, shame, guilt, resentment and even worry."

He was quiet on the other line.

I could hear him shuffling some papers, and in the background, the doorbell rang.

He said, "Hold on, Tina is here to carpool for hockey. I'll be right back."

I overheard the boys in the background talking about the cool cardboard forts and how they wanted to stay and play in them while blowing off camp. As much fun as some of their jam-packed activities and sports were, we did find that even at this young age, it was difficult to balance the times to let them take a break from sports while also teaching the importance of giving it your all—100 percent.

Bill got back on the phone, "I unpacked The Law of Success the other night. Remember the inside cover? Where my dad wrote, "Follow your light." It was a good reminder. I needed to hear him say that. And then I flipped it open, and I thought of you when I found this, **There are souls in this world which have the gift of finding joy everywhere and of leaving it behind them everywhere they go. Written by Faber.** When I read it, it reminded me of you."

"Well, that's weird, cause this trip has been a good reminder of a lot of things for me."

Just as I was about to say, thank you for saying that, I got a call from a Tucson-area code, and he encouraged me to take it. It was an upset mom that had a kid in the same floor hockey camp. Apparently, she had seen something happen with Marcus yesterday at camp and had to talk to one of us immediately. I let her give me the short, highlighted version of how Marcus was being bullied, then switched back to Bill and told him what she shared.

He responded, "Got it. Give me her number. I'll call her right now."

The fact he took that off my plate and did not keep me involved showed me the voice I was hoping he'd find; he just might be rediscovering. This call was night and day from the last call, and I wondered if he sensed the minister's prayer for us or felt me saying, "I love you, I'm sorry, please forgive me, and thank you."

Bill's attention to address this kind of bully would be his first. So often, I'd just handle these issues as they were usually midday while he was at work anyway. He was up to speed, as he had heard enough past episodes. Regularly, I was getting calls and notes home on updates of Marcus' bullies and how they were being sent to detention. Unfortunately, the bullying continued even after the discipline. Just like our lawsuits, these troubles were mounting and gaining momentum, rather than being resolved.

During last semester, after numerous stories about how awful the bus driver was to Marcus (who was quiet and polite), I played private investigator without the bus driver knowing whose children were mine, giving me the ability to see this bullying first hand. As excruciating as it was to see, I was then able to handle the situation effectively. I instantly recognized the mirror effect between our lives and Marcus'. His battles were ours and ours, his.

Bill and I finished our call with more grace than our last, and I sat relieved, in a peaceful state, soaking in his new way to provide for our family.

THE PROVIDER

After our phone call, unbeknownst to me, Bill decided to take the bull by the horns. The woman who originally called me shared with Bill that she was very upset about having watched many days of the floor hockey camp, and she had details of how Marc had become drastically bullied, not by other kids, but by a camp counselor in charge.

"This man humiliated him and made him sit out because he said, out loud, he wasn't good enough. Which is cruel, because he's at the same level as the rest of the kids! He uses a voice to mimic him... It's sickening... I was up all night worrying about this... I just had to do something to stop it," she explained.

Bill had a conference call set up with our attorneys in the late morning. He told Nick Mahoney, one of our lawyers, "Give me a couple hours. I have to take care of something."

Nick put immense pressure on him reminding him that this was a critical call and had to be handled today.

Bill showed up at floor hockey camp, with Nicole in tow, heading directly to the gym where the camp was held. He stood off to the side, unseen, to see if he could witness anything happening. Within a few minutes, he saw Marcus come off the bench he'd been sitting on and asked to go back in the game. The counselor started mimicking Marcus with a whining voice and said, "I want to go back in, my daddy paid for this camp, whah whah whah."

Just then, Clint took his stick and whipped it off against the wall and screamed "HEY!"

He looked as if, he too, had seen enough, just like the concerned lady.

Bill immediately walked in and said, "Excuse me!"

The counselor replied without concern and some sarcasm, "Can I help you?"

Bill replied, "No, but I'm gonna help you. You and I are going down to the office right now. Your assistant here can take over."

And he grabbed the back of the counselor's collar and escorted him out of the gym. Bill turned to the boys and Nicole, and said, "Stay here. Watch your sister. I'll be right back."

While heading to the office, the counselor tripped over a curb. Bill held him by his collar to keep his footing.

On the way, the guy was saying things like "What the hell are you doing? I'm going to sue you," and Bill replied, "Get in fucking line, you piece of shit."

Bill explained, "We're going to the office, and then you're going to quit."

The counselor said, "Are you fuckin' crazy?"

And Bill replied, "No, and I'm not fucking around. You and I both know you don't belong coaching kids. One way or another, you're done."

Bill stopped and looked him dead in the eye. "You have two choices right now: Quit and apologize to my kids, and the other kids in that gym, or I'm gonna beat the livin' shit out of you, the old-fashioned way. If you want to sue me, be my guest. It only highlights what an absolute coward you are."

Bill continued, "I'm guessing you're afraid to apologize, for fear I'll turn around and sue you, right? What a flat-assed circle-jerk this legal world has become."

When they reached the office, the counselor went from cocky, and sure to cautious, and scared about getting in legal or police trouble. The woman that had called us was already in the office, and, it was evident by the look on all faces, she had shared the details with his supervisor.

When Bill arrived, the supervisor walked up and said to the counselor, "What do you have to say for yourself?"

And the camp counselor replied, "I quit."

When they returned home, Bill canceled Nicole's play date and told the kids to put on their swimsuits.

"I have a surprise for you guys. I had an idea of something fun we could do."

He helped Nicole pick a bikini, and of course, she had to have matching flip-flops. This took some time because she had quite a collection to choose from, because of the access to past funds. He had never played that role before, so she soaked up his attention.

Bill flipped the stereo on and turned the volume up high enough to hear in the backyard. He gathered flippers, goggles and any pool toy he could find that hadn't been sold in the garage sale. He grabbed beach towels, laying them on a warm, dry table near the back door. He untangled the old hoses that came with the rental and started filling buckets with water. The day before, he had found an old bag of unused water balloons in a box marked kitchen junk drawer and instructed Marcus, "Get going on filling those up. And can you find a plastic bat? Were going to hit the water balloons with that."

Clint lined up the water guns we had, filling each one to the top, and testing them all out to make sure everyone had an even chance to dominate in the water games Bill told them they were going to play. Marc and Clint dragged one of the cardboard forts from the family room for use as a safe haven for the water fights. Bill made target signs with chalk on the stucco wall that wrapped around the backyard and asked Nicole to help him draw a hopscotch area, too.

They ran from one part of the small backyard to the next, but somehow he made it feel like a huge amusement park. This was, by far, the most fun they'd ever had with him as they slipped, slid, fell and laughed while running around. The boys let Nicole dominate with the water guns by giving her a water *rifle* that was practically the same size as her. They all faked being hit with dramatic falls to the ground. After a second or two, they'd rise like mummies and chase her, where she would hide by taking cover in Bill's arms.

The doorbell rang, and Bill decided he'd let it go. He wasn't expecting anyone and since he knew where I was and where his three kids were, he didn't feel a need to know who stood outside the front door. He watched the kids run around while the song Arms Wide Open by Creed, blasted through the house and back-yard. The words couldn't be more perfect for him on this very day. While watching them, he felt a welcomed shift that had been taking place. With arms wide open he could show them love and tell them to greet the world with the same.

The bell rang again, and then again, whoever it was decided to knock as well. So Bill started making his way through the sliding back door and entered the house. Water goggles sat on top of his head as he carefully walked with his flippers flopping on top of the slippery, white-tiled floor. He had worn them to give the kids a better chance to get away from him. Soaking wet from head to toe, he opened the door to find our lawyer, Nick Mahoney, dressed in his normal attire: a dark blue suit with a starched white button down underneath.

Nick stood stunned at the sight of Bill while looking him up and down.

Bill said, "You're a little overdressed for this party, don't you think?"

Exasperated, pointing to Bill's goggles, "Are you freakin' kidding me right now?" Nick asked.

"What?" Bill responded without shame for the unusual attire on his head and feet.

Nick had papers in his hand and waved them in front of Bill.

"Bill, this needs to be addressed right away. We had a fucking conference call. It's been hours since I've heard from you. I don't think I need to remind you, these lawyers know what they're doing. And you just gave them the upper hand and screwed yourself! They're coming for your jugular. I'm thinking, by the looks of you, you may have officially lost your mind. When is Judy going to be back? She'll need to sign these settlement papers as well. That is if I can even get these guys to return my call now."

"First of all, watch the language, my kids are nearby. Secondly, Judy's not signing anything. Neither am I. You have the last of the attorney fees that I want or can pay, and the total settlement charges paid out will be the last. I'm making an executive decision, and that is to tell you: take your money and run. And listen, Nick, a good friend told me, *there's an art to leaving*. I'm leavin'. I'm declaring bankruptcy. I sent the paperwork to a BK attorney a few days ago. And so these leeches… they can take what's left. If necessary, they'll answer to a higher power than me someday, and I'm comfortable with that. I'm letting go. I know what I want now. I want out."

"But we could win. You don't have to do this."

"Nick, I like to win. I'm a coach and former athlete, but *what* exactly am I going to win? There's nothing left, and these bastards will never stop. I'm sick and tired of trying to win a game played by cheats. In this deal, the law isn't about truth; it's about leverage. I'm letting go of the rope. As you know, I'm coaching pee-wee football. I've been coaching my kids that winning is about more than a score. It's about how you play and who you play for. I need to take my own advice and cut the ties to the game and these people. You know as well as I do that everyone, including the lawyers, are making a living off of this, but I don't see the value. I don't need to *win* this battle or to be *right* anymore. It's too destructive. Bottom line: I'm no longer attached to my money or the outcome of these lawsuits. I know what I should be fighting for now. If it's meant to be, I'll make the money back again. But I can't do it while dealing with these people. No mas. It's about my family and me now."

He continued, "And another thing: I'm done trying to resurrect i360 just so these guys can keep coming after me for more. They can have all my stock. I'm going bankrupt, and they can all find someone else to fight. They'll no longer have a second of my attention from here on out.

Nick stopped Bill, "But Bill…"

"Nick, stop, please. Over the last few years, I let this change me. I was unprepared for the loss of everything. There's no quick fix, and there's no long, drawn-out lawsuit that will fix it, Nick. The lawsuits distract me from the things worth more than money.

Listen, my whole life, I've been busting my balls to be the man I thought I should be. With money pouring in, it's easy to provide stuff you think your family needs. Even if things get screwed up, at least you have the money for therapy, a vacation or to cover medical bills. Being squeezed financially makes me unable to *provide* in that way. So, I'm going back to the basics. This path has slowly been destroying my family, my wife, my marriage, and our future. But not any more, brotha."

Nick pleaded, "Bill, you don't get who you're dealing with. These guys are going to come after you with a vengeance. And on top of that, the random anonymous tip made to the Phoenix bankruptcy department is now working against you. They are definitely onto your bankruptcy, claiming you are lying in regards to what you own. They mentioned furs, jewelry, and watches again, but added that you have cash hidden, and money offshore… whoever it is, they are relentless and will fight 'til the end. Do you hear me? It's fraud, buddy. You could face jail time if you're hiding anything. Things are tough, but this can make them brutal. I hadn't ever even heard of anything like this. I've never had a client endure this. So I don't even know how to prepare you."

"Don't. Don't prepare us. We'll survive whatever they got." Laughing, "What I disclosed is what we have, period. As a matter of fact, one of my financial buddies, just yesterday, said I was a dumb-ass for not having protected money offshore. Actually, I feel good that I didn't fall into that trap. And fuck them! Let them investigate. I hope it costs them a fortune. There's nothing to find. I'm an open book. It's interesting how liars and cheats always expect to find liars and cheats."

"Holy shit, you have lost your mind. Of all people, I can't believe *you* are giving up," Nick hopelessly said while he shook his bowed head from side to side.

"Here's the deal: I'm giving up by letting go, brotha, but I will never give up on what's *right* in my life… my family. I know what I did for that company and what my intentions were. I'm good with that."

Just as Bill finished that comment, he heard ice cream truck music from down the street. He stepped out onto the driveway, in full water gun fighting gear, while his eyes scanned past the lawyer, looking off to the left down the street. Every day during the summer, the ice-cream truck would make its way around. The kids were trained not to ask for these kinds of extras now. It was amazing how they let go of having those freedoms.

Bill lightly tapped Nick in the chest with the palm of his hand and said, "You have some change on ya, right?!"

"Oh dear God, Bill, you *have* officially lost your freaking mind. You need to see a doc and talk about getting on some meds." Still, Nick dug into his pockets, pulling out dollars and change, handing it over to Bill.

"HEY KIDS," Bill sang.

And they started piling into the doorway and out onto the driveway, wet swimsuits dripping and all.

"Lookie here; Uncle Nick is buying us ice-cream!"

"YAY!!!" as they ran past him with all their gear on. With water guns strapped in holsters and goggles on their eyes, they raced to the truck that pulled up right in front of our house.

"Come on, let's cheer you up," Bill said to Nick.

Nick reluctantly followed.

They stood at the end of the driveway and picked their ice creams. Nick refused to place an order, so Bill chose one for him.

"Two rocket pops please." They were the old fashioned red-white-and-blue rocket-shaped popsicles.

"God Bless our American Dreams," Bill said, as they cheered with their popsicles crossed like swords.

The kids ran back towards the house to get to the backyard festivities, shouting, "Come on, Dad!"

Marcus instructed Nicole to squirt Bill as he held the back part of her water rifle up, but she was in charge of aiming. She pulled the trigger, accidently shooting Nick right in the chest. His dark blue suit coat and starched, white button-down Oxford shirt, soaked with just one shot.

Bill laughed with a wink at Nick and said, "Perfect shot, Honey, you hit the bull's eye!"

When a willing victim who had committed no treachery was killed in a traitors stead, the table would crack, and Death itself would start working backward. The victim becomes the victor. C.S. Lewis

@PEACE

The afternoon's warm summer breeze put me in a trance-like state while I watered plants outside. I looked up to the sun hidden behind the puffy white clouds as I reflected on how intense that same sun was in Tucson compared to the gentle one here. *Get ready, girl.*

The dogs warmed themselves in sunny spots on the brick patio while watching me off and on. I plopped myself down between them as I pondered how awful it will be not to wake up to them, play with them, enjoy them. I tried to imagine how my re-entry to Tucson would be and felt better about it after the call from Bill. Fully enjoying these simple chores that made my existence easy here, I recalled Eckhart Tolle's messages about being present. Finding a way to offset and change the habitual, hurried routines in Tucson may be a challenge, but it helped first to become aware of it.

I'd been preparing for the blowback from this trip and expected there'd be a huge price to pay. But the phone call from Bill played over and over in my head. I found myself dissecting his words, his pauses, and his silence. I was happy for him, for the first time in a long time, and I welcomed the relief I was feeling. I was interested in knowing more of his details, but also felt a healthy detachment from his journey. It was as if I saw him stepping up to claim some independence for himself, and that gave me permission to let him go and do his own thing. The clarity that came from Skye about him not having a voice and his complacency in letting me go, "if that's what I wanted," was still an unknown. But because he took the phone number of that woman and didn't ask me to engage, it gave me the sense that good news was around the corner. I had forgotten what that even felt like.

I walked back into the house and my room. My white bed sheets and fluffy comforter lay there unmade, again. I'd spent so many years being so anal about making my bed and then after having children, I passionately carried the rule on as if it mattered. It felt good to make it now when I felt like it.

Thinking about being present... I thought to myself, *it's not easy, but I like that it's that simple.* I practiced with every step, moving from room to room. This

11-day space allowed me to uncomfortably miss the kids, and I dropped into a thought process about how I don't want to end up at 60, left with regret, that I was too busy to be present and overwhelmed with *to-do* lists when I could have been hugging, holding and kissing my little ones. I must find a way to, more consistently, embrace those little beings.

I settled on a new rule that I was going to announce when I got home. I was going to call it HOMEWORK. Any time we as a family felt disjointed, I was going to suggest that we do things with and for each other that had to do with giving us a round house…a peaceful, happy, safe house. I imagined myself randomly creating mental health days with them where we could go to a park or a zoo for the day. I could see myself teaching the kids how amazing it would be to take over a siblings chores when you know your sibling is overwhelmed. Just for the love of each other, for being present with one another and for the consistent practice of joy.

While standing in front of the cracked window, the cool breeze gently brushed against my face and arms with the smell of the flowering gardenia bushes outside wafting through. Standing straight up, with eyes open and bare feet planted onto the wood floor, I placed my arms out to my sides as I settled in with the intention of being present. Ahhhhh, I thought, as a tear of joy, rolled down my cheek while immense, solid peace filled me. Eventually, I plopped myself down, belly first, on top of the comforter, taking in the flowering scents and someone's fresh cut grass while listening to chirping birds and a lawnmower in the distance.

This is a good life.

DON'T JUST DO SOMETHING, STAND THERE. BUDDHA

I naturally went into clean and order mode, but while staying present. Sam I Am followed me to every space I entered. I stood in the quaint Crate and Barrel like kitchen, noticing the warm water rinse the soapy suds from my hands, and then watched the suds go down the drain. Noticing the tanned skin on my hands brought my attention to my fingers and nails. Mysteriously, they looked pretty to me today, the same nails I'd always hated and even covered with acrylic in the past. Because of very little-to-no sugar intake, I also felt the mental clarity spoken from people that fast. While continuing to scan my body, I appreciated it, and I mean ALL of it. Flaws and everything. *Weird.*

As I wiped the counters clean, I smiled as I realized, dieting and/or watching what I ate or drank in the past were always unsuccessful. The minute I'd decide to avoid sweets or fatty foods, I'd somehow feel overly deprived and find myself in the drive through, getting a happy meal at McDonald's or eating a pint of Baskin Robbins, mint-chocolate-chip ice cream. Leaving me to always gain weight on diets.

Here, I let it go. I really, let it go.

I'd shifted from unconscious eating and drinking to conscious eating. It's as if I finally let myself enjoy food now. The unconscious drinking of beers had not even tempted me, to my old ways, here. I imagined how different and how good it might feel to have a couple beers tonight while staying in this present conscious state of mind. With no fight, I'd regulated myself without great effort to bring everything into moderation. And then I remembered something Tom Callahan, the first healer I went to, said, "Everything in moderation, (and he smiled) including moderation."

That always struck a chord in me. Deep inside of me. Drinking a beer to celebrate with healthy friends and drinking to disappear are two different things.

Sam was now perched on the counter where I stacked Ed's and Tracy's mail.

Talk about being present; I thought as I petted him while he purred. "Hey, buddy. I'm glad that we've become friends." I lowered my face to him, "I'm gonna miss you guys."

It had been too long since I had an animal in my life. In my imagination, I could see our future puppy and our thrilled kids. Even though our finances screamed NO, I saw a greater benefit of peace coming into the house, not another chore or expense. If looked at in the right way, a pet was a reminder of how to stay present and seek joy. *Maybe a happy lab, with labitude, would give us that.*

Slowly, I dried the clean dishes with a fluffy, cream-colored towel, one plate, and glass at a time. Staying present and paying attention to the details in texture and color of each plate and glass, while also studying the way my hands moved around and held each piece. Sam lay perched beside me, watching my every move. I scooped a mound of bubbles left in the sink into my palm and watched as they slowly popped little by little. I held it out to Sam. He gently swatted at it with his paw, and the bubbles exploded in a little puff. We continued to hold the energy of being present together. *A master teacher, this cat was.*

Faintly, I heard a guitar in the background. I wondered if someone's stereo had just been turned on. *Was it Hottie?* As I tuned in more, I realized, it was him. He had plugged his acoustic guitar into an amp. I had heard him play a lot of music this past week, but it wasn't anything like that. This was slow and soulful, and I was drawn to hear every word. I slowly walked through the small house and towards the back door where I could hear more clearly. I gently pushed the screen door open and carefully closed it behind me. He was singing, and he sounded choked up. This song meant something to him, I could tell.

Oh... it's "Hallelujah." No wonder, I thought to myself. I sat off in the corner of the patio, where he wouldn't be able to see me. He had shared some personal stuff, so I could guess where he was coming from. I let the lyrics sink in showing me where every breath holds Hallelujah. It's interesting how a singer will sing a song you may be familiar with, but their rich personal background of joy and suffering can somehow magically be delivered as if it was a song you'd never been exposed to before. His heart and the wisdom he'd gained in life made it effortless to hear the faith and hope in his own future. This young man was comfortable with what he knew about life and seemed equally comfortable with how much he still had to learn.

That song spoke to me. It seemed that when a man loves a woman, and vice versa, it can break both of them open in a way that they may need in order to survive and embrace the rest of their life. It's not that they can't survive alone. They can. But if they have been filleted open, it leaves room for spirit to move in. Like Bill and me—it was obviously time to take another look inside while each tapping into our individual true natures and greatness.

I quietly slipped back into the bungalow after Hottie completed the song and packed a few things I knew I wouldn't need for my last days in Santa Barbara. As I was putting them in the truck, he came out, standing at the top of the stairs with no shirt on.

"Heyyy," I said to him. "What do you want? You here just to show off?" as I pointed to his chest. His hair was messy, and he looked like he'd been in his apartment all day. Maybe he was practicing for the open mic night. Dropping my awkwardness with him was such a relief. I truly treasured this brief friendship we had built in such a short time. And I had some peace in knowing I would most likely not stay in touch with him afterward. Our proximity, our age difference, and our paths would set us apart. But the one thing we had in common, needed no maintenance. His sex appeal and fresh, hopeful outlook on life and his adoration of me at my worst, unleashed me in an unexpected, yet transformational way. He reminded me of my own Goddess energy, my own feminine sexuality, and my own original fresh outlook on life. And while adoring him, he entertained me long enough to remind me of the joy and magic that can come when meeting a complete stranger.

"Hey, Jude," he sang from the top step.

"Stop," I would say again and again, as he'd done this many times during my stay.

"See you tonight, right? You chicken shit," he yelled.

"Oh geez, you really think name calling is going to motivate me to show up and make an ass out of myself?" I kidded him, "I was rethinking this whole thing. I don't want to do it."

His teasing was helping, but I wasn't going to tell him that I liked his support.

"You better be there," he said.

"Um hmm. We'll see," winking at him.

"You goin' to see Bayard right now?" he asked.

While putting some items in the Denali, "Yep, I'm gonna organize a few things first and take a long walk on the beach. I hope he comes tonight."

"You should just move here. You pretty much belong here. Like your hair is all bleached out, your tan, best of all, you're entirely all chilled out, like a real hippy chick. Honestly, I didn't think that would happen."

He laughed and continued, "You were a wound up girl, Jude. Thought I was gonna have to sleep with ya and give you my magic potion, so you could loosen up."

"Oh God. Okay, great. That would have wrecked me. I knew better than to go in that direction," I said laughing.

"Well, we still have one more night together. If you need any assistance at all, to calm the nerves, before your performance, you let me know. I'm here for ya girl." More laughing.

"Ugh. You're a brat. I'll see ya later."

SUNSHINEY DAY

It was still early afternoon, and the puffy, white clouds occasionally slipped in front of the bright sun. Hearing about Tucson's record-breaking 110-degrees enhanced my concern was for the kids who were practicing football every day. I let myself worry about it for just a second and then remembered Bill was the head coach, and because he still thought like a paramedic, he'd be on top of that. *No worries.* I let it go so that I could enjoy the drive to my second home, Arroyo beach. The radio was on, turned down low and I heard it, my all-time favorite song from Johnny Nash "I Can See Clearly Now." One of my earliest memories was singing it as a kid for my neighbors on Sussex Court in Buffalo Grove.

I had spent an entire lifetime since then forgetting about this song, only to have it come on, on some random station, at random divine times exactly when I needed to hear it. Just like it had come on in Tucson while I washed dishes before coming here.

Parked in my regular spot, I sat in the Denali and sang it at the top of my lungs. Before leaving the house, I'd already mentally prepared that this might be my second-to-last time at the beach before returning to Tucson. The idea of saying goodbye to Bayard was getting raw and real, as this exchange would be packed with so much more than a regular parting. I turned off the car and started towards the beach. Scanning the area, I looked all over for Bayard but didn't see him. Deep worry started to set in. *Yikes. Hello, anxious old friend. Where did my present self go? And what about the song, "I Can See Clearly Now" that just divinely played?*

My worry at this moment highlighted why practice was called practice for a reason. I had seen many satori moments in my life, those "A-HA" moments when I was flooded with immediate clarity on something. But because of the way I was wired to worry, it felt like I needed to have a more consistent practice of the art of being present.

Just then, my thoughts were taken over by my nearing goodbye to Bayard, his explanation on how these were his last months, and that he wasn't sure when he would go. I was attached to my bad luck story, where I often thought tragedy was probably coming my way. I temporarily spun out like I used to, picturing him on the floor of his tiny house, all alone. I was on a strong negative roll here, while I looked out onto the beach, already mourning my new dear friend.

"Hey there," I heard.

Bayard was standing there with his oxygen tank and fishing cap, sporting his big smile on his beautiful worn skin. He had a sweater on today, and I turned and ran into his arms. He held me for a long time.

"There, there," he said. "There, there child, everything is going to be all right, remember?"

"I thought, I thought the worst. Damn, I always go there."

"Always is a strong belief. Who would you be if you didn't believe that?" he responded.

"Want to walk?" I asked.

"A little, I'm a bit tired today," he admitted.

He took one look at me and knew where I was going in my mind.

He smiled. No lecture. Just an encouraging smile that said when he leaves this world, he'll be ready.

I'd mentioned the open mic early in the week, so I reminded him that tonight was the night.

"Wonderful, if I can keep my energy up, I'll stop by. The evenings are a little rough for me."

"Oh, that would be so great, but if it's too much, please don't push it."

He reminded me to stay present and to continue taking notes on all of my experiences and findings over the 11 days.

"Tonight could be a great chapter," he said.

"Maybe, but as the hours roll on, and I get closer and closer to this, I'm starting to legitimately feel sick," I said, laughing.

"And who would you be, if you never reacted to these fears with dis-ease?" he asked.

I didn't answer. That's what I liked about Bayard; he may pose a question like that, giving me silent permission to not immediately answer, encouraging to think and feel first before I spoke. I was so much quieter these days, even to the point of not over-explaining things to Bill in the last phone call. It made me feel better about my transformation here.

"So the private beach was a success for you?" Bayard asked.

I laughed, "A smashing success." Showing him the jellyfish stings on my ankles.

"OH, my... battle wounds," he said.

"I broke through initial fears I expected, and then just like the universe likes to do sometimes, the unexpected showed up," I explained.

Briefly, I told him of the day, and of my two new sexy tattooed friends while describing how scarcity dissipated from my senses. I shared that because of him and the others, I was sure I was living in the Land of Plenty now.

"He chuckled. "Ahhhh. I like it. The Land of Plenty. Will this be the title, or a chapter title?"

I smirked then quickly changed subjects, filling him in on the minister, the vows and how he spurred me onto redefining the new "F" word: Feminism.

"Good God, you're hitting every topic in 11 days," he remarked with a hearty "HA" afterwards.

He didn't offer any added profound words. But his smile beamed and joy emanated from him as he stared at me while walking arm in arm.

It was getting close to 5 P.M. and I had planned on yoga at 6 to get me calm before the open mic. So we said our goodbyes, promising to see each other later. Because of inviting him, I had committed myself. And I was pleased there was no way out now. How could I blow off Bayard, who may be forcing himself to get to this bar? If he would do that for me, I had to go.

As I stepped halfway into the truck, he playfully yelled from across the parking lot, "By the way, you're on to something here. I wholeheartedly agree with the Land of Plenty comment! It's a choice! To either live in it, or not."

WHAT'S UP?

Yoga was packed, but I found a small area in the back corner to lay my mat. Unfortunately, the stench of the man next to me was beyond distracting. It made my mouth water and I thought I was going to puke. Other then when pregnant, I've never really been super-sensitive to scents. I was hoping it would just pass. But, no. With every lengthy move he made into downward and upward dog, that scent rode on the breeze moving through the studio, finding its way into my nostrils. I was doing everything I could, to not outwardly gag. His stench convinced me he had poor bathroom etiquette. *Who the hell comes to yoga class like that, where we are packed like sardines bending and flowing, so close to one another?*

It occurred to me that maybe I should consider it a test to be present and non-judgmental. Maybe then I could find a way to work through this. So, I started coming up with excuses. What if *smelly guy* is homeless and was gifted the class for free? *God Bless him.* Or his water was turned off. Or maybe he's in the middle of a fast and has visited the toilet 25 times today. Or maybe he can't smell himself? Or Maybe he likes his scent, and he's flaunting it? This train of thought became humorous, and I forced myself to stifle a giggle. I took a deep breath in, and choked on his scent. I tried it again, another deep breath in and out. It got a little easier. Another deep breath, in and then out. A little better. I continued to move in and out of each position. I'm not sure of what others would have said if they were even watching me, but I felt fluid, each move graceful and gliding into the next one. One position would unfold, and then settle deeper into the next. I was finding that being present was possible even amongst *smelly guy.*

Sinking deeper and deeper into my breath and into the positions, I fell fast asleep in savasana. Next thing I knew, Violet was gently nudging me. I could smell a hint of bergamot essential oil just as I awakened. I remembered smelly guy and wondered where he had gone. The whole class had emptied. I shot up from the floor, and asked Violet, "How long have I been in savasana?" I asked.

"Not too long. I would have let you go longer, but isn't tonight the night of the open mic?"

"Yeah, it is!" I said while rolling my mat up, "I'm gonna take a shower and, OH, am I going to see you there? Are you still coming?"

"Of course I am," she said while she gave me a pat on the butt.

"Okay, see you in a bit," I said.

As I said that, my stomach flipped. Just for a second. Thoughts were starting to form, while trying to remind myself, *Why did I agree to this?*

On the walk to my car, I concentrated on being present with each footstep, and I let it calm me down.

It was good to see the dogs and I took them on a short stroll down the street and back. I had picked out clothes I wanted to wear, laying them on the comfy comforter.

For another second, I thought, *I could just forget all this silliness and crawl under that comforter. Stupid leap. Stupid net.* I couldn't though. I had committed to myself and most importantly, I may never forgive myself for not trying. And Bayard... he may be there.

I had two songs in mind but wasn't sure if either would work. I had a back-up choice, just in case, and I knew Hottie's band could play them all. With no idea of how they'd be played, I trusted I could wing it. The one time, I had choked on stage was now starting to creep into my mind, though.

Before having kids, I was asked to try out for a very successful wedding band performing in both Chicago and the suburbs. After practicing many hours on a song they always played, I showed up and felt ready. I was nervous because it was somebody's actual wedding, with hundreds of people in attendance, but I felt somewhat confident. The musicians in the group were used to playing it in their own style, and with their regular lead singer. So, I was unable to follow their key or rhythm, and I started to then forget the words. I'll never forget the look of horror on Bill's face as he stood in the back of the room of a wedding we had not been invited too. The bride and groom stopped dancing to see why the band didn't sound right. Bill's facial expression screamed, "Oh my God, how can I get her out of here fast." I was embarrassed, and we never spoke of it again.

Shaking that dreadful feeling, I jumped in the shower. My green summer cords were laid out on the bed with a fitted, charcoal-gray deep-V-neck top, which supported the fresh sex appeal I'd been finally feeling, off and on. I stood in front of the long length mirror and thought, *I would have never worn anything so edgy and unmatched before. This is something an artist would wear for sure.*

I liked how my hair was drying into slightly "beachy" waves. The sun had highlighted my hair in a way I hadn't seen since I was a kid. Tonight, I would treat my makeup like stage makeup, applying smoky-gray shadow on my eyelids while adding charcoal eyeliner. I had a soft peach lip-gloss that added mostly shine. I carefully applied mascara, laying on a few layers for a more dramatic look. Placing the crystal gemmed thin olive stretchy headband that the boutique owner had given me, over my relaxed hair gave me the vibe I was after. I had to admit though *I looked ridiculous in this bathroom.* I could tell by Sam's contemplative furry face that he thought it was a cat toy. It looked a little warrior princess like, and I decided to wear it for the Chumash people who'd once lived here. I thought: *maybe I will rock this, but I need to be in soft, low lighting in the bar with loud music, and people need to have some alcohol in them. Yeah, sure, that's when I'll feel like I belong in this outfit.*

Earlier today, Hottie suggested that I "take a shot, smoke a joint, meditate… whatever. Just do what you have to do to get yourself on that stage."

After walking into the kitchen, I studied the full bottles of alcohol lined up on the kitchen shelf. Apparently, these people were not big drinkers. I imagined they didn't find refuge in alcohol or shield themselves like I had for so many nights. Their lives appeared not to be filled with the turmoil ours was. But who knows? We humans get so masterful at hiding our pain from others. Even if they were the ones unscathed from a lot of suffering thus far, I was happy for them. It was refreshing to think of people like that now. At the same time, I liked this new feeling of knowing, trusting, hoping that we may come through this trying time, trusting that *This too shall pass.* It was empowering to feel that today, for myself and for others.

I reached for the tequila, pulled a small juice glass out of the cabinet, and poured out a tiny amount. I hate shots, never did them. But tonight, it felt right. Toasting, to myself, Maximillian, Titus and Sam I Am and to the rest of the world, "Bottoms up. Here's to us all experiencing as much ease, grace and fun as possible."

After taking a second shot, I sat next to the dogs on the kitchen floor. They had been watching my every move. *I can't imagine what they're thinking.* Sam I Am seemed to have had enough of me and retired for the evening in some unknown sleeping area I was never able to figure out.

An hour passed. I stalled long enough. Nervously, I gathered my sheet music and slid my ID with the $100 bill in my back pocket. Checking my phone to make sure I didn't have a call from home, I petted the dogs for a while, stalling some more. I slowly walked to the truck, staying present with each footstep, just trying to keep myself calm, so I'd actually go through with this. *I can't turn back now.*

I knew where the bar was, and Hottie mentioned hidden spots in the back where I could easily park. Driving down the alley behind it, just where he said, I was able to find a spot. I sat in the car and listened. And I prayed. And then listened some more. Loud music blasted from inside. Someone was already performing. They sounded good. Real good. *Damn it. Why am I doing this? I could be home with my kids right now. I look fucking ridiculous too.*

I carefully opened my car door, then quietly shut it behind me. I knew Hottie was probably on stage, but I didn't want anyone to see me yet. Just in case I want to bolt and get the hell out of here.

Doubt and embarrassment that I was attempting this performance started settling in deeper, and I wasn't feeling good. I started to feel sweat dripping down my back, and my face was flushed. My mouth started watering, and I was urgently seeking a place to puke. I found a corner against the building and an air conditioning unit and lost the two tequila shots I so courageously drank earlier.

Ugh. I should have eaten. I forgot again!

"Stick of gum?" Hottie appeared out of nowhere. He wrapped his arms around me, which we hadn't done yet with our friendship.

"Are you kidding me? You don't have to do this. I'm sorry for pushing you. Are you literally making yourself sick over this? It's okay, you don't have to do it, just come in, and let's have fun."

What a sweetheart he was. His buddy came out and asked what was going on, and Hottie told him, "She isn't feeling great, she's gonna pass on the singing thing tonight, and we're all just gonna have a good time."

Like gentlemen, they let me enter through the back door first. I walked past some chefs that were flipping burgers and entered into the lively bar.

"Those look good," I said.

The DJ was playing music during a break, waiting for the next open mic session to start. I was so relieved. *Hottie came to the rescue, and I don't have to do this tonight! It's ALL GOOD.* Just then, he came from the kitchen with a hamburger and a beer, "Here, looks like you lost your dinner. Eat."

He went back over to his buddy. While adjusting equipment on the stage. They laughed and talked, and at one point, waved to me. I waved back. I didn't see Bayard, Jenna, Jessie or Violet either. Thank God they didn't come. I won't be disappointing them then. They won't even know that I caved under the pressure. Only I'll know. *Maybe I can live with that. I already had in the past.*

Hottie got up to the mic and announced, "We'll be starting in 15. Those of you performing tonight, already have your space in line. We have 11 performers left."

For the next ten minutes, I cheerfully, and in the most relieved way, consumed the entire hamburger, the pickle and drank an entire beer sitting at the bar, while totally enjoying the comedian-like bartender, Eddie. While laughing out loud at his jokes, I noticed Hottie looking at me out of the corner of his eye, and I turned to wave to him. He waved back and then got Eddie's attention with a nod that basically said: "Give her another beer." Wow, this reminded me of the good old days with Bill, back when the beer and food kept flowing.

As Eddie gave me another frosty mug of beer, I said, "Hey thanks."

"No problem, it's on the house for out-of-town talent."

"Oh, no. I'm not singing tonight."

"Hmmm really? Aren't you the lady from Tucson? They've been practicing 'What's Up' all day. Got it stuck in my head and was looking forward to hearing a chick sing it, rather than those two bozos."

"Oh, well yes, I was going to, but I'm not feeling…"

Interrupted by Hottie's voice as he stood in front of the mic, I heard the band softly playing *my* song, "What's Up?"

"Tonight, I have a special friend from Tucson, Arizona, who has not sang since college, Judy Cochrane. Let's give her a hand. Singing 'What's Up' by 4 Non-Blondes."

What the hell? He's so dead!

Turning to look at the crowd, I noticed there were more people in there then I had seen when first walking in. Jenna and Jessie were standing and clapping with arms overhead. Violet sat with a distinguished male friend at a small round table in the back corner. Still no sign of Bayard. I was worried about him. I felt like puking again but refused to humiliate myself. Even though my legs wobbled, I paid attention to every step made to the stage, feeling the bottoms of my feet ground to the hard cement floor. I stayed present because it was the only safe place I could trust.

Hottie leaned into me laughing and said, "Sorry, I had to do it. You'll thank me in the morning."

Maybe Bayard was right. Maybe this would be a great chapter. I took the mic in my trembling hand, staying present and keeping my mind out of it, I listened to the music, while remembering the first words, and waited for my cue.

Starting off, it went okay.

Then I forgot the fricken words! *OH, how I needed a karaoke screen right now! I was choking! I was doing it again. I'M CHOKING!*

If Bill were here, he would be trying to strategize our escape. OH BILL! I NEED YOU RIGHT NOW! I'M A TOTAL FOOL!

Hottie stopped the band and walked up to me. He twirled me around, putting my back to the audience. He wrapped his hands around my hands on the microphone and squeezed. Knowing I was about to burst into tears, he said, "You have been talking about all this facing fear of speaking, singing, swimming and being present shit. Right now. Right here. You need to climb into this song. You personally have lived these words. You can fairly ask What's Up? You can talk about the hills of hope you've climbed and fallen off of. You've prayed and then prayed some more. You, Bill and the kids have lived these words. It's okay to own them. Sing this song for them. Okay? For them." He stared me down. "You good?"

That's IT! He was right. I knew that by losing myself in this song, I might find myself, just like in meditation, yoga, long walks, meeting new friends and in these 11 days. He got me, all right.

"For 8-21-88," I whispered below the microphone.

Before starting, I glanced out to the audience and saw Bayard. He must have entered when my back was to the crowd while getting coached by Hottie. An unfamiliar strength came through me, the kind I've never been able to describe, except to just say it like that. It didn't thrust me into a super serious place; it actually made me more emotionally flexible and free. I'm sure staying present and having a couple beers helped, but all of a sudden, I was not overly concerned with the outcome of things tonight. I was surprised by the feeling of safety, which was somehow present, as I looked out into the eyes of strangers in the audience and also at my new friends, whom I'd grown to love in a rapid way.

I heard the music starting over. My hands still shook, but with a looser grip on the mic, I was comfortable enough to continue. I connected to it, while I recognized there was a courageous part of me that had been asking myself all along… *what's up? What is up with all that's happened? What do you want me to do, dear God?* Relatively, it had been a rough road for me and so I just might have earned the right to sing it. We had been fighting the *good fight.* Trying to *stay gold.*

Moving through our struggles rather than around them had been key, and I'm not sure when it happened, but I was no longer worrying about what was coming my way or what the past had been.

The words moved me in a way that surprised me. I had felt like it had been twenty-plus years and I had still been trying to get up that mountain of hope for a destination that might never be. I felt tears welling up in my eyes. Yet, I was feeling only joy and all that's good. I let myself be vulnerable and sing it with all my heart. As I moved into the chorus, I caught the attention of many in the bar. Not because they saw talent, but they may have seen some truth. Their own. And the truth is: we all have times of struggle. It's a tribe, where we all belong. And nobody gets out of here alive. I could look into their eyes and see they could relate to the words too. Because I had prayed so much and often felt unheard, there were so many times where I would want to just step outside and scream *WHAT THE F*CK IS GOING ON?!* As if someone else was going to be able to tell me or help me.

Violet stayed on her chair in the corner of the room. Her eyes brimmed with tears, but she wasn't surprised by my "release." Jessie and Jenna swayed back and forth, singing the words along with me. Jenna stood in front of him as his hands rested on her hips. And Bayard, standing in the back, beamed amidst the heavy smoke and loud music, as I watched his tank and tubes pump the last of his life inside of him. His light-blue eyes shined while looking at me and, like always, he gave me some weird silent permission to keep being *me*. I turned to Hottie, with a smile plastered on his face while singing back up. The guys in the band could not have had a better vibe and naturally got into the smooth, but fierce raw beat.

Letting go of the stranglehold on a happy ending and truly staying present on the middle now... with continued focus on finding the light of God in self, others and circumstance, that's where I belong.

I placed the mic in the stand and turned to Hottie. He met me in the middle of the stage, gave me a kiss on the forehead and a hug. I thanked the band and the amazing audience with a wave and bee-lined for Bayard. We both laughed out loud and locked ourselves into an embrace. He rocked me back and forth. "You did it."

Violet and her friend appeared, and I introduced them to Bayard and then Jessie and Jenna. It was beautiful how they all had known, at least, a little about each other. They, too, just clicked as I had done with each of them individually. We ended up putting a couple tables together as if we had known each other for years, and let a great night unfold. We honored the motto for the evening, "Everything In Moderation, Including Moderation," while allowing Eddie to over-serve us the rest of the night.

The next open mic performances were experienced local professionals trying out some new music, and I was thrilled to be there for that.

Later on, Hottie's band and lead singer played AC/DC's "You Shook Me All Night Long," and its energy pulled me out onto the dance floor, where I motioned for my friends to join me. In between sets, the DJ played irresistible dance music, where I found myself sandwiched in between Jessie and Jenna moving to the groove most of the night. I hadn't felt pretty or sexy in way too long. My buzzed friends, the dim lights and the loud music, all made it work. I didn't make a firm decision to continue this look at the PTA meetings, or while volunteering for a future field trip, but I liked it for tonight in Santa Barbara, where moderation was not the goal. I loved this city, and she loved me back. Truly and deeply.

After dragging Violet onto the dance floor, Jessie and Jenna grabbed her and sandwiched her in for a dance. I went and put my hand out to Bayard. "I'll go slow," I reassured him.

He obliged, even though I could tell his fatigue had gotten worse. But I could also tell he was loving this night, as I was. We slow danced, and he said, "You have to admit, it'd be a good chapter."

I didn't respond because I didn't have to. But I could see how it might. I had to admit that meeting him was divine timing for us both. *When things get tough down here, does God, and our Angels deliver people like this all the time, and I just hadn't noticed? Or did I unknowingly pray for them to come, without realizing I had.*

The thought kept coming to mind: "Angels exist." I'd have to say that they do. *Cause, I'm dancing with one right now.*

The song ended, and I got Bayard to sit back down.

"One more song," I said to him.

I ran up to Hottie between songs and asked if I could do the Tracy Chapman song, for Bayard. Hottie winked and in front of the other guys said, "OH shit, we created a monster. We'll never get her off this stage tonight."

He then walked to the front of the stage, announcing, "Judy Cochrane again, people, singing Tracy Chapman's 'Give Me One Reason.'"

"This is for you, Bayard," as I pointed to him in a sultry way.

I turned my back to the crowd, and now without any inhibitions, started swaying and moving my hips in the way that a stripper would. The slow, jazzy tune allowed me to feel the beat with my whole body. I playfully sang to Bayard that I had 'his number', and I knew he had mine. Instead of descending the stairs, I hopped off the front of the stage with the microphone in hand and headed towards Bayard as he both clapped and laughed. I sang the last of the song up close and face-to-face, making sure to tell him that I loved him and there was just simply nothing left to say. Doubled over and clapping, he embraced the love and attention while fully enjoying the unleashed me. Jenna and Jessie were now giving me a standing ovation. After the song, Hottie met me out on the dance floor to get the mic, then handed that off to his buddy on the stage. He had two beers in his one hand. "Here's to no moderation tonight!"

The DJ played Van Morrison's song "Brown Eyed Girl." I never liked my brown eyes, always wishing they were green or blue. I had shared that with him. So, I thought it was sweet that he picked this specifically for me. Hottie grabbed my hand and twirled me around the floor. It was so fun to dance in public. And I'm not sure if I ever felt freer on a dance floor than this night. Bill being the best dancer out of the two of us, I wished he could see me now. I had always held back. Now I danced like I let myself dance at the bungalow, unconcerned with what anyone thought. Hottie was holding my hand up and noticed my henna tattoo, "What's it mean?"

"OH, geez, I forgot to ask her!" I tore off across the bar to our table, where Jenna was engaged in a conversation with Bayard.

"Hey, you never told me what this meant."

Hottie was standing by for the answer too.

Jenna explained, "I interwove the Virgin Mother Mary abd angelic beings of light into the intricate henna design. And I added the rosary beads that wrap the wrist and wrap around the middle finger."

I was seeing it upside down and hadn't made her out. Part of the design trailed up and around my right-hand ring finger. She explained that she loved my "prude" nature and just wanted to encourage me to continue to be me. I was so moved.

We closed the bar a few hours later than the regular scheduled closing time. Eddie, the bartender, was the only sober one and offered to drive Hottie and I home. The plan was to come and get our cars the next morning. If I had too, with the right shoes, I could walk back myself.

I'm still not sure why I didn't relieve myself before we left the bar; I think I was simply too drunk to be paying attention to my bladder's signals. With the carefree innocence of a toddler, I'd simply been having too much fun to stop and check in on that right now. We laughed hysterically the whole way home because Eddie was hilarious. He poked fun at me choking at first, then in a newspaper reporter way said, "Breaking news: Tucson woman takes the life of loved and deeply respected university professor Bayard Stockton by giving him a heart attack in a dive bar in Santa Barbara late last night."

I complained so many times about having to pee that both Hottie and Eddie were threatening me that if I peed in the car, they would make me walk. That just made me laugh harder, which was making the sensation to pee worse, of course.

He rolled into the driveway hot and screeched to a stop. "Get out. Get out. Get out." Hysterically laughing, at the horrific thought of ending the night that way, I was bent over as I scrambled to exit his car. I checked my pockets and couldn't find my house key, or my car key. Which was going to make things interesting, seeing as I needed to drive home in two days.

Hottie, in a drunk panic, slurred, "Well, there's a key under the mat, or under this frog." He picked up a ceramic frog figurine in the garden. "Nope, not there," he said, as he accidently dropped it, breaking its head off.

"AH SHIT!" he said, clumsily trying to put it back together.

I was now standing on the patio with my two hands holding my crotch in a full on, pee-pee dance, laughing even harder at Hottie destroying the garden sculpture, looking for a key that I had just remembered, I'd used a few days before. It presently sat on the kitchen table.

"It's in there. See? It's right there!" I hysterically laughed, as I pointed through the French doors to the kitchen table inside.

Eddie was trying to leave, but he couldn't get out of there soon enough. I went to the corner of the open patio, and around the side of the house, where I dropped my expensive corduroys and squatted to pee. I was still laughing hysterically because of the looks of shock on their faces. Because it was dark, Hottie didn't know if I had urinated right on the pavers, so he grabbed the hose and turned the nozzle on.

I screamed, "No. No. I peed in the bushes."

But it was too late; he sprayed the pavers, the bush and me. I was completely drenched in seconds. Eddie broke out laughing and with a quick pace started towards his car, "I'm gettin' the fuck out of here. You two are so messed up."

Hottie turned to Eddie spraying him from the back of the head all the way down to his feet.

"You are so dead!" He said as he charged back to Hottie to take control of the hose.

Hottie slipped and fell, trying to escape, and was now getting drenched by Eddie. Eddie then turned the hose back on me.

Finally. After turning the water off, Eddie told us, "It's time for bed kids!"

He checked his back seat, where I had been sitting as his passenger, and found my car keys and house key in the crevice of the seat.

Eddie left soon after, and Hottie helped me get the key in the door, which took him about 15 minutes. We were welcomed by the dogs and let them out. Now shivering in the cool July night air, we stood silent.

"When do you leave?" he asked.

"Day after tomorrow," I replied.

Right when I thought he was going to say something tender, he said, "Well, good, cause you need a day of recovery, you're gonna be so fucking hung-over." He slurred while laughing as he turned and started toward his apartment.

"Hey, that song 'Hallelujah,' you sang today. It was beautiful. Who broke your heart? Which one was it?"

"Ha, no. I've been singing that song for a long time, and always thinking of a 'her.' Today after I sang it, I realized whoever I attract into my life, I hope she loves me like you love Bill. You go to the depths." He winked and made his way back to me, leaned in and slowly kissed me on the cheek.

"Ahhh," I commented, with a smile, and then reached up with both hands and placed them on his cheeks. No words were needed as we exchanged our gratitude for each other.

I clapped for the dogs to come in, and we said our good-nights. I left my makeup on, brushed my teeth, peeled my contacts from my eyes and threw them in the trash because I was too buzzed to find the case. *I'm gonna hate myself for that in the morning,* I thought. Bill and I developed a system of how to care and keep our monthly throw-away contacts—making them last for six months to a year just to save money. But, tonight, I guess I was feeling abundant.

I pulled my pants down, kicking them to the floor, inside out. I stripped the shirt off over my head and threw it to the opposite corner of where the pants were. Maximillian and Titus sat at the doorway, watching articles of clothing being flung across the room in all directions. I pulled the white comforter back and slipped underneath the cool sheets. No pajamas tonight. Too drunk to find them; I was ready to pass out.

I remembered saying, "Thank you." Then I think I *literally* passed out.

DAY 10
GRAY

Technically, I may have still been drunk when I awoke the next morning. Immediately, I started thinking about what I'd have to do for my messed-up digestive system. I predicted it was going to be troubled today. Since I only had one more morning to wake up here, I lingered, and just lied in bed for a while. I could hear the dogs moving a bit under the bed. They slept there every night while they unknowingly, wholeheartedly convinced me that our family needed a dog, as soon as possible. When I peeked over the edge of the bed to check on them, I saw only Maximillian's nose and eyebrows twitching as he looked up at me. He normally went all the way under, but he thought I was getting up, so he was giving himself a head start. I scratched his head.

"Well, good morning, Max."

It was my last full day in Santa Barbara, and I noticed the twisted spiral of mourning taking place for my peaceful, easy existence here. While at the same time, I felt pure elation about seeing the kids and a cautious, yet comfortable, curiosity to hang out with Bill and see *what's up* with him and with us.

After lounging for a while, I was both surprised and pleased that I felt no ill effects from the previous evening. I got up and watered the plants outside in my new favorite attire; a pair of loose faded jean shorts and a white V-neck. My hair was pulled up in a just-rolled-out-of-bed bun. Loose and free... finally, that was me.

The dogs raced around my feet. The sun was out, and there was a slight breeze. I looked up at Hottie's apartment, wondering how he was feeling this fine morning. His Roman shades were still closed, and I figured he'd be asleep for a while. I finally looked at the clock, realizing it was just 6 A.M. *I shouldn't feel this good after only a few hours of sleep!*

As I stood in front of the bathroom mirror, I thought about what Bill would think when he saw me. I looked different. He was used to seeing my hair blow-dried, straightened, or in a styled way. In the past, I was pretty particular about my makeup being on before leaving the house. If I wore jeans they were rarely faded, and I usually paired them with complimentary blouses and sweaters that were refined and more appropriate for my age, matching the old income we had. *Wonder what he'll think now?* He's colorblind, so he may not notice the change in my hair color, but this whole natural thing, where parts of my hair were wavy and parts were straight, looked messy. *I'm messy but have never felt more pulled together.*

According to the highest fashion magazines, I was too tan. This was due to a loss of interest in sunscreen and wearing hats. I gave it all up here. I gave up all the fear attached to skin cancer and the desire to look 25 again. I somehow found permission to set aside the mask I had created.

As for the inside of me, I also wondered if Bill would reject that. Would he reject the part of me getting comfortable in my own skin again? I was bolder now. Even more so than in North Carolina. Just like back then, I was well aware of my weaknesses, yet now I was starting to see some new strengths. Was he going to be able to handle those? I wasn't sure of how Bill was going to emotionally feel about me, but I felt solid about not deciding on how I felt, based on how he felt about me. I could feel a quiet, new confidence in myself, and no matter how I was received when I returned home, I had faith that whatever happens was meant to be. Period.

Over the past ten days, I'd spent hours walking State Street. I loved the mix of people and activity. But, today, I felt drawn to explore it at this early hour, absent of others around. I grabbed an oversized cardigan and enjoyed a quiet walk heading towards the bar to get my Denali. Driving down the empty streets mesmerized me. It was serene and easier to see the soul of a street with no locals, no tourists and no Ferraris to distract me. The stores were closed for at least a few more hours. I parked right in front of a jewelry store.

I hopped out and found myself attracted to something in the jewelry-store window. *That's a first.* It was always Bill who would make me look at random jewelry in stores. I never had an interest. In fact, I so often returned numerous pieces of jewelry that he stopped buying them for me. Today, something drew me to the window. With my face planted against the glass, I studied a three-carat aquamarine ring. My birthstone. Just a solitaire shape. But the most brilliant ocean-colored aquamarine I had ever seen. *Why now? Why didn't that catch my eye for the last ten years when we could have afforded it? Was it simply a want it cause you can't afford it kind of thing? No, it wasn't.*

I immediately recognized where the guilt and shame of having material things in the past made me feel *filthy* rich, not comfortably rich. I was shocked I even had this vocabulary laying dormant in my mind. Now it made sense why I was always questioned by Bill—and even Jimmy, the valet guy—about "not taking ownership" of our material things. I could see how the woman emerging today could get comfortable with these things while still being genuine, reminding herself she was not the car she drove, the house she lived in and the jewelry she wore. Relief was felt with this shift. Becoming clearer on what I wanted and more comfortable with wanting it, I could see myself allowing wealth in, rather than attaching guilt and shame (when we had money) or hunger and desperation (when we did not.)

Want not, fear not, came back to mind. *Goodbye poverty consciousness.*

I could now see there was a part of me that wanted to rise and shine, not just lay down and accept our poverty, but to move my feet in the direction of my dreams. I knew enough to understand that if I tried to desperately manhandle every single angle on how to have wealth again, it wouldn't be as fruitful as I could imagine. Allowing it was key.

A tree in the middle of the forest does not demand that the sun serve it with light, it *allows* it to bring it light.

While looking at this piece of art in the window in a different way, I could appreciate the cuts in the aquamarine gem, and I was in awe of the art of it. It was stunning. So standing there, financially broke as could be, I was okay with wanting it for myself... someday. And I wasn't bothered that I couldn't afford it, or afford a lot of other things, today. I felt myself sigh with relief.

Being broke may just have taught me to be more comfortable with abundance. *I'm not what I do, or what I have. I'm not what I don't have. I've been enough and had fair enough all along.*

All the sudden, I heard a sweet man's voice say, "When we dream it, we dream it for free."

Turning to face this angelic voice, I saw a face to match. He looked like a big strong cherub who stood probably 5'9" with a belly like Santa. His name was Gray. He may have been in his late 60s. His scruffy round face was framed with long, messy gray hair, and his dark green-hazel eyes twinkled, seeming to dance all around me. He held a Bible under one arm and was carrying a backpack on the other. His skin was weathered, tanned and leathery; the crow's feet around his eyes ran deep and hinted at an interesting life. *I want to know of this life.*

He smelled liked the streets, but it wasn't offensive. I remembered seeing him before. I accepted his invitation for me to walk the streets where his friends lived and were waking for the day. He introduced me to them like I was his long-lost daughter. We talked and talked and talked some more. In a short period of time, gaps were miraculously being filled. He had my whole life story, and I had his. A beautiful being, he was. I wasn't sure if he was the leader here, in the homeless world on State Street, but he emanated love and light like no other. One of the younger groups of homeless were waking and starting to enter the streets, and they were thrilled to be in his presence. I was amazed how wonderful it was to be the only one here with all of them. I wanted to pinch myself. *Is this actually happening?*

The younger boys were immediately interested in why I was there, and he protected me like the Angel he was. Gently, but assertively, he shooed them away when they got a little out of line. One of the kids whipped out a little boom box and yelled, "LETS DANCE!" The Kool & the Gang song "Celebration" played. About 15 homeless people gathered, mostly male, but a few women appeared as well. We all stood in the middle of the empty street as the music blasted out of this tiny old-fashioned time machine. A 70-ish African American man had just joined us and started break-dancing so intensely that I hoped he wasn't going to hurt himself. We all danced around him, to make sure that didn't happen. It was crazy to see the rhythm and joy spontaneously erupt. *Was this normal practice for them to break out like this?* I wondered if I should look for a candid camera. This can't be real. Someone started dancing The Hustle, and I joyously dropped into the line as Gray held my hand. In unison, we filled the entire street while moving up and down a small strip of State Street.

As business hours approached, a car occasionally would need to get by, so we'd move over, and then flood the street again. I felt like a part of this community. As the sidewalks and streets started to roll with more foot traffic, we slowly stopped the dance, shared some high-fives and went our separate ways.

Gray and I stayed together and without discussing it, we spent the entire day together. As we snuck off for a walk on the beach to share more of life's treasures, I told him how I felt about my marriage, our future, our kid's futures, and how I was feeling broken and hopeless when I first got here. I explained our American Dreams had been crushed but was finally feeling there would be a silver lining in it all. I just couldn't see the details of it, yet.

"My dear, if I were to share with you something about being broken, would you listen to me?"

I turned to look him in the eyes, "Of course I would."

"And why would you listen to me?"

"Hmmm. 'Cause you seem to be someone that may have dealt with feeling broken?"

"I have only experienced being financially broken. But never broken. A soul never breaks. The same soul you came in with is the same soul you leave with. It's whole, never broken. And you didn't start this trip broken. You've been whole all along. Our souls don't keep track of our earnings, degree, title, assets, status or credit scores."

I squeezed his hand and smiled with an agreeable nod.

"What you could work on is maybe a little patience," he said laughing.

He shared a verse: *JEREMIAH 29:11* "*For I know the plans I have for you, declares the Lord, plans to prosper you and not harm you, plans to give you hope and a future.*"

Grays smile made his eyes squint as he looked right at me—through me. Smiling, I reached back for his hand again and squeezed. I found him fascinating and his faith, real.

We people-watched together for hours, and I spent a lot of that time, studying him. I noticed a "thing" he did after a kid had passed us and kicked his Coke to kingdom come: he gently nodded his head. It reminded me of a Buddhist thing to do. A sign of respect. Or what we do in yoga, at the end of class, when we say, "Namaste," with a nod. Roughly translated, it means, "The Divine in me bows to the Divine in you," or "The Spirit within me salutes the Spirit in you." It's about a knowing we are all made from the same One Divine Consciousness. And we are one race—the human race. He acknowledged that in every person that acknowledged him, and he did this whether it was a good or bad acknowledgment.

"What is that?" I nodded as an example. "What does that mean for you?"

"I silently am saying, *I love you.*" He turned to look at me. "All you need is love, Judy. You've heard that before, haven't ya?" He smiled.

"Have you been like this your whole life?" I sincerely asked.

Seriously contemplating what I'd asked, he replied, "Yep, I have."

"You know what you are Gray?" I exclaimed as I shot up and stood in front of him, "You are soulshiney! That's what you are! Soulshiney people heal things, they clear things up, they redefine things; they silently transform people and their ways. That's what you do here on State Street. This is some job you have here, Gray. You sure picked a whopper one to master!"

He broke out laughing, and I joined in.

An idea popped into my head, and I switched subjects by asking, "Hey, do I have permission to buy you a new shirt?" as I pointed to the drugstore nearby.

"Sure, if you wish my dear," he answered.

I took off at a fast pace to see the selection of T-shirts. Certainly, they will have a few to choose from here. Right on top was a white XL. I noticed the tag said, "Irregular." *Well, that's perfect because he was irregular in the best of ways.* I grabbed a few colored T-shirts and set those aside as I followed my desire to create something on the white shirt. I asked the cashier if I could borrow a black Sharpie. He looked up to see me, and as he said "Yes," but he had a strange look on his face. A look of excitement, like he'd just recognized a famous person in a public place. He tried making eye contact with others in the line before and after me as if to get them to help him put a name to *my* face. Finally, the guy behind me got his courage up while cautiously and politely asked, "Hey, who are you?" He slid his sunglasses down his nose as if to observe me closer in the fluorescent lighting. The cashier chimed in before I had a chance to stop their questioning, "OH, OH, I know where I've seen you!" He turned to the guy with the sunglasses, snapping his fingers, "I got it, I got it! You're the actress from that movie… um, hold on… I'll get it."

I stopped him by saying, "No, no, I'm not an actress."

"OH, OKAY, maybe you're in the music world then?"

"No, nope, you guys are way off. I'm just here temporarily. Housesitting."

This guessing game became so funny it made me laugh out loud. I had an urge to say, "I'm nobody," but stopped myself in my tracks. That did not feel accurate. The guy in line with the sunglasses refused to believe me.

With some annoyance and certainty, he said, "She's an actress for sure. She's somebody. She's just not gonna say it."

My hypnotherapy practice and love for words kicked in. I could feel that familiar friend, *creativity*, as I was inspired by how Gray made me feel.

I laid the white T-shirt out on the counter. The customers in line, who were still waiting for me to admit I was "somebody," graciously stepped around me, leaving me to my project. I drew something on the back and wrote on the front. I didn't *think* about it. I just wrote what I *felt*. I studied it for a bit, paid for the shirts with the extra ten bucks I had and walked back to the park bench.

I handed Gray the bag with the various colored tees, which he loved, but I held the white tee close to my chest.

"I made this for you," I said, handing him the white tee.

He raised it up and saw I had put a cross on the back of the tee.

Explaining the obvious, "Because you love Jesus."

He gave me the *I love you nod.*

He flipped the shirt around to the front, and it read, "BROKE BUT NOT BROKEN".

His twinkling eyes filled with tears, as he pulled me close, but not without asking "May I?" first.

We hugged.

"I love you," I said. I could feel him nod his head.

Clarity surfaced with this thought of *not* being broken. Not ever. Gray gave me permission to embrace being broke, but with the way he made me feel, it convinced me I was not broken, now, nor have I ever been. The exchanges with all of the people I had met, and now him, helped me to dig deep past our obstacles, happenstance, fate, circumstances, opinions, choices, good luck and the bad that had appeared in our lives and I could see our souls intact. While remembering who I am, and where I'd come from, my Faith may have wavered, but my soul did not break, crumble or even grow. It's the same one I came here with, and it's the same one I'll leave here with. Period.

The harder times in Gray's life *might* have bent him, beat on him and maybe left him bloody at times, but it didn't break him. The spirit living in him remained whole. He'd said it earlier today, "The spirit that lives inside me is in all of us. It knows the truth. It creates miracles. It's quiet and powerful. I was born with this spirit, and I'll die with it. So will you. Thank God."

I left him on that park bench and mentioned I'd be rolling down State Street the next day around 8 A.M. for my departure.

GOOD TO GO

Before taking off, while still parked in front of the jewelry store, I flipped the vanity mirror down to take a closer look at myself. I was curious about what those people in the drug store saw that made them so certain I was "somebody." I started this day after an evening of too many beers, minimal sleep, followed by a lot of laying on the beach and sitting on curbs and benches with Gray. I stroked my neck and noticed dried sand sprinkle away, and I simply sat perplexed in front of the little rectangle mirror. *I'm grungy.*

And then I recognized something new. Looking into my own eyes, as I had looked into Gray's. I saw some love for self, and my self-talk shifted. My eyes seemed bright and pretty, even from behind what was left of last night's makeup. I also was miraculously having a good hair day, despite the fact that it hadn't been washed since yesterday. My skin somehow looked flawless, even though it was sunburned and sweaty. For the first time, my lip color and shape were acceptable, even though I had not even applied lip balm. I could have critiqued the messy-grunge look I displayed, but somehow saw some beauty instead.

While being in a genuine state of power, remembering who I am and where I come from, the light inside me had progressively made its way outward. And the only way the people in the store could "name it" was to assume it was star power.

Later that afternoon, back at the bungalow, I reflected on the past ten days. It was ridiculously easy and even fun to pack and organize my things, just being one person. I played music and danced around the house off and on while belting out songs from the radio. "American Woman" came on. It empowered me as I could see the energetic shift since last cranking that song.

I planned on seeing Hottie so that I could say goodbye. I told him I'd be leaving before he'd be up tomorrow. But he was nowhere to be found. I had gotten used to his schedule and was surprised he wasn't there. I was dreading it, but I knew I had to go to the beach. It was time to say goodbye to Bayard. We had talked at the bar and made a plan to meet at 3 P.M. I parked the Denali and watched him from my car for a while. There he was, sitting on his bench. He was serene, and it blew me away that he seemed authentically at peace with his deterioration.

As I walked up, he stood, turned and pointed his cane towards me. "Judy, we go our whole life, seeking. Most of us unaware of what it is we are looking for. And that's okay. But I must say, you have a way of seeking joy. And I love that

about you. And I love that I now have a part of that living in me. Keep it up, doll."
He said this as he gave me a wave, with his back toward me, while walking away.

"That's it? That's your goodbye?" I said, laughing.

He turned back to me, and laughed, "No, No, how about, you come to this beach one last time at seven tomorrow morning, right before you depart. You know, a proper goodbye to the beach, we'll be alone."

"Great idea. I will see you then."

"Yes, doll," he said. He gave me another wave, again with his back toward me as he walked away.

The same little boy who'd thrown heart-shaped rocks into the ocean with me last week started heading toward me, "Want to play with me?" he asked.

We played our rock-throwing game. One by one, we threw them while saying things we were grateful for.

He screamed, "Cherry Slurpees!"

"Yeah, Slurpees!" I repeated with agreement.

His parents were off in a distance, but we grabbed their attention with the screaming of "Slurpees."

"Cheese pizza," I screamed.

"And chocolate cake!" he added.

"And for being broke." I hurled a rock so hard; I nearly threw my shoulder out.

I continued, "And for HER! YES! HER!" I hurled another rock.

The little boy stood there confused from my last two statements.

I was about to say "Never mind" but heard a voice coming out of the water. "HEY! OW! SHIT. What the F ?"

The little boy's parents were heading in our direction now.

The last rock I'd hurled, had hit a surfer in a wet suit, emerging from the water. He was carrying a surfboard, looking pissed off and heading straight for me.

The little boy was giggling.

It was Hottie, rubbing his collarbone area. "What the Hell, Jude?"

I said, stopping him from his rant. "No swearing, we have a little boy here."

His parents were standing nearby now, encouraging him to stop giggling about the surfer's injury.

"Oh it's okay, I know him," I explained.

Hottie looked perplexed and playfully annoyed. "Yeah, we know each other, and I allow her to hurl rocks at me."

The little boy lost interest in us. He meandered off continuing to gather the rest of the rocks, screaming on his own, "Disneyland, Bottle Rockets, Baseball..."

"What the heck did you start here?" he said while watching the kid throw rocks into the ocean with all his might.

"You should try it. It's an awesome feeling." I handed him a rock.

"Are you throwing rocks with good things attached to baptize them in the sea or something?"

"Kind of, but not just the good, also the bad. Cause you know, it's all good. It can serve you right, if you let it."

"So you say." He rubbed his collarbone.

Hottie hurled a rock into the ocean, and shouted, "For meeting you."

"Aw, aren't you sweet?" I said.

I went to grab my beach bag and towel. He waited for me to gather everything up and said, "You're excited to see them aren't you?"

While heading toward the parking lot together I answered, "Totally flipped-out excited."

"What about Bill?"

"Ummm, I'm feeling cautiously optimistic about Bill. I have no idea how he's feeling about me, though. But, the last time I talked to him he sounded solid. Different than when I first left. It's all good Sean. Don't ever forget that. I'm gonna try not to." I winked.

Together, we slowly walked through the parking lot to my truck.

In a sincere tone, he said, "This is where we first met. Hold on, tho'," he said, as he took off to his car.

I watched him run to and from his Jeep. He was so gorgeous—inside and out—I hoped he'd find somebody good enough for him.

He returned with the guitar pick I borrowed at the open mic night.

He had pierced a hole in it and ran a thin guitar string through, "For good luck," he said, as he put it around my neck.

"OHHHHH! I loooove this! It is so cool. What a priceless present."

We reminisced and laughed about that first meet-and-greet. He admitted he had thought he was going to get me into bed, even though I was totally wound up. But he said, "Once I got to know you, I was totally turned off." He cracked up laughing.

And I punched him. "You're such a shit!"

"Just kiddin'. No, once I got to know you and the family through you, it became clear to me the five of you had something untouchable. Like it's weird, 'cause I don't have a family yet, but I see a tribe, as you call it. Even if you didn't end up still married and every kid lived in different places, there would be this bond. I don't know. It's hard to explain. Like I said before, I just know that I feel sorry for any guy that would try to disrupt it." He whipped his bangs off to the side.

I reached out to him, and he pulled me in for a hug. He kissed me on the forehead. "I have a study group tonight. I'm headin' that way now and class tomorrow mornin'. I may not see you. So, take care, Jude. Stay in touch. Oh, and I hope your friendship with Alvarez stays alive and well," he said with a wink.

I watched him pull out of the parking lot. While leaning against the truck, I basked in gratitude for my new friend and the feeling of my own personal power surging through me. It had been so long since I felt this grounded. Like Glinda the Good Witch had said to Dorothy in *The Wizard of Oz*, "*You always had the power.*"

I felt like I just realized this truth for myself. Feeling compelled after Hottie drove away, I ran back to the beach just one more time, I picked up one rock and threw it in. Silently, I screamed, "THANK YOU. THANK YOU. THANK YOU."

I quickly glanced around, hoping to find a heart-shaped rock for Bill. After many attempts over the last few days, and then not finding any—I trusted that I could let the search go. And I headed back to the Denali.

I attended the 6 P.M. yoga class and said goodbye to all my new friends there. Violet and I giggled about all the fun we'd had at the bar. She cradled my face with her hands, pulling it close to hers, and with a kiss on the lips, she said, "Continue to be the Goddess you are."

As we left the studio together, I looked to see if the minister might be watering outside, but he wasn't. I gave a silent, *I love you nod* to both the church and the studio and drove off.

I popped over to the tattoo parlor, sticking my head in the door, yelling, "HEY!" Holding my henna tattoo up in the air, "LOVE YOU GUYS!!!"

Jenna and Jessie came flying up to the front of the store to give me big hugs. Jesse leaned into my face, all serious and sexy, with his tongue out, like he was going to French kiss me goodbye. And then he burst into hysterical laughter as I laughed and pushed him away.

They walked me out to the sidewalk, demanding I come back and see them soon. After a short walk, I heard Jesse yell to get my attention, "Hey, JUDE!"

Turning to look at him, I saw he had lifted his shirt and was unzipping his pants, "Hey, how 'bout one for the road? Ya know, for a preventive measure?"

"Oh my God," I said, hysterically laughing.

While walking away, I waved behind my head. And I wondered if these two would ever know what they truly did for me. I felt deeply awakened to my own sexual charge. This feeling combined with the rest of my explorations and remembrances of self left me feeling excited for the rest of my life to unfold.

awakened on Day 11 to a slight cool breeze coming through the cracked window. I noticed the birds were even more vocal this morning. A feeling of strength, both physically and emotionally, plus the excitement of reuniting with my family, had been building with each passing day—I was simply ready to explode.

I had set an alarm but woke up two hours earlier than planned. After I had laid my yoga mat down in the family room, the dogs took their regular places on either side of me. All of my moves were fluid… at least, I felt like they were. I set an intention with each move: grateful, abundant, peaceful, loving, joyful, open, calm and ready for my departure.

As I walked to the bedroom, I noticed my wedding ring, which sat on the nightstand. I placed it on my finger, hoping I could say whatever I needed to say when I saw him.

Ready or not, here I come.

I had everything organized and already had the car packed. I had washed and dried my new green summer cords and planned on wearing them into the triple-digit degree Tucson desert, no matter how roasted I got. My white V-neck was probably a dangerous choice for attire today, as I imagined over the next eight-to-nine hours, I would likely have something spilled down the front of it.

I let the dogs enjoy their sunbathing on the patio while I showered and packed my toiletry bag, staying present with my moves. It was just another serene Santa Barbara morning, one I hoped I had memorized and locked in me for safekeeping and for easy access later when things in Tucson unfolded, exploded or whatever.

Sam I Am entered the bedroom. I picked him up, holding him in my arms and I buried my face in his fur, listening while feeling the vibration of his purr. "Awe Sam, I'm gonna miss you, buddy."

I fished through my wallet to make sure I had a few bucks, just in case I needed food on the road. I don't know why I hadn't noticed it on the drive here, but I had one last gasoline credit card, tucked away behind an old grocery list, for gas. I was grateful we still had that. I was also pleasantly reminded that I still had the $100 crisp bill I'd never used for a spa treatment, bar or lunch. I thought it was so funny that I'd been here for 11 days and barely spent any money, besides a little on food and for Skye's session, which was well worth it.

Clearly, I was effortlessly manifesting abundance here in Santa Barbara.

Good God, follow me home.

I put the dogs in the house and left a note I wrote the night before to Tracy and Ed, thanking them for this opportunity. I gave Maximilian, Sam I Am and Titus big hugs and kisses.

"Thank you, thank you, thank you," I said to them, knowing they were a huge part of my healing.

Before locking the door, I whispered, "Thank you," to the bungalow. *What a perfect place for me to Be.* I hid the key under the ceramic frog Hottie had decapitated the night before. I looked up at his window, but the shade was still drawn. After getting in the car and buckling up, I focused on staying present, because I could feel anxiety creeping in, challenging me with the thought, *Is this really over? Will I ever feel this way again? How will I manage and endure my busy life after this?*

I pressed my forehead against the steering wheel, noticing the sand and some tar on the floor mat that traveled via bare feet and flip flops, and my anxiety calmed. The sand and tar proved, *I was here, and when needed, I'll get there again.*

I then bounced back to the excitement of seeing them.

For a minute, I reflected on how I felt when I first pulled into this driveway compared to today. I thanked God that I had come here by myself. This quest was meant to unfold while traveling alone. This glorious reflection made me feel kind of proud. A part of me laughed at myself because of *what a big deal* it was for me. I imagined the ultrasensitive parts of myself might be stronger now. It was clear that so often the cliff I thought I was standing on really was a curb. I couldn't help but think of the many others in the world before me, presently and in the future, enduring things of much greater magnitudes than financial and marital issues. But I loved myself enough today to let the thought pass, allowing myself to celebrate embracing these past 11 days the best I knew how. I vowed to remind myself that I have to start from where I am in order to grow, and I felt both peace and joy for myself. It reminded me of the quote I loved from Joseph Campbell.

IF YOU DO FOLLOW YOUR BLISS, YOU PUT YOURSELF ON A KIND OF TRACK THAT HAS BEEN THERE ALL THE WHILE, WAITING FOR YOU, AND THE LIFE THAT YOU OUGHT TO BE LIVING IS THE ONE YOU ARE LIVING. Joseph Campbell

Looking up, I saw Hottie in the window. He had pulled his shade up and was peeking out. He must have heard my truck door. Picking up the guitar-pick necklace around my neck, I kissed it and he flashed me a peace sign. Having taken the time to get to know one another, I felt deeply grateful to be reminded that while studying the Hottie that dwells inside him, I saw the same dwelling inside us all. Truth is, no matter how drop dead gorgeous, homeless, ill, sexy, depressed, anxious, colored, discriminated against, rich, or poor... you are first a soul. And if one can manage not becoming distracted by everything else, it's easier to see that the whole human experience is secondary to our spirit that dwells inside.

I drove to Arroyo Beach, where I'd promised to meet up with Bayard. I was on time, and I knew he'd be timely as well. I drove in silence this time, without the radio. I was torn between being excited to see him and also torn up to have to share this good-bye. His departure may be soon, and how do you say good-bye to someone in that situation?

We had spent hours discussing *My Book of Paul* and Paul's message on a doormat that hung in his loft studio when he passed: "GET HOME." Bayard was deeply moved, and I felt if I did anything for him, it may have been that I gave this brilliant writing professor two words he could someday hang his fisherman cap on.

I decided that today the goodbye would be all about him. I was going home to my family after this amazing 11 days, which he'd poured endless amounts of hours and love into. And, this morning, I was pulled to declare it was going to be ALL for him. If I sensed he didn't want me to cry, then I was going to suck it up. If he needed to see emotion, I was going to be open and true.

That was the plan. And I was going to stick to it... no matter what.

I parked the Denali in the same spot and headed toward the beach. The waves were rolling up as the tide was starting to come in. It was an intimate thing for me to get a glimpse of what I had spent years fearing: *what lives under these waters*. I always loved this time of the morning, when I could explore, without fear, the rocks, shells and sea creatures on shore before the tide rolled all the way up only to pull them all back into her. It was the oceans way of showing herself to me, as I had been showing myself to her over these past days.

Even though I had let it go yesterday, I was hoping to *finally* find a heart shaped rock for Bill. I planned on handing it to him tonight and having it possibly open a door for us to begin talking, maybe process, or at least understand and possibly move through this hard time.

I moved closer to the ocean and couldn't help but stand in awe of it. As I picked up my pace towards shore this morning—this shore had a different message for me.

There was no sign of Bayard, but he had most certainly been there, before my arrival.

In the sand he wrote, "GET HOME."

And, knowing of my search for one last heart rock for Bill, he had found a large smooth one with various lines in it. Not perfect, which was perfect. It sat next to this message, which I had not considered for myself, but only those that were going to the other side.

I dropped to my knees, landing in the sand. I placed the rock in the palm of my hand. Stunned, I watched the waves slowly absorb his message, as they gently rolled over, eventually filling the lines he'd made. I felt a profound peace in comfortably knowing my search for a happy ending had ended for real, and it will always be about the middle… the present. And when facing any suffering, it's always good to GET HOME, in whatever way that may mean. It tied into doing the necessary work on yourself, others and circumstance—creating a round house…a house in order…emotionally, mentally, physically, spiritually. The entire trip was about beginning within, where the light is… the light that created me. For me today, his message and Paul's message gave me clear direction and permission, to check in on that ROUND HOUSE of mine. *What order can I provide?*

It was time to GET HOME and reconnect with my family. I am ready for this.

My original plan was to give Bayard what he wanted and needed today, although I thought about waiting for him to return or even tracking him down at his house or going to the coffee shop he liked. But I stayed strong, sticking to the plan. He wanted it this way, and I would honor that. This was one of those moments, yet again, that deserved silence, and I embraced it like the treasured gift it was.

I was alone, but not. I could imagine and feel Paul behind me with his hands on my shoulders, gently pushing me back home. I made my way slowly back to the truck, turning to look at the ocean several times. I would miss her so, and I dreaded the fact that I may never see Bayard again here on this beach. The only thing I could feel okay about was that the time we did spend together was fully embraced by us both. I couldn't have given or received anymore than I did.

I drove down State Street one last time, hoping to see Gray. It was early morning, and there he was, in his spot, with all his glory.

I yelled, "Gray!"

He looked up from his Bible, excited to see me.

He was wearing his *broke but not broken shirt*, as he slowly wobbled, bow-legged, across the street to my drivers side window, "Gooood morning Sunshine," he said, cheerfully. "You headin' home, dear?"

I handed him the $100 bill. "Yes, and here. I found this in my wallet this morning. My dad calls this a voucher. Will you accept this voucher?"

He reluctantly accepted, but knew me well enough, to know I wasn't going to let him refuse it.

He patted the top of my hand, "Got your Angels with ya. I can feel it. Stay gold, dear."

"Thank you, Gray." And with a nod from him, I drove off.

I watched him wave for several minutes in my rearview mirror.

I entered Highway 101. It was hard for me to not become distracted by the white-tipped waves as they rolled and crashed into the sandy shore as I drove by. The deep blue sky and scattered puffy white clouds that had been the norm for the last 11 days still stole my attention, just as they had on Day One.

As I made my way out of town, I contemplated how this whole trip continued to have 11s popping up in it. I recalled the numerous things written about the number 101: that the 0 represents a ground zero, and the 1s on either side represented pillars that one would walk through for new beginnings and at the same time, leave behind what was necessary. It went along with Skye's explanation of ground zero, and I found myself reflecting on all the ground zeros I'd hit during these 11 days. I felt a smile on my face.

I opened the sunroof and turned on the radio and of course, "Drift Away" played. My window was still down, as I held my left arm out, flapping it just as I had coming out of The Canyons—like an eagle. I drifted away into the song knowing that when my mind is free, I'm able to gratefully experience the joy of life more harmoniously. The rhythm of music and the rhyme in lyrics does that for me. I could see how it had always helped me in my life and simply made me strong. The music blasted, and I thought I might blow the speakers. I was air drumming, and with my right hand straight up and out of the sunroof, I felt the cool morning air hit my palm.

I had left a message yesterday for Bill and the kids, stating I would be leaving in the late morning. Looking at the clock, I realized I would surprise them by getting there earlier today as I was ahead of schedule.

With my cruise control set at 85 mph and the few stops for gas and food breaks, I expected perfect timing to arrive before they left for football and cheerleading practice. That would give me about two hours with them and then we would all go to practice together. I wanted to watch Bill do what he loved and watch the boys run around with all their friends. I desired to get back in the groove, but with the new re-membered version of me. It would be the perfect re-entry.

Stopping for gas right outside L.A., I bought a small bag of crackers, an apple, and two large waters.

"$11 dollars please," said the cashier.

"Even? Eleven dollars and no cents?" I asked.

The cashier looked at the cash register again, "Yeah, that's weird. It never comes out even."

I made a mental note to show Bill that receipt later. It would be one more of many examples of this 11-thing.

Whenever I have entered a large city, I've been elated to be in the middle of it. Growing up and having access to downtown Chicago was a blessing, and the vibrancy in people with varied backgrounds, the food, the music, the art... it just made me feel progressive, creative and alive.

While having the sunroof open, I don't know what made me scream it, but I yelled, "HOW GOOD CAN IT GET?"

I started to take the idea of a jewelry business seriously. Because of the previous day's inspiration, with *broke but not broken* on Gray's T-shirt, my thoughts spiraled into complimentary products. Hmmm. *T-shirts!*

When Gray slid that shirt on, the reaction on people's faces on State Street told me it could be a good idea. Why not? With all the .COM companies tanking, plus the stock market crash… and a surge of bankruptcies these days, it was like *broke was the new black.*

I rationalized, "I can keep looking for a job, just like Bill keeps looking for his career job. But what if I started this on the side? I would, for sure, be doing something I love. If done right, this actually could be a viable business, with a little bit of revenue. I started figuring out costs for inventory, silk screening, supplies, tools, packaging, marketing, shipping costs, web development and travel to trade shows where I could sell them. I even thought, I could use recycled T-shirts from Goodwill and tear them up, dye them, put random stitches on them. Make them one-of-a-kind edgy and market them as recycled tees.

I pulled out my little handheld recorder and hit "Record."

The creativity was unleashed yesterday with *broke but not broken* and now numerous phrases, favorite quotes, and ideas started to pour out of me. That tiny recorder was smoking, as I rifled the ideas off. I felt a spark of vibrancy with this direction, letting out a loud "WHOO-HOO" that actually startled me.

I had been making great time. Bill had taught me well on how to drive by following, and also sharing the lead, with other experienced drivers. Since L.A., I had been traveling behind a male driver, in a black two-door Mercedes. He knew how to drive in this same orchestrated fair way, sharing the risk of a ticket. We traveled all the way through Phoenix and into Casa Grande, Arizona, where we encountered less-experienced drivers who tried to hitch a ride if you will, and we both took turns shaking them off.

My mind was settling down from the massive download of product ideas. I even came up with a name for the potential company. I was feeling centered. *I may just have a plan of action.* I wasn't expecting to come home with that.

The black Mercedes let me take the lead while driving through the last of Phoenix and entering Casa Grande. I was only 70 miles from home now, and I was elated!

The temperature display showed 111 degrees outside. It made me smile as I said out loud, "Oh goodness, that is *blazing* hot! Literally going back into the fire!"

GET HOME

After pressing "play" on my favorite Dr. Wayne Dyer CD, which was already loaded, I listened to him talk about paying attention when getting stopped dead in your tracks. Whether it's a car accident, a detour, or even ending up at a wrong address... *Trust you're exactly where you are supposed to be. The universe may be in play. Don't judge whatever and whoever shows up. Just be open to needing this opportunity for some reason or they need you, or both.*

I immediately reflected on every person I met in the last 11 days and how true that was for me. Just as I had that thought, I heard a loud explosion. It sounded like a bomb! Followed by an excessive flapping noise, and then metal scraping and screeching. My car started losing control, and I quickly glanced at the black Mercedes behind me. He swerved sharply to the left to get out from behind my truck, as he watched me struggle. Gripping the wheel, I tried to remember my Chicago city-girl driving skills and carefully pressed the accelerator, which was counterintuitive. It didn't make the vehicle accelerate. It helped to stabilize it. That blown tire made the truck feel as if it was dragging a parachute. Continuing straight in the lane, I allowed the drag of the failed tire to slow the vehicle down before even considering turning the steering wheel off to the side of the road.

Stunned, I sat there parked for a second and just took a deep breath. Holy shit. I was sure I'd blown a tire. It felt like the front driver's side but wasn't sure. That had never happened to me before.

I looked around, noticing I was literally in the middle of nowhere. The OnStar program with this truck had been canceled, and my heart sunk, knowing I may be sitting here for a while. *There's no way I could surprise them now.* I scanned the area to see if there were any nearby gas stations I could walk to and ask for help. On my right was an abandoned building that was all boarded up. "KEEP THE FAITH" was spray painted in bright red spray paint on the old boards. I smiled. How divine. *Maybe Santa Barbara was following me home.*

I pushed the OnStar button anyway, hoping and praying for satellite connection.

And then I heard, "ON STAR, may I help you, Mrs. Cochrane?"

Still looking at the 'KEEP THE FAITH' message, I smiled, "Yes! I'd like some help."

"Are you in a safe spot, Mrs. Cochrane?"

"Yeah, thank you. I'm off on the side of the road."

"What seems to be the trouble today?"

"Well, I haven't checked to make sure. Hold on. Let me look," and I stepped out of the car.

"HOLY SHIT!" I yelled.

I hopped back in the car, "Oh, my God, I don't even have a front drivers side tire left on this truck, and there's metal missing on the rim. I had a severe blowout. It's 111 degrees, and I've been driving for eight hours or so now. I canceled this OnStar a while back, but can you still contact AAA?"

"Sure thing, Mrs. Cochrane, I already dispatched them. They are 45 minutes away. They seem to be a bit backed up this afternoon. Just sit tight. They'll be there as soon as possible."

"Oh, darn. I was trying to make it home to see my family, any chance you can call another technician?"

"No ma'am, this is the soonest. Well, look at it this way: if it's as bad as you say, we are very grateful that you'll be seeing your family at all. I have here that your Denali is an SUV and with a left front tire blowout driving 75 mph, the chances of you flipping the car at that speed was very high."

Oh, Lord, I had the cruise control set at 84, in temperatures of 111 degrees. I can only imagine how hot the pavement was. That would have been a very sad reunion for my family for sure.

There was so much to share with them. They would have to go through all my things in the Denali: my journals, the full and half-written songs, and the tape recordings of inspirational T-shirt and jewelry ideas probably would have made no sense. I couldn't imagine not getting to smell their sweaty faces from practice and hold their little hands, and have them crawl in my lap and follow me around... read books, get a puppy, share vacations, and adventures, go to the zoo, watch more of their games, be there for their graduations, weddings and precious babies to be born. While also possibly never knowing what this marriage was capable of.

No! no! no! This was not the time for my departure! I silently concluded.

"Will there be anything else, Mrs. Cochrane."

"No. But thank you for being there, On-Star, I am ever so grateful."

Laughing while she responded, "You are very welcome, Mrs. Cochrane. Have a good day."

I waited and waited for AAA. It had been over an hour now, so I continued to add to my list of T-shirt and jewelry ideas. I was disappointed I wouldn't make it home in time to see everyone, but was in such a state of gratitude that I wasn't in a hospital, so the disappointment effortlessly passed.

I remembered Wayne's CD and what he said: I had to wonder who was about to show up.

Finally, the AAA truck pulled up behind me. A small-framed guy in his 50s got out. Worn work boots, a dirty white T-shirt, with frayed hems around the collar and a well-worn baseball cap. He had Arizona-weathered skin, with deep-set wrinkles surrounding his light blue eyes.

When he saw the lack of tire, he yelled, "WHOA, WHOA, WHOA! What in the h e l l do we have here?"

My window was down, and he leaned in with his elbow resting on the window frame. "Sugar," he began, checking my front seat to see if I was alone. "You either have an Angel sitting in that there passenger seat, or you're the luckiest damn broad I've ever known, and we need to high-tail our asses to Vegas right freakin' NOW!"

Laughing and instantly loving this character, I said, "I think it's an Angel in the passenger seat, plus someone gave me this for good luck." I raised the guitar pick necklace up, so he could see it. I continued: "I know this is gonna sound bizarre, but listen to this…"

I reversed Wayne's CD to the point just before the tire blew and hit play.

His mouth dropped open, "I'll be damned, so we were supposed to meet?" He held his hand out. "Name is, Frankie."

I nodded and we shook hands, "Nice to meet you. I'm Judy."

We had a great ole time discussing the danger of this blowout, and he asked where I was coming from and going to. I gave him a quick synopsis, and he was strangely intrigued. He opened the back of my truck, where my guitar and bags were. We had to move everything around, and each item included a story he seemed to want to hear more of. Like the rest of my new friends, we didn't need a lot of talk time to understand one another. He smelled like cigarettes, but for some reason, I wasn't bothered. He looked like a real cowboy, and I recognized how much I loved Arizona's ability to capture all different kinds of people to dwell here. You had to be durable, though, that's for sure. Similar to the durability needed in Chicago winters; one needs to be equally as tough to endure summers in the desert. Especially those working out in the elements, as he did.

I could tell my intuition was kicking in, and I asked him if he was recently sober. I felt like it was okay to ask for some reason.

He looked at me, shocked. "How'd you know that?

"An Angel told me," I said, half-kidding.

"What are ya, a witch?" He was also half-kidding, "I'm sober 29 days." We just stared at each other.

"What are ya thinkin'?" he asked.

"I'm thinking you're a tough son of a bitch and a bit stubborn, and if you throw that stubborn part of you at staying sober, you'll stay sober."

"My wife left me because of my stubbornness. She hated it."

While moving my things around, I said, "Well, she may not have loved it, but you will. It could serve you well. Would you like to have someone in your life in the future?" I asked.

"Yeah, sure do, but I'm a used up..."

"Oh... stop with your sob story," I commanded while laughing, "Just use that stubbornness to stay sober. When you're comfortable and trusting your sobriety, remember to unlock your heart so a woman can get back in there."

I wasn't sure why I went on with this *reading*, or *whatever it was*, I just had this feel and couldn't stop myself.

He opened the area where the new tire was and realized the lock to the jack was missing.

"I bet some dumb ass that changed your oil or something, hoisted it." They're hard to find, little missy, but I may have one in my shop. You'll have to ride with me or stay here and wait for me to return. What's it gonna be?"

"I'll go with," I replied.

"I have to stop for a couple people that have locked keys in their car, okay?" he warned.

Ugh, I thought, *I just want to get home.*

Then I said, "Oh, I don't know. Maybe I should call my husband. Maybe he has that in the garage or something." I said.

"Give him a call then. I'll wait," he replied.

I dialed Bill's phone, and there was no answer.

So I left a message, "Surprise. Hey, it's me... I'm in Arizona ahead of schedule. I was going to surprise you guys, but I have a flat tire, and AAA is here, and we don't have a lock for the jack. I'm wondering if that's in the garage. You're probably running errands before practice. I'm in Casa Grande, AZ at the Trekell Road, Exit 174. Anyway, that's a hike for you. No worries, I can go back to this guy's station, 'cause he thinks he has one there. So much for my big surprise, so surprise."

I jumped onto his truck's running board and waited to hop in while he scrambled getting his fast food wrappers and AAA paperwork together. He wiped and slapped the seat off, creating billows of the Arizona dust in the air. Noticing the scent of raw gas spilled inside, I took a deep breath, having always loved that smell coming from old cars and trucks.

Like a travel guide he said, "First stop—'A camper with big family.' That's all they said. Dumb asses in the office. I don't even have a crossroad. Keep a look out for a family in a 1985 camper on the side of the road up ahead."

"Oh, goodness. In this heat? A whole family? Ugh," I said.

"Yep. Blazing hot, like witches' titties," he looked at me apologetically,

"That came out without me thinkin'."

"Yeah, and when you get your stubborn-self directed to sobriety, make sure you tame inappropriate talk about witches' titties amongst the ladies," I said, smiling.

"Calling All Angels" by Train was playing on the radio, and I turned it up.

"Angels exist," I said to him. "I have 11 days of proof."

His eyes stayed on the road, "Seems ya do, pretty lady, sure seems ya do."

"Oh, geez, there they are," I said, pointing to the opposite side of the highway.

"Oh, crap doodles!" He looked at me cautiously, "Is that better?"

I nodded yes.

Like a desert sand truck racer, he pulled a sharp, aggressive left into the ditch of the median of the highway. The dust poured through the open windows as his air-conditioning was out of service. *A AAA guy with a broken air conditioner? Classic.*

The song pumped through his scratchy speakers, *"I won't give up if you don't give up, I need a sign, to let me know you're here..."* I sang along and directed it to him. He swayed his head to and fro. As much fun as I was having, the thought of not seeing the kids was driving me crazy. Oh, how I missed them. It's like I missed them off and on in a controlled way while away, but I dropped the flood gates managing that this morning and wanted nothing more than to feel all of them in my arms. *I was so close!*

He pulled up behind the ancient-looking camper, just as he had with my truck. He positioned the truck to shield them from passing traffic. He hopped out, motioning for me to stay put.

"This'll just take me a sec."

I was burning up in his truck, but didn't want to interfere with his business, so stayed put. I started counting the family members on the side of the road. There were 11 of them. *Of course, there were!* I thought. They ranged in age from a brand new baby to an 80-year-old woman. They were from Mexico as they had Mexico license plates.

While visualizing the reunion I'd have with all of them tonight, I heard Frankie whistle. With a wave, he motioned me to join him and the family. I took one step out of the truck, and a swarm of kids ran towards me. I loved it, dropping down low to welcome them. *Oh, how I missed my kids*. They were all speaking Spanish in an excited tone, so I couldn't make out what they were saying. With two kids attached to my legs while their tiny feet were mounted on top of mine, I slowly walked, making it over to Frankie.

He said, "Look at this shit."

I gave him a quick glance with a look of disapproval on the word "shit."

"What? Don't worry. They don't speak no English."

I tossed him another look of disapproval.

I noticed an elderly woman sitting comfortably under a mesquite tree. Her legs were out in front of her, and she seemed peaceful. I was so drawn to her but wasn't sure why. She had dark brown skin, long shiny black hair and brown eyes that were mesmerizing. She was watching me, as I was watching her.

With the kids still holding on to my legs and my hands, I said to Frankie, "What's up? What'd ya call me out here to see?"

"Her." He pointed to the old woman under the tree.

Her entire family had shielded her from the blazing sunshine by propping her under this tree in the shade. She sat on a handmade woven blanket that was beautiful. The desert motif had intricate detail. I could tell it was a cherished family heirloom, as the little ones were careful not to step on it with their shoes. Her peace continued to emanate, as she wasn't sweating and appeared to remain comfortable, even in this heat. He motioned for me to go to her. I entered her shaded area with caution. She felt majestic to me. This family tradition of honoring the elderly seemed so lost on Americans.

It's something I hoped for myself, as an older lady. *But have I been doing the groundwork she so clearly has done?* A family doesn't just do this on a whim. I'm not just entitled. This has to be genuinely earned. This takes years of tradition and service to one another. This bond they all so clearly had was something I wanted for our family. If these 11 days ever come off as a selfish thing on my part, then the karma, or what goes around comes around, would wind up with them leaving me to my own devices as well. I hoped that wasn't going to be the case.

I waddled over to her, with the tiny kid's arms still wrapped around my calves. She welcomed me with her eyes. And then I saw it. On her shirt, there was a small gold angel pinned to her collar.

'Well, there's your sign, Twinkles."

I turned to him, wanting to address the "Twinkles," but was distracted by seeing the angel on her. I nodded in agreement. *I did just sing that I wanted a sign.*

"Angels exist." I turned to him to confirm.

And then she spoke as if she understood my English. I immediately turned back to her.

"Mother Mary, queridotiene muchos 'angeles. Entiende?"

Because of the kids' Spanish and a little assistance from one of her great grandchildren, I was able to understand that she thought I had a lot of Angels around me. With her hands in prayer, she repeated it. I stood there continuing to soak in the message she so wanted to share with me. She reached out, and I gave her my hand.

She said, "Viste a la Madre Bendita. Sera oido."

The great grandchild translated in English, "Call on the Blessed Mother. You are heard."

"Holy shit balls!" Frankie exclaimed as he listened in.

Laughing and turning towards Frankie, I said, "Ya just can't stop yourself, can ya?"

He had both hands on his head, "We got to go. I'm late for the next gig. Say your goodbyes."

I exchanged long hugs with the woman and the kids, and off we went.

We entered a high-school parking lot, where an annoyed teenage boy, with tightly folded arms, leaned impatiently against his car. He'd been at football practice and was beyond annoyed that we were late.

"Come with me," Frankie suggested.

I followed him to the car, and in about three seconds, he unlocked the kid's door. Frankie reached in and found the keys on the floor. As I was making small talk about Bill being a football coach and having played in college, Frankie yelled, "WHAT THE SHIT?"

The teen and I directed our attention to Frankie. He was holding an angel pin on a lanyard that had hung on the boy's rearview mirror. I think Frankie's language amused the crabby teen. I cracked up laughing. Frankie was bent over laughing, too. "You are a frickin' witch or somethin'." He put his hand up in the air, as to ward me off. "Son, stand far away from her, she's probably got some potion or voodoo shit, she's gonna do on ya."

The boy enjoyed Frankie's raw humor, but asked, "What's up? What witch shit?"

I explained about the song, and the darling Mexican family, and how there had been eleven of them, and I just did this 11 days... then the teen turned to me with a serious tone, "Holy shit. That's trippy. I prayed for a sign today. This morning before school."

He lowered his voice so Frankie wouldn't hear the details, sensing there was potential that he'd make fun of him.

"The whole day passed, and then football practice passed, I hadn't seen nothin' and I thought, 'I'm so F'd.' I thought if locking my keys in the car is 'the sign' that's somehow telling me everything's gonna be all right, I'm screwed."

Frankie noticed the seriousness in the boy's tone while walking up and put his hand on the boy's shoulder. I stood silent, listening to him explain where he was emotionally, and we both noticed the danger zone this kid had entered. I encouraged him, because of his age, he'd need to be courageous and ask for help from a professional or someone older, or that has lived through what he's feeling. Frankie was moved and stayed silent through the whole talk. I could see that possibly his drinking and destruction of self may have started at this very age. I recognized that I was going to have three teens at the same time, and this could make my life very interesting in the near future. I could be grateful today that I was still on this earth to provide any assistance during those trying teen years.

I shared, "Maybe locking your keys in the car was a good thing. I'm here, and Frankie's here to tell ya, we have lived a few years, and some of them have not been cheery. But it's all right. The good, the bad, the ugly. If you're feeling depression and having thoughts of departing this place, then it's time to cooperate by learning about that, and seek and find help for it. Maybe you needed to know you are in this world for a reason, and we showed up to make you see you're not alone. I've believed we all have Angels, here and on the other side. Whether you believe in it or not, I think they believe in you. Have you ever noticed how sometimes in life, people show up right when you need them and not a second sooner? So you have to hold on, with faith that everything is all right and as it should be. Then you find peace and relief from there. Listen to me. This too can pass, but you need to move your feet in that direction. You need to cooperate. Take my number and Frankie's to start with."

He thought about what I said for a while, and I hoped when my kids were teens, they would hear me like this kid did.

Frankie said, "Call me for whateva' ya need kid. I live in this town. And get me a goddamn football schedule. I wanna see you make some plays."

We got back into Frankie's truck, "What the hell is with you, girl? All this Angel shit... it's crazy. I need a quick break here. I need to get some gas around the corner."

He pulled into the gas station. I got out and headed into the welcoming air-conditioning. This was so different from Santa Barbara's summer weather, but enduring the heat wasn't as bad as I had imagined. I grabbed a water bottle and nothing else. I placed it on the counter and waited for the cashier to announce the total: $1.01. *Of course.*

The third customer Frankie needed to see before we could go to the shop was an elderly white lady in her late 70s. Her sweaty gray hair was plastered to the sides of her face as she patiently waited outside the grocery store. She was hunched over and had groceries on a wheeled cart of her own. Sitting in the truck, I watched Frankie assist by holding her arm while pushing the cart for her. I looked around and thought this might not be my first choice of places to live, but the people sure were nice, and we could probably afford it more easily than the foothills of Tucson. Then I heard Frankie yell, "HOLY shit balls! What is going on?"

"Geez Frankie! I thought I had a potty mouth!"

He was waving ferociously for me to join him and the sweet old lady. The woman's face was aghast. She probably hadn't heard that language in 40 years. While apologizing for him, I noticed he was pointing to a gold Angel pin, on her collar.

Now, I'm stunned. I stared at the gold Angel pin. It was slightly different from the rest.

This is divinely interesting. Is this going to stop, or did Santa Barbara open the floodgates to something really miraculous here?

"Ma'am, is that something you got today? Like at a church or something or... *thinking maybe there was an establishment handing angel pins out in town today.*

"Oh no, this was given to me by my late husband." She pointed to her plates on her car. "He was my *Superman.*"

I had noticed the Purple Heart license plate as I walked up.

She went on to explain, not only about his amazing service, but also her deep love for and devotion to him, and how her love had nothing to do with his medals. His passing had been recent, yet she wasn't mournful, which I found fascinating. She was more grateful. Whatever time they had spent together was enough. She had peace and was left whole. She insisted the reason they cherished each other was because they weren't trapped in a romance novel while trying to compare to it or live their marriage out in that way.

She said, "We were spiritually connected, not superficially connected. I believe, if there was ever a secret to a good marriage, it would have to do with something like that."

It reminded me of a Joseph Campbell quote: **When people get married because they think it's a long-time love affair, they'll be divorced very soon, because all love affairs end in disappointment. But marriage is a recognition of a spiritual identity.**

My life with Bill flashed in front of me, as I considered and scanned our spiritual connection. I could see my initial questioning and hesitation back in college. Should I go out with this *Super*man? I recognized the pull to him. That gut feel. The one that you can't prove, but just know, and I knew. I could see it now... The Plan, for us, and for our three kids. It's like I knew everything that I knew today while sitting on that bar stool. That gut feel had nothing to do with a fairy-tale love affair and seemed to have everything to do with the plan that had been in play all along.

Immediately, I thought about what Skye said when she mentioned that he would let me go, if it served me well. He would let me leave him behind. He would give up this marriage without benefit for him, in order for me to survive and thrive. *Sounds like a fairy-tale romance novel, not a part of our plan. I don't want to be married to, or divorced from a man like that.*

I wondered how I was going to download all of this information to Bill. It could take me weeks. Or it will be like meeting everybody over these 11 days, where with ease and grace, the stories unfold without huge amounts of dialogue. *But will he want the download? Does he want me?*

For me, it was crystal clear: we're not completely done. We have some things to sort out, maybe some work to do together or maybe more done apart. Bottom line is, sleeves need to be rolled up, and we need to get at it... get whole... *get home*. The heart-shaped rock will be the perfect offering, and opening to start our conversation.

My eagerness to get home was rapidly multiplying by the minute.

Frankie and I briefed the dear woman on the whole Angel thing, and with certainty, she replied, "Oh, you kids, of course, Angels exist. Mine does, and he and the others are with me all the time."

We stopped by Frankie's shop, as planned, and, of course, there was no tool that would work. But I instantly knew it wasn't bad luck; it just simply was what it needed to be.

"It's okay, this too shall pass, everything was going to be all right, and we'd find a way," I said, with a smile, while he smirked and rolled his eyes, mocking my positivity.

I studied his shop and found it intriguing to dive into his private space here— his underworld.

"It's nice in here," I said.

"Oh, it's a piece of shit garage, that's all."

"Hmmm. Maybe this will help." I picked up a black marker and wrote on his white board, "KEEP THE FAITH—Judy."

I turned and winked, and set the pen down. "And Hey! You have to admit, I told ya Angels exist."

"Um, little lady, that was a permanent marker, not a dry erase, which is made for that actually," he explained.

"Um-hm. I know," I said knowingly while smiling.

"Not such a bad place, I guess," he admitted as he scanned his shop.

"Yep," I agreed, looking around, ceiling to floor. "I like it here. Hotter than a witch's titty, but it'll do. Good place to heal, stay sober and attract a fine woman. Sometimes, it's good to get another set of eyes on your situation or space, so you can get a different perspective."

Frankie and I made our way back to my truck and the blowout.

He offered, "I'll sit and wait with you until you get a hold of Bill."

I assured him that could be a long wait, knowing I missed my window of getting to see the kids before practice, and now Bill was probably in the middle of coaching football.

Frankie pulled up behind the Denali. He was a hardass, but a beautiful softy and he'd let me in his world today, to see the part of him that was open and true. Dr. Wayne Dyer was right: if you can trust, the unexpected person entering your world may be there for a reason, either for you or for them or both... it's a divine gift.

We sat without words in Frankie's truck. It surprised me how the blazing heat was not a bother. I encouraged him to leave, but he refused. He didn't want to leave me there; it was against his nature.

All of the sudden, he said, "What in the Fuck?"

I didn't correct him, because I was equally shocked. Barreling across the median and then crossing the middle of the multi-lane highway, at high speed, I saw Bill's pickup. He was now driving straight, head-on, toward my truck on the side of the road.

"It's him," I whispered, "it's Bill."

With my feet up on the dash, I felt everything shift to slow motion. I stayed put, and watched, waiting for him to stop his truck and show me his every move. I knew this man better than any other, and I needed to see him and his eyes to get an idea of where his heart and head were.

The billowing dust kicked up on the side of the road, making his truck practically invisible. Slowly dropping my feet down to the floor I leaned up closer to the windshield to get a better look. He had just exited his truck and was heading toward the front of the Denali. As the dust settled, Frankie and I studied Bill's face as he charged up to evaluate the absent tire. He looked panicked and squinted to scan the front seat, looking for me. Knowing how fast I drive and that I was trying to surprise the family, he put two and two together and recognized how lucky I had been. He then realized I was in Frankie's truck.

It dawned on me, If I died today, he wouldn't feel like that sweet old woman with the angel pin. If he died today, I wouldn't have felt like we had enough time. Not only would I mourn him, I'd mourn the potential for us to love each other, deeper... which felt like part of the plan.

Frankie and I studied Bill's reaction. I don't think I've ever seen anything like it. Terror had moved to relief in one facial expression.

Frankie said, "Aw, crap, this shit can make an old geezer cry. A real legit re-uniting goin' down right here." He turned his hat backward and leaned forward on the steering wheel.

Nicole had unbuckled herself, and I saw her sweet face pop out of the front driver's window. Her blonde hair was in high pigtails that only Bill would've been able to do for her. The boys were strapped in the back.

I had to remind myself, it had only been 11 days, yet it felt like I'd been gone a year.

When Frankie saw her cute face pop out of the window, he said, "Oh great, your killin' me right now, look at that face. Oh crap, she's cryin'... Go Go GO..." he leaned over me and flung my door open.

I sat tight because I wanted an even deeper read on Bill.

Frankie hopped out and headed toward Bill to see if he had the key to the lock, for the spare. And he did.

Frankie read Bill's face. "YEAH, I know what you're thinkin'. Thought the same myself. There ain't a stitch of rubber left. Lookie here at the metal shards off the rim... and then I take your ole lady on my route, and all these frickin' people have Angel pins and shit. It's crazy, flat-out crazy, Brotha. And it's mind-blowing that she didn't roll this thing. It's raining Angels over here."

Bill shook his hand like he did with past teammates, pulling him into his chest with a half hug, "Thanks for stayin' with her, brotha."

Giving Bill a "you're welcome" nod, Frankie started working on the spare.

While still in Frankie's truck, I waved to the kids, who were all popping out of the sunroof and windows. Then I locked eyes with Bill. I hopped out of the truck and slowly walked toward him. Nicole was screaming "Mommy, Mommy, Mommy," and the boys were chiming in. Bill had told them to stay in the truck, safely away from the busy road.

"Hold on, Daddy will come gettcha," he said, never taking his eyes off of me.

Bill walked towards me not with a sprint, but with what I recognized from a while ago: My *Superman*, with quiet confidence and the purpose that I had missed seeing in him. It was clear he had no question in his mind of what he wanted and was after: it was *me*.

"Judy, you could've rolled that thing!" His arms were wide open as he came toward me.

"I know, I know, close call," I said.

He grabbed me, and I felt his hands effortlessly lift me up as I jumped up on him, wrapping my legs around his waist. Grabbing my hands in his, he pulled them into his chest. We second-guessed ourselves and hesitated to kiss. Then Bill felt my wedding ring on my finger and looked down to confirm it was what he thought. He looked at me, and with no more hesitation, he kissed me. I had already noticed his ring.

I had deeply missed his full lips on mine, and we kissed again. He kept turning to observe the absent tire and just shook his head.

I declared out loud, "I promise, I'll never drive like that again... too much to lose."

All doubt of how I'd be received by Bill melted away like a lemon drop. We had work to do, but we've had to roll our sleeves up before. And it felt like we would be able to do it again.

Nicole and the boys had unfastened their seat belts and were all trying to get out of the driver's side, so we turned and ran toward them. Bill swung Nicole around and into my arms. She was crying literal tears of joy. This journey had been hard on her. Apparently, she'd spent many nights crying herself to sleep. She giggled as I kissed every part of her face while saying, "I love you, I love you, I love you, my baby girl."

The boys attached themselves to me with hugs around my waist and held on tight. Their sweaty heads smelled sweet to me. Oh, how I'd missed this tribe. Marcus spent a lot of time staring at me. I wasn't expecting words from him, but I could tell by the strength in his hug around my waist, he was pleased and relieved to have me home. When I bent over to hug Clint, he remained shy and cautious while he played with my hair and whispered, "Welcome home, Momma."

Bill, with a perplexed look on his face, pointed to the "KEEP THE FAITH" on the abandoned building wall. "Wow?" he said.

"Yep. Wow is right. Bill, I have quite a bit to share with you. This trip was rich with synchronicities like that. Kept reminding me, that we're living in the Land of Plenty."

"Agreed," he said, as we stared at each other.

Aligning with the plan… again.

We stood there, all of us wrapped together in a strong embrace. I think Frankie was having a rare moment, while in observation mode, as he was quieter than he'd been all day. I could feel him study us, and I wondered if he saw what Paul, and the others did. I sure did. Then, now and again.

After the spare tire was in place, Frankie was ready to go.

He said, "Well, this has been one crazy ride, Twinkles! Yer set. You all can **get home** now."

While standing in the middle of our family of five, I stretched out my arms and said, "I am home, Frankie, it's all right here."

EPILOGUE: I KNOW BETTER
BY JC COCHRANE

That same night, one by one, I tucked the kids into their beds. While snuggling up to them I ran my fingers through their freshly shampooed hair, smelling like fruity coconuts alongside the scent of minty brushed teeth. It's good to be here… in Heaven… at Home. I felt different. Practically unrecognizable.

I knew then that the 11 Days divinely shredded me while miraculously supported me at the same time. Just as my entire life had been doing all along. I felt strong. Because I had walked through the imaginary 11—the pillars—for a new beginning while leaving the past behind with some peace and understanding, instead of leaving with my middle finger up in the air—I claimed this evening to be my glorious finish line and also my new starting line.

My love for this family hadn't changed or even grown, but the depth of the love and my role in this family was clearer. My gut was right when first meeting Bill. Maybe the hesitation was because I also knew that our relationship wouldn't always be filled with ease and grace in every moment. But these rough and smooth rides with my marriage up until now have gotten me to where I am today, and that's a good thing. And not backing this *Super*man into a corner, demanding him to always be what I think is super, excited me about our more authentic future. A future I trusted; if we stayed married or split, we could always be who we are supposed to be. That's where we soar.

It's as if a curtain had been drawn back in the last 11 days, letting the light in while shining on our purpose and the plan in play all along.

I belong here.

While lying by the kid's sides, my throat ached from stifling a relieved-to-be-happy cry. After they were all sound asleep and while Bill showered, I walked outside into the backyard. I laid myself down on that old lawn chair with the dangling, broken straps. I didn't know it then, but, it was going to hold me, not just one more night, but many. I looked up to the sparkling stars popping off the night sky.

What if… I did attempt to write about these 11 days, I let myself think.

The absence of experience and having no previous desire to do such a thing left me void of how I would ever begin a massive project like that. But somehow, the ending popped into my head—the afterword, the epilogue—whatever they call it.

Dear Bill, Marcus, Clint, and Nicole,

I started this book for myself, but I will finish it for you.

If it never reaches the hands of another being, I would be ever so grateful that it will be in yours. It can serve as a family document, a trust fund, if you will. It can remind you kids of how hard your Dad and I fought; to understand ourselves individually, each other, our marriage, and our circumstances. It was a good fight filled with failures and victories while we pushed, pulled and let go to provide in different ways while being both divinely focused and distracted by life… driven by love with the five of us in mind.

Even though words can only take it so far, my hope would be to have you know how deeply loved and treasured you are, that you will always be enough, your flaws are welcome, life can be tough, but so are you. Don't be afraid to fail; it's impossible to avoid failing at something eventually. Unless of course, you are so careful and fearful of failure that you don't live at all—then that's a backdoor failure.

There's a song in you, so sing it. Just begin and be bold. Trust yourself. Everything is going to be all right. Don't worry too much.

And finally, I love you, and there's not a damn thing you can do about it.

in love & in joy, Mom/JC

I readjusted my seat on the loose straps. First, with quiet guttural sobs, feeling a release, I slid my hands over my face, hoping a neighbor wouldn't hear, and then I heard a voice—my voice.

Drop your hands. No more hiding. Show 'em what you got. If you are this grateful—don't be afraid to express it. You're free. You don't have to apologize for being you, or for being vulnerable, happy, sad, or mad.

No need to doubt anymore. Be bold. You no longer have to say things are okay when they're not. You don't have to worry so much or over-react to tough news. You know there's a possibility of it eventually serving you right.

You don't have to attack your fears, just allow them to do their job and nothing more.

Don't wait for the rescue, the lucky break or a lottery ticket. You got this.

In the future, you don't have to forgive everyone and everything immediately. Don't force transformation; it's a process—let it unfold.

You don't have to say yes when you really want to say no.

You don't have to fixate on happy endings, you know it's more about the middle.

Don't underestimate your role in things, keep taking your fair share.

Don't think for one second you're broken, you never were.

You don't have to worry about what's coming your way. It will come, and it will eventually work out.

Don't discount your thoughts. They become things.

Don't give up on the belief that there is good in the world. And don't allow others to fence you into believing otherwise. Dare to be good for goodness sake.

You can let the laundry wait and not make every bed every day. Anyone who judges your messy house (physical & emotional), shouldn't be in your house.

What you do need to do—is authentically show up. Genuinely connect and seek to understand: self, others and circumstance.

Take good care of your very best friend—yourself.

When you ask—should I stay or should I go? Whether it's a marriage, a job, a friendship, a belief system, or a city... know there is an art to leaving. So do your Homework: when getting your house in order, Begin Within and work your way out. Be grateful for where you are. Start from that point rather than the place you think you should be. Some marriages, friendships, etc need a final finish line. Some need a fresh start, again and again.

Remember who you are. Thank God, your Angels and all your beings of the Light on the other side.

Laugh, sing and dance your ass off, often.

Share your discoveries. Someone else is on the same hunt.

Passages filled with turmoil need to be gone through, not around.

Repeat: I love you. I'm Sorry. Please forgive me. Thank you.

Stay aware and alert to the Land of Plenty you live in,

where God can unfold in you, others and circumstance.

And if for some reason, you forget any of this: then recall what just divinely unfolded in these last 11 days. And LOVE. Come on. Let understanding continue to lead you to love.

After these 11 Days—You know better—while practicing these things, you and those around you can enjoy each other on the road to GET HOME.

Your sacred space is where you can find yourself, again and again.
Joseph Campbell

AFTERWARD: 11 YEARS LATER
BY BILL COCHRANE

To the Reader:

Judy asked me to share my commentary on the 11 DAYS and also on the last 11 years. That's hard to do having lived it from a similar, yet unique vantage point. But here it goes.

Losing it all, got real, real quick. I wasn't prepared, and it turns out I didn't have to be. Eventually, after I shook off the lawsuits, declared bankruptcy, became grateful for the work I could get, took responsibility for parts of our marriage and simply just enjoyed the kids... I was rich again...not according to my bank accounts—but I felt rich.

I prayed a lot but kept my feet moving. I never let up, at least not for too long. I kept turning every stone to find solid work, a career with meaning and focused on finding good people where I could make a difference and knew the money would eventually follow. My free time was spent coaching our kids and others. These were definitely the times that ask you to not give up. Even when it looked like many dead ends.

The morning after Judy arrived back to the rental, federal agents from the Phoenix Bankruptcy Department, arrived at our home banging on our door at 8 A.M. Our lawyer was right; someone anonymously claimed that the bankruptcy I had applied for, was fraudulent. We were back in the fire again, but this time had a better handle on it. We let them fully search the house while assisting in opening drawers and cabinets. They were at first strictly professional and eventually turned friendly as it became obvious we had nothing to hide.

I wish I could place a happy ending here, but the truth is, after the 11 days, we had a decade of taking one step forward and two or three back.

I was on the 11th job when Judy started writing this book. I was overweight, out-of-shape and tired from flying all over the country for my job. With no reserves, 401K or savings, we were still financially starting over—living paycheck-to-paycheck.

Judy was still running Spiritualitee, the business spawned by the boutique owner and Gray. She operated off of folding card tables set up in the kitchen, often making the hand-silk screened tees and jewelry late into the night. When we could afford the entrance table fees at conventions and shows, she'd sell them at weekend events in Arizona, California, and Florida.

At this time, we had the same struggles that a lot of families have paying for kids sports and extras and then barely able to assist with college tuitions. Marcus had just come out of a half-way house after a cocaine addiction. And we had just painfully scraped 5000 dollars together to purchase our first home in 11 years—a small foreclosure. Shortly after the home purchase, the company I was working for changed directions and I was let go. This forced me to find another job. One that I wouldn't have been looking for otherwise. Today, I work on my own, which ended up being the right move. My point is that it temporarily felt like another kick in the teeth, but in fact, it was a blessing.

Now that you've read this book, though, you probably have a good idea of why I'm still standing. I had to work at it by becoming a different provider, but my wife, who is not only the love of my life but my real-life partner is the one I give credit to.

She operated like this during our most challenging times and continues to this day—on good days and bad—she finds the goodness in people and continues to have these great exchanges with everyone including complete strangers. A Buddhist monk once called her a Warrior of Goodness—I'd have to agree.

Thank you for letting her share her voice. I hope it helps you the way I've seen it help others.

I hope your paths are filled with as much ease as possible. But if you are in the midst of a struggle—Keep the faith. And as my dad would say, "Follow your light and fight the good fight.

Peace, Bill

Life is thickly sown with thorns, and I know no other remedy than to pass quickly through them. The longer we dwell on our misfortunes, the greater is their power to harm us. Voltaire

A letter to Judy from Bill: *written after first reading the book:*

JC

In so many ways I am very happy that I suggested not reading or discussing this book as you went through the process of writing it. Somehow, I knew it had to be free of my opinions and perspectives. Now having read it, I'm confident that it was meant to only be told by you.

It was to heal the final wounds for us, the kids and perhaps others.

It is hard to have so many emotions at one time, to relive details that brought up so many feelings of doubt and pain. Honey it is real, it was painful. You nailed it. I guess I had put so many of those challenges away in my head separating them as a way to minimize the total impact. But in one 12-hour sitting, it brought it back as if it were yesterday.

I have always been grateful for you and the way you kept us positive and moving forward but as I read this cover to cover with the pain, the shame, the hurt I caused and what we survived, I am left overwhelmed and amazed by you... thankful, humbled, really and grateful you and I made it.

Reading this tore me up in so many ways. The heartache, fear, and hopelessness came back like a raging storm and brought me to tears more than once. It also made me smile, laugh and appreciate you, our family and my life in general.

In the beginning, you said you wanted to write something about the last 11 years, if for no other reason, to help our now, adult children, understand how hard we worked on ourselves and each other. I really had no idea where you would take this. I'd like to say, I had no idea of all the things you went through. I, of course, thought I did from my perspective but to see it laid out made it even more clear how lucky I am that we're still together. I'm glad I read it through, at night, alone, unable to stop, to ask you what and why you felt or did something or try to share how I felt at a particular point. I wanted to scream at times and hide at others. Hug you, but then at certain points, I got pissed.

I sat in my office with the light of the computer and the moon at my back, reading and trying to justify, rationalize, maybe just process the whole thing at once. I remember thinking my God, how did she live with this, to begin with, and then how did she relive this for the past year as she wrote it? But then it sank in. I could see the little girl and the woman that went through it and how she came out the other side, and it all just made sense—your obstacles tend to become your strengths.

I looked up as I closed the book and said to myself, Thank God our family pulled through that.

Your story, our story, I assume, is not so different from others. Everyone lives their life with tragedies and victories, loves and losses, and I hope this encourages someone. Helps them know that the finish line and starting line is coming and they, like you, can make a difference in how things turn out by how they deal with it.

I have watched you put this to paper. Anyone, I think, can imagine the time and dedication it takes to write a book, but a book like this that bears your soul is altogether something more. I know you left your heart on those pages while unafraid of failure or the kind of criticism we learned to expect from those who knew us during the fall. So I am proud of your effort and dedication, but I am most proud of your willingness, to be honest, and share your real you.

So my love, my partner, my friend, know I love you more today than ever before, not because of the book but because of who you are. My respect for you is not seeded in the effort it took to write the book or even that you are courageously publishing it. It is based on the life you have led and character you are filled with. The love that you share and the happiness that you bring. You're willingness to engage this story head on and be real, honest, raw and responsible is inspiring to me. And your courage to look back and choose not to be bitter but to find your heartbeat and soul and then to share it...

Well Done My Love, Well Done!

BC

ACKNOWLEDGEMENTS

For Bill, thanks for stepping up, stepping out
& for staying strong
Marcus, for staying calm
& for keeping it real
Clint, for keeping it light
& for staying focused
& Nicole, for staying in a
state of authenticity

Thank you dear God and for all those you sent as this book would have never seen completion without your guidance.

Thank you to my ancestors of the light and those on the other side; I couldn't have written it without you: Paul Dickerson (pauldickerson.org), Professor Bayard Stockton – who got home in 2006 – after many emails and phone calls between us. Exact dates are unknown, but I was told the minister and Gray have also passed. Tommy Moskal, Bill's college teammate, did end up standing up in our wedding but left the planet early in 2005, Sandy and their three boys are living in the midwest. Also leaving early – in 2012, the North Carolina healer, David Cree.

R.I.P. and thank you to Monty Klemmer, Aunt Corinne, Mr. Daniel, Bill Cochrane Sr., A. P., Walter Payton, Chuck Bowden, my grandparents Milt and Alid Bondus, and other profound beings and writers who directed and supported this project.

Thank you to my dear and divinely placed friends that loved me no matter what: Hottie, Violet, Katie, Skye, Eddie, Jenna and Jesse… and the generous boutique owner… all still residing in, around and near California.

Thank you to Frankie and your hilarious foul mouth. Thank you, Tracy & Ed for your bungalow where I pulled it together. And for your precious animals Maximillian, Titus and Sam I Am.

Thank you to my glorious North Carolina friends—Claire, Mike & Anne Anderson, and Dr. Kate Stewart & Alex Stewart. I'm ever so grateful for all of you.

Thank you to the warriors that marched through the fall of i360 and Infocast. Special thanks to Steve Ridley and his family who faithfully forged through right alongside of us, enduring the same financial battlefield. **GOOD GOD! GOOD GRIEF! GOOD TIMES!**

A special canine thank you to our girl, Adobe, our chocolate Labrador, adopted shortly after the 11 days.

She came with ticks, fleas and a deformed jaw which made her teeth funky. She chased the kids in the backyard, soaked up the cold tile in Horehole, chased lizards without killing them, liked long walks, slept in our beds, gladly wore Christmas bows on her head and joyfully explored every corner of all nine houses thereafter. You know what you did for us. It was your plan all along. You were the clay that helped keep this roundhouse together. May you rest in peace in your magnificent and glorious labitude.

While editing the last chapters in Dallas, she endured her last chapter. She took her last glorious breath while she laid in the grass with Marcus, me and a home care Vet (& with Bill on facetime while out of town) www.Lapsoflove.com

On that note, a special thanks to Jill Angelo—author of Sacred Space. She's my badass warrior friend from Chicago who helps Lions in South Africa and is also the owner of a foster organization www.the moondogfarm.com. Days after Adobes passing, she had a huge adoption event where she named a puppy, ADOBE, and he was rescued out within hours.

Thank you, Nicole Cochrane, for carrying this book in paper form (with 40,000 more words than it has today) to Sri Lanka so that you could be the first to edit it. Also, I deeply thank you for creating the tagline! Thank you, Marcus Cochrane, for being the second to edit and for suggestions like "The Land of Reflection" Part two-title. And thank you, Clint Cochrane, for offering your lightening bolt insight on how it reads.

Deep thanks for contributions too long to list on all; Thank you to all my friends that walked along side me during this time and the following eleven years to follow. I love you. To my dear friend Karen Callan. Author of Just In Time – *How to find joy and synchronicity in every moment* and RosaYoga.com – for your inspired service to this world, your precious family and for your spiritual energy toward this project. And for the hundreds of hours of time you gifted me in both editing and simply loving me and protecting my voice.

Thank you, Gene Armstrong, for editing. What a pleasure it was to work with you. Ava Blank, Cara Houck, Sherril Howard & Tim Harrington, Jay Meyer and Caroline Yacu for beta-reading. Thank you to my incredibly gifted author friends: Windy Harris – windylynnharris.com and Susan Pohlman – susanpohlman.com. You're genuine and profound encouragement to keep at it was deeply appreciated—always divinely appearing when I most needed it. Thank you to Stewart at Stewart Kuper Jewelers for handling us with compassion as we sold off our jewelry. Thank you Dennis Rhodes for cover design. And thank you to Laura Bravo Mertz for the author photo.

Thank you to Dr. Wayne Dyer, RIP, for passionately encouraging me to write this story in 2005, and then also pushing me to sell my tees (created on my drive back home) at my first I Can Do It event in San Diego. I sold out because he wore the first tee I created, BEGIN WITHIN, on stage.

Thank you to my entire Wilson family & Cochrane family for all things too vast to mention.

Thank you, Aunt Barbara and Uncle Klindt, for the seeds you plant and continue to support. Thank you, Dad, for understanding me and for loving me no matter what. Thank you Bill Salisbury and thank you, Mom, for being my rock. Thank you to my sister Cary, for always reminding me where I come from. Thank you to my brother Johnny, for reading my first draft and not laughing at it, but pointing out my courageousness in being able to share it. That helped to inspire me to continue to courageously carry on… which was mandatory in order to finish.

Thank you to Abby and the women at the fundraising lunch who were the first to arrive at my door after I requested gently used tee shirts to practice silk screening for my then, new business www.spiritualitee.com.

Now found on my new website **www.jccochrane.com.**

To those hero's that swooped into our lives, after the 11 DAYS and offered a loan for a down payment on a home after rental #5 or so… you know who you are. And after that didn't work out, and the next hero stepped up to save the day only to have it crash again… I want you all to know that after 11 years passed, it became clear that we will forever be grateful for your heroism even though the attempt of generosity did not pan out for any of us as our friendships ended. Truth is, we were the ones we were waiting for. I wanted to take this time to acknowledge your gesture. I hope that you are your own hero in your own lives, and all is thriving in your world.

What a glorious ride filled with grit and grace.

And thank you… yes, you, for reading this. Even though we may not meet face to face, I hope you're seeing and feeling your light. If not, read the book again. It's a mirror. Anything you like in it already lives brightly inside of you. in joy, jc

11 DAYS PLAYLIST

CHAPTER · · · · · · · · · · · · · · · · · · SONG TITLE – ARTIST

THE CANYONS · · · · · · · · · · · American Woman – Lenny Kravitz
SUPERMAN · · · · · · · · · I Want To Know What Love Is – Foreigner
CAN'T FIGHT IT · · · · Can't Fight This Feeling – REO Speedwagon
DAVID · · · · · · · · · · · · · · Truly Madly Deeply – Savage Garden
THY WILL BE DONE · · · · · · · · · · · · · · Angel – Sarah McLachlan
TRULY MADLY DEEPLY · · · Feels Like The First Time – Foreigner
LET IT RAIN HERE · · · · · · · · · · · · Let It Rain (live) – Jesus Culture
KEEP THE FAITH · · Don't Let The Sun Go Down On Me – Elton John
ALL IS NOT LOST · · · · · · · · · · · · I Shall Be Released – Bob Dylan
WHAT'S YOUR STORY? · · · · You Should Be Dancing – Bee Gees
FOR RICHER AND FOR POORER · · · Come To Jesus – Mindy Smith
SUNSHINEY DAY · · · · · · · · I Can See Clearly Now – Johnny Nash
@ PEACE · · · · · · · · · · · · · · · · · · Hallelujah – Jeff Buckley
A HOUSE IN ORDER · · · · · Wild Horses(acoustic) – Rolling Stones
PROVIDER · · · · · · · · · · · · · · · · With Arms Wide Open – Creed
WHAT'S UP? · · · · · · · · · · · · · · What's Up? – 4 Non-Blondes
WHAT'S UP? · · · · · · · · · · You Shook Me All Night Long – AC/DC
WHAT'S UP? · · · · · · · · · · Give Me One Reason – Tracy Chapman
WHAT'S UP? · · · · · · · · · · · · · Brown Eyed Girl – Van Morrison
GRAY · · · · · · · · · · · · · · · · · · Celebration – Kool & The Gang
HWY 101 · · · · · · · · Drift Away – Uncle Kracker Feat. Dobie Gray
GET HOME · · · · · · · · · · · · · · · · · Calling All Angels – Train
added during editing to the very end of:
GET HOME · · · · · · · · · · · · · · · Thinking Out Loud – Ed Sheeran

COMING SOON

JC Cochrane on her next book—*This is a letter I wrote to my son, Marcus, just as I started this eleven DAYS book...*

CARRY ON – PROLOGUE –
3 GRAMS (COPYRIGHT © 2014)

Dear Marcus,

Jan 2014. I'm sitting at the kitchen table in the middle of our busy house. It's the craziest time of the year, and I decide, it's time. Time to write the book about the 11 days in Santa Barbara.

I created some kind of energetic balloon around me because once I started looking at everything within the box; I dropped into an intense tunnel vision. The chaos in the house drifted away as I sat in clear focus of our recent past. After years of postponement, I knew today was the day. I was ready to write 11 Days, but, more importantly, with a decade of patience on the universe's part, it was ready to *right* me. I felt manic as I scribbled details of the 11 days with a dry erase marker, covering every sliding glass door and window on the first floor, including a large decorative mirror.

Slowly, while going through the box, I found sticky notes and magazine clippings of pictures that either came from or reminded me of the events that happened in Santa Barbara along with receipts, quotes and even the original map printed with red marker highlighting the places to stop for gas, which, as you know, your Dad created, not me. HA

Thoughts of my new friends flooded my heart, and I feel so grateful for them. The lessons of those 11 days have proved to carry on in this last decade. Thank God.

Vision boards I created before and after the trip lined the interior walls of the box. I studied my hopes and dreams on those pages, and I see how they follow me. Maybe this is why they aren't realized because they've been tucked away in a box, waiting for me to "open" to them. It just seems they are part of a plan that is not meant to be resisted any longer. One I just have to fearlessly keep aligning with.

In that box, our attorneys' names, numbers, tax forms, bankruptcy dates, mortgage letters, job interviews, declined job applications with attached resumes, credit card, and banking statements—all holding negative messages with more bad news or flat-out declines. (my note to self—release these items ASAP.) I uncovered our food stamp and state health insurance card that had been tucked away.

The dates of things started drawing me in, and I noticed that it had been exactly 11 years since the 11- day trip. Dad was on his 11th job. We were in our 11th house. You turned 11, the week before the 11- day trip. I can safely say; it could not be clearer that I'm supposed to be spending time on this now.

I went through the box of notes and one by one, I studied each item and read each page of my journal. I thumbed through the spirals partially used by you from past classes. Thinking of you, Marcus, I read all your notes, reminding me of your early beginnings of curiosity, innocence, and pure heart. Wow, has time whipped by.

When I got to the bottom of the second box, I saw a pack of Newport cigarettes. I could tell by the weight that it wasn't a full pack. Up until now, I remembered everything I'd been pulling out, but this. I shook it and felt its contents. Then opened to find three small folded pieces of paper with $ amounts and quantity amounts next to each name. Behind the paper were three tiny zip lock baggies, each filled with one gram of cocaine. All the bags had little red hearts on them.

And then it all came back... I'd completely forgotten that these were the first drugs I'd confiscated from your Mazda RX8, and I had hidden them in this box. It was like finding an old friend. The friend that boldly told me the truth about what was really happening to you. Warning me that your foot was on the pedal, full throttle. Our family was vulnerable, and I worried about not being ready for something like this. I recalled that early morning sitting in your front seat with the smell of cigarettes lingering in the air. You had just rolled in at 6 A.M. The relief that you were safely home was always tainted with the silent question... How do we fix this? But on the flip side, I also recalled wondering, What kind of an addict would keep cocaine in baggies with tiny red hearts? A part of me smiled inside because I could still recognize my kind & gentle Marcus, and that gave me some hope.

It was the beginning of my search and rescue for you. And for myself, who felt I had failed you.

Taking this all in while standing at the kitchen table, I felt my knees unlock, and I uncontrollably slammed down onto the chair behind me, drawing the attention of Clint and Nicole, who were watching TV just a few feet away. I was grateful you weren't there to see me recover these drugs, as I know it's still an open wound for you... for us. I know now, though, that I can't really shield you anymore.

I was surprised that it hit me like a bag of bricks again. Had I not processed enough? I quickly slipped the cocaine back into the box and threw some things over it to keep it hidden from the world. Hidden from me. Definitely hidden from you. Even though things are not the same in our lives, this memory reminded me of the ripped-to-the-core feelings of this time period. The battlefield, I recall, is one that practically slayed us all while we painfully waited to see if we would have to bury you.

My dear son, the reason I share this now is because I have clarity that this book wants to be written, as well. Not sure why, cause I don't think we have this all figured out, and so I'm not sure we have a platform to even help others yet. You can't say AA is your answer. You can't say RR–Rational Recovery is your answer. I don't think any of us were exceptionally brave or courageous or even unlucky or plain stupid, so there's not much of a story there. We just got caught up in the slippery shit, just like any other family does.

We can probably say something about the love and trust that grew while learning to understand addiction and also each other, in a deeper way. But I'm not sure people will care to hear about that. So, with your permission, I'm going to write it for you and me, Dad, Clint, and Nicole. Cause, if nothing else, I want to document, the best that I can: my love, my sometimes crazy-ass-mad-insane devotion, intention, guilt, blame, fear, and mistakes through it all. And, in the end, the one thing that can be clear, is that I'm grateful, so deeply grateful, for how it served us right in the growth and lessons it brought our family in the search, rescue and the excruciating, but mandatory release of you. With your permission, this will be the prologue of:

Carry On... the secret language, lessons, and heart-wrenching love a family experiences when a child endures addiction.

Husa, Momma

YOU CRACK ME UP copyright © 2014
from broken bones to broken homes and
monsters, bullies & stuff
a children's guide

YOU CRACK ME UP, tells an inspiring sweet story of boys and girls that face their first troubles (nightmare, bullies, etc...) while gently and simply explaining that whatever cracks us up (giggles or even tears), lets the light in... making home life and school life happier.

YOU CRACK ME UP is one of 11 children's books – from the OAKIE DOAKIE (copyright 2015) series.

For Mom & Dad: Ideal for reading before bedtime. It's suitable as a read-aloud book for preschoolers, or a self-read book for older children.

...and it is done.

Made in the USA
Middletown, DE
05 December 2016